Regulae Iuris in the Medieval and Modern Age

Legal History Library

VOLUME 78

The titles published in this series are listed at *brill.com/lhl*

Regulae Iuris in the Medieval and Modern Age

Essential Stability vs. Evolving Contexts

Edited by

Ilya A. Kotlyar

With a Conclusion by

James Gordley

BRILL | NIJHOFF

LEIDEN | BOSTON

The work on this volume was partially funded by Research Foundation – Flanders (FWO).

Cover illustration: Digestum Novum (Venice: Nicol Jenson, 1477), D.50.17.1, ICo 2347, by A. Panzanelli.

Library of Congress Cataloging-in-Publication Data

Names: Kotlyar, Ilya A. editor
Title: Regulae iuris in the medieval and modern age : essential stability vs. evolving contexts / edited by Ilya A. Kotlyar.
Description: Leiden ; Boston : Brill Academic Publishers, Inc, 2026. | Series: Legal history library ; volume 78 | Includes bibliographical references and index.
Identifiers: LCCN 2025034011 | ISBN 9789004736078 hardback | ISBN 9789004736092 epub
Subjects: LCSH: Legal maxims (Roman law)--History | Legal maxims (Roman law)--Early works to 1800 | Roman law--Interpretation and construction | Law, Medieval | Ciceronianism
Classification: LCC KJA100 .R44 2026 | DDC 340.5/4--dc23/eng/20250910
LC record available at https://lccn.loc.gov/2025034011

Typeface for the Latin, Greek, and Cyrillic scripts: “Brill”. See and download: brill.com/brill-typeface.

ISSN 1874-1793
ISBN 978-90-04-73607-8 (hardback)
ISBN 978-90-04-73609-2 (e-book)
DOI 10.1163/9789004736092

Contents

Acknowledgements

This volume has been prepared in the course of the project "Medieval juristic *regulae*. Origin. Evolution. System", funded by Research Foundation – Flanders (FWO.OPR.2020.005001).

Notes on Contributors

Ilya A. Kotlyar
is an Assistant Professor at the Francisco Vittoria University, Madrid. He obtained his law degree and a postgraduate research degree at Moscow University (2008, 2011) and obtained his Ph.D. in Law at the University of Edinburgh (2017). His research interest and experience lie primarily in the field of legal history, especially in Roman law, Canon law and the *ius commune*. His particular areas of expertise are the early modern law of Scotland and the Low Countries, the law of succession, obligations, and procedure. Recently he has concentrated his attention on the *regulae iuris*, especially from an interdisciplinary perspective of law and linguistics.

Adolfo Giuliani
(M.Sc. LSE 2000, M.Phil. Cambridge 2001 and Ph.D. Cambridge 2007) works at the intersection of legal history and legal theory. He has published on various topics in historical legal epistemology, e.g. legal evidence, presumption, interpretation, plurinormativity. In legal theory, he focuses on the impact of philosophy of information on legal thought. He currently works for the Italian Ministry of Education, University and Research and previously for the University of Helsinki (2017–20) and the Max Planck Institute in Frankfurt for legal history and legal theory (2020–22).

Maria Kola
is a doctoral candidate in law at Adam Mickiewicz University in Poznań (Poland). She is currently working on her dissertation at the Department of Roman Law, Legal Traditions and Cultural Heritage Law. Her principal scholarly interest is legal reasoning, while her interdisciplinary Ph.D. project is being pursued as part of research in Germany (Münster) and Italy (Padua). She holds a master's degree in Law and obtained a post-graduate diploma in International Law.

David Deroussin
is a full professor of legal history at the University of Lyon. His publications include papers and books (*Histoire du droit des obligations*, Paris, 2012, 2nd ed.; *Histoire du droit privé*, Paris, 2018) on the history of private law. He currently heads the Doctoral School of Law at the University of Lyon.

Piotr Alexandrowicz
is an assistant professor at Adam Mickiewicz University, Poznań (AMU). He holds an M.A. in law, theology and canon law. In 2019 he defended his Ph.D. thesis in legal history at AMU in which he discussed the medieval Canon law argumentation in favour of binding force of all agreements and the later influence of this argumentation on the contract law in the Western legal tradition. He has published on the reception of Roman law in medieval canon law, on the incunabula of the Decretals of Gregory IX, on the early modern moral theology and contract law and on *differentiae iuris civilis et canonici* as an example of early modern comparative approach to law.

Ger (Gerard) Coffey
B.A (UL), LL.B. (NUI), M.A. (NUI), Ph.D. (NUI), Associate Professor in Law, Centre for Crime, Justice and Victim Studies, School of Law, University of Limerick, Ireland. His research and teaching interests lie in the areas of criminal law, criminal justice, criminal procedure, and legal history. With a particular focus on the Common law double jeopardy principle and Civil law *ne bis in idem* principle he has published his research widely in high-ranking national and international journals. He is the editor-in-chief of the Irish Criminal Law Journal and Council Member of the Association for Criminal Justice Research and Development (Ireland).

Harry Dondorp
is an assistant professor (retired 2023) at Department of European Legal History, Vrije Universiteit Amsterdam. His main field of interest is comparative legal history, esp. the law of delict, limitation and prescription, third-party contracts, and specific performance. He focuses on the medieval *ius commune*, the jurisprudence of both canonists and civilians. The topics of his publications vary from the required two-thirds majority in papal elections to decreeing specific performance in (Roman) Dutch law.

Emanuel G.D. van Dongen
is an associate professor at the Molengraaff Institute for Private Law, Utrecht University. He studied at Tilburg University (2005, 2007), received his Ph.D. at Maastricht University (2013), and was an assistant professor at Utrecht University (2013–2022). He has been a visiting professor or scholar at RomaTre (2019), LUISS (2017, 2019) and Turin University (2018–2024). He also held the TPR Exchange Chair in Private Law at Ghent University (2021–2022). Since 2023 he has also been a Deputy Justice (*raadsheer-plaatsvervanger*, civil law) at the Arnhem-Leeuwarden Court of Appeal.

James Gordley
is a J.D. Harvard Law School, 1970; MBA University of Chicago Graduate School of Business 1968; B.A. University of Chicago, 1967; W.R. Irby Distinguished University Professor, Tulane Law School; Distinguished Professor of Legal History, *Università Bocconi* (joint appointment); Shannon Cecil Turner Professor of Jurisprudence Emeritus, Berkeley Law School; Fellow, The American Academy of Arts and Sciences; Corresponding Fellow, The British Academy; and *Membre titulaire, Académie internationale du droit comparé.*

Introduction

Ilya A. Kotlyar

1 The Background of This Volume

This volume is based on the online workshop "*Regulae iuris* and maxims of law in the legal historical perspective", organised by Ghent Legal History Institute on 21 January 2022 and funded by Research Foundation – Flanders (project number FWO.OPR.2020.005001). However, it is not a simple publication of the workshop proceedings. The organisers have analysed and identified the common theme of the workshop presentations. The list of contributors does not fully coincide with the scholars presenting at the original workshop. Nevertheless, all the contributors to the volume were participants in the workshop and are scholars, both young and experienced, working in the field of *regulae iuris*.

The 2022 workshop has revealed a common theme in the scholarship of *regulae* – the contradiction between essence and context within them. On the one hand, the *regulae* may be seen as real entities, essential in themselves and stable. The presentations by David Deroussin and other scholars have shown that already the Roman jurists, e.g. Cicero, dreamt of using the *regulae* as the underlying legal principles, helping to "reduce law into art". Similarly, the presentation by David De Concilio has indicated that medieval jurists, especially those of the Bologna school in the 13th century, tended to see the *regulae* as objective generalisations of the solutions to the groups of related legal cases: they revealed certain "reasons of law" (*causae legis*) underlying the solutions.

On the other hand, the presentations have also revealed that, at all historical stages of the usage of *regulae iuris*, a more utilitarian and contextual approach was prevalent: the "rules of law" were often far from having any stable meaning. They could change their meaning and their wording under the influence of each other, of contradicting fragments of the authoritative legal text, and of the evolving social context. For example, as shown by Paul Du Plessis's presentation, the Justinianic title *De diversis regulis* was rather a heterogeneous collection of rules, united not by any essential theory of law but by the idea of acceptable modes of argumentation. David De Concilio has stressed that the 11th- to 12th-century Glossators collected *regulae* and *brocarda* not for systematic purposes, but rather to argue cases more convincingly and to teach students to do the same. The presentation of Emanuele Conte has demonstrated the preference of the variant "*coniunctio*" rather than

 | DOI:10.1163/9789004736092_002

the original *"coniectio"* in the medieval Mss. of the Digest D. 50.17.1; this suggests that even the wording of the *regulae* and definitions tended to be adapted to the predominant juristic context. Gero Dolezalek showed how the *regulae* started appearing in juristic Mss. very early; yet, later on, the interest to them was declining, and the old *regulae*, formulated by the early Glossators, were often erased, as, probably, not fitting the new conceptual legal contexts. David Deroussin, by the example of Dupin the Elder, demonstrated that the *regulae* can be intentionally adapted and reformulated to function in a codified system of law. Harry Dondorp, in the example of the rule "*Duorum in solidum dominium esse non posse*", has shown that exceptions to the rule and juristic "explaining away" of those exceptions could produce more legal content than the rule itself and, essentially, determine not only the scope of application but also the whole meaning of the rule. The presentation of Emanuel van Dongen, dedicated to the *regula* of D. 50.17.203, showed how important was the mental (conceptual) context in which a *regula* was read for its interpretation and implications. Finally, the presentation by James Gordley, the main tenets of which have been published elsewhere,[1] stressed that *regulae*, maxims and similar entities which we consider "fundamental principles of law" often come into existence through rather random processes; we select the "principles" we find useful (in a particular context) and reject others.

This volume is the first English language collaborative publication to assess the topic of *regulae iuris* from a certain methodological perspective: essentialism vs context. There have previously been published collections of articles on the topic of *regulae*: e.g. an Italian language publication by Jovene Editore in 2016.[2] A minor deficiency of that volume is the lack of uniform methodology: it simply looks at the *regulae* as a historical phenomenon in need of a theoretical assessment. The participants of the 2022 workshop have been invited to submit their articles for the volume, united by the common theme of "essence vs. context", or, more precisely, "essential stability" of the *regulae* as opposed to their evolving context (social or structural). The contributions to the volume are expected to explore what was more important in the formation or the existence of *regulae iuris*: their underlying and stable social value or their ever-evolving relation to each other, to their exceptions and changeable cultural phenomena?

1 James Gordley, "*Regulae Iuris* and Legal Principles: Whence and Whiter?", *Tulane European and Civil Law Forum* 37 (2022): 201–207.

2 Valeria Di Nisio, ed., *Regulae Iuris. Ipotesi di lavoro tra storia e teoria del diritto* (Naples: Jovene Editore, 2016).

The novelty of this proposed volume is in its methodological unity. It attempts to look at *regulae iuris*, first of all, as a dynamic system with an ever-evolving structure. The *regulae* were interconnected, having various relations among each other, based on similarity, contradiction, or juxtaposition. Rather than looking at the "rules of law" as phenomena lying strictly within a topic of "Roman law", of "Canon law", of "Natural law", of "legal theory and philosophy of law", the articles of this volume attempt to liberate the *regulae* from "slavery" to the legal order or culture that created or influenced them and to look at the *regulae* in themselves, in their ever-evolving interrelationship in the changing social and cultural contexts. There was a time when a similar endeavour in linguistics gave rise to a whole new school of thought when Ferdinand de Saussure proposed to look at language as a structure independent from the social, political or economic phenomena that influence it. The *regulae iuris* present an opportunity to attempt a similar groundbreaking approach to law.

2 Methodology and Summary of This Volume

The articles of the volume address the theme of the relative importance of essence vs context among the *regulae* and maxims of law either holistically, looking at the system of *regulae iuris* in general (articles by Ilya Kotlyar, Adolfo Giuliani, Maria Kola, and David Deroussin), or by looking at particular *regulae* and their context (articles by Piotr Alexandrowicz, Gerard Coffey, Harry Dondorp, and Emanuel van Dongen). A conclusion is provided by James Gordley.

The editorial article by Ilya A. Kotlyar presents the main hypothesis lying behind the volume. It addresses the relationship between the *regulae* and the medieval dialectical method, pointing out that the *regulae* in the medieval period of their development were, probably, determined not by objective social principles, but rather by the contextual relationships, which was typical of the dialectical epistemology. The article argues that the extent to which the *regulae* were, indeed, dialectical may be determined by the application of the structural method, developed in linguistics, which assumes that the *regulae* were akin to arbitrary signs, whose scope and meaning were determined by the order of relations (structure) among them. This provided the methodology applied during the preparation of the contributions and editing of the final manuscript.

The article by Adolfo Giuliani further develops the topic of the interrelationship between the *regulae,* or maxims, and the dialectical method of reasoning, with a focus on the early modern period. Besides demonstrating a fundamental dependence of maxims on the dialectical epistemology, the author also shows how the "new Aristotelianism" of the late 16th to mid-17th centuries fundamentally altered the attitude towards the maxims, by drawing a distinction between the maxims as "verisimilars" and the "signs" as individual facts. This approach turned maxims into the "first principles" in the hierarchy of law and other social sciences, while simultaneously decontextualising them and making the analogy with language and the structural method less relevant. The author's observation on the "spatial idea of knowledge", predominant in pre-modern science, potentially speaks in favour of the applicability of the structural method to this era.

The article by Maria Kola is dedicated to a topic related to that of Adolfo Giuliani – the development of the *regulae* in the context of logic and epistemology in the early modern period. It focuses on the *regula* "*Ubi eadem ratio ibi idem ius*", which was one of the fundamental *regulae*, defining the principle guiding the operation of all others. The article provides proof of the rapprochement between the *regulae* and logical rhetorics in the aforesaid period. Importantly, it contributes to verification of the main hypothesis of the volume by showing how the key terms constituting the *regulae* (such as the term "*ratio*") were gradually "precised down" and becoming more technical under the influence of dialectical and rhetorical context; this even involved a conscious "rephrasing" of the *regula*, with an addition of the term "*aequitas*" to it.

The article by David Deroussin reflects the next historical stage of the usage of *regulae*, when the "first principles" as the essential basis for the *regulae* persevered in their importance, but the context of the *regulae* rose back in prominence, as well. The author shows how both pre-codification (Domat) and post-codification (Dupin the Elder) French jurists saw the need for the "laws for the laws" for the French legal order, helping to organise the more specific legal rules and providing guidelines for the interpreters. They used the Roman *regulae* as the vehicle for the perennial "first principles" of law, a source of stability and authority; at the same time, they adapted the *regulae* to the context of their contemporary legal order. This article shares many common points with the article by I. Kotlyar, especially in comparing the *regulae* with signs and the system of *regulae* with language, in the notion that the function of the *regula* to a greater extent than its origin determines its meaning, and in dealing with the cases of the development of new *regulae* out of the old ones, in order to adapt the old *regulae* to the new context.

The article by Piotr Alexandrowicz is dedicated to the development and significance of the *regula* "*Utilius scandalum nasci permittitur quam veritas relinquatur*" from its origins in medieval Canon law (X 5.41.3). The article confirms many tenets of the main hypothesis, such as the central importance and the often arbitrary character of the *traditio regulae* in medieval jurisprudence, and the fact that the jurists formulated a new *regula* while being aware of its many exceptions and limitations. The article also shows the key importance of the meaning of terms, such as "*veritas*", in defining the scope of the *regula*, and the importance of different contextual paradigms of meanings (*veritas bonae vitae, veritas iustitiae,* etc) for that purpose. It also shows how a *regula* tended to be defined more and more precisely with time. On the other hand, the article seems to contradict the main hypothesis by showing that medieval jurists (Hostiensis, Panormitanus) often kept going back to the theological "essence" of the rule, as well as paying attention to the inconsistency of the original legal source of the *regula* (*Liber Extra* with the Ordinary Gloss), instead of trying to develop a uniform interpretation of the rule "here and now".

The article by Gerard (Ger) Coffey provides quite a challenge for the main hypothesis of this volume. The author sees the Common law rule against "double jeopardy", as well as the Continental Civil law principle "*ne bis in idem*", as based on the "universal law of reason, justice, and conscience". Even if this thesis might be debated, the author rightly points that this principle may already be identified in certain Roman fragments (e.g. D. 48.2.14), and it was not by chance that the 11th- to 13th-century English ecclesiastics referred to it in their attempts to establish jurisdictional immunity for clergy. The mystery lies in the fact that neither medieval civilians nor canonists attempted to make a *regula iuris* out of this principle. The most prominent collections of *regulae* omitted this principle; those that included it (e.g. *Flores legum* of 1496)[3] referred only to a single isolated fragment of the Digest in its support. It was unsurprising, then, that the similar principle would only be recognised in English law by the 18th century, as shown by the author. We have a clear case here where the jurists wanted a *regula* to exist to perform a particular function, so, the analogy with language suggests that the *regula* would be created; yet, this did not happen. This suggests that the structural context might not explain all the processes occurring with the *regulae iuris* in the medieval period.

The article by Harry Dondorp is dedicated to the emergence and development of the *regula* "*Duorum in solidum dominium esse non potest*" in medieval jurisprudence. The example of this *regula* shows how the exceptions (or *fallentiae*) were key to understanding its *ratio*, forcing the jurists to find appropriate meanings to the terms "*dominium*", "*in solidum*", etc. The article, nevertheless, shows how unsystematic the *fallentiae* could be, often duplicating each

3 *Flores legum secundum ordinem alphabeti* (Paris: Guy Marchant, 1496).

other, thereby obstructing a precise definition of the scope of the *regula*'s application.

The article by Emanuel G.D. van Dongen is dedicated to the development of the interpretation of the *regula* "*Quod quis ex sua culpa damnum sentit, damnum sentire non videtur*" (D. 50.17.203). The article shows how the same *regula*, with unchanging textual expression, significantly evolved in its meaning and implications, after Accursius in the 13th century placed it in the new mind scheme, within the normative context of delictual liability. This allowed applying this *regula* to cases of contributory negligence, demonstrating the power of normative context in the shaping of the *regulae*. At the same time, the article provides an example of how two *regulae* (D. 50.17.203 and VI. 5.13.86), similar almost to the point of confusion, were treated separately by the jurists, without submitting them to an identical interpretation. This speaks in favour of the relative importance of the normative essence of the *regula*, as opposed to its varying contexts.

CHAPTER 1

Roman and Medieval Juristic *Regulae* and *Brocarda* from the Structuralist Perspective: Real Entities or "Signs"?

Ilya A. Kotlyar

1 Medieval Dialectics and Its Epistemology: "Probable Truth" as Contextual Truth

One of the problems discussed by the researchers of *regulae iuris* in recent decades has been their relation to the medieval dialectical method. This problem is also the focus of the present work. Nevertheless, we first need to define what is meant by the medieval dialectical method. There seems to be no doubt that such a method existed, and it was relatively uniformly implemented in the practice of late medieval universities.[1] There is also little doubt that this method was strongly inspired by the dialectics (logic) of Aristotle, from which it adopted such key features as the separation of dialectics from ontology, strict distinction between demonstrative and probable conclusions, importance of the "commonly held assumptions", and close association with rhetorics, with mutual adoption of dialectical and rhetorical *loci* (*topoi*) as arguments in the disputation. The medieval scholars themselves associated their method with that of Aristotle.[2] Nevertheless, it must be remembered that the adoption of Aristotelianism in medieval thought was a complex process, only finished in the 13th century – long after the "dialectical method" had started being actively implemented, including in legal disputation. The views of Aristotle, including those on dialectics, were known to the pre-1200 European scholars mostly through Latin writings of Boethius: more specifically, his translation and commentary to Aristotle's *On Interpretation*, his translation and commentary to the Porphyrius' *Introduction* (*Isagoge*) to the *Categories* of Aristotle, his commentary to the *Topics* of Cicero, as well as his own *De topicis differentiis.* These texts together ended up being referred to as *vetus*

1 Olga Weijers, *A Scholar's Paradise: Teaching and Debating in Medieval Paris* (Turnhout: Brepols, 2015), 95–97, 107–110; Hans-Ulrich Wöhler, *Dialektik in der mittelalterichen Philosophie* (Berlin: Akademie Verlag, 2006), 126–129.

2 Wöhler, *Dialektik,* 22, 31.

 | DOI:10.1163/9789004736092_003

logica, in juxtaposition to *Prior Analitics, Posterior Analitics, Topics,* and other original works by Aristotle, rediscovered in the 12th century and designated as *logica nova*. The *vetus logica*, nevertheless, was never superseded at the medieval faculties of arts: the students always began their studies with Boethius, only later passing on to the newly discovered texts.[3]

From this selection of texts, one could not form an appropriate understanding of Aristotle's metaphysics and physics, and the place of his dialectical method in that system. From the legacy of Boethius, one would primarily study the formal logic (or term logic) of Aristotle, his Ten Categories, his juxtaposition of matter and form (hylomorphism), together with the related juxtaposition of *genus* and *species*. The reader could learn the distinction between universal and particular propositions through the "square of opposition" ("Porphyrian square"), learn that contradictory propositions could not both be false but contrary propositions could, as well as that indefinite (i.e., neither clearly universal nor particular) propositions, though seemingly opposed to each other, could both be true. At the same time, Boethius and other Late Antique authors often mixed Aristotelian ideas with their own Neoplatonic or Stoic interpretations. Unlike Aristotle himself, Porphyrius and Boethius, holding to a more "realist" understanding of "universals", exaggerated the controversy over them. They exacerbated the juxtaposition between genus, uniting uniform "matter", and species, based on a *differentia* of "form".[4] The "form", besides individualising and actualising the "matter", also becomes the basis for "universals", containing the essence of individual things: the predicates are "intrinsic" (*insunt*) to the individual things upon which they are predicated.[5] Boethius also joined the Aristotelian 'term logic' with the Stoic 'propositional logic', with its conditional propositions (e.g. *modus ponens*).[6] Finally, Boethius significantly influenced the subsequent tradition of dialectics by stressing the importance of "maxims" in dia-

3 Weijers, *A Scholar's Paradise*, 54.

4 Severinus Boethius, "*In Isagogen Porphyrii Commentarium,*" *Corpus Scriptorum Ecclesiasticorum Latinorum* 38 (1906): 135–348, https://www.logicmuseum.com/wiki/Authors/Boethius/isagoge/CPorII, IV.11.

5 Hugh Chisholm, ed. *Encyclopaedia Britannica*, 11th ed. (Cambridge: Cambridge University Press, 1911), "Predicables," https://en.wikisource.org/wiki/1911_Encyclop%C3%A6dia_Britannica/Predicables; Severinus Boethius, *De differentiis topicis libri quattuor* (Paris: apud Prigentium Calvarin, 1533), 11.

6 Thomas Bénatouïl, "Introduction: Dialectics in Dialogue," in *Dialectic after Plato and Aristotle*, ed. Thomas Bénatouïl and Katerina Ierodiakonou (Cambridge: Cambridge University Press, 2019), 4–5; Katerina Ierodiakonou, "Dialectic as a Subpart of Stoic Philosophy," in *Dialectic after Plato and Aristotle*, 120–121, 123–127; Sophie Aubert-Baillot, "Terminology and Practice of Dialectic in Cicero's Letters," in *Dialectic after Plato and Aristotle*, 256–258.

lectical reasoning. He identified as "maxims" the propositions which did not require proof and could not be proven. The maxims were universally true and could be identified in any argumentation. This is yet another example of how Aristotelian dialectic evolved into a more "realist" and "universalist" variety in the late antique writings, that transmitted it to medieval readers.[7]

In the end, one may argue that the medieval intellectuals have received, and even developed further, Aristotle's dialectical method of study and argumentation (mixed to a significant degree with methods from Stoicism), without necessarily receiving the substantive philosophy, or metaphysics, of Aristotle. The culture of organised debates and disputations was omnipresent in medieval European universities; however, its purpose was usually didactic: it was more often an exercise, or a game, instead of pursuing the goal to resolve a real theoretical issue "once and for all".[8] The questions were set, theses brought forward, opposing arguments raised, and the question finally resolved – all these stages were aimed primarily to train the skill of the debaters, both in the method of argumentation and in the knowledge of the substantive topic (law, grammar, natural philosophy, etc.). This was because the final goal of dialectical disputation was not to achieve a certain truth, but rather a "provable truth", a "probable knowledge". Thomas Aquinas famously wrote that "essential principles of the things are unknown to us" (*principia essentialia rerum sunt nobis ignota*),[9] expressing the caution of medieval philosophy to make final and definite judgments about truth in the actual reality. Only the truths of logic, arithmetic and geometry, based on unquestionable axioms, were certain and demonstrable. All the other truths, based on assumptions held by "the many, the wisest, or the many among the wisest", were subject to doubt and discussion. When medieval doctors and students staged disputes on the topics like "Do all roses have spikes?", they were trying to produce not "necessary knowledge" (in the classification of Boethius), but rather probable knowledge, i.e., knowledge with high convincing power. Being true and being convincing did not necessarily coincide.[10]

And, yet, dialectical truth and knowledge were still truth and knowledge, even if of the "lower order", so to say. Aristotle himself insisted that "probable truth" was truth in the majority of cases. The more probable was a proposition,

---

7 For more details on the influence of Boethius in the creation of maxims, see the contribution of A. Giuliani to this volume.

8 Weijers, *A Scholar's Paradise*, 101–104, 121–135; Wöhler, *Dialektik*, 126.

9 Thomas Aquinas, *Sentencia libri De Anima*, 1.1 n. 15, https://www.corpusthomisticum.org/can1.html.

10 Boethius, *De differentiis topicis*, 16–18.

the closer to the truth it was.[11] The same idea we may find in Boethius, with his distinction of "necessary" and "probable" knowledge – knowledge that convinces people could also end up being true and "necessary". Boethian "maxims" reflect the same principle: if a certain premise is tacitly used in syllogisms and argumentation and never fails to support the arguments and convince the scholars, it must be necessarily true. Similarly, medieval dialecticians, e.g. William of Conches (1090–c. 1170), would often hold that the results of disputations and setting opposing arguments against each other were not necessarily true, but they were "true opinions", with a high probability of being true, in contrast to unsubstantiated "false opinions".[12] The truth of propositions in the dialectical discourse could be described as "contextual truth". Various theses, proposed and opposed at scholarly disputations, could be true under certain circumstances of the real world context and false under other circumstances. Nevertheless, the final product of a disputation, effectually tested "by fire" of the opposing objections, reevaluated and made more precise by the learned debaters, eventually taking account of all or almost all imaginable circumstances – after all these "filters", the final solution would end up more universal, and, therefore, closer to the "Truth", in this epistemological system. It was not by chance that disputations in medieval universities would often allow questions and objections to be raised by the general public (*a quolibet*): the idea was to make sure that all possible contradicting cases could be considered and, thus, ensure the "universality" of the conclusions.[13]

Besides the circumstances of the real world, to approach the level of verisimilitude and universality, a thesis was supposed to take account of the context of related and opposing concepts and propositions, so that a proper distinction could be made where one proposition applies and where another takes its place. This often involved distinguishing between different meanings of terms, as well as between matter and form, between substance and accident, between concepts taken as a genus and as a species. For example, Thomas Aquinas masterfully uses such distinctions in his *Summa Theologiae* in order to reconcile seemingly contradictory passages from authoritative texts. Thus, he distinguishes between the particular virtue of justice (*iustitia*), which deals with a behaviour of one individual towards other individuals, and the so-called "legal justice", which he sees as a general virtue, uniting all other virtues in so far as they contributed towards the common good of the whole society. In this way, Aquinas reconciles the authorities that enumerated "just-

11 Wöhler, *Dialektik*, 23–24.
12 Wöhler, *Dialektik*, 71.
13 Wöhler, *Dialektik*, 131–133.

ice" among other special virtues, alongside prudence, temperance, etc, and the other authorities, that held that "justice is every virtue".[14] On another occasion, Aquinas distinguishes between the sin of 'unbelief' (*infidelitas*) in general, as encompassing all kinds of sins against faith, and 'unbelief' as a special sin, on par with Christian heresies and Judaism. In this way, he reconciles the contradicting opinions on who sins more: the pagans, the Judaists, or the heretics. His solution explains that subjective guilt in the case of heresy is the greatest, because the sin is against the faith, which the sinner has already accepted as true; on the other hand, objectively, the "corruption of faith" is greater with the pagans, and the gravest objective extent of their unbelief is when they commit apostasy, returning to paganism, which is not a special kind of 'unbelief', but an aggravating circumstance of such.[15] Moreover, Aquinas uses the Aristotelian distinction between subjective, integral, and potential parts of a whole, to resolve the conflicting classifications of virtues and synthesise one uniform classification. For example, in the virtue of justice, he finds such subjective parts as distributive and commutative justice, such (quasi-)integral parts as "doing good" and "avoiding evil", and such (quasi-) potential parts as religion, piety, observance, and equity. The vices against these virtues were classified accordingly.[16]

All this demonstrates how a holistic approximation of truth was achieved, or at least, believed to be achieved, in the medieval dialectical method, by setting various concepts and conceptual systems against each other and integrating them together. Even though the positions of particular elements in the system formulated by a scholar could be mistaken, the whole system achieved an approximation of reality and possessed explanatory power. Even though the philosophy of Thomas Aquinas, and most of the late medieval philosophy in general, was Aristotelian, based on the rediscovered corpus of works by Aristotle, this epistemology and dialectical method were marked by Neo-Platonist and Boethian characteristics. All in all, this methodology was distinctively a medieval creation, deeply influenced by the Christian notion that the truth is knowable and that it may be found in the corpus of authoritative texts and traditions if proper effort is made.

---

14 Aquinas, *Summa Theologiae,* IIa-IIae, qu. 58, art. 5–8, https://www.corpusthomisticum.org/sth3057.html.

15 Aquinas, *Summa Theologiae,* IIa-IIae, qq. 10–12, https://www.corpusthomisticum.org/sth3001.html.

16 Aquinas, *Summa Theologiae,* IIa-IIae, qq. 48, https://www.corpusthomisticum.org/sth3047.html, 61, https://www.corpusthomisticum.org/sth3061.html, 79, https://www.corpusthomisticum.org/sth3079.html, 80, https://www.corpusthomisticum.org/sth3080.html.

The method of dialectical scholastic disputation, as implemented in medieval learned practice, involved the following stages/elements: (1) raising of a thesis on the basis of authoritative sources, (2) juxtaposition of the thesis to other theses, also found in the texts of authority, (3) bringing of the arguments in support of either thesis and their analysis, (4) resolution of the contradiction through the introduction of a *tertium* (a concept or a condition, allowing to distinguish between the theses and connect one or both of them to an established truth or a logical maxim), (5) confirmation of an old thesis or synthesis of a new one, (6) responses to the objections brought against the thesis.[17] In the universities, this procedure was routinely institutionalised through the appointment of *repondens* and *opponens*, or even allowing the general public to set their questions to the *respondens*.[18]

2 *Regulae Iuris*: To What Extent Dialectical?

To what extent do the *regulae iuris* fit within the tradition of dialectic? This question has been addressed by the scholars a few times, but a clear answer seems to have never been given.

Perhaps the most influential researcher of the *regulae iuris* of the last century, Peter Stein, touched upon the influence of Greek dialectics on Roman jurisprudence in the 2nd–1st centuries B.C. He explored the importance of the concept of "rule" in dialectics, as a means of distinction between right and wrong, and the importance of Cicero's use of the term "*regula*" in application to rhetorical, dialectical, and legal issues.[19] The focus of Stein, however, is on the influence of other liberal arts, rhetoric and, especially, grammar, on the Roman notion of *regula*. In particular, he pays much attention to the debates between "analogists" and "anomalists" among the grammarians of the 2–1st-centuries B.C., described by Varro. The "analogists" (notably, Aristarchus of Samothrace) sought to reduce all grammar to general rules and eliminate exceptions, while the "anomalists" (e.g. Crates of Mallus) sought to preserve the exceptions. Stein posits as the main thesis that the attitude of the Classical Proculian and Sabinian schools of jurisprudence reflected the attitudes of the "analogists" and "anomalists", respectively, in application to law.[20]

17 Wöhler, *Dialektik*, 127.
18 Weijers, *A Scholar's Paradise*, 131–133.
19 Peter Stein, *Regulae Iuris: From Juristic Rules to Legal Maxims* (Edinburgh: Edinburgh University Press, 1966), 49–52.
20 Stein, *Regulae Iuris*, 53–61.

Stein also mentions the relevance of medieval dialectics in the debates among medieval jurists, noting that Placentinus scorned dialectics and other sciences of the *trivium*, while his opponent Johannes Bassianus, as well as his students/successors Azo and Accursius, were appreciative of the liberal arts. Stein provides a few examples of how dialectical thinking affected the views of the jurists of the line of Bassianus, the prime example being the principle that a species is always a part of the genus and thus cannot contradict it.[21] Stein also mentions how the notions of Boethius influenced Azo's comment to D. 50.17.202 on the relation of *regulae* and *diffinitiones*, and how they help to identify the substance of the legal cases.[22] Yet, unfortunately, Stein fails to explain all the implications of the application of dialectical categories to *regulae* by medieval jurists. From Stein's book, it is not clear what was at stake in the debates between Placentinus and Bassianus, how the medieval jurists understood "substance", what "general" and "special" meant for them, and many other relevant questions.

Stein also pays attention to the logical maxims of medieval dialectics, including those developed by Robert Kilwardby, William Shyreswood, and other medieval dialecticians. Nevertheless, the only purpose of this reference for Stein is to explain why the term "maxim" rather than the term "*regula*" came to dominate English legal discourse.[23] Notably, Stein also uses the term "maxim" retrospectively, in order to describe particular rules formulated by Classical Roman jurists, which did not qualify to be classified as *regulae iuris* proper, lacking sufficient level of abstraction and a clear scope of direct application. Such rules were rather empirical criteria to solve legal cases in a particular way; Stein provides "*Ignorantia iuris nocet*" (D. 22.6.9pr)[24] as an example of such "maxims".[25]

All in all, it may be said that Stein viewed the *regulae* as a legal phenomenon, first and foremost. Even if it was inspired by the influences from rhetorics, dialectics and other disciplines, an impression is made that, having taken its shape in law, the cross-disciplinary influence becomes negligible and the phenomenon starts following the logic of law, practical and theoretical.

Roughly contemporaneously with Stein, research on the medieval stage of the development of the *regulae* was performed by Peter Weimar. The most

---

21 Stein, *Regulae Iuris*, 139–142, 144–145.

22 Stein, *Regulae Iuris*, 143.

23 Stein, *Regulae Iuris*, 153–162.

24 Editor's note: In the FWO.OPR.2020.005001 database, this *regula* is registered under No. 120.

25 Stein, *Regulae Iuris*, 105–108.

significant contribution of Weimar was demonstrating, through the history of the evolution of 12th-century collections of "*brocarda*", that "maxim"-like assertions of the early Glossators performed a function similar to that of the *topoi*, or *loci communes*, used as sources of argument in dialectical and rhetorical disputations. Hence the etymology of the term "*brocarda*", which Weimar connected to the stem '*broccus*' ('fangs', 'protruding teeth') – they were initially seen primarily as "weapons" for the lawyers to argue their positions.[26] The first collections of *brocarda*, such as the *Perpendiculum* (c. 1180), contained the arguments both "for" and "against" a particular position, without providing a solution. *Regulae iuris*, according to Weimar, were initially distinguished from *brocarda*: they were a product of the juxtaposition and resolution of contradicting *brocarda*. Weimar demonstrated how the Glossators developed new *regulae* in three stages, which may also be seen as three elements of a 'brocard': (*1*) *notabile*, (*2*) *generale*, (*3*) *solutio/regula*.[27] Gradually, the final solution came to be identified with the whole process, and the *regulae* and *brocarda* came to be seen as synonymous. Despite establishing the similarity of functions between the *brocarda* and *topica*, Weimar does not develop further the topic of the extent and productivity of the influence of dialectics and dialectical epistemology on medieval jurisprudence. In his later article he, despite identifying the juxtaposition and solution of contraries, as well as the involvement of the *generalia*, as indispensable elements of the method of arguing and expounding law among the Glossators (according to their own witness), does not touch upon the issue of the relation of that method to medieval dialectics, at all.[28]

Gerhard Otte was one of the few scholars who directly addressed the extent to which medieval Glossators took advantage of dialectical categories and principles in their legal reasoning. He demonstrated that the superficially dismissive attitude of some jurists towards the liberal arts, including dialectics, did not entail either ignorance of those disciplines or a refusal to employ their methods. Quite to the contrary, probably, in contradiction to the assumptions of Stein, Otte showed that even Placentinus was aware of the categories of Cicero and used them in his legal discourse.[29] The categories of Aristotelian dialectics, in their Ciceronian-Boethian interpretation, were very much inte-

26 Peter Weimar, "*Argumenta brocardica*," *Studia Gratiana* 14 (1967): 95–107, 112–114.

27 Weimar, "*Argumenta brocardica*," 111–112.

28 Peter Weimar, "Die legistische Literatur und die Methode des Rechtsunterrichts der Glossatorenzeit," *Ius Commune* 2 (1969): 43–83, in particular at 48–49.

29 Gerhard Otte, *Dialektik und Jurisprudenz, Untersuchungen zur Methode der Glossatoren* (Frankfurt: Vittorio Klostermann, 1971), 31, 83–84, 143–144, 157–158, 160.

gral to the method and discussions of the medieval jurists. Following this interpretation, the jurists identified the special *differentia* with "form" and strived to classify genera into species only on the basis of a "substantial form". Following this system, Glossator Azo criticises the idea that the division of law into public and private was based on the regulated subject matter, because otherwise there would be an infinite speciation of law into the "law of donkeys", "law of horses", etc.; instead, this division was supposed to be based on the, presumably, more substantive "interests of the whole vs interests of the individuals" criterion.[30] The jurists also demonstrated the ability to distinguish between subjective and integral "parts" of legal phenomena, holding, for example, that a usufruct (as the right to collect fruits) was an integral part of the ownership (*dominium*), but not a part of the genus "ownership", because it was a species of servitude. A full ownership (*plenum dominium*), being a union of "property" (*proprietas*) and the right to fruits, was therefore not possible without a usufruct; and, yet, the *proprietas* was seen as the key material component of the genus "ownership".[31] But Otte also pays attention to the peculiarities of the legal discipline, noting, for example, that the term "species" was often used by the jurists not in its dialectical meaning, but in the meaning used in the Roman juristic texts, referring to individually defined goods, as opposed to "genus", referring to goods measurable in weight, volume, etc.[32]

The deficiency of Otte's account was in not drawing significant distinction between rhetorics and dialectics and, therefore, misrepresenting the method of medieval Glossators. Otte insisted that, unlike medieval theologians, the jurists were not oriented towards discovering a juridical truth, but only towards developing convincing methods of legal argumentation. In support, he referred to seeming inconsistencies in the juristic disputations, preserved to our days, as well as to the fact that the earliest juristic *brocarda* had no solutions. Referring to Weimar, Otte held that the *regulae* and *brocarda* were a product of inductive reasoning from particular legal *casus,* while their primary function was similar to the rhetorical *topoi* – to convince, not to generalise the law in an authoritative way.[33] That the probable truth was also "the truth" and that high convincing power in the dialectical method meant a high probability of truth seem to have escaped Otte's attention. The arguments

30 Azo Portius, *Summa super Codicem* (Torino: apud heredes Nicolai Bevilacquae, 1578; Torino: ex officina Erasmiana, 1966), 348, Inst.Just. 1.1.

31 Otte, *Dialektik und Jurisprudenz*, 46–47; D. 7.1.4; D. 50.16.25.

32 Otte, *Dialektik und Jurisprudenz*, 47–48.

33 Otte, *Dialektik und Jurisprudenz*, 220–225.

brought by Otte in favour of his thesis do not stand. For example, the fact that *Quaestiones Sabbatinae* by Pilius (1200s) often resolved the disputed questions in a "*deus ex machina*" fashion[34] was actually a typical characteristic of the medieval dialectics, where the "accidents" of the phenomenon could help to identify the "substance" and, lacking "necessary" conclusions, the more convincing conclusions would often be adopted. This cannot serve as a proof of irrelevance of truth for medieval Glossators.

A new wave of interest to the *regulae* and their methodological ramifications seems to have arisen by the 2010s. David Deroussin in 2008 and 2012 dedicated articles, respectively, to the Roman and the early modern ideas for the *regulae*. Particularly telling is his observation on the Platonic influence on the rise of the *regulae*, which could be seen as 'ideal types' of solutions for groups of similar legal cases. His observation that the *regulae* were an instrument of the Ciceronian programme to present the law as 'art' (hence, '*Ius est ars boni et aequi*') is also very important. Nevertheless, Deroussin insisted that the *regulae* were a purely legal phenomenon, derived from positive law rather than from extra-legal ethics or dialectics.[35]

In 2016, an important collection of articles was edited by Valeria Di Nisio, looking at the *regulae iuris* not only from a legal historical, but also from a legal theoretical point of view.[36] In particular, the contributions by Vincenzo Giuffre and Alessandro Corbino further develop Stein's history of Roman *regulae*. An important claim is made that universally worded rules are *a priori* used in a "jurisprudential legal order", i.e., in a legal order where opinions of jurists bear authority.[37] The contribution by Corbino attempts to reconstruct a Roman "theory" of *regulae*, explaining the relationship between a *regula*, a legal precept and a legal *casus*, the applicability of newly formed *regulae* to newly emergent *casus*, etc.[38] There seems to be a disagreement between

34 For example, by bringing a citation not mentioned in the 'pro-contra' sections as an argument for solution (Pilius Medicinensis, *Quaestiones Sabbatinae* (Modena: Presso l'Universitá degli studi, 1935), 14 (*quaestio* 3)), or by referring to an established custom as the decisive argument (ibid, 33 (*quaestio* 8)).

35 David Deroussin, "Le droit romain a-t-il connu des principes? Sur les significations (possibles) de *principia, praecepta* et *regulae iuris*", in *Les principes en droit*, ed. Silvie Caudal (Paris: Economica, 2008), 132–139, 147–148. For the 2012 article, see bibliography.

36 Valeria Di Nisio, ed., *Regulae Iuris. Ipotesi di lavoro tra storia e teoria del diritto* (Naples: Jovene Editore, 2016).

37 Vincenzo Giuffrè, „Regulae Iuris. Prospettive di approfondimenti," in *Regulae Iuris. Ipotesi*, 12–13.

38 Alessandro Corbino, „Caso, diritto e regula. Limiti della funzione normative del caso deciso nella visione romana", in *Regulae Iuris. Ipotesi*, 35–76.

Thomas Finkenauer, who stresses the mnemonic function of the *regulae*,[39] and Cosimo Cascione, who insists the *regula* always has an abstract legal value and "resists invasion of the case".[40] The deficiency of the volume is its unidisciplinarity, the lack of a perspective on the *regulae* from the point of view of grammar, dialectics, rhetorics, and other disciplines relevant in Antiquity and the Middle Ages.

In contrast, the influence of rhetorics on law comes to the fore in the upcoming monograph by J.W. Tellegen and O.E. Tellegen-Couperus, to be published soon by Brill.[41] The authors have revealed that many of the *regulae iuris*, assembled in the title 17 of the book 50 of the Digest of Justinian, originated from rhetorical *topoi*, with Cirero's *Topica* being particularly influential. For sure, the influence of rhetorics cannot explain the origin of all the Roman *regulae*. Yet, it is an important reminder that juristic thinking can never be taken in isolation from other disciplines.

David De Concilio has recently defended a thesis, confirming and qualifying the observations of P. Weimar. He confirms that the 12th-century collections of *brocarda* were inspired by rhetorical and dialectical *topoi* and pursued predominantly an educational task. Nevertheless, he noted that the early 13th-century collections, especially those associated with the school of Bologna, demonstrated a tendency to routinely solve the contradictions between the *brocarda*, with a view of the systematisation of law.[42]

The provided literature review by no means attempts to be exhaustive on the topic of the *regulae iuris* in general, or on the topic of the relation of the *regulae* to dialectics. In summary, much of the debate taking place in the literature in the course of recent decades revolves about the extent to which the *regulae iuris*, either in Roman or medieval times, reflected the "Truth" in law, the "contextual" or dialectical truth. In other words, was there among them, at any point in time, a certain system, or uniformity, shared by "the many, the wisest, or the many among the wisest" of jurists? Or, rather, vice versa, every *regula* had only that meaning and scope of application that any individual jurist ascribed to it, without any clear uniformity?

39 Thomas Finkenauer, „Le *Regulae iuris* come strumenti mnemotecnici," in *Regulae Iuris. Ipotesi*, 77–86.

40 Cosimo Cascione, „Profondita e margini di una ricerca," in *Regulae Iuris. Ipotesi*, 210–211.

41 Jan-Willem Tellegen and Olga Tellegen-Couperus, "The *Regula* as a Rhetorical Device in Roman Law" (unpublished manuscript, 10 July 2023), PDF.

42 David De Concilio, "Via Brocardica. The Development of Brocards and the Western European Legal Tradition (c. 1160–c. 1215)" (Ph.D. diss., University of St. Andrews, 2022).

Setting the question properly is by itself a step in the direction of answering it. In order to find out whether there was an overarching system among the *regulae iuris*, it is natural to compare them with the system that originally gave rise to rhetorics, dialectics, and all Western philosophy in general. The *regulae* should be compared with language – not with a particular one, but with the language as a general phenomenon, on which grammar, dialectics, and other liberal arts were based. Therefore, now we will look at structural linguistics and see how implementation of its methodology by analogy to law may help us to understand the *regulae* better and evaluate the degree of their uniformity and standardisation.

3 Structural Linguistics as a Method: Connections with Dialectics and Law

Structural linguistics is a combination of approaches, inspired by the works of Swiss linguist Ferdinand de Saussure (1857–1913), in particular by his posthumous *Cours de linguistique générale* (1916). The basic feature of this methodology is the distinction between actual human speech (*parole*) and language proper as an abstract entity (*langue*). Language proper, in this approach, is presented as a system of signs. A "sign" is defined as a unity between the "signifier" and the "signified". The signs are "arbitrary" – not in the sense that there is no order among them, but in the sense that they are not predetermined by the objective reality which they signify. Taken in isolation, no sign has any meaning. The signs have meaning only in their relations with other signs. The relations can be those of juxtaposition (e.g. English noun 'advice' vs. English verb 'to advise'), analogy (e.g. words similar in some ways being similar in other ways, too), syntactic function, and so on. In any case, the meaning of every sign within the system of signs is fundamentally 'negative' and 'relative', in the sense that the users of language do not define 'apple' through any positive characteristics of an apple, but rather through the denial of other words which could be used. The apple is not 'pear', 'peach', 'banana' or any other word for fruits known in the given language. Thus, the structure existing in the language (in this case – a vocabulary of various fruit names) serves as a limit of arbitrariness in the language – a delimitation on what is possible and not possible in it. The structuralist approach sees those structures as the proper subject matter of linguistics, in contrast to 'extra-linguistic' influences on language by psychological, social, cultural, and physical phenomena.

Most importantly, taken as a structure, the language is viewed 'synchronically', i.e., as a fixed in time, 'dogmatic' system. Saussure did not deny the importance of diachronic research (i.e., evolution of languages) but saw it as a fundamentally random process. Dynamic changes in the languages, allegedly, do not change the whole system but only particular elements within the system; they can, nevertheless, undermine the steady equilibrium of the system and make it switch to another equilibrium.[43]

Structural linguistics post-Saussure was represented by several linguistic schools: Prague school, Moscow circle, Copenhagen circle. With all the differences between various authors, there is a significant degree of conceptual unity. Louis Hjelmslev, from the Copenhagen circle, even attempted an ambitious task of creating a fully formalised theory of language. Thus, like in a math theorem, Hjelmslev defines "system" and "process", "correlation" and "relation"; he distinguishes linguistic "functions" acting in dynamic processes and those acting in static systems.[44] The "signified" and "signifier", in Hjelmslev, become designated as "content" and "expression", and the distinction between "form" and "substance" is added, so that the sign becomes a relationship of four elements: "content-substance", "content-form", "expression-substance", and "expression-form".[45] A sign is primarily a function of the "content-form" and "expression-form", in that the word "pink" in the English language designates a certain colour spectrum (content-form). That English has a different word, "rose", for a slightly different spectrum, while Dutch has the word "*roze*" to designate both spectra, is an example of how the language creates "content-form" and applies it to the "content-substance". Meanwhile, English "rose" and Dutch "*roze"* are one and the same "expression-form": their difference in pronunciation and spelling reflects different "expression-substances".

Thanks to structural linguistics, such concepts as "correlation", "combination", "solidarity" and similar have become technical terms in linguistics, designating certain types of relations between sounds and other linguistic units. Thus, Roman Jakobson actively applied the same concepts and introduced some of his own: e.g. in distinguishing between "opposition" (when one of two the two alternative sounds is chosen) and "contrast" (when two different sounds are used together to highlight each other).[46] Jakobson saw language as

43 Ferdinand de Saussure, *Course in General Linguistics,* trans. Wade Baskin (New York: Philosophical Library, 1959), 83–87.

44 Louis Hjelmslev, *Prolegomena to a theory of language* (Madison: University of Wisconsin Press, 1963), 28–47.

45 Hjelmslev, *Prolegomena,* 51–56.

46 Roman Jakobson and Moris Halle, *Fundamentals of Language* (Berlin: Mouton de Gruyter, 1971), 14–15.

a form that shapes the "sound matter", a certain "code" that the listeners learn to decrypt. The linguistic units constituting the "code" have "distinctive features" – minimal features, allowing to distinguish one phoneme or morpheme from the other. There are also less essential "redundant features" (helping to stress the distinctive features) and "configurative features" (helping to arrange the distinctive features). Binary contrasts and oppositions are crucial in this "code", but they are always relative: two "opposed" phonemes may together be opposed to a third one.[47]

The "code" is meaningful and decipherable because there are rules on what is possible and what is impossible in it. The dialectic of possible and impossible is very important in structural linguistics. Words from another language are incomprehensible to us because they use "unacceptable combinations".[48] Moreover, a language is a multi-level structure, with ascending degrees of freedom and widening borders of possible as we move from the lower-level simple sign-units (phonetics) to the higher-level and complex ones (grammar).[49] Every sign, e.g. a word, finds itself in the context of larger units and simultaneously provides context for the smaller constituent units, and the whole and the parts are equally dependent on each other. The more is the word dependent on the larger context of the sentence or the text, the less it is disturbed by speech or spelling errors.[50] This reflects the abovementioned principle of the relativity of binary oppositions: the features distinct in one context may be confused or even equalised in another context.

What is noticeable to an outside observer about structural linguistics is the strong influence of the notions of hylomorphism in the works of that school. Many of the concepts used by Saussure, Hjelmslev and Jakobson: "form", "matter", "substance", "essence", – look as if they were taken straight from Aristotle and Aristotelian tradition, with its juxtaposition of form and matter and the idea that reality is made up by the joining of the two. Yet another typically Aristotelean feature is the contrast between universal and particular, the whole and the parts. This is not very surprising if we remember that Aristotelian dialectics started, essentially, with an interpretation of language, of concepts used within language, and assertions formulated thereof. It is not by chance that even modern analytical philosophy tends to see philosophical disputes as linguistic misunderstandings.

---

47 Jakobson and Halle, *Fundamentals of Language*, 26.

48 Jakobson and Halle, *Fundamentals of Language*, 15.

49 Jakobson and Halle, *Fundamentals of Language*, 74.

50 Jakobson and Halle, *Fundamentals of Language*, 78.

Another significant overlap between structuralism and dialectics is that, while the language from the structuralist perspective is seen as a structure setting apart possible and impossible combinations, the dialectic was also traditionally seen as a structure distinguishing acceptable and unacceptable arguments, probable and improbable knowledge. Just as rules of grammar determine acceptable combinations of words, the logical maxims and *topoi* determine acceptable arguments to prove particular points, while the legal *regulae* may be seen as determining acceptable legal arguments.

The *regulae iuris*, according to P. Stein, came to be when controversies about grammar, between "analogists" and "anomalists", were extended to jurisprudence. Yet, both sides of the debate were united by the essential recognition that the *regulae* were different from the more specific legal precepts, that they were abstract, as opposed to specific, and were juxtaposed to the specific precepts. For example, in Gaius (2nd century), a late representative of the supposedly "anomalist" Sabinian school, we find a strong enthusiasm to define *rationes* underlying particular legal precepts into abstract *regulae*, and even to reconcile several *regulae* between each other and define the borders between them.[51] This assumes the idea that the *regulae* lie on a higher plane of abstraction than the rest of the law, that their interrelationships are independent of the "plane" of specific legal precepts, and that, in the end, the whole legal order is based on the system *regulae* or even reducible to them. The "analogist"–"anomalist" controversies seem to have revolved predominantly not around the existence of the abstract "level" of general rules but on the exact relationship between that level and the level of more specific precepts and practices. Is a *regula* with exceptions still valid? does a *regula* create new law in yet unresolved situations? – these questions were at stake, but not the special status of *regulae*.

It is safe to assume that, just as the rules of grammar have since the Hellenistic period been a subject of theoretical discourse, so were the *regulae* a subject of a theory, or theories, of *regulae*, especially in the medieval period, when knowledge was predominantly produced theoretically, with the help of the dialectical method. We should have a look at the medieval theories of law, and especially of *regulae*, compare them with what structural linguistics tells us about the evolution of language, and see if there is a similarity. Particular attention will be given to the relationship between the universal and the particular, because in this aspect we can see particularly strong similarities.

51 Stein, *Regulae Iuris*, 93–95.

4 Dynamic vs Static, Particular vs Universal in Language Compared to Medieval Jurisprudence

Linguistic evolution, from a structuralist perspective, may be presented in the form of four stages: (1) destruction of the initial static law, (2) accumulation of multiple solutions of the emergent vacuum, formation of a dynamic law, (3) generalisation of one of the solutions into a new norm, with a formation of the new static law, (4) regularisation/standardisation of the new static law, determining the scope of its application. One illustration of this scheme is the evolution of "ykavism" – a phonetical rule of Ukrainian language, whereby sounds [o] and [e], when they turn up in a closed syllable, transform into [i]. In the initial state of East Slavic dialects, before the year 1000, there was a high diversity of vowel sounds, while the closed syllables were a rarity. The 11th century saw a disappearance of "extra-short" [ĕ] and [ŏ] sounds in some dialects of what is now Ukraine, which led to a sudden appearance of "new closed syllables". The Proto-Slavic norm was, essentially, destroyed. During the stage (2), spanning roughly from 1050 to 1400, various dialects were inventing new phonemes for the "new closed syllables", so that they could remain distinguishable. Gradually, the sound [i] became the most popular substitute for [o] and [e] in such syllables. During the generalisation stage (3), approximately 1400–1700, the speakers started to associate (even if unwittingly) the closed syllables with the sound [i]: the use of [i] in all closed syllables becomes the new static norm. Finally, the regularisation phase (4), encompassing the 18th century, saw the social elite starting to reflect on the "correct" language and set the boundaries of application for the new rule. The phenomenon of "hypercorrection" appeared, whereby [i] started being used even in some open syllables, in imitation of the perceived "correct" language. At the same time, the rule stopped being productive and was no longer applied to newly adopted words from Church Slavonic, Greek, and other foreign languages. Exceptions to the rule were formulated. Thus, a new stable equilibrium was achieved.[52]

Significant similarities may be found in the process of *regulae* formation, at least in the form it was envisioned in the preserved Roman and medieval texts. Above we have already mentioned the three stages of the formulation of *regula* in medieval texts, through *notabile*, *generale* and *regula* proper, as identified by P. Weimar. These stages are well grounded in the sources: jurists, such

52 For more information about this process, see: George Y. Shevelov, *A historical phonology of the Ukrainian language* (Heidelberg: Winter, 1979).

as Azo, were often quite self-conscious about them. Thus, in his *Brocardica aurea,* Azo routinely distinguished between *notabilia*, which mostly had a rhetorical force of persuasion, *generalia*, which generalised the law for a particular genus of situations, and *regularia*, where a contradiction between opposing *generalia* was resolved, with one of them usually taken as a standard (regular) solution and the other as an exceptional solution.[53] It does not escape our attention that especially the last two stages, the 'generalisation' and 'regularisation', correspond pretty well with the process of linguistic evolution from the structuralist perspective, as described above. In both cases, first an inductive generalisation occurs, where empirical occurrences are associated with a particular *genus*; then, the newly generalised rule becomes the new norm, obtains a "life of its own" and starts being consciously extended to new cases, while also being consciously restricted by various exceptions.

Even more similarity we find if we look at the distinctive "theory of *regula*", which we can identify in the works of medieval jurists. Some beginnings of that "theory" we may find already in the work of Classical Roman jurists, who used a distinctive concept of "*traditio regulae*". It referred to the moment when a particular jurist in his writings "discovered" and formulated a *regula*, while his jurist colleagues accepted it as a *regula*. Normally, a jurist who formulated a *regula* was not the one to call it so – it was up to other jurists to do that.[54] There does not seem to have been much formal elaboration of what the *traditio regulae* was precisely to look like. But the juristic responses had an obligatory legal force in late Roman law, as enshrined by the 426 A.D. Law of Citations, and therefore the *traditio* was indeed seen as a legally significant event.

In the writings of certain medieval jurists, we find *traditio regulae* in a more elaborated form, strongly reminding of the "regularisation" phase of linguistic development, described above. *Traditio* was seen as a generalisation of the pre-existing law and the legal *casus*, previously resolved by the legislator or juristic responses. This is why the *regula,* in the 12th century juristic writings, was often associated with the "*ius commune*" – the usually applied law, resolving the cases that occurred "*frequenter*" rather than "*raro*".[55] The "rarity" of a

---

53 Azo Portius, *Brocardica aurea* (Venice: apud Franciscum Bindonum, 1566), fo. 2–3, 5, rub. I, fo. 36, rub. XI, fo. 54, rub. XVIII, fo. 62, rub. XXIII, fo. 98, rub. XLVI.

54 Stein, *Regulae Iuris,* 92.

55 "Omnis enim exceptio, vel excusatio, sua utitur aequitate contra regulam, quae est ius strictum et commune" (Azo, *Summa super Codicem,* C. 3.1, citation by: Severino Caprioli, "Tre capitoli intorno alla nozione di 'regula iuris' nel pensiero di Glossatori," *Annali di storia del diritto* 5/6 (1961/1962): 335); "Quandoque vero ponitur regula pro iure

situation was seen as one of the reasons why no *regula* could be formulated about it.[56] At the same time, from the point of view of the predominant and "orthodox" line of medieval juristic thought (Johannes Bassianus, Azo, Accursius), a *traditio regulae* was always supposed to identify a particular *genus* of cases, to which the *regula* would, from now on, apply directly and abstractly.[57] Notwithstanding that, every generalisation of that sort was imperfect and could "overstretch the wings of the *regula*".[58] Thus almost every *regula* was, strictly legally speaking, "false" and had exceptions: preexisting legal precepts that specially excluded a certain *species* of *casus* from rule(s) applying to the *genus*. The opposition of the *regula* to its exceptions was seen in the early writings as the opposition of "*ius commune*" and "*ius strictum*" ("strict law") to "written equity" (*aequitas scripta*).[59] In later writings, the association of *regulae* with *ius strictum* and *ius commune* was no longer as explicit,[60] seeing that *regulae*, too, were based on "equity"; nevertheless, the underlying idea remained that the *regula* was rooted in preexisting legal practice and, simultaneously, had a direct general legal force, corrected by exceptions. The exceptions were said to derogate from the *regula* (or, rather, from the field of *regula*'s direct legal force) in certain special fields, while simultaneously confirming the *regula* "stable and immovable" in non-excepted cases[61] and helping to define the *regula* by "declaring the *genus* to which the *regula*

communi" (Pascipovero, *Concordantia utriusque iuris*, citation by: Caprioli, "Tre capitoli", 331); "[...] ex iure quod est[...] scilicet generale plurium et commune, fiat regula" (*Glossa Magna* ad D. 50.17.1, s.v. '*Regula Est*'); "Item sumitur regula pro iure communi" (Guido da Baisio, *Rosarium super Decreto*, citation by: Caprioli, "Tre capitoli," 331). Cf. "regula iuris communis" (*Glossa Magna ad* D. 1.3.16(15), s.v. '*Ius Singulare*').

56 "... propter eorum nimiam raritatem" (Azo, *Summa super Codicem*, 411, D. 50.17).

57 "Regulae enim, licet indifinite proponantur, generaliter tamen exaudiuntur ..." (Azo, *Apparatus* ad D. 50.17.1, citation by: Caprioli, "Tre capitoli," 362); "... ubi ergo nulla est exceptio, facit ius generale" (*Glossa Magna* ad D. 50.17.1, s.v. '*Regula Est*').

58 "... et quia nimium alas suas ampliat sibi derogatur in aliquibus" (Azo, *Apparatus* ad D. 50.17.80.1, citation by: Caprioli, "Tre capitoli," 363).

59 "Item in qualibet regula quae habet exceptionem: nam exceptio est de equitate et regula de stricto iure; et sic magis exsequenda est exceptio" (Azo, *Apparatus* ad C. 3.1.8, citation by: Caprioli, "Tre capitoli," 355); "Item poni potest fere in omni regula, cum quaelibet patiatur exceptionem ... & exceptiones sunt de aequitate ..." (Azo Portius, *Lectura super Codicem* (Paris: Nivelle, 1577; Torino: ex officina Erasmiana, 1966), 167, C. 3.1.8).

60 Caprioli, "Tre capitoli," 336–337.

61 "..ipsa lex vel regula firmatur, quae remanet" (*Glossa Magna* ad Nov.7.2.pr, s.v. '*In auxilio*'); "[exceptiones] ostendunt [regulam] firmam in [casibus] non exceptis" (Dynus of Mugello, *Tractatus super regulis iuris* (Paris: Georges Mittelhus, 1498), ad rubr, https://gallica.bnf.fr/ark:/12148/bpt6k9926161/f13.item#).

applies".[62] *Traditio regulae,* in medieval jurisprudence, was thus seen as inseparable from the definition and conservation of the *regula*'s existing exceptions, turning them into a *numerus clausus*. This was understandable from the point of view of dialectics: when a *regula* was associated with a *genus*, it was attached not to a determinate material set of *casus* but rather to the form defining that *genus*, and therefore it allowed for exceptions. But, more importantly, the *traditio regulae*, as understood in medieval jurisprudence, bears a strong resemblance to the linguistic regularisation, described above, in that it was a conscious creation of a new abstract rule, which gives a start to both the direct application of that rule to newly discovered cases, falling within a certain *genus* or *species*, and to the conscious restriction of the rule's application to the identified exceptional situations.[63]

Yet another parallel with linguistics is that the newly consciously formulated rule was not, generally, applicable to completely new situations, i.e., dialectically speaking, new "forms" shaping new "matter". Thus, in the example with "ykavism" above, the newly shaped rule stopped, at some point, being applied to words newly borrowed from other languages, i.e., new combinations, consisting of what was perceived as the new "sound-matter". We find in the medieval jurisprudence a similar juxtaposition of "old law", to which old *rationes determinationis*, analogies and established *regulae* were applicable, to the "new law", regulating completely new situations, which could not, even in principle, be foreseen by the old law. Fiefs, seen as created and regulated by custom, were the prime example of such "new matters". This juxtaposition of "*nova negotia*", requiring a new resolution, to the cases already resolved by law, precedent and the established forms of interpretation, we find in the writings of Azo,[64] as well as the Accursian Gloss. Bartolus, too, in his discourse on customs, held that, in the fields covered by old law but not explicitly resolved by it, a new custom was not to be applied by analogy, because the *ratio legis* was to prevail, but in the fields completely ignored by old law the custom could completely abrogate law and its *ratio*; behind this *ratio legis*, we can recognise the *regula,* seen as a *coniunctio rationum legis*.[65] Elsewhere, Bartolus, essentially, recognises that the *regula*'s non-application to new laws means that it has no

---

62 "Exceptio declarat regulam: quia ex qualitate exceptionis declaratur de quo genere regula loquatur" (Philippus Decius, *In tit. Ff. De regulis iuris* (Lyon: Antoin Vincent, 1562), 9, D. 50.17.1).

63 "..ubi autem [regula] habet exceptionem, facit ius speciale praeterquam in exceptis" (*Glossa Magna* ad D. 50.17.1, s.v. '*Regula Est*').

64 Azo, *Lectura super Codicem,* 44, C. 1.14(17).11(10); Azo, *Summa super Codicem,* 9, C. 1.14(17).

65 Bartolus de Saxoferrato, *In primam Digesti Veteris partem Commentaria* (Venice: Giunti, 1590), fo. 18v, *repetitio* in D. 1.3.32(31).

direct legal force other than in respect of the cases with an already established *ratio* and context.[66] A *regula* could, in theory, be applied by analogy to newly occurring and rare situations, as Bartolus himself demonstrates in his treatment of the case with a newly emerging island in the sea;[67] but his application of the "*Quod in nullius bonis est prius occupanti conceditur*"[68] *regula* to this situation is not blanket but careful, with a careful weighing of which *ratio* was best in resolving various issues emerging in such a situation.[69] All in all, just like in the case with linguistic development, the theory of *regula* reveals the notion of a never-ending process of "discovering" new rules, which both extends and restricts their application, but always according to the defined criteria: the "similarity of reasoning", newness and oldness, form and matter.

In addition, both linguistic development and the medieval theory of *regula* demonstrate the alignment of the "rule-exception" and the "static-dynamic" juxtapositions with each other. Indeed, already Saussure described static (synchronic) rules of language as "universal but not imperative", meaning that they are perceived by the speakers as binding but always allowing for exceptions. He contrasted them to the "particular but imperative" dynamic (diachronic) laws, meaning that changes of particular elements with in a language are always caused by extralinguistic factors (social, psychological, etc.) and consist of multiple individual changes.[70] These changes always affect particular forms existing within the language, such as sound or word combinations, or only individual words or sounds, but, within the form that they affect, they have no exceptions and are always consistent. In other words, while the static laws represent "abstract forms" in the language, dynamic changes are always specific and material, changing the "sound-matter" within the static "forms". This suggests that, when a new static rule is generalised, the exceptions to it tend to be more "material": they are collections of individual cases, to which the linguistic innovation failed to extend. In the example of Ukrainian "ykavism", while the static rule applies to closed syllables in general, the multiple

66 For example, when speaking about the *regula Catoniana* (on invalidity of legacies) and the reasons why it is not directly applicable to subsequently introduced legal grounds for invalidity of legacies (Bartolus de Saxoferrato, *In secundam Infortiati partem Commentaria* (Lyon: Harcaeus, 1552), fo. 121r, D. 34.7.5).

67 Bartolus de Saxoferrato, *In secundam Digesti Novi partem Commentaria* (Venice: Giunti, 1590), 237r, D. 50.17.1.

68 Editor's note: In the FWO.OPR.2020.005001 database this *regula* is registered under No. 305.

69 Bartolus de Saxoferrato, *Tractatus Tyberiadis seu de fluminibus* (Rome: Herolt&Riessinger, 1483), Liber II, s.v. '*Nullius enim*', '*Sed quaero*' & '*Sed quid si ille*'.

70 Saussure, *Course in General Linguistics*, 92–95.

exceptions to it reflect the more conservative situations, which were not affected by the disappearance of extra-short vowels at the stage (1) above, and were thus not affected by the dynamic law at the stage (2). These exceptions are "epenthetic" vowels, words with an extra added syllable, "apocopic" words, "vowel – liquid consonant" combinations, as well as suffixes, prefixes, and many other generic situations. Yet, there are no "exceptions within exceptions", not counting a few isolated words, explainable through either linguistic analogy[71] or through peculiarities of the word itself.[72] The relation of the rule to the exceptions is, thus, a binary one, like that of a genus and a species, not allowing for additional complexities. This context of a binary relation ends up being decisive in determining the scope of the rule's application at the regularisation stage (4), in contrast to the original causes for the linguistic change, lying at the stages (1) and (2).

In a similar way, in the medieval jurisprudence, we see a clear juxtaposition of *regulae,* as universal and abstract "pure forms", and all other types of legal rules, which were ultimately seen as "legal matter" of sorts, reducible to particular *casus*. Metaphors comparing ordinary laws to "precious metals, from which coins are forged", or to "construction materials for the building", were quite widespread.[73] Of course, many different kinds of legal rules were distinguished by the criterion of generality. There were *iura singularia* – local statutes and customs, aimed to resolve more mundane and limited issues. Their provisions were not to be used to disturb the general logic of law (*rationes iuris*); interpreting them extensively or applying them by analogy was restricted to a narrow set of circumstances.[74] In contrast, there were general laws, which formed the standard legal order, the "*ius commune*". They were held together by *ratio iuris*; they were subject to extensive interpretation whenever possible. General words of the laws were to have a literal and universal effect, according to their proper meaning.[75] Yet, even the general laws were not fully universal. A law, according to Azo, was a "general response for

71 E.g. the word "*Zaporizhzhia*", instead of the older "*Zaporozhye*", which, by the logic of exceptions, was not supposed to evolve.

72 E.g. the word "*Boh*" ("God"), which retained its [o].

73 Dynus, *Tractatus super regulis iuris,* https://gallica.bnf.fr/ark:/12148/bpt6k9926161/f10.item; Giovanni d'Andrea, *Gl.* ad rub VI 5.13 (*Corpus Iuris Canonici* (Rome: in aedibus populi Romani, 1582), vol 3, fo. 776–778).

74 Bartolus, *In primam Digesti Veteris partem,* fo. 12v–13v, commentary and *repetitio* in D. 1.1.9.

75 Bartolus, *In secundam Infortiati partem,* fo. 38v–39r, D. 31.1.44.pr; *In primam Codicis partem Commentaria* (Lyon: Harcaeus, 1552), fo. 34r–34v, C. 1.14(17).5.

all people with the same *casus*";[76] its "generality" was based on applying to a material class of people, who have encountered the same legal situation. Yet, because the law is still enacted to resolve a particular *casus*, it is not fully abstract and remains connected to the "legal matter". This is enough for Azo and Accursius to distinguish the law and the *regula* and explicitly stress that not every general law is a *regula*.[77] Remaining "material", general laws, statutes, and customs, for the sake of their proper interpretation, were equally dependent on an extra-legal factor – the intention of the law-giver (*mens constituentis*). All these rules were called to resolve particular social problems that the lawgiver had in mind, either generally for all people or in a more specific application.

This is what distinguished all these rules from the *regulae*, which were perceived as "incorporeal forms" juxtaposed to the "matter". The existence of incorporeal forms was well-known in dialectical philosophy, although their exact nature was debated.[78] For the *regula*, the subjective intention of its maker (legislator, jurist, etc) was irrelevant. Only the objective *ratio* mattered, seen as an objectively equitable resolution of a legal conflict. Therefore, "*eadem ratio*" and "*non eadem ratio*"[79] were seen as the only way to determine the *regula*'s scope of application.[80] Disconnected from the legal matter, the *regulae*, were to abstract the most general *rationes* lying behind several laws. Indeed, the analogy of law, applying a resolution of one legal *casus* to a similar *casus*, was possible precisely because these *casus* had the same *ratio* behind them, i.e., the same *regula*, either already formulated (*tradita*) or not yet formulated.

There was a theoretical dispute between Dynus of Mugello and Giovanni d'Andrea (Johannes Andreae), whether it was the *regula* or the analogy that was the more essential element in the extrapolation of one *casus* to another. Giovanni insisted that a *regula* was born only at the moment of *traditio regulae*, while after the *traditio* it applied because it contained law (*ius*) and extended it by analogy to new *casus*. Before the *traditio*, there was no *regula*, but only a *ratio iuris*, from which a *regula* would arise. In contrast, Dynus, and Bartolus who followed him, saw the *traditio* as joining of the "matter" of law

---

76 Azo, *Apparatus* ad D. 1.3.2, s.v. '*Diffinitio*' (citation by: Caprioli, "Tre capitoli," 358).

77 Azo, ibid; *Glossa Magna* ad D. 1.3.8(7), s.v. '*Iura*'.

78 Severinus Boethius, *In Topica Ciceronis Commentarius* (Lyon: Gryphius, 1536), 58–59; Ierodiakonou, "Dialectic as a Subpart," 125.

79 For more detail on the *regula* "*Ubi eadem ratio ibi idem ius*" and the evolution of the concept of *ratio* in it in the early modern period, see Maria Kola's contribution to this volume.

80 Bartolus, *In secundam Digesti Novi partem*, fo. 237r, D. 50.17.1.

with the "form" of *regula*, distinguishing between "*ius quod est regula*" and "*regula quae est ius*".[81] This debate reminds of the general "nominalists vs realists" debates among medieval dialecticians. The practical implications of the debate, nevertheless, were not very clear.

Exceptions of *regulae*, usually referred to as "fallacies" (*fallentiae*) in the late medieval and early modern literature, collected in medieval and early modern collections, also related to the *regulae* as matter to the form. Exceptions to the *regulae* were of various kinds: some were quite wide, excluding a whole species of cases from the *regula*'s genus, while others were very narrow, limited to just a single *casus* identified in the corpus of law. The important phenomenon was that many exceptions seemed to "except" from a slightly different or wider rule. For example, in the collection of *regulae* by Bartolomeo Socini, first published in 1533, the *regula* "*Cedens bonis a debito liberatur*" ("*One is freed from debt by giving up his goods*")[82] is associated with multiple exceptions, one of which runs: "*Post bona debitoris confiscata et gratia Principis restituta*" ("[Except], after the goods have been confiscated and returned by the grace of the Prince"), with a reference to C. 9.51.12-13. The peculiarity is that it seems to be a completely different genus from that implied in the text of the *regula*. The *regula* speaks about *cessio bonorum*, an act of voluntary giving up by the debtor of his estate in favour of the creditors, akin to the modern voluntary bankruptcy. In contrast, the exception speaks not about the *cessio bonorum*, but about a completely different situation – the debtor's property has been confiscated by the government for his criminal offences. The exception assumes that the *regula* speaks about all situations where the debtor has been deprived of all his goods, although the *regula*'s text speaks only about *cessio bonorum*. The fragment C. 9.51.12-13 is brought here in opposition not to the direct application of the *regula* but to the application of *regula* by analogy, on the basis of a vague and more general principle.

There are many "exceptions" like that to be found in various medieval and early modern collections. Their abundance may be explained by the low importance of the text of the *regula* in determining its scope of application. The text of the *regula* was determined rather arbitrarily: it could always be

---

81 See: Giovanni d'Andrea, *Gl.* ad rub VI 5.13 (*Corpus Iuris Canonici*, fo. 776–778); Dynus, *Tractatus super regulis juris*, https://gallica.bnf.fr/ark:/12148/bpt6k9926161/f10.item; Bartolus, ibid.

82 Bartolomeo Socini, *Regulae cum suis ampliationibus et fallentiis* (Lyon: Nicolas Petit, 1540), fo. XXIIIIv. In a later edition, the same *regula*, with a slightly different wording ("Cessione bonorum quis a debito liberatur") is mentioned a second time (Bartolomeo Socini, *Regulae et fallentiae iuris* (Cologne: Johan Gymnich, 1592), 131–132). In the FWO.OPR.2020.005001 database, this *regulae* is registered under No. 356.

wider or narrower than needed. After all, a *regula* was a probable, dialectical knowledge. Being an "incorporeal form", the *regula* was a model of legal resolution, applicable wherever the model seemed to be applicable and the same *ratio determinationis* applied. The exceptions fulfilled the function of designating the fields with a divergent *ratio*, where the *regula* for sure could not apply. Just like in the case with "ykavism" above, the "*regula-fallentia*" relation was a binary one, determined by arbitrary and formal criteria. "Exceptions from the exceptions" were not an element in this scheme of relationship. Indeed, in the early modern works, we find "*limitationes*", which remind of "exceptions from exceptions".[83] Yet, unlike the exceptions, these *limitationes* do not directly derogate from a wider genus or species: instead, they "precise down" the borders of application of the exception and thus do not destroy the binary relationship of the *regula* and the exception. The importance of this binary context was such that we find in the later authors, such as Philippo Decius, a readiness to legally expand (amplify) the scope of a *regula* in order to match its exceptions: for example, if the *regula* applied to agents, while the exception applied to agents and judges, the *regula* could thereby be extended to apply to judges, as well.[84]

The above shows us that in the theories, current among medieval learned jurists, there was a rather fleshed-out notion about the role of *regulae* in the legal framework. And this assigned role of *regulae* was that of maintaining a structural cohesion in law, determining the borders between the possible and impossible, acceptable and unacceptable legal argumentation. This role strongly reminds us of the role of grammar and other static rules in the functioning of language. It also achieves a dialectical systematisation of legal material, approximating the legal truth. However, in order to fulfil this function, the *regulae* were themselves supposed to have a structural cohesion among themselves above all else, be clearly distinct from each other and recognizable, like words, letters and other signs within a language. It is not obvious that *regulae* and *brocarda* ever had such a structural cohesion, instead of that being just a theory. It is quite possible that, quite to the contrary, many *regulae* were defined by their wording, by their text, to a greater extent than by their context within the system of *regulae*. It is equally probable that certain *regulae* may have been defined by particular legal *casus*, specific fragments in the *Corpus juris* and other authoritative legal texts, which, in their turn, could

83 E.g. Socini provides multiple *limitationes* to the *fallentia* of the *regula "Dotis causa aliis creditoribus praeferatur"* (Socini, *Regulae cum suis ampliatinibus et fallentiis*, fo. XLIIV–XLIIIV).

84 Decius, *In tit. Ff. De regulis iuris*, 11–13, D. 50.17.1.

reflect particular social or moral considerations. In both of these situations, the *regulae* could not be considered sufficiently detached from the particular "legal matter" and resemble an abstract "sign"-like ideal entity. Nevertheless, it might be possible to establish these properties of *regulae* using empirical research methods.

5 Establishing Structural Cohesion among the *Regulae*: Preliminary Results and a Programme of Action

As described in several publications,[85] there is a project at the University of Ghent, funded by the Research Foundation – Flanders (FWO.OPR.2020.00 5001) and dedicated to finding signs of structural uniformity among the *regulae iuris* developed in the Roman and medieval times, to the extent that they formed a system of "signs", determined by their legal context more than by the considerations of morality, social interest, fidelity to the original text, and other "external" considerations. It is not the aim of this article to repeat in much detail the description of the goals and methodology of the project, as well as of the structure of the database of *regulae iuris* developed in the course of the project.[86] The reader may find them in the attached references. It will suffice here to restate the main methods of the project, share the preliminary results, and set out the questions yet to be answered.

The work on the *regulae* within the project was based on assembling them from later (early modern) collections, which was to ensure the maximum coverage of all known *regulae* and their various textual variants. The collected *regulae* were subjected to logical analysis, with the purpose of identifying their subjects and predicates, as well as the concepts/notions each *regula* consisted of. All this was intended to imitate the way of thinking typical for medieval dialectical method. The analysed *regulae* were then compared with each other, and relations were established among them on the basis of similarity and opposition. The aim of this was to allow for a network analysis of the *regulae*, in order to see which of them were closer to each other and

85 Ilya A. Kotlyar, "Medieval juristic *regulae*: unity or disunity?," *Tijdschrift voor Rechtsgeschiedenis* 89 (2021): 409–438; Ilya A. Kotlyar, "Potential Application of Structural Linguistics Methodology in the Network Analysis of Roman and Medieval *Regulae Iuris*," *Journal for Digital Legal History* 1, no. 1 (2023): 1–22, https://doi.org/10.21825/dlh.85999.

86 The database in its preliminary form("DatabaseStructuralism3.accdb") is open for free download at OSF: Ilya A. Kotlyar, "Medieval Juristic Regulae. Origin. Evolution. System," OSF, updated 22 September 2024, https://doi.org/10.17605/OSF.IO/4WQZS.

which were further, in order to predict their possible mutual influences. Significant attention was paid to determining whether two similarly sounding "maxims" are substantially one *regula* with two textual variations or two similar *regulae*: this was determined on the basis of substantial identity of their underlying *ratio*, taking into account their conceptual content and citations brought in support of them.

The analysis was enriched by adding into it *fallentiae* and *ampliationes* of *regulae*, which also may be found in abundance in the extant collections. This was expected to show, to what extent the *regula* and its *fallentiae* determined the scope of each other, which was what the legal theory expected from them, as was described above. Two main methods of doing that were developed. One is to look at how one and the same *fallentia* relates to several related or contrary *regulae*. Indiscriminate mixing of *regulae* and *fallentiae* in the sources would be a sign of the absence of structural coherence among them. Another method is to see if unlimited speciation of *regulae* was done in practice. As was mentioned above, in medieval dialectics, unlimited speciation of a substance was seen as unacceptable: any substance could be fully described by a combination of a material genus and a "substantial form". It was stated elsewhere[87] that certain medieval jurists followed this rule by not allowing *fallentiae* on the basis of a "substantial form" to a *regula* produced through a binary juxtaposition to another *regula*, because it was seen as sufficiently "special" already. Thus, the task was to test this theoretical limitation in practice.

The first obvious result of the project, which also turned out to be its main difficulty, is the low coincidence rate of the *regulae* found in various collections, combined with their sheer number. Strict implementation of the objective criteria of distinction between similar *regulae* has led to the vast majority of the *regulae* found in the collections being unique. This difficulty is crucial because it prevents the developed database of *regulae* from being representative enough to determine the frequency of citation and reproduction of particular *regulae*. A sign, in order to be a part of language, needs to be used often and repeatedly; otherwise, it is just a temporary moribund "experiment", used by a few speakers. The same applies to the *regula*, if we try to determine if the system of *regulae* may be compared to a language.

Nevertheless, this preliminary result is already quite significant. It seems to contradict the often repeated thesis that the *regulae* were used as mnemonic

87 Kotlyar, "Medieval juristic *regulae*: unity or disunity?," 427–430.

devices, memorised by jurists and reproduced in the almost unchanged form from source to source.[88] If this were so, we would have seen a smaller and easier-to-memorise pool of *regulae*, with a high coincidence rate across collections. This observation seems to discard the idea that the *regulae* were defined by their wording. The wording was not very important in identifying a *regula*.

Another important observation is that connecting the *regulae* into groups by the criterion of similarity and opposition has produced relatively small groups, mostly of two-three *regulae* in a group. For example, one of the biggest groups, analysed elsewhere in much detail,[89] includes only seven *regulae*. This obstructs the efficient application of the network analysis. One of the key concepts of network analysis is that of "centrality", which measures the "privileged position" of some elements in the network over others. Yet, as the use of Gephi (network analysis tool) demonstrates, the *regulae* in each group tend to be relatively equally interconnected, with no clear "central" nodes emerging. Nevertheless, the analysis of similar *regulae* has allowed for the development of criteria of proximity, or closer and remoter similarity, among them.[90]

Another observation is that several distinct *regulae,* based on different sources and fragments of the *Corpus iuris*, often sound very similar: e.g. '*Alteri per alterum non debet iniqua conditio inferri*', '*Negligentia unius alteri nocere non debet*', and '*Alterius temeritas non debet alii nocere*'.[91] On the one hand, too strong a similarity between the *regulae* could speak against the main hypothesis of the project: this could be evidence that the borders between the *regulae* did not allow for distinctive features and that there was no limit as to how much two *regulae* could overlap. On the other hand, this could also be evidence in favour of our assumptions: this could mean that the two *regulae* were interacting in time and influencing the wording of each other, remaining distinct.

Research of contrary and contradictory *regulae* has also produced some results. For example, sometimes seemingly contrary and irreconcilable *regulae* ended up being well "aligned" with each other, having an unspoken, but clear, boundary of application.[92] Quite fruitful turned out to be the analysis of

---

88 See, e.g.: Finkenauer, „Le *Regulae iuris* come strumenti," 82–86.

89 Kotlyar, "Potential Application," 14–17.

90 Ibid.

91 'One may not put another into an unfair condition', 'Negligence of one must not harm another', and 'Someone else's temerity must not harm another', respectively. In the FWO.OPR.2020.005001 database these *regulae* are registered as, respectively, No. 33, 155, and 798.

92 For example, "Cedens bonis a debito liberatur" ("One is freed from debt by giving up his goods") and "Cedens bonis non tenetur nisi in quantum facere potest" ("Giving up one's

the *fallentiae* to contrary *regulae*. All in all, the border between the *regulae* and the *fallentiae* seems to have been real: the two phenomena were quite distinct and did not coincide one with another. At the same time, the rule against further speciation of "special *regulae*" seems not to have been followed. Yet, probably, our adopted definition of a "special *regula*" was not precise enough; some additional research may be necessary here.

There is a potential for a lot of additional research, in continuation of the project. The most obvious one would be its expansion into new collections of *regulae*. In this way, sufficient representation of the *regulae* will be achieved, which will help to determine, which *regulae* and their variations were cited often and on a stable basis, and which ones were not well-accepted and remained standing outside of the stable pool. Another method that has not yet been sufficiently implemented is the analysis of the scope of the concepts used in various *regulae* within the network. For example, in the two opposing *regulae*, "*Casus fortuitus liberat debitorem*" and "*Casus fortuitus non liberat debitorem*",[93] it would be interesting to see if the term "*Liberatio*" was used by the sources in intentionally different (adapted) meanings, so as to allow reconciliation of the two rules.

The analysis of the *fallentiae* and *ampliationes* of *regulae* may also be expanded. So far, we have divided *fallentiae* into "substantive" and "accidental", depending on whether they are based on a substantial or accidental *ratio determinationis* in relation to the genus of the *regula*, from a dialectical perspective. The next step may be to single out the *fallentiae* which expand the genus of the *regula*, in the mechanism described above. This will show how often the *fallentiae* provided a context helping to determine the scope of the *regula*.

Another useful addition to the analysis would be adding a dynamic (diachronic) element. We have already started to register the origin of particular *regulae* within our database, including the identification of the moment of *traditio regulae* in the sources. This may help to test the already performed network analysis, in particular the proximity of relations between the *regulae*. If the *regulae* were indeed a coherent language-like system, then, if two *regulae* are closely related conceptually, they should be expected to originate

goods, one is liable only in so far as he can pay"). Their border of application lay along the distinction between the obligation as a legally enforceable burden (civilis obligatio), which was taken away, and the obligation in the absolute sense (naturalis obligatio), which was limited.

93 Editor's note: In the FWO.OPR.2020.005001 database, they are registered under No. 64 and 254, respectively.

at approximately the same time, preferably with a shared "genealogy". This hypothesis may be tested. Moreover, research into the origin of particular *regulae* may allow for an enhanced network analysis, taking into account not only the conceptual similarities but also mutual references among the *regulae*. In this way, the *regulae* may be further integrated into one graph, allowing to identify *regulae* with increased centrality and expected significance.

6 Conclusion

We have explored above the many similarities that the Roman and medieval *regulae iuris* shared with a language, defined as a structured system of signs. These similarities reflect that both language and law are dialectical systems, based on "probable truth", abstract thinking, and the majority consensus. In both systems, the context is important, especially the context of similarities and binary oppositions – more important than the origin of this or that element, or its "original" meaning. Whereas in languages this overarching importance of structural context has been accepted as important for a long time now, it still remains to be shown that the *regulae iuris*, in the way they have been inherited from Roman and medieval times, had a similar contextual interdependence. It was shown above that the research performed at the University of Ghent has provided some mixed preliminary results, as well as a promise for future discoveries in this field.

It is beyond doubt that the *regulae iuris*, as well as various modern "maxims" derived from them and often associated with fundamental legal principles, have each their unique meaning and a long tradition of interpretation behind that meaning. Many *regulae*, e.g. "*Benignior sententia in dubio est praeferenda*" ("*In doubt, a more benign decision is to be preferred*"), make up part of what is seen today as a democratic legal order with the rule of law and are widely considered ethically significant. From this perspective, a *regula* may be seen as having a separate and very concrete essence, determined by social reality. Nevertheless, the history of these legal principles often reveals the indispensability of context for their full understanding: the context of the social and cultural circumstances of their formulation, but also the peculiarly legal context, provided by the internal structure of the *ratio iuris*. This importance of legal context should always be remembered when dealing with the *regulae iuris*.

Bibliography

Corpus Iuris Civilis. 5 vols. Lyon: Hugues de la Porte, 1558–60. https://historica.unibo.it/home.

Corpus Iuris Canonici. 3 vols. Rome: in aedibus populi Romani, 1582. https://digital.library.ucla.edu/catalog/ark:/21198/zz0014rx5v.

Aquinas, Thomas. *Sentencia libri De Anima*. www.corpusthomisticum.org.

Aquinas, Thomas. *Summa Theologiae*. www.corpusthomisticum.org.

Azo Portius. *Brocardica aurea*. Venice: apud Franciscum Bindonum, 1566.

Azo Portius. *Lectura super Codicem*. Paris: Nivelle, 1577. Reprint, Torino: ex officina Erasmiana, 1966.

Azo Portius. *Summa super Codicem*. Torino: apud heredes Nicolai Bevilacquae, 1578. Reprint, Torino: ex officina Erasmiana, 1966.

Bartolus de Saxoferrato. *In primam Codicis partem Commentaria*. Lyon: Harcaeus, 1552.

Bartolus de Saxoferrato. *In primam Digesti Veteris partem Commentaria*. Venice: Giunti, 1590.

Bartolus de Saxoferrato. *In secundam Infortiati partem Commentaria*. Lyon: Harcaeus, 1552.

Bartolus de Saxoferrato. *In secundam Digesti Novi partem Commentaria*. Venice: Giunti, 1590.

Bartolus de Saxoferrato. *Tractatus Tyberiadis seu de fluminibus*. Rome: Herolt & Riessinger, 1483.

Bénatouïl, Thomas, and Katerina Ierodiakonou, ed. *Dialectic after Plato and Aristotle*. Cambridge: Cambridge University Press, 2019.

Boethius, Severinus. *De differentiis topicis libri quattuor*. Paris: apud Prigentium Calvarin, 1533.

Boethius, Severinus. *In Topica Ciceronis Commentarius*. Lyon: Gryphius, 1536.

Boethius, Severinus. "*In Isagogen Porphyrii Commentarium*." *Corpus Scriptorum Ecclesiasticorum Latinorum* 38 (1906): 135–348. https://www.logicmuseum.com/wiki/Authors/Boethius/isagoge/CPorII.

Caprioli, Severino. "Tre capitoli intorno alla nozione di '*regula iuris*' nel pensiero di Glossatori." *Annali di storia del diritto* 5/6 (1961/1962): 221–374.

Chisholm, Hugh, ed. *Encyclopaedia Britannica*. 11th ed. 29 vols. Cambridge: Cambridge University Press, 1911. https://en.wikisource.org/wiki/1911_Encyclop%C3%A6dia_Britannica/Predicables.

Dębiński, Antoni, Magdalena Pyter, and Michal Skřejpek. "Regulae Iuris: A Lasting and Universal Vehicle of Legal Knowledge." *Bialystok Legal Studies* 27, no. 4 (2022): 49–67. https://doi:10.15290/bsp.2022.27.04.04.

Decius, Philippus. *In tit. Ff. De regulis iuris*. Lyon: Antoin Vincent, 1562.

Deroussin, David. "Le droit romain a-t-il connu des principes? Sur les significations (possibles) de *principia, praecepta* et *regulae iuris*." In *Les principes en droit*, edited by Silvie Caudal, 127–48. Paris: Economica, 2008.

Deroussin, David. "Remarques sur les "*regulae iuris*" et les principes en droit (Temps Modernes)." *Revue historique de droit français et étranger* 90, no. 2 (April-June 2012): 195–235.

Di Nisio, Valeria, ed. *Regulae Iuris. Ipotesi di lavoro tra storia e teoria del diritto.* Naples: Jovene Editore, 2016.

Domingo, Raphael, Javier Ortega, Beatriz Rodríguez-Antolín, and Nicolás Zambrana. *Principios de Derecho Global: 1000 reglas y aforismos jurídicos comentados.* Cizur Menor: Editorial Aranzadi, 2006.

Dynus of Mugello. *Tractatus super regulis iuris.* Paris: Georges Mittelhus, 1498. https://gallica.bnf.fr/ark:/12148/bpt6k9926161/f1.item#

Flores legum secundum ordinem alphabeti. Paris: Guy Marchant, 1496.

Hjelmslev, Louis. *Prolegomena to a theory of language.* Madison: University of Wisconsin Press, 1963.

Jakobson, Roman, and Moris Halle. *Fundamentals of Language.* Berlin: Mouton de Gruyter, 1971.

Kotlyar, Ilya A. "Medieval Juristic Regulae. Origin. Evolution. System." OSF. Updated 27 December 2022. https://doi.org/10.17605/OSF.IO/4WQZS.

Kotlyar, Ilya A. "Medieval juristic *regulae*: unity or disunity?" *Tijdschrift voor Rechtsgeschiedenis* 89 (2021): 409–438.

Kotlyar, Ilya A. "Potential Application of Structural Linguistics Methodology in the Network Analysis of Roman and Medieval *Regulae Iuris*." *Journal for Digital Legal History* 1, no. 1 (2023): 1–22. https://doi.org/10.21825/dlh.85999.

Otte, Gerhard. *Dialektik und Jurisprudenz, Untersuchungen zur Methode der Glossatoren.* Frankfurt: Vittorio Klostermann, 1971.

Pilius Medicinensis. *Quaestiones Sabbatinae.* Modena: Presso l'Universitá degli studi, 1935.

Saussure, Ferdinand de. *Course in General Linguistics.* Translated by Wade Baskin. New York: Philosophical Library, 1959.

Shevelov, George Y. *A historical phonology of the Ukrainian language.* Heidelberg: Winter, 1979.

Socini, Bartolomeo. *Regulae cum suis ampliationibus et fallentiis.* Lyon: Nicolas Petit, 1540.

Socini, Bartolomeo. *Regulae et fallentiae iuris.* Cologne: Johan Gymnich, 1592.

Stein, Peter. *Regulae Iuris: From Juristic Rules to Legal Maxims.* Edinburgh: Edinburgh University Press, 1966.

Tellegen, Jan-Willem, and Olga Tellegen-Couperus. "The *Regula* as a Rhetorical Device in Roman Law." Unpublished manuscript, 10 July 2023, PDF.

Thomasettis, Thomas de. *Flores legum, cum suis exceptionibus et declarationibus.* Venice: Baretius, 1603.

Weijers, Olga. *A Scholar's Paradise: Teaching and Debating in Medieval Paris.* Turnhout: Brepols, 2015.

Weimar, Peter. "*Argumenta brocardica.*" *Studia Gratiana* 14 (1967): 91–123.

Weimar, Peter. "Die legistische Literatur und die Methode des Rechtsunterrichts der Glossatorenzeit." *Ius Commune* 2 (1969): 43–83.

Wöhler, Hans-Ulrich. *Dialektik in der mittelalterichen Philosophie.* Berlin: Akademie Verlag, 2006.

CHAPTER 2

Knowing through Maxims

Adolfo Giuliani

1 Maxims: A View from the 21st Century

After the huge wave of studies on legal maxims published during the 1950s and 1960s, we return to this theme but with a different mindset. These studies sought a broader normativity, distinct from legislative rules, and believed that legal normativity extended beyond the state. As the legal philosopher Michel Villey put it in 1968: "le droit c'est la loi?"[1] Legal maxims answered. They were evidence of a normative world without legislator, whose architecture was structured not according to a descending stairway of deductive syllogisms but by flexible dialectics.[2] Another methodological world came to view. Maxims were rules not made but found, unsuitable for logical deduction ("*non*

1 Michel Villey, *La formation de la pensée juridique moderne* (Paris: PUF, 1968), 550. Among the most well-known studies, Peter Stein, *Regulae iuris, From Juristic Rules to Legal Maxims* (Edinburgh: Edinburgh University Press, 1966); *id.*, "The Digest Title *de diversis regulis iuris antiqui* and the General Principles of Law," in *Essays in Jurisprudence in Honour of Roscoe Pound,* ed. Ralph A. Newman (New York: Bobbs-Merrill Co, 1962), 1–20 (=Peter Stein, *The Character and Influence of the Roman Civil Law* (London: Hambledon Press, 1988), 53); *id.*, "Civil Law Maxims in Moral Philosophy," *Tulane Law Review* 48 (1973): 1075–85; Theodor Viehweg, *Topik und Jurisprudenz, Ein Beitrag zur rechtswissenschaftlichen Grundlagenforschung* (Munich: Beck, 1952); Dieter Nörr, "Spruchregel und Generalisierung," *Zeitschrift der Savigny-Stiftung für Rechtsgeschichte: Romanistische Abteilung* 89 (1972): 18–93; Bruno Schmidlin, "Horoi, pithana und regulae – Zum Einfluß der Rhetorik und Dialektik auf die juristische Regelbildung," *Aufstieg und Niedergang der römischen Welt* 2.15 (1976): 101; *id.*, "Regulae iuris, Standard, Norm oder Spruchregel? Zum hermeneutischen Problem des Regelverständnisses," in *Festschrift für Max Kaser zum 70* (Munich: Beck, 1976), 91–110; Josef Esser, *Grundsatz und Norm in der richterlichen Fortbildung des Privatrechts* (Tübingen: Mohr, 1956). See also Laurens C. Winkel, "A Note on Regulae Iuris in Roman Law and on Dworkin's Distinction between Rules and Principles," in *Critical Studies in Ancient Law, Comparative Law and Legal History: Essays in Honour of Alan Watson*, ed. John W. Cairns and Olivia F. Robinson (Oxford: Hart, 2001), 413–18.

2 In a positivist perspective there is no room for maxims. For example, Jeremiah Smith, "The Use of Maxims in Jurisprudence," *Harvard Law Review* 9 (1895) 13–14: "[maxims] are phrases, solemn and imposing in form, which seldom or never render any real assistance in the solution of a legal puzzle; but on the contrary actually retard that solution. They are mere truisms; or mere identical propositions; or moral precepts; or principles of legislation; but not working rules of law".

 | DOI:10.1163/9789004736092_004

ex regula jus sumatur", D. 50.17.1), not dispositive but regulative, not to be analysed by formal logic but by the rich dialectical methodology dismissed by the rise of modern states. These studies succeeded; there was a broader normativity beyond the state: they made their point.

Today, I think, we should take a further step and building upon previous results, return to this theme with new questions. The distance that separates us from that distant epistemic world is huge, but maxims are nevertheless an essential point of reference for finding answers to one broad question that can only be answered by legal-historical analysis: the creation of law. Legal actors used legal maxims (collective name for a broad typology) to give order to their world, to make it knowable, and to look better into it; they were instruments to produce normative knowledge.[3] But to make such an inquiry possible we need first a serious effort to connect legal history and legal theory and to place it in the broader field of historical epistemology.

To better define my inquiry, we need to consider the dual function of a maxim. If we take as an example the iconic statement "mothers love their children" which was the basis of King Solomon's judgement, we will find that it fulfils two different functions: (i) a concise representation of reality ("this is how the world looks like") and (ii) a standard to confirm the disputed fact ("the presumed mother confirms, or not, how the world looks like"). While the first aspect has been the familiar concern of previous research, which focused on the formative process, as John Cairns and Paul du Plessis put it, "from cases to rules",[4] this paper takes a step forward turning to the other function, in which maxims move "from rules to cases", and their concise representation of reality is used to confirm a disputed fact. Moreover, if previous research moved within a framework inspired to the philosophy of language (which characterised legal science throughout the 20th century) and saw the formative process of maxims guided by a concern about "how to do things with words",[5] this paper turns to the rising concern with "how to do things with models, patterns, forms […] and maxims", which is presently defining a broad field of research studied by the philosophy of information, the philoso-

3 Thomas Duve, "Legal History as a History of the Translation of Knowledge of Normativity," *Max Planck Institute for Legal History and Legal Theory Research Paper Series*, No 2022-16, https://doi.org/10.2139/ssrn.4229323; Jürgen Renn, "The Globalization of Knowledge in History and Its Normative Challenges," *Rechtsgeschichte* 22 (2014): 052–060, https://doi.org/10.12946/rg22/052-060.

4 Paul J. Du Plessis and John W. Cairns, ed., *The Creation of the Ius Commune: From Casus to Regula* (Edinburgh: Edinburgh University Press, 2010).

5 John L. Austin, *How to do Things with Words* (Oxford: Clarendon Press, 1962).

phy of presence, the concern with representation, the knowledge of the present, conceptual design.[6] Briefly: how to know through maxims.

Two points will be emphasised throughout this essay. The first regards terminology. In this paper, I will use the term "maxims" not only to follow John Fortescue (c. 1394–1479) and others, who Anglicised the Roman term "*regula juris*" to "maxim", but also to keep close to the medieval logical lexicon, derived from Boethius (*infra*, 1.1), which treated *maxima* as a *genus* encompassing a family of almost interchangeable terms including *regula, aphorism, axiomata, theoremata*, and others.[7] My point is that an inquiry on maxims must transcend the boundaries of legal science. Maxims were a shared feature of practical disciplines (*disciplinae practicae*, i.e. whose object is unfit to be analysed by the methodology of abstract disciplines, namely without factual content, e.g. geometry),[8] which included law, ethics, moral theology, economics, political theory, and others. This idea runs throughout the medieval and early-modern logical tradition. We find, for example, the scholastic logician Gilbert de la Porrée (c. 1085–1154) listing the following terms:[9]

6 The reader interested in exploring these connections may wish to see: Luciano Floridi, *The logic of information: a theory of philosophy as conceptual design* (Oxford: Oxford University Press, 2019); Christopher Alexander, *Notes on the synthesis of form* (Cambridge MA: Harvard Univ. Press, 2002); and P. N. Johnson-Laird, "Mental models and human reasoning," *Proceedings of the National Academy of Sciences* 107 (2010): 18243–50. For an overview of the normative dimension of types, see Lorenzo Passerini Glazel, *La forza normativa del tipo: pragmatica dell'atto giuridico e teoria della categorizzazione* (Macerata: Quodlibet, 2005). I discussed the shift from language-based to information-based legal-historical research in: Adolfo Giuliani, "After Comparative Legal History," in *Liber Amicorum Luigi Moccia*, ed. E. Calzolaio (Rome: Romatre, 2021), 215–41.

7 John Fortescue, *De laudibus legum Angliae* (1st. publ. 1543, London: Henry Lintot, 1741), Ch. 8, p. 6: "Principia autem [...] sunt quaedam Universalia, quae in Legibus Angliae docti, similiter et Mathematici, Maximas vocant, Rhetorici Paradoxas, et Civilistae Regulas Juris denominant"; Christopher Saint German, *Doctor and Student* (London: S. Richardson and C Lintot, 1761), Chap. 8 p. 26: "The fourth ground of the law of England standeth in divers principles that be called in the law maxims, the which have been always taken for law in this realm, so that is not lawful for any that is learned to deny them".

8 Aristoleles, *Metaphysica*, lib. 6, cap. 1, 1025^{b} 25; Thomas Aquinas, "*Sententia libri Ethicorum. Textus editionis Leoninae 1969*," in *Id, Opera omnia*, ed. Roberto Busa (Stuttgart: Frommann-Holzboog, 1980, p. 145^{a}, to. 4, I, 2, 9 and 11; Henning Arnisaeus, *De republica seu relectionis politicae libri duo*, in *id., Opera politica omnia duobus tomis distincta*, (Argentorati: Sumptibus haeredum Lazari Zetzneri, 1648), to. 1, II, Prooemium, 3, 1–37, pp. 280^{a}–291^{a}; Merio Scattola, "Dialectics, Topology and Philosophy in Early Modern Times," in *Traditions of Controversy*, ed. Marcelo Dascal and Han-Liang Chang (Amsterdam: John Benjamins Pub, 2007), 181–206.

9 Nikolaus Häring, *The Commentaries on Boethius* (Toronto: Pontifical Institute of Mediaeval Studies, 1966), 190; see also Gillian R. Evans, *Getting It Wrong: The Medieval Epistemology of Error* (Cambridge: CUP, 1998), 144.

> "communes loci" rhetorum et "maximae propositiones" dialecticorum et "theoremata" geometrarum et "axiomata" musicorum et "generales sententiae" ethicorum seu philosophorum continentur universalitate unius regulae qua dicitur: "communis animi conceptio".

That those terms were to a certain extent interchangeable was commonly recognised in legal writings. For example, Petrus Peckius (Pieter Peck the Elder, 1529–89), a professor of Civil and Canon law at Leuven University, spoke of the similarity of legal maxims and medical aphorisms, both growing from the repeated observation of reality (since a certain herb heals cholera in Titius, Seius, and Sempronius, the conclusion is drawn that this specific herb heals cholera).[10] At the same time, the collections of adages, emblems, *loci communes*, *argumenta* and presumptions were a common pursuit of 16th-century legal scholarship.[11] These terms shared one specific feature which, as Gilbert de la Porrée put it, was to be a "shared mental conception" (*communis animi conceptio*). The idea is that social communities possess a repository of cognitions that summarise what its members know about human experience. As mentioned above, each of them performs a double function: (i) a small-scale model of reality that summarises some formal features of what we know ("the herb XY heals cholera"), and (ii) a blueprint to be used as a guide to look better into future cases.[12]

The second point is that, as an object of study, maxims are unintelligible if viewed in separation from their epistemic background. Until the mid-17th century rise of philosophies based on first principles, legal science was largely based on Aristotelian scholasticism. Even a superficial look at the legal texts used in the pre-modern period shows the persistence of medieval arguments and authorities, which continued to be cited throughout this period. This continuity was insured by largely unchanged methods of legal education, deeply rooted in medieval scholasticism and, on the other hand, by unchanged pat-

10 Petrus Peckius, *Ad regulas Iuris Canonici commentaria* (Helmstedt: Iacobus Lucius, 1588), fol. 228v.

11 Andrea Alciato's works on emblems and presumptions are a clear example.

12 See on this Severino Caprioli, "Tre capitoli intorno alla nozione di 'regula iuris' nel pensiero dei glossatori," *Annali di storia del diritto* V–VI (1961–1962): 221–374. A great source on *communis animi conceptio* is William Hamilton, "The philosophy of common sense," in *The works of Thomas Reid* (Edinburgh: Maclachlan and Stewart, 1895), 742–803; this deep engagement with Aristotelian scholasticism should not be surprising considering earlier models, e.g. the medieval Scottish philosopher John Mair, on which see A. Broadie, "Medieval notions of the theory of ideas," *Proceedings of the Aristotelian Society* 87 (1986–7): 153–67.

terns of argument and modes of reasoning. Legal science unquestionably registered methodological innovations (e.g. the 12th-century *logica nova*, the 16th-century revival of Aristotle's *Rhetoric* and *Analytica Priora*, the pansemioticism of the early 17th century) but the legal profession always tried to reconcile any new influence within a continuity of texts, as Edward Coke put it: "*natura, sicut jus, non facit saltus*". If we turn for example to the standard procedural manual, Guillaume Durand's *Speculum iudiciale*, we find a text written in 1260–76 and still in use the in mid-17th century, at the time of René Descartes and Thomas Hobbes. Scholasticism offered a foundational methodology whose veritable impact would be missed without realising that university education, monopolised by scholasticism, was based on a canon of Aristotelian texts that remained in use until the 17th century. If it were possible to find a foundational point in this methodology, it would be a question such as: "What is reality?" The characteristic answer was to make explicit the inner rationality of reality. Scholasticism provided intellectual actors with a mental habit (Aquinas: "the principle that guides action","*principium importans ordinem ad actum*") that patterned the structure of their creations, from the medieval *summae* (see their texts ordered in a hierarchy of titles, numbers and paragraphs) to the architecture of early gothic cathedrals. Bartolus must be taken seriously when he boasted that about half of his library consisted of theological works.[13]

This paper offers a different view from the traditional and dubious characterisation of maxims as "generalisations". It is incorrect because this feature is intrinsic to any rule, as Schauer put it: "there are no rules for particulars". It is misleading because it suggests connections to a legislative statement, or even to a *Rechtssatz*.[14] Papinian, Bulgaro, Accursio, Paolo di Castro, Andrea Alciato, Francis Bacon and others did not produce "generalisations" but *regulae, max-*

13 Thomas Aquinas, *Summa Theologiae*, I-IIae, qu. 49, art. 3. The influence of early scholasticism on Gothic architecture has been studied by Erwin Panofski (to whom I also owe Aquinas' quote): Erwin Panofsky, *Gothic Architecture and Scholasticism* (New York: Farrar, 1976), 16. Bartolus' library seemingly included "volumina triginta in iure civili et canonico et triginta quattuor in sacra theologia", according to *Thomae Diplovatatii Liber de claris iuris consultis. Pars posterior*, ed. Fritz Schulz and Hermann Kantorowicz (Bologna: Institutum Gratianum: 1968) (*Studia Gratiana* x), 286.

14 Ennio Cortese, *La Norma giuridica* (Milan: Giuffré, 1962), I: 337: "Che i giuristi medievali abbiano negato alla regula iuris una sua qualità di *Rechtssatz* autonomo non sembra tesi da potersi sottoscrivere senz'altro" ("That medieval jurists denied the *regula juris* its quality of an autonomous *Rechtssatz*, cannot be denied"). Of course, medieval jurists were unaware of a juristic conception that legal positivism developed in the 19th century. The clearest introduction to generalisation is F. Schauer, *Playing by the rules* (Oxford, Clarendon Press, 1991).

imae, *axiomata*, *dignitates*, *principia* and other normative statements, whose rationale was in their brevity (D. 50.17.1: "*regula* [...] *brevis narratio*").[15] They were created according to a principle of economy, which proceeded by subtraction, eliminating superfluous factual elements in order to arrive at its essence, compressed into its smallest size, as a stone. Logical elaboration moved not by expansion to the broad, but by reduction to the small. In the background was the Aristotelian statement that "principles which are least in magnitude are greatest in power".[16]

2 Maxims: The Internal Architecture

Legal maxims were an integral component of the fluid system of the *ius commune*, the internal organisation of which depended largely on a specific epistemic background. Before the mid-17th century demise of Aristotelian scholasticism (see § 5), legal knowledge was internally arranged according to a topology. This term (from its unit, the Greek *topos* or Latin *locus*) indicated a network of 'places', which specified a set of basic points of reference that offered guidance (similarly to road signs, as specified by some 16th-century texts), provided points of view, ordered experience, interpreted facts, and had the authority that was conferred upon them by consensus. In the background was a spatial idea of knowledge that self-contained all the cognitions current within a bounded context, be it an academic discipline, a profession, or a social community.[17]

In legal science, for example, the *loci* were the basic points upon which the discussion in the discipline was articulated and it shaped the internal structure of books, teaching manuals and academic writings. Their guiding power was based on the fact that legal actors produced normative knowledge work-

15 Note the emphasis on *brevitas* in Paulus' definition: D. 50.17.1: "regula est, quae rem quae est *breviter* enarrat; non ut ex regula ius sumatur, sed ex iure quod est regula fiat. Per regulam igitur *brevis* rerum narratio traditur". See similar emphasis on *brevitas* in Cujas' definition in his introduction to the Digest title *De regulis juris*: "multarum rerum quae eodem se habent modo *comprehensiones breves*: vel ex eo quod plerumque fit rerum *definitiones breves*". Jacques Cujas, *Paratitla in libros quinquaginta digestorum seu Pandectarum Imperatoris Iustiniani* (Lyon: apud Gulielmum Rovillium, 1570), 303.

16 Aristotle, *On the heavens*, Bk. 1, 5, 271b10. Or, as Julius Paci put it: "principium vi maius, quam magnitudine esse" in his translation of Aristotelis *De coelo* (Frankfurt: apud Claudium Marnium, 1601), Lib. 1, cap. 6, p. 17.

17 Maxims woven into a social community is the theme of the painting "Flemish proverbs", made in 1559 by Pieter Bruegel the Elder (c. 1525/30–1569), which shows scenes of village life that illustrate about one hundred maxims.

ing out from a set of assumptions (each place or *locus* was a source of arguments) and according to some formal features. The overall structure had a particular architecture, as Merio Scattola observed:

> … [T]he arguments are not disposed in a logical order, in the descending stairway of the deduction, but are grouped within a dialectical disposition. It is impossible to link together all pieces of human knowledge in a descending deductive chain (*per modum conclusionis*). They must be compared together in order to understand which among them is compatible with all others. In general, since every one of them is proved to be true, each element or argument of practical knowledge must be compatible with each other element. But this relationship is not evident immediately and must be searched for, and this search is a typical dialectical duty. The tradition is often full of arguments that are apparently opposite.[18]

At the same time, it was believed that the order of knowledge reflected the order of the mind. There was no separation between the two, since knowledge, in the Aristotelian-scholastic tradition, was considered to be a relation between a knowing subject and a knowing object.[19] This connection is clear in the concern with memory. The process of memorising objects (as medieval students routinely did with the Digest title *De regulis juris*) relied heavily on how the mind works, for example, visualising them distributed in physical places ("a house, an intercolumnar space, a recess, an arch, or the like").[20]

2.1 *Medieval Foundations: Boethius*

The topological structure of knowledge noted above was based on a doctrine that went back to the fountainhead of medieval Latin logic: Anicius Manlius Severinus Boethius (485–526), the author credited with being the bridge between ancient Rome and the medieval logic tradition. He wrote two standard textbooks that remained in use until the 16th century (*De differentiis topi-*

18 Scattola, "Dialectics, Topology and Philosophy," 184.

19 Wiliam Hamilton, "Of presentative and representative knowledge," in *Id., The works of Thomas Reid*, 804–815 at 808a: "All knowledge is a relation […] between that which knows (in scholastic language, the *subject* in which knowledge inheres) and that which is known (in scholastic language, the *object* about which knowledge is conversant); and the contents of every act of knowledge are made up of elements, and regulated by laws, proceeding partly from its object and partly from its subject".

20 *Rhetorica ad Herennium*, trans. Harry Caplan (Cambridge MA: Harvard University Press, 1981), III: 16 and 17–20.

cis and *In topica Ciceronis*), which transmitted the doctrine of *loci* (*regiones, capita, signa, notae, fontes, sedes*) as it was found in Cicero, who in turn believed it to be derived from Aristotle.[21] At its heart was the concern to show how the mass of current cognitions contained a latent structure. Some self-evident principles, from which all reasoning proceeded, gave its inner form. They were concentrated pieces of knowledge, whose heuristic power was in being self-evident (*per se nota*).[22] Two ideas in his doctrine proved to be enormously influential.[23]

The first idea is the distinction between a maxim-proposition and a maxim-pattern.

(1) The maxim-proposition (*maxima propositio*) is a self-evident statement, which being known in itself (*per se nota propositio*) does not need to be proved by anything else: it is indemonstrable.[24]

> Maximas propositiones (propositiones supremae principales, indimostrabiles, per se notae) vocamus quae et universales sunt, et ita notae atque manifestae, ut probatione non egeant, eaque potius quae in dubitatione sunt probent. Nam quae indubitatae sunt, ambiguorum demonstrationi solent esse principia; qualis est "Omnem numerum vel parem vel imparem" et "Aequalia relinqui si aequalibus aequalia detrahuntur" caeteraeque de quarum nota veritate non quaeritur.[25]

A maxim-proposition is the rational basis that sustains any argument, and may fulfill its role even if unexpressed; as Boethius says, if we discuss "whether the kingdom or the consulate is better, and we will say that both being good, the kingdom is more long-lasting than the consulate",

21 For an enlightening reconstruction of this theme see Benedetto Riposati, *Studi Sui "Topica" Di Cicerone* (Milan: Vita e pensiero, 1947), 684. See also the contribution of I. Kotlyar to this volume on the significance of the philosophy of Boethius in medieval scholastic tradition.

22 A. M. Severinus Boethius, "*De differentiis topicis*," in *Patrologia Latina* LXIV (1847), ed. Jan Paul Migne, col. 1185A: "Hoc enim ita notum est, ut extrinsecus probatione non egeat, et ipsum aliis possit esse probatio".

23 Boethius, *De differentiis topicis*, col. 1185A: "Argumenti enim sedes partim propositio maxima intellegi potest, partim maximae propositionis differentia."

24 Boethius, *De differentiis topicis*, col. 1184D: "maxima et universalis, et principalis, et indemostrabilis, atque per se nota propositio, quae in argumentationibus, [...] vim tamen argumentis et propositionibus subministrat".

25 The test of Boethius, as it appears in: Petrus Hispanus, *Summulae logicales*, tractatus V (*de locis*), lectio 3, cited in: Hamilton, "The philosophy of common sense," 767.

we are implicitly grounding our argument on the higher principle that "long-lasting goods are more valuable than the short-lived ones".[26]

(II) The maxim-pattern (*maximae propositionis differentia*) is more abstract. It surmises that humans reason and frame their arguments according to a finite set of patterns. Some simple examples: (1) the pattern "from similarities" ("*a similibus ad similia*") is the blueprint for an argument such as "As the eye cannot see clearly when the air is impure, so the mind is unclear if the soul is troubled"; (2) the pattern "from the major to the minor" ("*locus a maiore*"): "He ruins his own family, what would he capable of with strangers?"; (3) the pattern "from the minor to the major": "if the ecclesiastic cannot sell the goods of the church, he is not entitled to dispose of the church".[27] Boethius offers other examples: "The question is put forward whether the wise man is not envious. The person who is envious is by other's fortunes; the wise man, however, is not oppressed by other's fortunes; therefore, the wise man is not envious". In this case the argument proceeds from the topic of definition: things whose definition is different, are themselves different ("*quorum diversa est diffinitio, ipsa quoque diversa esse*").

The second idea is the dualism of *loci interni* and *loci externi*. Drawn from Cicero and familiar to any law student until the eclipse of rhetorical learning during the 17th century, this distinction offered an ordering criterion by which any cognition had its place according to its source of argumentative power: internal arguments (*loci interni*) derived it from their own rational coherence; external arguments (*loci externi*, conceptualised as *testimonia*), from the authority of external sources. In the background is the recognition of two sectors of knowledge. The first is grounded on its own internal rationality; the other is made of cognitions whose rationality is not original but derived from external sources, summarised under the heading of testimony, whose rationality is derived from the source's authority. One is original, the other is second-hand knowledge. On this separation is built a dualism between testimonial and non-testimonial knowledge. This distinction was full of potential.[28]

---

26 Boethius, *De differentiis topicis*, col. 1185.

27 Examples 1 and 2 come from Giambattista Vico, *Institutiones Oratoriae*, trans. G. Crifó (1st ed.: 1711; Napoli: Ist. Suor Orsola Benincasa, 1989); example 3 from Pietro Andrea Gammaro, *Legalis Dialectica* (Bononia: Benedictus Hector de Faellis, 1524), 14.

28 For example, 17th-century scholars criticised Johannes Bertachinus' legal vocabulary (*Repertorium juris*, late 15th c.): being structured by alphabetic order it mixed internal and external *loci*.

It seems worth noting that some medieval writers expanded beyond Boethius' precise logical doctrine of *maximae propositiones*. They dropped the word *propositio* and spoke of *maximae* using this term in vernacular languages to cast a wide net that included broadly rules of conduct, moral principles, legal canons, such as *articuli, aphorismi, veritates, assertiones, regulae, loci communes, conclusiones, propositiones*, and other terms. They were, nevertheless, unified by being understood as "commonly held opinions" ("*communes animi conceptiones*").

3 Maxims' Ordering Function

One of the functions of the maxims was to give order to the text. As is well known, the Roman compilation lacked any meaningful order; it seemed to have been piled up by hands working at different times, piecing together heterogeneous material made up of snippets of texts, decisions on individual cases and fragments of doctrine. Medieval jurists felt compelled to order the text. They sometimes moved on from their function of interpreters who focused on elucidating individual words, to a philosophical task. They sought logical patterns which held the text together and made it coherent. Just as philosophers sought *universalia*, jurists used induction to reduce complexity by abstracting a unifying rationale from similarly decided cases. A textbook example is the formation of the *regula* "that which belongs to no one, naturally belongs to the first occupant" (*quod nullius est id occupant conceditur*) lengthily examined by the Gloss (Gl. s.v. '*Regula*' ad D. 50.17.1), which, focusing on relations between *genus* and *species* and "*signum universale denotans universalem affirmationem vel negationem*", explains how a *regula* emerges from the inductive connection of similar cases, specifically instances of occupation of various wild animals:

> Wild beasts, birds, fish and all animals, which live either in the sea, the air, or the earth, so soon as they are taken by anyone, immediately become by ius gentium the property of the captor.
>
> Ferae igitur bestiae & volucres & pisces, & omnia animalia quae in coelo & terra nascuntur, simul atque ab aliquo capta fuerint, iure gentium statim illius esse incipient.[29]

29 Inst.Just. II.1.12: "Ferae igitur bestiae & volucres & pisces, & omnia animalia quae in coelo & terra nascuntur, simul atque ab aliquo capta fuerint, iure gentium statim illius esse

University education provided the necessary skills. By wrapping the Roman text in a dialectical apparatus legal actors were able to uncover latent patterns, connect scattered texts and sometimes bring to light doctrinal micro-systems.[30] Such efforts produced coherence, intellectual sophistication, and ultimately authority. This methodology was an engine for producing new normative knowledge from Roman rules, and its results were accepted by courts as learned opinions, whose authority was grounded not on the Roman text, but on the legal profession that produced it.[31]

4 Knowing through Maxims

How can a disputed fact be determined through a maxim? From this perspective, maxims are a cognitive device based on the relationship between the general fact summarised in the maxim, and the puzzling fact to be determined; in the example of King Solomon's judgement this is in the relation between the *universal* Mother of the maxim "mothers love their children" and the *particular* presumed mother in front of his eyes.[32] To begin to understand the relation between the maxim and the fact we must turn to Aristotelian scholasticism. Judging involves a cognitive problem. This question concerned Thomas Aquinas, who discussing the nature of *judicium*, emphasised its cognitive dimension ("*sapientia, per quam formatur judicium*"). While the

incipient". For an analysis of the Gloss to D. 50.17.1, see Ennio Cortese, *La Norma giuridica* (Milan: Giuffré, 1962), I: 322–338, and Herbert F. Jolowicz, "Roman Regulae and English Maxims," in *L'Europa e il diritto romano. Studi in memoria di Paolo Koschaker* (Milan, Giuffre: 1953), I: 221–34.

30 Andrea Alciato in 1537 explained how *regulae* were functional to the solidification of the *ius civile* in micro-systems: "Bartolus, Baldus, and Paulus mastered everything better: and by certain rules, doctrines or, so to speak, fetters, enclosed the whole ius civile" ("Bartolus, Baldus, Paulus diffusius omnia attigerunt, & certis regulis atque doctrinis seu compedibus quibusdam ius civile concluserunt"), cit. in: Andrea Alciato, "Oratio," in *Opera Omnia* (Basilae: apud Thoman Guarinum, 1582), IV, col. 1051. See also Alain Wijffels, *Introduction historique au droit* (Paris: Presses Univ. de France, 2010), 199–201.

31 The productive involvement of the legal profession in producing normative knowledge, which comes under the broad heading of *interpretatio*, declined in the late sixteenth century. I afforded an explanation in A. Giuliani, "From presumption to interpretation," in *Per Saturam. Studi per Severino Caprioli*, ed. F. Treggiari (Spoleto: Fondazione Centro italiano di studi sull'alto Medioevo, 2008), 447–74.

32 I Kings 3:16–28 in *Decretales Gregorii*, lib. II, tit. XXIII *De praesumptionibus*, cap. II [X 2.23.2].

judicial decision must be correct to carry out an act of justice, this result is based on a logically and temporally prior phase: the knowledge of the fact: the disputed fact must be correctly determined.[33] The awareness that their determination (*quaestio facti*) was the crucial and most complex chapter of judicial procedure runs deeply throughout pre-modern legal writings.[34] Facts must be determined correctly, but they are infinite, each one unique and different, and there is no science of contingent facts. The judge has various *media* to know facts, falling under the collective term "*probationes*", which raises a natural question: what is the position of a maxim, and what sort of knowledge does a maxim provide?[35]

33 Aquinas, *Summa Theologiae* [hereinafter ST], II-IIae, qu. 60, art. 1: "Videtur quod iudicium non sit actus iustitiae. Dicit enim Philosophus in 1 Ethic. [I.iii], quod unusquisque bene judicat quae cognoscat, et sic iudicium ad vim cognoscitivam pertinet videtur. Vis autem conoscitiva per prudentiam perficitur. Ergo judicium magis pertinet ad prudentiam quam ad justitiam, quae est in voluntate ut dictum est [q. LVII, art. 4]". Developing his argument, Aquinas concludes that a correct judgement requires two components, an act of reason and an act of justice: "In omnibus tamen ad rectum judicium duo requiruntur: quorum unum est actus rationis; dicere enim vel definire aliquid, rationis est. Aliud autem est dispositio judicantis, ex qua habet idoneitatem ad recte judicandum; et sic in his qui pertinent ad justitiam, judicium procedit ex justitia; sicut et in his quae ad fortitudinem pertinent, ex fortitudine. Sic ergo judicium est quidem actus justitiae sicut inclinantis ad recte judicandum; prudentiae autem sicut judicium proferentis". Similarly, Aquinas writes that "ad quod judicium sit actus justitiae tria requirantur: primo quidam ut procedat ex inclinatione justitiae; secundo quod procedat ex auctoritate praesidentis; tertio quod proferatur secundum rectam rationem prudentiae". Following the Aristotelian principle "quod unusquisque bene judicat quae cognoscat" (*Nichomachean Ethics* I. iii) Aquinas concludes that "judicium ad vim cognoscitivam pertinere videtur" (ST, qu. 47, art. 4). For an overview of this doctrine see Prospero Fagnani, "De constitutionibus c. Ne innitaris," in *id., Jus Canonicum, Sive Commentaria Absolutissima in V. Libros Decretales* (Cologne: Widenfelt et Berges, 1699), 30–112.

34 Adolfo Giuliani, "Civilian Treatises on Presumptions, 1580–1620," in *The Law of Presumptions: Essays in Comparative Legal History*, ed. Richard H. Helmholz and David Sellar (Berlin: Duncker & Humblot, 2009), 21–71.

35 The logical nature and thus the probatory function of maxims is a notorious crux of judicial procedure. It is crucial to note that the rise of natural law conceptions of procedure disempowered maxims, until the pathbreaking work by Friedrich Stein, *Das private Wissen des Richters: Untersuchungen zum Beweisrecht beider Prozesse* (Leipzig: C.L. Hirschfeld, 1893), on which see: A. Piras, "Le massime d'esperienza e la motivazione insufficiente," *Jus* (1955), 79–121, – and for the historical context: K. W. Nörr, *Naturrecht und Zivilprozess: Studien zur Geschichte d. dt. Zivilprozessrechts während d. Naturrechtsperiode bis zum beginnenden 19. Jh.* (Tübingen: Mohr, 1976).

4.1 *Knowing by Seeing and Knowing by Non-seeing: (i)* scientia, *(ii)* fides *and* opinio

We turn to Aristotelian Scholasticism for a very brief overview of its map of knowledge, in search for the place of maxims. We will be guided by the original and never challenged characterisation of a maxim as a self-evident statement (Boethius: "*per se nota propositio*"). A guiding idea that repeatedly emerges from texts is a fundamental dualism between: (i) a conception of knowledge (*scientia*) as a mental state based on the direct or immediate contact between mind and reality: the mind grasps the material object by the senses or the intellect;[36] (ii) another mode of cognition (belief, opinion, *fides* and *opinio*) characterised by the absence of a direct contact between the mind and the object; this is source of cognitions resulting from voluntary assent. Those two modes of cognition, very briefly, may be characterised as knowing by seeing or knowing by non-seeing.[37] This dualism was in the mind of Durand of Saint-Pourçain (1275–1332/4) who wrote:

> Intuitive knowledge is that which tends immediately to a thing which is objectively present according to its actual existence; as if I see the colour of the wall, or the rose that I hold in my hand. Abstractive knowledge is any cognition which is received from an object that is not present to the mind of the object immediately known.
>
> cognitio intuitiva, est illa quae immediate tendit ad rem sibi praesentem objective, secundum ejus actualem existentiam; sicut cum video colorem existentem in pariete, vel rosam quam in manu teneo. Abstractiva,

36 M. Ayers and M. R. Antognazza, "Knowledge and Belief from Plato to Locke", in *Knowing and Seeing: Groundwork for a new empiricism*, ed. M. Ayers (Oxford: Oxford University Press, 2019), 5–11. The locus classicus of the dualism of knowledge and opinion is Plato's Republic 477a–478d.

37 The source of course much older, going back to Plato's distinction between intelligible and sensible, reality and appearance, knowledge and belief as distinct powers or faculties: knowing is seeing/believing is indirect cognition through appearances, see on this: Maria Rosaria Antognazza, "The Distinction in Kind between Knowledge and Belief", *Proceedings of the Aristotelian Society* 120 (2021): 277–308. Antognazza correctly remarks that the standard analysis of knowledge in terms as "justified true belief" (based on a continuum from belief to knowledge) is absent in medieval and early-modern texts. See also: Luciano Floridi, "'Objective knowledge': the disappearance and revaluation of 'knowledges' from John Sergeant to Karl Popper," 18 March 1994, http://dx.doi.org/10.2139/ssrn.3854449.

> dicitur omnis cognitio, quae habetur de re non sic realiter praesente in ratione, objecti immediate cogniti.[38]

This dualism recurs in the texts. Consider, for example, its illustration through reference to the words of Paul: "For now we see through a glass, darkly; but then face to face" (*Videmus nunc per speculum in aenigmate: tunc autem facie ad faciem*; Paul, I Corinthians 13.12) – to emphasise the dualism between the face-to-face vision of intuitive cognition and the blurred cognition unaided by eyesight. Various intellectual strands can be discerned in the background. On the one hand, there is an intellectual line that goes back to Plato's conception of knowledge as seeing: the faculty of seeing the pure, atemporal, unchanging forms, and thus arriving at the vision of "the universe in its necessary, permanent, and wholly perfect being"; on the other hand, there is the Aristotelian emphasis on sense and experience in the acquisition of knowledge. However, it was in the medieval tendency to present Aristotelian texts in agreement with Plato that this conception flourished. It was expounded in texts that showed the continuing presence of Aristotle. As it will be seen below, the philosophical questions they pose, the framework of the arguments and the vocabulary itself show an intense engagement with Aristotelian texts.[39]

The dualism of knowing by seeing and knowing by non-seeing is confirmed by the contrast between two mental states characterised by the contact between mind and reality or its rejection. The first is characterised by the presence of the object to the cognitive subject; in the second such contact is absent, and the cognitive process is characterised by a gap. This dualism separates what is known *per se* (*scientia*) and what is known *per aliud* (*fides* and *opinio*). Let us examine them separately.

(1) Knowledge (shorthand for *episteme, nous, scientia, scire, intellectus*) is identified by reference to seeing (mentally perceiving) and is thus radic-

---

38 Durand of Saint-Pourçain (Durandi de Sancto Porciano), *Scriptum super IV libros Sententiarum, Prologus*, q. 3 n. 6. I cite from: William Hamilton, *Discussions on Philosophy and Literature, Education and University Reform* (London: Longman, 1853), 59. This text is discussed in Alain de Libera, "Présentation et représentation. Aux origines du 'représentationnalisme'," in *The Language of Thought in Late Medieval Philosophy*, ed. Jenny Pelletier and Magali Roques (Cham: Springer International Publishing, 2017), 417–435. For a clear introduction to this theme, with particular reference to Duns Scotus, see Maria Rosaria Antognazza, "Intuitive cognition in the Latin medieval tradition," *British Journal for the History of Philosophy* 31 (2023), 675–92.

39 Joseph Owens, "Aristotle and Aquinas," in *The Cambridge Companion to Aquinas*, ed. Norman Kretzmann and Eleonore Stump (Cambridge: Cambridge University Press, 1993), 38–59, esp. 38–40.

ally different from *fides* and *opinio*. With all Aristotelian resonances, we find Aquinas reiterating that knowledge is the state of mind moved directly by its object which is present in a primitive and irreducible way to the mind of the knower. The knowing object is present and perceived in its essence (*quidditas: quid res est*) to the knowing subject.[40] Between mind and object there are no gaps: the object is "present" (*prae-esse*: being in front of the observer) to the mind, as if it were here and now.[41] It is crucial to note that the mind adheres immediately to the knowing object in a process that is moved either by the object itself (*per seipsum cognitum*) or by something else which is already known (*per aliud cognitum*): the object is grasped by sense or through representation.

(II) Belief (*fides, credere*) is characterised by the absence of an immediate contact with the knowing subject: the object is known indirectly by hearing ("*ex auditu*"),[42] and cognition is given on grounds external to the object. While knowing (*scire*) is the state by which the object is grasped by sensory perception or clear mental intuition ("*ex visu, vel alio sensu vel alio mentis intuitu manat, et ita est clara*"), belief is obscure ("*fides autem obscura, quippe quae ex auditu est*"). It would be misleading, however, to suppose an inferior cognitive state; on the contrary, the assurance by which fides or opinion are embraced lies in the source of assurance, not in its degree. Belief, being identified by its source *ex auditu*, would not change into knowledge, namely, a mode of cognition *de visu*.

(III) *Opinio* has a special place in juristic thinking, being the cognitive faculty that operates on the mutable and contingent state of reality, populated by things "that happen most of the time" (*quae ut in pluribus accidunt*). Humans, unlike angels and other creatures whom Aquinas called "*intel-*

40 Aquinas, *In 3 Sent.*, Dist 26, II, 4: "certitudo proprie dicitur firmitas adhesionis virtus cognoscitivae ad suum cognoscibile", cit. in Antognazza, *Distinction in kind*, 10.

41 Antognazza, "The Distinction in Kind," 277–308. Giovanni Mascardo, qu. 8: "dispicere non possum, unde clarius, & manifestius Iudex veritatem cognoscere quaeat, quam si res ipsa ob ipsiusmet oculos observetur". Mascardo cited Didaco Covarrubias, *Variarum ex iure pontificio, regio et caesareo resolutionum*, lib. 1, cap. 1, n. 7 ("notorium est quod ante oculos situm est"). Baldus, *in l. cives, Cod. de appelat.* (=C. 7.62.11), and Mascardo, *De probationibus,* conclus. 1101, cited in C. Ghisalberti, "La teoria del notorio nel diritto comune", *Annali di storia del diritto* 1 (1957), 403–51 at 419, n. 51. Cyprianus Soaresius, *Introductio in dialecticam*, lib. 4, cap. 30, fol. 160: "Prima & vera sunt, quae non per alia, sed per se ipsa fidem habent".

42 Martinus Azpilcueta, *Relectio c. Novit De judiciis* (Roma: J. De Angelis, 1575), 22: "credere est firmiter adherere alicui iudicio, non eo quod vidit, sed ob aliorum relationem". See also R. Feldhay, "Thomist Epistemology of Faith: The Road from 'Scientia' to Science," *Science in Context* 20 (2007): 401–21.

lectuales", have limited cognitive capacities. By reasoning, however, they extend their cognition of the moral world through inferential processes. Laboriously proceeding step-by-step they infer new knowledge from what they already know.[43] The source is a passage from the *Nicomachean Ethics* (Lib. 1, c. 3, n. 4) that had an immense influence on scholastic and humanistic thought:

> it is the mark of an educated man to look for precision in each class of things just so far as the nature of the subject admits.[44]

According to Aristotle, mathematics and ethics demand different methodologies: mathematics requires demonstrations, the moral world requires arguments, but they imply the coherent inferential processes offered by dialectics and rhetoric, being the appropriate modes of cognition of practical disciplines. There are two observations to be made to better frame this mode of cognition.

The first is that an opinion is a basis for a morally safe action, including pronouncing a judgement.[45] We find for example the theologian Francisco de Vitoria (c. 1480–1546) lecturing in Salamanca on the *Secunda Secundae* of Aquinas, adding a comment on Aristotle's text mentioned above:

> I maintain that in order to act morally opinion is sufficient, so that neither science nor faith is required. This is proved, because moral actions are about contingencies, about which we cannot have evidence; as Aristotle states [*Ethics*, lib. 1, c. 3, n. 4], in moral matters we must be content with imperfect and human conjectures, which do not amount to evidence and certainty, but produce a certain appearance, certainty, and human probability.

> Dico nihilominus quod ad bene moraliter agendum sufficit opinio, ita quod non requiritur scientia nec fides. Probatur, quia actions morales

43 For an enlightening reconstruction see Scott Macdonald, "Theory of Knowledge," in *The Cambridge Companion to Aquinas*, 160–95 at 161–2.

44 Aristotle, *Nicomachean Ethics*, in *The complete works of Aristotle: the revised Oxford translation*, ed. Jonathan Barnes (Princeton NJ: Princeton University Press, 1984), 1730, I, 2, 1094^{b} 24–25.

45 Aquinas, *ST* II.IIae, qu. 70, art. 11: "Respondeo dicendum quod, secundum Philosophum, certitudo non est similiter querenda in omni materia. In actibus humanis, super quibus constitutuntur judicia non potest haberi certitudo demonstrativa [...] sufficit probabilis certitudo".

> sunt circa contingentia de quibus non possumus habere evidentiam; sed, ut dicit Philosophus [Aristotle, *Ethics*, lib. 1, c. 3, n. 4], in moralibus debemus esse contenti crassis et humanis conjecturis, quae non faciunt evidentiam et certitudinem, sed faciunt quaendam apparentiam et certitudinem et humanam probabilitatem.[46]

The second is that inquiries on opinion are guided by experience, which makes the mass of mutable facts knowable:

> in contingent matters of action an individual can be directed, not by those things that are simply and necessarily true, but by those which occur most of the time (*quae ut in pluribus accidunt*) [...] But to discover what is true most of the time we need experience [...] experience is the result of many memories.
>
> in his (sc. singularibus) autem non potest homo dirigi per ea quae sunt simpliciter et necessitate vera, sed ex his quae ut in pluribus accidunt. Quid autem in pluribus [II II 49 a.1] sit verum oportet per experimentum considerare [...] experimentum autem est ex pluribus memoriis.[47]

What is "experience"? In the Aristotelian-scholastic lexicon, this word indicates a repository of cognitions that grows from the accumulation of sensory instances.[48] It is the product of a solidified process of stratification of continuous investigations on contingent things (*ea quae ut pluribus accidunt*), which over time reveal recurring patterns. Since each new finding is set against the standard of "what usually happens", this stratification excludes individual and unregulated discoveries and, through accumulation, produces a collective commonplace knowledge.[49]

---

46 Francisco de Vitoria, *Commentary of Aquinas' II-IIae*, qu. 47, art. 4, cited in T. Deman, "Probabilisme," *Dictionnaire de Théologie Catholique*, 15 vols. (Paris: Letouzey et Ané, 1931), XIII, cols. 417–619 at 458–9.

47 Aquinas, *ST*, II-IIae, qu. 49, art. 1. Oldend per Calv: "Experientia cognitio quaedam nullo docente, per usum contingens. Et in hoc distat ab arte, quae certis traditur praecepti. Oldend."

48 Aristotle, *Post. Anal.* 2.19.100a4-6: "So from sensation comes what we call memory, and from memory, when it is generated repeatedly of the same thing, there comes experience. For memories that are many in number constitute a single experience".

49 Ian Maclean, *Logic, signs and nature: learned medicine in the Renaissance* (Cambridge: Cambridge University Press, 2002), 197, and Peter Dear, "Miracles, experiments and the ordinary course of nature," *Isis* 81 (1990): 663–83 at 666.

The triadic map of *scientia, fides* and *opinio*[50] recurrently appears in theological and juristic texts. It is discussed, for example, for example, in the *Manuale confessariorum* by the jurist and theologian Martin de Azpicuelta (1493–1586) who sets it out as follows:

> science, or visual cognition of the thing (*scientia, vel cognitio visiva rei*)
>
> faith, or cognition, by which we firmly judge that which we cannot see is so (*fides, vel cognitio, qua firmiter ita esse iudicamus, id quod non videmus*)
>
> opinion, or cognition by which we judge something which we cannot see is or is not; but which we cannot firmly believe is so, though concerned that the contrary might also be true (*opinio, vel cognitio qua iudicamus aliquid esse vel non esse, quod non videmus, nec firmiter credimus ita esse, sed cum formidine ne contrarium sit verum*)[51]

This theory also appears in one of the *consilia* by the influential jurist Jacopo Menochio (1532–1607).[52] He discusses the case of an old man, Bernardus Patavinus, caught up in the toils of the Inquisition and charged with heresy for having declared to the judges, who were testing his orthodoxy, that he was "certain" to go to Heaven. Examining "what is certainty" (*certitudo quid sit*), Menochio spoke of three kinds of certainty: (i) evident certainty (which pro-

---

50 How the triad *scientia/fides/opinio* morphed in time is beyond the scope of this essay. In 16th-century legal writings, the standard citation is the *Summa* by Antonin of Florence (1389–1459), which in turn draws from Albertus Magnus (c. 1206–80), who in his *Liber de quatuor coaequaevis* wrote: "Opinio vero est acceptio unius partis cum formidine alterius, ita tamen quod ad illam quam formidat, non habet rationem expressam, formidatur tamen propter debilitatem rationis alterius partis. Fides autem est perfecta persuasio unius partis per multa probabilia. Sed scientia est eorum quae cognoscuntur per causam, et quoniam impossibile est aliter se habere". (Albertus Magnus, *Liber de quatuor coaequaevis*, Tr 1, q. 2, a. 3, in *Opera Omnia*, 38 vols. (*Paris:* Vives, 1895), vol. 34, 327a). See on this Stanley B. Cunningham, *Reclaiming moral agency: the moral philosophy of Albert the Great* (Washington D.C.: CUA Press, 2008), 32–33. Apparently, this triadic scheme belongs to the first wave of scholasticism at the university of Paris. Hugh of St Victor (1096–1141) wrote: "Faith is a form of mental certitude about distant realities that is greater than opinion and less then science" (*De sacramentis* I.10.2).

51 Martinus Azpilcueta, *Enchiridion sive Manuale confessariorum et poenitentium* (Venice, 1584), 1004–5, cap. 27, n. 279. See also P. Dear, "From truth to disinterestedness in the seventeenth-century," in *Social Studies of Science* 22–4 (1992): 619–31.

52 Jacopo Menochio, *Consilia* (Venice: Ziletti, 1609–13), I: fol. 211v, cons. 82.

ceeds from the evidence of the thing) (*certitudo evidens: a rei evidentia provenit*); (ii) certainty of conviction or faith (*certitudo credulitatis seu fidei;* (iii) moral or human certainty (*certitudo moralis, seu humana*).

4.2 *Representing "What Usually Happens"*

Medieval jurists routinely acknowledged that maxims represented "what usually happens" (*id quod plerumque accidit*). They produced itemised lists of maxims that summarised instances of what is normal in a social context ("from robustness it is presumed that the weakling did not provoke but was the one attacked";[53] "from evil physiognomy it is presumed that he committed the crime"; "once evil, always evil"; "if he is poor today, he was poor before"). They were accepted as temporary truths, until contradicted.

Those maxims, grounded on the trust in a regular pre-existing ordered pattern, were another word for presumption. The reference to "what usually happens" is a central feature of presumption that appears in the Gloss: "*praesumitur ex eo quod plurimum accidit*"[54] and persists in legal writings, in admonishing, for example, that "the just judge should not presume what is incompatible with human experience and rarely occurs" ([*j*]*udex iustus non debet presumere ea, quae repugnant experientia humana, & quae raro eveniunt*).[55] Medieval jurists routinely acknowledged this similarity. In his *Vocabularium Juris* Alberico da Rosate (c. 1290–1360) wrote that a maxim is "a collection and conjunction of many similar things" ([*r*]*egula* [...] *est multorum similium collectio vel coniunctio*) and established a parallel between *plerumque* and *regulariter*.[56] A broadly similar account appears in the commentary on the *Digest* title *De regulis iuris* by Philippus Decius (1454–1535). He saw their connection in summarising "what commonly happens"; being descriptions of *plerumque* (most of the time), they are grounded on a basic trust in regularity.[57] Any claim based on a maxim, reflecting the common course of nature, re-establishes normality; if contradicted it must be proved, shifting the burden of proof to the other litigant.[58]

53 This maxim comes from Aristotle, *Rhetoric*, 1402a 17–28.

54 Gl. S.v. '*Praesumptionem*' ad D. 22.3.25.

55 Jacopo Menochio, *De Praesumptionibus, conjecturis signis & indiciis* (Venetiis: Apud haeredes Francisci Ziletti, 1587), 818, lib. 6, pr .49, n. 5

56 Alberico da Rosate, *Vocabularium Iuris* (Paris, 1525), fols. 195v and 178.

57 Philippus Decius, *In tit. ff. De regulis iuris* (Lyon: Antoin Vincent, 1562), 8, *Reg.* 1, § 11: "Et ideo dictio plerunque regulam facit [...] Sic etiam praesumptio insurgit a communiter accidentibus".

58 Doctrine of the *fundata intentio*, e.g. in Everharus Bronchorst, *In titulum digestorum de diversis regulis iuris antiqui* (Frankfurt: apud Emmelium, 1626), 31–32, Prolegomena:

The human world, seen through a maxim, becomes explainable. Human actions are not singular, unexpected, and unique but are recognisable by their being patterned along types or models. The various references to verisimilitude, normality, a common order of nature, innate preconceptions, and others suggested a web of connections between facts, which creates maps to look better into reality. They highlight an inner network of relations (causal, temporal, natural) in which everything is connected to everything else. Without such patterns or if the knowing process were to operate in a *vacuum* in separation from such patterns, reality would be impenetrable.[59] If we take for example, the maxim "once evil, always evil" (*semel malus semper malus*) we find a fragment from the repository that records what has been experienced over time in a social context. What happens in social life is reflected in its maxims and is a variant of the commonplace knowledge that is current within its boundaries.[60] The natural corollary is that normality cannot explain the singular, unique, or diverging event, which must be proved individually (*facta non praesumuntur*):[61]

"certe qui regulam iuris pro se habet, is certam, claram & fundatam intentionem suam habere dicitur [...] secundum regulam pronuntiandum est, nisi de contrario, aut specialiter probetur".

59 On the maxim "once evil, always evil", see H. Kiefner, "Semel malus semper presumitur esse malus," in *Zeitschrift der Savigny-Stiftung für Rechtsgeschichte, Romanistische Abteilung* 78 (1961): 308–54. J. C. Westerhoff, "A world of signs: Baroque pansemioticism, the polyhistor and the early modern Wunderkammer," *Journal of the History of Ideas* 62 (2001): 633–50; Hans U. Gumbrecht, "Typology of cultures and history of emblems," *Emblemata: revista aragonesa de emblemática* 16 (2010): 37–44; and Dear, "Miracles," 663–83.

60 Alciato in his treatise on presumptions wrote that "Patres praesumunttur amare filios suos" (pr. I), "Mulier praesumitur de facili decipi, maxime propter viri seductiones" (pr. XLII. I), "Minores praesumuntur de facili dicere mendacia" (pr. XLII.7), "Vir praesumitur constantior muliere" (pr. XLVII), "Agricola diligens praesumitur innocens et quietus".

61 On *traditio rei* see Menochio, *De praesumptionibus*, 754, lib. 6, pr. 14, n. 1: "praesumptionem transactionis non induci, nisi hoc specialiter approbetur", and "non praesumitur solennitas extrinseca, nisi probatur". On the deterioration of a thing in price or substance see Nicolaus Everardus (Nicolaas Everaerts), *Loci argumentorum legales* (Louvain: Servatius Sassenus, 1552), 310: "non praesumitur deterioratio rei in precio vel substantia, nisi probetur". Moreover, Antoine Favre, *Codex Fabrianus* (Lyon, 1681), 58: "[p]ossessio quoniam facti magis quam iuris est, per testes probari debet". Menochio, *De praesumptionibus*, 753–5, lib. VI, praes. 14: "Facti quae sunt non praesumi". See also Mascardo, *Conclusiones,* t. II, concl. 732. The source is D. 45.1.137.2: "in eo vero, quod tempore vel facto finitum est, nullus est coniecturae locus". The Gloss s.v. *'Nullus'* explains that "[i]n incertis, non certis, est locus coniecturis". Augustinus Barbosa, *Variae tractationes iuris* (Lyon: Bordes et Arnaud, 1631), 59, axioma 93: 'Factum, Facta,' n. 26; Giovanni Mascardo, *Conclusiones probationum,* concl. 732, n. 5.

> Note that those facts which happen at random and do not belong to human nature, cannot be presumed: they must be proved.
>
> Nota quod non debent praesumi ea quod accidentaliter proveniunt, et non insunt homini a natura, nisi probent.[62]

Legal writings provided lists of such facts (a marriage, a baptism, the delivery of an item (*traditio rei*), a possession, the deterioration of something in value or substance). There was an underlying coherence in this doctrine, for normality covers only typical, usual and expected facts (*factum praesumitur, quod fieri consuevit*).[63] At the same time, it reflects accepted social values ("if she is the mother, she would love her child" and "there is no one who does not desire that his or her children be safe and happy"),[64] as well as the tendency to streamline decisions based on the principle of economy, since any fact that can be explained by normality or nature's regularity does not need to be proven.[65]

An idea of how maxims worked in practice can be gathered from the legal advice (*consilium*) Menochio gave in the following case.[66] Albert, an old man from Padua, died leaving all his possessions to a convent. Sometime later, one Francisco turns up with another will which names him universal heir. The question is brought to court, and Menochio, offering an argument entirely based on maxims, draws the conclusion that the donation is forged. The kernel of his argument is based on three presumptions: first, the notary who drafted the second testament had been condemned some years before for forgery (*de falso*), from this fact a presumption arises that he is dishonest. Second, another presumption of dishonesty emerges from the circumstance that the notary fled the town hoping to avoid prison once the forgery was

62 Alberico da Rosate, *Dictionarium juris tam civilis quam canonici* (Venice, 1573), s.v. 'Praesumptio'.

63 Nikolaus Everardus, *Loci*, p. 310; Menochio, *De praesumptionibus*, VI, pr. 14, n. 20, 755, and pr16, 754: "Nam in consuetis atque ita in a communiter accidentibus ea quae facti sunt, praesumuntur", "Facti, quae sunt in his, quae fieri solent, & a communiter accidentibus, praesumuntur".

64 Cicero, *De Inventione*, I, 30, 48: "Credibile est quod sine ullo teste auditoris opinione firmatur, hoc modo: Nemo est, qui non liberos suos incolumes et beatos esse cupiat".

65 Menochio, *De praes.* lib. I, q. 3, n. 2 "Haec violenta praesumptio a naturalibus causis et principiis nata, contrariam probationem non admittit [...] n. 5: est hoc argumentum concludens a necessitate naturae, quae vi humana, ut aliter se habeat, effici non potest. Qua enim ratione et medio probari poterit contrarium eius, quod natura ipsa, quae evidentem adfert certitudinem, docet atque comonstrat?"

66 Menochio, *Consilia*, V: fols. 67–70, *consilium* 422.

detected. Third, a presumption is based on the maxim that what is unlikely is presumed to be false (*falsum praesumitur quod non est verisimile*). In fact, in the *probandum* three facts were not verisimilar. First, it is not likely that Albert, an avaricious old man, was willing to make a donation; such a human character, argues Menochio, shares one trait with women: "*genus mulierum dicitur avarissimum, donatio a muliere facta non praesumitur*".[67] Second, it is not verisimilar that Albert wished to grant a donation to someone, like Francis, with whom there was no relation of reward, friendship or any other reason of benevolence (*non est verisimile Albertus voluerit donare D. Francisco, de se non solum non benemerito verum etiam nec amicitia nec aliqua benevolentia coniunctio*). Third, it is not verisimilar that Albert changed his mind; a maxim, registered by Alciato, states that "change is not presumed" (*mutatio non praesumitur*).[68]

5 Early Modern "Artificial Reason"

Sixteenth-century maxims lived in a special cognitive environment. We will be able to understand it by turning to the epistemic background against which jurists conceptualised the knowledge of facts. The most immediate observation is that their points of reference were gradually moving towards the models offered by a recently revived Aristotelian text: the *Rhetoric*, a work whose relevance to legal science was enhanced by the promise of an artificial method in the knowledge of facts. In this context we will place the question considered above: what is the relationship between the maxim and reality, between the statement "every mother loves her child" (*omnis mater diligit filium*) and real life? This question was in the mind of the *consiliarius regius* Pierre Du Faure de Saint-Jory (Petrus Faber/Fabrius, c 1540–1600) who in 1585 suggested (quoting Seneca) that the guidance offered by verisimilarity was based not on truth but on reason:

> It is hard to conjecture on the human mind … and we should never expect to get a totally certain comprehension of things because explor-

67 On the maxim "*genus mulierum avarissimum*", see Stein, "Civil Law Maxims," 1082–5.

68 Andrea Alciato, *De praesumptionibus*, reg. 3, pr. 16. The source is D. 22.3.22 (Ulpian): "Eum qui voluntatem mutatam dicit, probare hoc debere". Peckius, *Ad regulas iuris canonici*, fol. 56r: "Mutatio non praesumitur: quia mutare est quid accidens, & accidentia non praesumitur".

> ation on the truth is difficult; but we go where verisimilitude leads us. We then follow where reason, not truth, leads us.[69]

What did he mean by "reason"?

5.1 *Artificial Method*

Du Faure's reference to reason was particularly significant in those decades. From the 1530s, the theory of judicial proof was radically reshaped. It was recast according to the methodology of a newly recovered Aristotelian work, the *Ars Rhetorica* (AR). This work was first revived in Venice in the late 15th century by a group of emigrés in Venice (George of Trebizond, 1395–1484),[70] and was then disseminated by a flood of commentaries and translations into Latin and vernacular languages. This work had a deep effect on the epistemology of the knowledge of facts, contributing to a turn from Latin to Greek sources, and more broadly, it announced the demise of Cicero as a literary model.[71] This work furthered the epistemic project of an investigation of facts based on a rational method. This epistemological impetus was further reinforced by a philological re-reading of the *Analytica Priora* (*APri*) by the jurist and logician Giulio Paci de Beriga (Julius Pacius, 1550–1635).[72] His translation and commentary on this text became standard textbooks during his lifetime. From these works, legal scholars gleaned the idea that the knowledge of facts could be elevated to the broader Aristotelian project of explaining human reasoning in terms of logical inference. The immense attention

---

69 Petrus Faber, *Ad tit. de diversis regulis iuris antiqui ... commentarivs* (Paris: Duvallus et Beysius, 1585), 441, *ad* D. 50.17.114: "Difficilis humani animi coniectura est: ideo numquam expectamus certissimam rerum comprehensium: quoniam in arduo est veri exploratio: sed ea imus qua ducit verisimilitudo. Sequimur denique qua ratio, non qua veritas trahit".

70 John Monfasani, *George of Trebizond: A Biography and a Study of His Rhetoric and Logic* (Leiden: Brill, 1976).

71 Morris W. Croll, *'Attic' and Baroque Prose Style: The Anti-Ciceronian Movement* (Princeton, N.J: Princeton University Press, 1969); Gumbrecht, "Typology of cultures and history of emblems," 37–44.

72 Giulio Pace studied at Padua both law (seemingly) with Jacopo Menochio, and logic, mentioning Jacopo Zabarella as "praeceptor meus". His edition of the *Organon* became a standard textbook during his lifetime, *Aristotelous Organon Aristotelis Stagiritae Peripateticorum principii Organum* (Genève: ex typis Vignonianis, 1605). On Giulio Pace studies at Padua with Jacopo Menochio see Jacques Berriat-Saint-Prix, *Notice sur Julius Pacius a Beriga, jurisconsulte et philosophe des XVIe et XVIIe siècles* (Paris: P.-J. Langlois, 1840). His mention of Zabarella as "praeceptor meus" is in the opening of his edition of the *Analytica Priora* I.1.

attracted by those works shows the impetus for bringing to life a fresh and challenging project that promised a new beginning; one word summed up its appeal: an *artificial* method.[73] The legal profession was taken by storm by the epistemic possibilities offered by these Aristotelian texts. They offered what the professionalisation of the supreme courts needed: a method of knowing facts that was objective, precise, and impersonal.[74] No human touch was needed; it was "artificial". That the mind was an emotionless reasoning machine suited the legal profession because it conferred an epistemic superiority that justified the authority of the growing class of Supreme Courts. They were staffed by authoritative academics and leading practitioners who boasted of their superior reasoning and experience; if the profane found them obscure, that was part of the general idea of artificial reason.[75]

The main idea, expressed in the opening lines of Aristotle's *Rhetoric* (*AR* I.1), is that humans are primarily reasoners but are prone to errors, and those who reason correctly do so either by natural talent or by chance. But a superior form of reasoning can be created, one that imitates the mind of a perfect reasoner, unencumbered by passions, and that explicitly brings forth the rationality of human thought. It is based on the idea that reasoning is patterned along a general syllogistic form, and the aim was to make it explicit, which Aristotle, using an archaic Greek word, called *enthymeme* (literally: "internal to the mind"). His efforts to set out a reasoning method in the *Ars rhetorica* contribute to the broader project carried out in the *Analytica Priora*, to formulate a general formal theory of syllogistic reasoning.[76] At its heart was

---

73 Francesco Patrizi of Cherso (1529–97) registered this climate writing in 1562: "[j]ust before the present time, Cicero was considered the best, and Quintilian the second, and others prized Hermogenes. But now that Aristotle has been discovered, he has gone thousand miles ahead". Francesco Patrizi, *Della retorica, dialoghi dieci* (Venice: Francesco Sanese, 1562), 9, Dialogo II: "Poco sopra a questa etá, Cicerone era stimato il migliore, et Quintiliano era il secondo, et alcuni tenevano per primo, et altri tenieno Hermogene in maggior pregio. Ma hora, scopertosi Aristotele, e' loro ito avanti mille miglia nel credere di ognuno".

74 The Aristotelian text (A 1, 54a 11–55a3) asserts that the inquirer's mental operations must be unaffected by emotions but concerned only with logical demonstration. See e.g. Paolo Beni, *Disputatio in qua quaeritur, an sive actori, sive reo, liceat in iudiciis & concionibus affectus concitare: ac Iudicum animos flectere & permiscere* (Venice, 1594).

75 This is the context of the clash between Sir Edward Coke (1552–1634) and King James I. Coke, then Chief Justice, asserted that the law used an artificial reason that was inaccessible to the outsider, even if highly educated in other ways. *The Reports of Sir Edward Coke*, (Edinburgh and London: W. Green & Sons, 1907), VI: 1343.

76 Aristotle's project for a universal syllogism-based reasoning is in *APri*, lib. II, cap. XXIII; Pacius introduces the chapter writing "Cum syllogismo aut inductione fides fiat, omnis probatio ad syllogismum reducitur" p. 246. See on this: Catarina Dutilh Novaes, "The

the aim of extending reasoning by means of a method that transcended and enhanced the natural human reasoning capacity, which was qualified as "artificial" by offering a technique that purposefully expanded their capabilities.[77] The word "ars" in the title stands for a methodology for producing things. As Giulio Paci tells us, rhetoric was an art (*tekne*) that was functional for the production (not the contemplation) of knowledge; it was like the making of harnesses, which is instrumental for riding and functional for military art.[78] Some translations and commentaries of the *Rhetoric* produced at this time presented its subject-matter as "ratio disserendi", another word for logic.[79]

Jurists borrowed this artificial method to reconceptualise the question of fact and its operative instrument: judicial proofs. And because of the centrality of the knowledge of facts in framing the juristic phenomenon, the artificial method reverberated in major areas of legal science. In a few decades, jurists rewrote entire sectors of their discipline (judicial proof, contracts, interpretation) according to a protocol that connected facts and legal rules according to an impersonal logical connection.[80] Most profoundly affecting the legal

---

Syllogism as Defined by Aristotle, Ockham, and Buridan," in *The Language of Thought in Late Medieval Philosophy*, 217–31, and Myles Burnyeat, "Enthymeme: Aristotle on the Logic of Persuasion," in *Explorations in Ancient and Modern Philosophy* (Cambridge: Cambridge University Press, 2012), 152–202.

77 According to the Paduan logician Jacopo Zabarella (1533–89), rhetoric was part of logic: Jacopo Zabarella, *Opera logica* (Basel: Waldkirch, 1594), 19e: "quia rhetorica est pars quaedam logicae [...] quoniam Rhetorica secundum essentiam suam est logica, & sub logicae parte universali tanquam specialis sub genere continetur".

78 Pacius, Commentary on *Analytica Priora*, in *Aristotelous Organon*, 111. As Aristotle explains: "All Art deals with bringing something into existence; and to pursue an art means to study how to bring to existence a thing which may exist or not, and the efficient cause of which lies in the maker and not in thing made." Aristotle, *Nicomachean Ethics*, trans. H. Rackham (Cambridge MA: Harvard University Press, 1999), Book VI.4.4, p. 335. See also on this: Wiliam Grimaldi, *Studies in the philosophy of Aristotle's Rhetoric* (Wiesbaden: Steiner, 1972).

79 This point is made in the most influential commentary, authored by Pier Vettori (1499–1585) who in the Introduction writes "[w]hen Aristotle used this word [*scil.* rhetoric] [...] he affirmed that rhetoric is part not of civil science but of *ratio disserendi*". The latter term is illustrated by Boethius: "omnis ratio disserendi, quam λογικέ logicen Peripatetici veteres appellant," in Boethius, *De differentiis topicis*, col. 1173 C. Another argument was to free rhetoric from connections to political discourse: Petrus Victorius, *Commentarii in tres libros Aristotelis De arte dicendi* (Florence: ex officina Junctarum, 1579), *Praefatio*: "[Aristoteles] non civilis scientiae, sed rationis disserendi partem rhetoricam esse affirmavit".

80 I believe that late sixteenth-century legal thinking would be fruitfully explained in terms of its concern to link Roman law with Aristotelian scholasticism as discussed in Giuliani, "Civilian Treatises on Presumptions, 1580–1620". In *The Law of Presumptions: Essays in*

field was the view of reasoning as a generalised inferential process based on a syllogistic form that governed precise connections between premises and conclusions.

5.2 *Maxims in the Context of Artificial Reason*

It is time to return to our major focus on maxims. They are one of the components of the artificial method and interact with its overall dynamics. Let us turn to the Aristotelian text. Aristotle introduces artificial proofs in the opening sections of the work (AR, I. i–ii), adding that he wanted to go beyond earlier writings by offering an epistemic method focused solely on proofs (*apodeixis*):

> *AR* I.1.3: this method is about proofs and at its heart is the enthymeme, which is a demonstration (*apodeixis*); the rest is just an appendage (*prostekay*). (*my translation*).

> *AR* I.1.11: it is evident that a method formed artificially is about proofs; and proof is a kind of demonstration.

> *AR* I.1.11 (Victorius, *Commentarii,* 17): "quia autem perspicuum est rationem ac viam quae sequitur artem, circa probationes versari. Probatio autem est demonstratio (*apodeixis tis*) quaedam"

The doctrine is supported by two distinctions (Diagram 2.1). The first distinguishes artificial from non-artificial proofs according to the presence or absence of reasoning:

(1) Artificial proofs are produced by reasoning. A fact is ascertained, inferential steps push the reasoning forward, connections are sought, the combination of syllogistic terms produces the conclusion. Artificial proofs can be described as sources of information about the existence of a fact generated by a specific syllogistic form, very distant from what it is usually understood by syllogism, which Aristotle named "*enthymeme*".[81] The main idea is that reasoning is not structured according to abstract forms but to the actual inferential patterns internal to the

Comparative Legal History, edited by Richard H. Helmholz and David Sellar, 21–71. Berlin: Duncker & Humblot, 2009.

81 The jurist and logician Giulio Paci in 1597 rescued the enthymeme from its reductive characterisation as a "truncated" syllogism, noting that the word "truncated" (*aletes*) was missing from the Greek original text and had been added by a medieval commentator, in AP 2.27 Pacius.

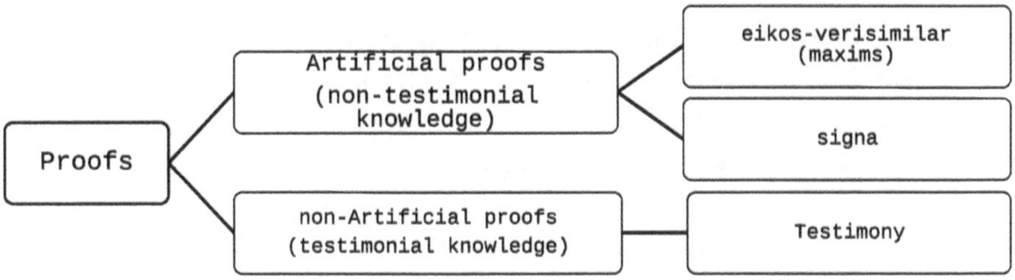

DIAGRAM 2.1 A summary view of the dualism of artificial and non-artificial proofs according to *AR* I.2.2 and *AnPri* II. 27

mind (enthymeme: "in the mind"). This syllogistic form produces either strict or loose arguments in relation to the premisses it processes (*AR* II.22.4-9): when the premise is necessary, the argument is strict; when the premise is "for the most part", the argument is loose (*AR* II.22.10).

(II) Non-artificial proofs, another word for testimony, are received passively. A testimony is a data provider that provides a narration. The inquirer listens to the witness who describes what they have perceived or looks at the document that represents it. This process does not require reasoning. The Spanish jurist Francisco Sarmiento de Mendoza (d. 1595) wrote that the perfect testimony would be given by an animal that could speak, it would tell what it sees without elaboration.[82]

The second distinction is internal to artificial proofs: it distinguishes between the two premises that are elaborated by the syllogistic form offered by the artificial method (*enthymeme*): (1) *eikos* or verisimilar and (2) signs. We shall leave signs aside being a separate branch of artificial proofs, although it is crucial to note their expansion at the expense of *eikota* during the early 17th century, at the time of the decline of maxims (see *infra*). *Eikos* (plural: *eikota*, from *εἰκών*: image, painting, representation) is a philosophically loaded term that 16th-century translators turned into the Latin "*verisimilis*" (*veri-similis*: similar to the truth) and illustrated with maxims, the commonest of which was the standard "mothers love their children":

82 This observation is owed to Francisco Sarmiento de Mendoza, "*Selectae interpretationes,*" in *Opera omnia* (Antwerp, 1661), 5, lib. 1, cap. 1, n. 9: "Probatio vera est, quae sensu corporeo immediate percipitur, ut si testes hominem occidere videant: praesumptio vero, quae non sensu corporeo immediate, sed per discursum colligitur. Prima adeo sensibus capitur, ut animalia irrationabilia si loqui scirent, possent probationem priorem facere, non secundam; sed homini rationali adeo potest res evidenter ostendi ex secunda, sicut ex prima".

AR I.2.15: The verisimilar is what happens most of the time, however not at random as some say, but it regards those things or events that can happen in different ways, and happen in regard to what is verisimilar as the universal is related to the singular.

AR I.2.15 (Victorius, *Commentarii,* 50–1): verisimile enim est, quod plerumque fit, non simpliciter autem, quaeadmodum definiunt nonnulli, sed quod versetur circa ea, quae contingit aliter se habere, ita se habens ad illud, ad quod verisimile est, ut quod in universum fit, ad singulare.

AnPri II.27.1: The verisimilar and the sign are different, but the verisimilar is a probable proposition, about what it is known that can happen or not happen or can be or not be: as, for example, that envious hate and lovers cherish.

AnPri II.27.1 (Pacius, p. 452): Verisimile autem et signum non sunt idem, sed verisimile est propositio probabilis, quod enim plerumque sciunt ita fieri, vel non fieri, aut esse aut non esse; hoc est verisimile: ut invidentes odisse, aut amantes diligere.

5.3 *Maxims as Small-Scale Models of Reality*

At the heart of *eikos* (Latin: *veri-similis*) is a relation. Variously translated as image, painting or representation, *eikos* is the perceptible side of an aspect of reality. In his *De memoria et reminiscentia,* Aristotle speaks of *eikos* in relation to a painting: the painted animal (*eikos*) is in relation to the real animal. The representation and the represented cannot be separated, like the two sides of a page. It suggests that, to know reality, the mind needs models, but in a particular way that includes the study of the mind. *Eikota* are products of experience that are stored in the memory and are probable (i.e. believable) when the mind recognise them in its objects of cognition.[83] In the puzzling fact the mind seeks a model or pattern which is stored in the memory, hoping to find a relation, Aristotle says, "as the universal is related to the singular" (*AR* I.ii.15). Consider

83 (Pseudo-)Aristotle, "*Rhetorica ad Alexandrum,*" trans. Francesco Filelfo, in *Aristotelis Rhetoricorum libri omnes* (Lyon: apud haeredes Iacobi Iuntae, 1561), Ch. 7 De probationibus, p. 199: "eikos dicitur, quod probabiliem propositione dicimus, illud est quod cum dixeris auditoribus, in mentibus eius exempla teneant". For a full discussion of *eikos* see Aristotle, *De memoria et reminiscentia*, 450a30: "it is obvious that one must consider the affection which is produced by sensation in the soul [...] as a kind of picture (*eikos*)". (Aristotle, *On memory and recollection*, trans. WS Hett (Cambridge MA: Heinemann, 1957), 293–5).

how we relate the strange insect we see in the garden to our experience of biology. We connect the puzzling thing to a model and use the latter as a standard which, separating all random phenomena, brings to light the regularity intrinsic to the fact or thing under scrutiny. Hence, the connection to the model discriminates relatively stabilised facts and can therefore be an appropriate premise to infer further knowledge.[84] At the same time, the relative closeness to the model gives it a prescriptive quality making it a standard that dictates what can or cannot be seen.[85]

There is a point in time, in the early 17th century, when the relationship between the puzzling fact and the model, at the heart of knowing through maxims, is overshadowed by other concerns. A wave of rationality invested judicial reasoning, and the first attack was launched in the direction of maxims (in their various denominations). At this point the distinction between verisimilitude and sign becomes unclear. If the puzzling fact is connected to the model by inferential reasoning, the common ground that verisimilarity shares with sign is apparent. Commentators routinely raised the question: Is the truth-content of a maxim based on self-evidence or on logical reasoning? If they are both processed by syllogism, what is the difference between verisimilarity and sign? Commentators framed the question in brutally outspoken terms citing an argument to be found in Quintilian: "Atalanta is not a virgin, as she has been roaming the woods in the company of young men" (*non esse virginem Atalantam, quia cum iuvenibus per sylvas vagetur*).[86] Is the argument based on a maxim or on sign-inference? The question was highly controversial.[87]

Given this background, we may understand the significance of the blurred distinction between verisimilar and sign. While Aristotle asserted that "the

84 An enlightening discussion in Wiliam Grimaldi, *Aristotle's Rhetoric I, A commentary* (N.Y.: Fordham University Press, 1979), Aristotle, *Rhetoric*, 57 a 34, p. 62. See also *id.*, *Studies in the philosophy of Aristotle's Rhetoric.* Wiesbaden: Steiner, 1972, 107.

85 In this context it could be placed the formalisation of *factum* into *species facti* as e.g. in Hieronymus Verrutius, Novum lexicon utriusque Iuris (Paris: Apud Michaelem Sonnium, 1583), s.v. 'factum', 85: "Factum idem nostris iurisconsultis quod casu seu species facti seu hypothesis dicitur sine cuius notitia non potest de iure responderi, quippe quod in facto casuve ius est positum".

86 Quintilian, Institutio Oratoria, V, 9, 12, who specified that the example was drawn from Hermagoras. See on this Marie-Luce Demonet, "Les signes probables (eikota) au temps de Montaigne," *Bibliothèque d'Humanisme et Renaissance* 63, no. 1 (2001): 7–29 at 14.

87 For example, Menochio stated in 1587 that "all those arguments which are drawn from senses are called signs [...] those that are drawn from the intellect and opinion are verisimilitudes" (*haec igitur omnia quae a sensibus ducuntur argumenta, vocantur signa* [...] *quae vero ducuntur ab intellectu vel opinione, verisimilia dicuntur*).

verisimilar and the sign are not identical" ("*verisimile autem et signum non sunt idem*," *APri*, II, 27, Pacius), those 16th-century commentaries saw the dividing line increasingly blurred. They could not clearly see the autonomy of cognitions received directly by intuition from cognitions received indirectly by reasoning, or in the scholastic parlance, cognitions *per se* (maxims) and cognitions *per aliud* (signs).[88]

Those doubts reflected the cracks in the medieval belief system. It is true that in a particular social setting, based on the self-image of a repository of shared experiences, arguments from verisimilarity could have some validity. However, the lengthy discussions on that question indicate what a raw nerve they touched. They signalled a move from a culture grounded on "presence" to another culture tending towards signs and to the subject producer of meaning. The medieval mind believed in the possession of a repository of experience that reflected an ordered course of nature. Everyone, be them humans, animals, and even inanimate objects had their place from which they derived their explanation. The new setting raised a question that was not just epistemic but ontological: whether the social world could be accepted as it is, including its common beliefs as they are embedded in nature, or rather was a pansemiotic reality wholly explainable by sign reasoning.[89]

6 Conclusion

Mid-17th century marks the turning point of our inquiry. This time saw the demise of Aristotelian scholasticism, which crumbled under the philosophies based on the first principles announced by Hobbes, Leibniz, Descartes and other writers. They made their anti-Aristotelianism one of the most visible features of their projects, producing one of the most radical turns in the European intellectual tradition. By launching an attack against Aristotle they also dismantled the intellectual tradition that governed the internal architecture of legal knowledge according to the dialectical structure of maxims. Legal thinking reformulated its internal architecture according to a philosophy of first principles. The leading idea was that legal rules could be derived from a set of first principles and expanded by deduction to cover all cases. The corollary was that legal rules address the general, not the particular. But when legal

88 The relevance of this distinction is very well argued in Antognazza, "The Distinction in Kind"; for a classic statement see: Hamilton, "Of presentative and representative knowledge," 804–815; *id.*, "The philosophy of common sense," 804–815.

89 I owe this observation to Gumbrecht, "Typology of Cultures".

rules are conceived as generalisations that never fail, maxims cannot be justified, as they reflect "what usually happens". If the proper function of legal rules is to be all-inclusive, exceptions cannot be justified. The substance of this point is that law, as it addresses the general, not the particular, and being not related to any specific context, is interpreted according to logical and binding rules. It is precisely on these grounds that law, overlooking the contingent, was elevated to a science based on general principles. It is not just a coincidence that by the mid-16th century the goddess of justice Themis began to be represented blindfolded.[90] This perspective also dismissed innate ideas since they could not be rationally explained. It actually postulates that the human mind at birth is empty of content. Humans come to the world with no pre-existing notions inscribed in the soul but with a reasoning faculty by which the individual comes to know the laws that govern the natural and human world. Humans do not carry with them preconceived ideas; their mind at birth is a *tabula rasa*.[91]

As I have argued in this essay, maxims cannot be separated from Aristotelian scholasticism, not only for its flexible dialectical methodology but also for its foundational perspective that knowing is a relation between subject and object. In this context, the aspiration should be read as constituting a sector of knowledge that is objective, namely non-testimonial, but at the same time expression of a multiagent rationality, be that the common knowledge of a profession, or of a social community, but which concerns everyone.[92] Its meaning is objective, being not made by an individual but "found". The compilers of the lists of maxims, *loci*, arguments, and presumptions were in fact finders who sought patterns in the observation of experience.

90 For a very good example see Ulrich Zasius, "*In titulos Digesti veteris commentaria*," in: *Opera omnia* (Frankfurt: Feyerabend, 1590), 1: fol. 101: n. 105: "Legislator considerare debet, quid in universum utile sit, non quid mihi vel tibi vel Titio vel Sempronio, utile est". See also Nikolaus Vigelius, *Dialectices juris civilis libri tres* (Basel, 1581), 458; the source is D. 1.3.8 (Ulpian): "iura, non in singulas personas, sed generaliter constituuntur". Mario Sbriccoli, "La benda della giustizia. Iconografia, diritto e leggi penali dal medioevo all'eta' moderna," in *Ordo iuris. Storia e forme dell'esperienza giuridica*, ed. Mario Sbriccoli, P. Costa and M. Fioravanti (Milan: Giuffré, 2003), 41–95, and D. E. Curtis and J. Resnik, "Images of Justice," in *Yale Law Journal* 96 (1987), 1727- 72 at 1755.

91 For an detailed analysis of this theme see Merio Scattola, "Models in History of Natural Law," *Ius Commune. Zeitschrift Für Europäische Rechtsgeschichte* 28 (2001): 91–159. A cogent argument against the *tabula rasa* in Steven Pinker, *The Blank Slate: The Modern Denial of Human Nature* (London: Allen Lane, 2002).

92 For a recent assessment of this theme see Hugo Mercier and Dan Sperber, *The enigma of reason* (Cambridge MA: Harvard University Press, 2019).

In this essay, I tried to answer a question about the function that maxims had in pre-modern legal systems. I felt that this question is timely since it reflects the present awareness that knowledge is moving toward conceptual design and one of its functions is to design small-scale models of reality for the purpose of looking better into facts. This question of course is immense but finds in maxims a miniature view of the problem. I tried therefore to elucidate some basic points: (i) that the premise for maxims to be operative is a specific epistemic structure; (ii) their function is to give order to a knowledge base; (iii) they guide the deliberator in giving sense to the data of experience; (iv) and finally, that they work well so far as the reality they summarily describe is well-ordered.

Acknowledgements

I wish to express many thanks to Guillermo Merck for fruitful discussions. I acknowledge some insights from Alessandro Giuliani and Peter Stein received in past years on this theme.

This essay sometimes uses *they/their* as a gender-neutral pronoun and adjective, following a convention that goes back to the 15th century.

Bibliography

Primary Sources

Albertus Magnus. "*Liber de quatuor coaequaevis.*" In *id., Opera Omnia*, vol. 34. Paris: Vives, 1895.

Alciato, Andrea. "*Oratio*". In *id., Opera*, vol. IV. Basileæ: apud Thomam Guarinum, 1582.

Azpilcueta, Martinus. *Relectio c. Novit De judiciis*. Roma: J. De Angelis, 1575.

Barbosa, Augustinus. *Variae tractationes iuris*. Lyon: Bordes et Arnaud, 1631.

Boethius, A. M. Severinus. "*De differentiis topicis.*" In *Patrologia Latina* LXIV (1847), edited by Jan Paul Migne.

Fagnani, Prospero. "*De constitutionibus c. Ne innitaris.*" In *id., Jus Canonicum, Sive Commentaria Absolutissima in V. Libros Decretales*, 30–112. Cologne: Widenfelt et Berges, 1699.

Fortescue, John. *De laudibus legum Angliae*. London: Abel Roper, 1660.

Menochio, Jacopo. *Consilia*. 13 vols. Venice: Ziletti, 1609–13.

Menochio, Jacopo. *De Praesumptionibus, conjecturis signis & indiciis*. Venetiis: Apud haeredes Francisci Ziletti, 1587.

Peckius, Petrus (Pieter Peck the Elder). *Ad regulas Iuris Canonici commentaria*. Helmstedt: Iacobus Lucius, 1588.

Rhetorica ad Herennium. Translated by Harry Caplan. Cambridge MA: Harvard University Press, 1981.

Rosate, Alberico da. *Dictionarium juris tam civilis quam canonici*. Venice, 1573.

Rosate, Alberico da. *Vocabularium Iuris*. Paris, 1525.

Vico, Giambattista. *Institutiones Oratoriae*. Translated by G. Crifó. Napoli: Ist. Suor Orsola Benincasa, 1989.

Secondary Sources

Alexander, Christopher. *Notes on the synthesis of form*. Cambridge MA: Harvard Univ. Press, 2002.

Antognazza, Maria Rosaria. "The Distinction in Kind between Knowledge and Belief." *Proceedings of the Aristotelian Society* 120 (2021): 277–308.

Broadie, Alexander. "Medieval notions of the theory of ideas." *Proceedings of the Aristotelian Society* 87 (1986–7): 153–67.

Byrne, Edmund F. *Probability and opinion. A study in the medieval presuppositions of post-medieval theories of probability*. The Hague: Martinus Nijhoff, 1968.

Caprioli, Severino. "Tre capitoli intorno alla nozione di 'regula iuris' nel pensiero dei glossatori." *Annali di storia del diritto* V–VI (1961–1962): 221–374.

Cortese, Ennio. *La Norma giuridica*. 2 vols. Milan: Giuffré, 1962–64.

Dear, Peter. "Miracles, experiments and the ordinary course of nature." *Isis* 81 (1990): 663–83.

Du Plessis, Paul J., and John W. Cairns, ed. *The Creation of the Ius Commune: From Casus to Regula*. Edinburgh: Edinburgh University Press, 2010.

Esser, Josef. *Grundsatz und Norm in der richterlichen Fortbildung des Privatrechts*. Tübingen: Mohr, 1956.

Evans, Gillian R. *Getting It Wrong: The Medieval Epistemology of Error*. Cambridge: CUP, 1998.

Floridi, Luciano. *The logic of information: a theory of philosophy as conceptual design*. Oxford: Oxford University Press, 2019.

Giuliani, Adolfo. "Civilian Treatises on Presumptions, 1580–1620." In *The Law of Presumptions: Essays in Comparative Legal History*, edited by Richard H. Helmholz and David Sellar, 21–71. Berlin: Duncker & Humblot, 2009.

Grimaldi, Wiliam M.A. *Aristotle's Rhetoric I: A commentary*. N.Y.: Fordham University Press, 1979.

Grimaldi, Wiliam M.A. *Studies in the philosophy of Aristotle's Rhetoric.* Wiesbaden: Steiner, 1972.

Gumbrecht, Hans U. "Typology of cultures and history of emblems." *Emblemata: revista aragonesa de emblemática* 16 (2010): 37–44.

Hamilton, Wiliam. "Of presentative and representative knowledge." In *The works of Thomas Reid,* 804–815. Edinburgh: Maclachlan and Stewart, 1895.

Hamilton, Wiliam. "The philosophy of common sense." In *The works of Thomas Reid,* 742–803. Edinburgh: Maclachlan and Stewart, 1895.

Häring, Nicolaus. *The Commentaries on Boethius.* Toronto: Pontifical Institute of Mediaeval Studies, 1966.

Horowitz, Maryanne C. *Seeds of virtue and knowledge.* Princeton NJ: Princeton University Press, 1998.

Johnson-Laird, Philip. "Mental models and human reasoning." *Proceedings of the National Academy of Sciences* 107 (2010): 18243–50.

Kiefner, Hans. "Semel malus semper presumitur esse malus." In *Zeitschrift der Savigny-Stiftung für Rechtsgeschichte, Romanistische Abteilung* 78 (1961): 308–54.

Macdonald, Scott. "Theory of Knowledge." In *The Cambridge Companion to Aquinas,* edited by Eleonore Stump and Norman Kretzmann, 160–95. Cambridge: Cambridge University Press, 1993.

Maclean, Ian. *Logic, signs and nature in the Renaissance.* Cambridge: Cambridge University Press, 2002.

Mercier, Hugo, and Dan Sperber. *The enigma of reason* (Cambridge MA: Harvard University Press, 2019).

Owens, Joseph. "Aristotle and Aquinas." In *The Cambridge Companion to Aquinas,* edited by Eleonore Stump and Norman Kretzmann, 38–59. Cambridge: Cambridge University Press, 1993.

Passerini Glazel, Lorenzo. *La forza normativa del tipo: pragmatica dell'atto giuridico e teoria della categorizzazione.* Macerata: Quodlibet, 2005.

Scattola, Merio. "Dialectics, Topology and Philosophy in Early Modern Times." In *Traditions of Controversy,* edited by Marcelo Dascal and Han-Liang Chang, 184. Amsterdam, John Benjamins Pub, 2007.

Scattola, Merio. "Models in History of Natural Law." *Ius Commune. Zeitschrift Für Europäische Rechtsgeschichte* 28 (2001): 91–159.

Stein, Peter. *Regulae iuris, From Juristic Rules to Legal Maxims.* Edinburgh: Edinburgh University Press, 1966.

Viehweg, Theodor. *Topik und Jurisprudenz, Ein Beitrag zur rechtswissenschaftlichen Grundlagenforschung.* München: Beck, 1952.

Villey, Michel. *La formation de la pensée juridique moderne* (Paris: PUF, 1968).

Westerhoff, Jan. "A world of signs: Baroque pansemioticism, the polyhistor and the early modern Wunderkammer." *Journal of the History of Ideas* 62 (2001): 633–50.

Winkel, Laurens C. "A Note on Regulae Iuris in Roman Law and on Dworkin's Distinction between Rules and Principles." In *Critical Studies in Ancient Law, Comparative Law and Legal History: Essays in Honour of Alan Watson*, edited by John W. Cairns and Olivia F. Robinson, 413–18. Oxford: Hart, 2017.

CHAPTER 3

Regula "ubi eadem ratio, ibi eadem iuris dispositio" through the Prism of Early Modern *locus a simili*

Maria Kola

1 Introduction

In a nutshell, the eponymous rule asserts that where the same reason exists, there the same law prevails against the background of analogy.

The shape of the concept of analogy is a product of a centuries-old tradition. Hence, various elements of it have come to the fore throughout its timeline. Also, it is discernible how paths (not only conceptual but also etymological) of "reasoning by analogy" have crossed along the way. Looking back, one will find the Greek roots of the notions and their Latin counterparts, interpretations based on similarity and argumentation relying on specific *loci a simili* – what we would later call analogy – causing history to come full circle.

This study seeks to clarify a few issues. Firstly, I intend to assemble a jigsaw puzzle out of language pieces, showing connections between analogy (*a simili*) and legal topics (*loci argumentorum legales*). I briefly outline the terminology, referring to Greek language transplants, and then mention roots of the *regula* excerpted from the gloss *Æestimari* to D. 9.2.32pr. Secondly, I overview a number books on legal argumentation from the 16th century to identify authors whose works on *topica* seem to have been important for that genre of legal literature, and subsequently determine whether the *regula* appears in their writings and, if so, how it is formulated there. This part cites sources, i.e. legal texts of the *ius commune* which describe reasoning by analogy and invoke the *regula*. Finally, I face the challenge and attempt to dispel doubts as to impact of "topical thinking" on the shape of the *regula*.

2 Greek Transplants with Borrowings Involving Analogy

The body of work concerned with the concept of analogy is so large that any attempt to measure it would be beyond the scope of this study. Nonetheless, the title of this study deliberately draws attention primarily to the language

 | DOI:10.1163/9789004736092_005

component. Translating "the unknown by the more unknown", as some would render the Latin phrase (*ignotum per ignotum*), is best avoided. In this case, I would qualify it quite contrariwise – it was necessary to maintain a balance between a particular period (16th century) and the perception of analogy among the early modern jurists. Hence, I describe a mutual meshing of analogy and similarity, "*topos*" and "*locus*", argumentation and reasoning by analogy.

The term "analogy" has an ancient Greek origin ("ἀναλογία"); it is composed of "ἀνά" and "λόγος", with both having appeared in different contexts. Prefixing λόγος with ἀνά[1] implies a doubling of content that captures the relationship between magnitudes whilst taking certain features into account.[2] The second word (i.e. "λόγος") is derived from the verb "λέγειν" and can be roughly translated as "collect", "gather", "count", or "say".[3] The word "ἀναλογία" is descended from the mathematical term "ἀνάλογον", i.e. a proportion[4] defined in Euclid's *Elements*, "Τὰ δὲ τὸν αὐτὸν ἔχοντα λόγον μεγέθη ἀνάλογον καλείσθω", which has been recently translated into "And let magnitudes having the same ratio be called proportional".[5] Analogy can be defined as a relation of identity which occurs between pairs of different magnitudes.[6] These magnitudes share a measure, or reason ("*ratio*"), which allows them to be juxtaposed, weighed against each other or counted in relation to each other.

Etymologically, "analogia" seems to predate the Latin "*similitudo*". However, it came to be used as a term ("*analogia iuris*" and "*analogia legis*") in the context of legal reasoning much later. The phrase "*procedere de similibus ad similia*" found in ancient Roman legal sources, was used by judges in a decision-making process on similar facts. Besides the above-mentioned expression other were employed as well, including "*simili modo*", "*similia*", "*similitude*". In fact, one may look in vain for the word "analogia" in ancient Roman sources; such a course of action (procedure *de similibus ad similia*) did function, albeit

1 Robert S.P. Beekes and Lucien van Beek, *Etymological Dictionary of Greek* (Leiden: Brill, 2010), I: 97, cf. along, upwards.

2 Mieczysław A. Krąpiec, *Teoria analogii bytu* (Lublin: Redakcja Wydawnictw Katolickiego Uniwersytetu Lubleskiego, 1993), 252.

3 Beekes and van Beek, *Etymological Dictionary*, I: 841, 868, cf. λέγω – to collect, gather, count, say. Another term "λόγος" may be understood as a word, explanation, or reason – see: Pierre Chantraine, *Dictionnaire étymologique de la langue grecque. Histoire des mots. Λ–Ω* (Paris: Librairie C. Klincksieck, 1984), 625.

4 Chantraine, *Dictionnaire*, 82, cf. 'proportionnellement'.

5 Richard Fitzpatrick, *Euclid's Elements of Geometry* (Austin: University of Texas at Austin, 2008), 130.

6 Józef Herbut, "Kilka uwag o definicji analogii," *Roczniki Filozoficzne* 14, no. 1 (1966): 117.

under a different name. It is said that "analogy was constantly used by Roman jurists both in legal concepts and as tools of legal procedure. However, it was treated as neither an *applicative* nor an *interpretative* criterion, nor for theorising about operations, but as a *technique of ability*, the aim of which was to identify *similarities* and *differences*".[7]

The particular procedure *de similibus ad similia* has become the technical expression of any interpretation beyond the *Corpus Iuris Civilis*, according to A. Steinwenter.[8] Linguistic variations of the term *similitudo* appear among texts included in Corpus Iuris Civilis multiple times, the otherwise labelled "analogy" emerged centuries later. In the legal literature, it is called by some "a child of natural law", which appeared at the end of the 17th century; thus, "it cannot be expected in this wording in ancient Roman law, and one must be careful not to pit ancient forms against modern ideas and discover *analogia iuris* therein".[9] However, it does not seem that the analogical mode of reasoning was absent. Consequently, were the term "analogy" used in the title, it would likely lead to a slight misinterpretation when discussing the *regula* and some early modern collections of arguments. Nevertheless, the broadly accepted word "analogy" will be predominantly used throughout this text.[10]

3 Greek Transplants with Topics (τόποι)

The Latin "locus" corresponds to the Greek "τόπος" which in the most general sense means a "place".[11] Its origins should be sought in Aristotle's work, and later in Cicero's and Boetius' writings. Leaving aside all discussion on the subject, it may be worthwhile just to mention Quintilian's *Institutio Oratoria* (V.10.20) where one can find an outline of *sedes argumentorum*, i.e. the "secret

7 Letizia Vacca, "L'interpretazione analogica nella giurisprudenza classica," in *Fides humanitas ius. Studi in onore di Luigi Labruna*, ed. Cosimo Cascione and Carla Masi Doria (Napoli: Editoriale scientifica, 2007), VIII: 5746. Unless otherwise noted, all translations of quotations from Italian or German are by the author.

8 Artur Steinwenter, "Prolegomena zu einer Geschichte der Analogie," in *Festschrift Fritz Schulz* (Weimar: Hermann Böhlaus Nachfolger, 1951), II: 349.

9 Artur Steinwenter, "Analoge Rechtsanwendung im römischen Recht," in *Studi in memoria di Emilio Albertario* (Milano: Giuffrè, 1953), II: 106.

10 Nevertheless, there are a lot of nuances when jurists speak about analogy. One might suggest that there is clearly a metaphorical use of analogy (with its Greek connotation) and similarity. A separate subject, the scope of which is beyond that of this chapter, is the relationship of analogy to similarity and *vice versa*.

11 Beekes and van Beek, *Etymological Dictionary*, 1494.

places" where arguments reside and whence they must be extracted ("*sed sedes argumentorum, in quibus latent, ex quibus sunt petenda*"). Thus, some would paraphrase them as "treasure trove of trains of thought" (*Fundgruben für den Gedankengang*).[12]

Besides the term being present by virtue of linguistic legacy, the idea itself was also disseminated. The concept of topics appeared in antiquity and was also present from the 12th to the 17th century, as the issue of "*topica* was an integral part of legal methodology".[13] As may be inferred from the tables of contents in books on *topics*, there were hundreds of examples of legal arguments.[14] Furthermore, a particular place (*locus*) was an argumentative habitat comprising a plethora of legal disquisitions to legitimise a given argument. Moreover, it was employed as a comprehensive arsenal of argumentative options ("ammunition for lawyers"),[15] and once the issue had been identified, then *loci* (commonplaces) provided the rhetorician with a set of ready-made points to be raised in an argument.

Besides that practical purpose, topics proved applicable in another significant domain, namely as tools for the interpretation of law. Although the scholastic method had already been used in the Middle Ages and legal issues were addressed in writings that employed dialectics, fundamental works on legal logic did not emerge until the 16th century. Jan Schröder noted that "some of the first independent treatises were written in the 15th century, while a more in-depth theory of law is in evidence since the sixteenth century."[16] According to Stefan Vogenauer "that time became the golden age for the subject of interpretation, which was then discussed not only in special treatises, but also in special collections of arguments called *topics*, and in comprehensive works."[17] A particular topic would describe a certain manner of interpretation or, given the standpoint of this inquiry, legal thinking about analogy (*locus a simili*).

---

12 Ernst Robert Curtius, *Europäische Literatur und lateinisches Mittelalter* (München: A. Francke Verlag, 1954), 77.

13 Stefan Vogenauer, *Die Auslegung von Gesetzen in England und auf dem Kontinent* (Tübingen: Mohr Siebeck, 2001), 1: 438.

14 E.g.: *ab absurdo, a maiori, a minori, ab ordine, a contractibus ad quasi contractus, a dote ad alimenta, ab emphyteusi ad feudum, a legatis ad fideicommissa, a minoribus ad furiosos prodigos mente captos seu dementes, a sententia ad libellum.*

15 Jan Schröder, *Recht als Wissenschaft. Geschichte der Juristischen Methodenlehre in der Neuzeit (1500–1933)* (München: C.H. Beck, 2020), 1: 31.

16 Jan Schröder, „Juristische Methode," in *Handwörterbuch zur deutschen Rechtsgeschichte. Band 2. Geistliche Gerichtsbarkeit – Konfiskation*, ed. Albrecht Cordes et al (Berlin: Erich Schmidt Verlag, 2012), col. 1450.

17 Vogenauer, *Die Auslegung*, 434–435.

Significantly, it was considered "an integral part of legal topics and brocard collections in the sixteenth and seventeenth century."[18]

In short, two linguistic crossflows could be observed, while the development of interpretation and various attempts to define its forms was taking place in the background. The Greek language was making a visible comeback, though not only in conceptual terms, but in writing as well. The authors of the 16th-century collections of *loci* put Greek terms (e.g. Everardus' *Topicorum seu de locis legalibus liber*) and even single letters (e.g. Reberteria's *Topicῶn iuris libri quatuor*) in titles of their works, even though they remained faithful to Latin otherwise.[19]

Hence, one of the factors which I considered while selecting works on legal argumentation was the occurrence of *topica* or *loci* in the title, as a way to determine the numbers and authors whose books on *loci* proved the most prolific for the topical method. Thus, since those jurists pointed out the argument by analogy (*a simili*), I will focus on its description and the formulation of the *regula* therein.

4 *Ratio*: The Essence of the *regula*

The logical subject of the *regula* "*ubi eadem ratio* …" centres on the word *ratio*. The second part of the *regula* refers to law in that it uses the words *ius* or *iuris dispositio*, depending on whether it is stated as a direct excerpt from the gloss to *lex Aquilia* (*ubi est eadem ratio, et idem ius*) or as its enhanced formula (*ubi est eadem ratio, ibi eadem iuris dispositio*).[20] However, the minor language variations do not affect its general meaning.[21]

The *regula* was conceived in the context of liability for destruction or damage to certain goods described in *lex Aquilia* (D. 9.2.32pr).[22] Without

---

18 Vogenauer, *Die Auslegung*, 497.

19 Even so, contemporary usage gives preference to terms such as *analogy*, *analogia*, *Analogie*, as well as *topical thinking*, *pensiero topico*, *topische Denkweise* (with *locus a simili* being their 16th-century counterpart).

20 Detlef Liebs, *Lateinische Rechtsregeln und Rechtssprichwörter* (München: C.H. Beck, 2007), 235, cf. "*Ubi eadem ratio, ibi eadem juris dispositio* (as "Bestimmung"), while in "*Ubi eadem ratio, ibi idem jus*" (as "Recht"); Krzysztof Burczak, Antoni Dębiński and Maciej Jońca, *Łacińskie sentencje i powiedzenia prawnicze* (Warszawa: C.H. Beck, 2013), 306.

21 Editor's note: In the FWO.OPR.2020.005001 database, this *regula,* in the version „Ubi est eadem ratio, et idem ius esse debet", is registered under No. 239.

22 *Gaius libro septimo ad edictum provinciale.* Illud quaesitum est, an quod proconsul in furto observat quod a familia factum sit (id est ut non in singulos detur poenae perse-

going into extensive discussion and the abundant literature on that matter, it should be noted that the interpretation based on *lex Aquilia* was expanded by the activities of jurists and praetors, whereby legal protection was expanded to include similar cases of wrongful damage. Thus, the reasoning concerning one delict would be applied in the assessment of another delict. Medieval Glossators commented on the word "*æstimari*" (to estimate), used in that Roman law source with reference to *lex Aquilia*, inferring that the same kind of valuation should be made. It was "permissible to apply a provision to a situation which, although not covered by the wording of the *lex*, was covered by its meaning".[23] A few source references were invoked by the Accursian Gloss in order to justify the *regula* (D. 2.13.9.2, D. 4.9.5.1, D. 37.13.1pr, D. 43.22.1.3, D. 48.5.28.13, Inst.Just. IV.7.2a). As the main purpose of this study is to look for the *regula* in collections of loci, I leave the analysis of those sources aside. It is noteworthy, however, that they are not cited in the *loci a simili* described by the analysed authors (apart from D. 48.5.28 used by Cantiuncula in his description towards the end of general remarks about *locus a simili*).

The word "*ratio*" is the key to decode the meaning of the *regula* in *loci a simili* and the circumstances of its use.[24] My task is to identify the context in which "*ratio*" appears, including an overview of the accompanying texts as its background.

5 Authors of Collections of *loci legales* in the 16th Century

Numerous books have been published on early modern legal argumentation and interpretation, but it needs to be noted that their editors often drew

---

cutio, sed sufficeret id praestari, quod praestandum foret, si id furtum unus liber fecisset), debeat et in actione damni iniuriae observari. Sed magis visum est idem esse observandum, et merito: cum enim circa furti actionem haec ratio sit, ne ex uno delicto tota familia dominus careat eaque ratio similiter et in actionem damni iniuriae interveniat, sequitur, ut idem debeat aestimari, praesertim cum interdum levior sit haec causa delicti, veluti si culpa et non dolo damnum daretur.

23 Vogenauer, *Die Auslegung*, 496.

24 It should be mentioned that *ratio* features prominently in a vast number of topics on legal argumentation. Thereby, its presence can be considered as a natural component of many *loci*, including the argument under current discussion (on *a simili*). Not only is *ratio* determined in the *regula*'s wording, but also observed in the content of *topoi*. Hence, it can be considered that the notion *per se* (*ratio*) plays a crucial role in any legal argumentation.

attention to particular qualifying characteristics of works concerning topics. Therefore, I decided to focus only on the collections of legal "topics" and such titles and authors who were cited repeatedly and can be distinguished by certain features. I adopted the following criteria: titles (*topica* or *loci*), places and dates of publication, numbers of editions, reprint frequency, ordering of selected arguments (*loci*), and their level of detail. Thanks to this litmus test, the following were chosen for further inquiry: Petrus Andreas Gammarus (Pietro Andrea Gambaro), Nicolaus Everardus (Nicolaas Everaerts), Iohannes de Arnono (Giovanni d'Arnono), Claudius Cantiuncula (Claude Chansonnette), and Ioannis à Reberteria (Jean de la Reberteria).[25]

Having made a comparison of those books, it became apparent that Everardus' work stood out. His work was considered an innovation "although interest in legal argument was not new, the author for the first time sets out fully and systematically the various kinds of argument that can be used in legal matters".[26] Entitled *Topicorum seu de locis legalibus liber* (Leuven, 1516), the book was indeed popular, as it remained in print for around 150 years and extensively affected contemporary legal practice,[27] which may have been due to the practical approach informed by his judicial career. It appears that Everardus' work was written in such a way or, in other words, was characterised by such qualities in terms of legal methods of argumentation, that led to its presence on the European publishing market for many years until 1662, when the last edition came out in Frankfurt.

Nonetheless, I have researched several other collections of *loci* whose authors were indicated within literature on legal argumentation. I tentatively collated their legal arguments on analogy (*loci a simili*) to observe whether the *regula* "*Ubi eadem ratio* …" could be discerned. I verified first editions of these works chronologically, nonetheless, Everardus' book remained the focal point.

25 See earlier bibliographic references: Martinus Lipenius, *Bibliotheca Realis Iuridica* (Frankfurt am Main: Cura et sumptibus Johannis Friderici, 1679); Roderich von Stintzing, *Geschichte der deutschen Rechtswissenschaft* (München, Leipzig: R. Oldenbourg, 1880); as well as recent ones discussing jurists: Schröder, *Recht als Wissenschaft*; Peter Mack, *A History of Renaissance Rhetoric 1380–1620* (Oxford: Oxford University Press, 2011); Rafael Domingo, ed., *Juristas universales. Vol. II: Juristas modernos* (Madrid: Marcial Pons, 2004).

26 Alan Watson, *The Evolution of Western Private Law* (Baltimore: Johns Hopkins University Press, 1985), 28.

27 Robert Feenstra, "Everaerts (Everardi), Nicolaas", in *Juristen. Ein biographisches Lexikon. Von der Antike bis zum 20 Jahrhundert*, ed. Michael Stolleis (München: C.H. Beck, 2001), 194.

6 Petrus Andreas Gammarus (Pietro Andrea Gambaro)

The first book about *loci* worth mentioning is *Legalis dialectica in qua de modo argumentandi et locis argumentorum legaliter disputatur* written by Petrus Andreas Gammarus (1480–1528).[28] It has been claimed that Gammarus' work presented the earliest approach to legal argumentation in the form of topics,[29] prompting some sort of new trend in the argumentative legal experience. He was closely associated with Bologna (probably born in the nearby town of Casalfiumanese, as one can find his name followed by the cognomen "de Casali"),[30] where he obtained his *doctor iuris* title and became a professor. The affiliation with the University of Bologna is evident in Gammarus' manner of presenting topics: in Bologna scholars used medieval sources and basic forms of Aristotelian-Scholastic reasoning and perceived dialectics to be more of an art of discourse rather than a speculative science.[31] Gammarus attached particular importance to theories of legal logic approached as dialectics, which to some extent had a methodological character.[32]

The first edition of Gammarus' *Legalis dialectica* was published in 1507 in Bologna,[33] but it propagated to various cities in Europe,[34] e.g. Cologne (1513), Leipzig (1522), Krakow (1526), Basel (1540), showing the impact of the author's *loci*. As noted above, the books by Gammarus and other authors were com-

28 Gammarus was a Roman Catholic clergyman who held various church positions, including the office of *auditoris rotæ* and, at the end of his life, the bishopric of Faenza. Having been appointed to the office, Gammarus died on his way to assume it – see: Pellegrino Antonio Orlandi, *Notizie degli scrittori Bolognesi e dell'opere loro stampate e manoscritte* (Bologna: per Costantino Pisarri, 1714), 234; Andrea Padovani, "Gammaro, Pietro Andrea," in *Dizionario biografico dei giuristi italiani* (*XII–XX secolo*), ed. Italo Birocchi, Ennio Cortese, Antonello Mattone and Marco Nicola Miletti (Bologna: Il Mulino, 2013), 941–942.

29 Schröder, *Recht als Wissenschaft*, 29; Merio Scattola, "Scientia Iuris and Ius Naturae: The Jurisprudence of the Holy Roman Empire in the Seventeenth and Eighteenth Centuries," in *A Treatise of Legal Philosophy and General Jurisprudence. Vol. 9. A History of the Philosophy of Law in the Civil Law World, 1600–1900*, ed. Damiano Canale et al. (Dordrecht: Springer, 2009), 10.

30 See: Umberto Dallari, *I Rotuli dei lettori legisti e artisti dello Studio bolognese dal 1384 al 1799* (Bologna: 1888), I: 194.

31 Vincenzo Piano Mortari, *Dialettica e giurisprudenza. Studio sui trattati di dialettica legale del sec. 16* (Milano: Giuffrè, 1955), 7.

32 Piano Mortari, *Dialettica*, 6–7.

33 Petrus Andreas Gammarus, *Legalis dialectica, in qua de modo argumentandi et locis argumentorum legaliter disputatur* (Bologna: per Benedictum Hectori, 1507).

34 See: Otto Maria Dominicus Franciscus Vervaart, *Studies over Nicolaas Everaerts (1462–1532) en zijn Topica* (Arnhem: Gouda Quint, 1994), 248–250.

pared in terms of dates and places of publication, and the number of subsequent editions; I also conducted a preliminary examination of the *locus a simili* and examined the structure of the argument by analogy. Thus, I verified certain technical elements, such as the name, the order in a particular book, the place in the table of content (*locorum divisio*), and, on the other hand, looked at the legal sources describing the *locus a simili.*

Among Gammarus' dozens of arguments, analogy (*de loco a simili*) was placed in the second volume, which "is devoted to intermediate and external topics and hypothetical syllogism".[35] The author engaged in some theoretical deliberations, as well as provides specific examples of reasoning about similarity. Gammarus listed nearly 40 various instances, including *a matrimonio igitur carnali ad spirituale, a contractu ad ultimas voluntates, a tempore ad locum* and *a re ad tempus.*[36] This distinguishes the latter from Everardus, who treated the above-mentioned examples as separate topics.

However, regardless of Gammarus' attitude to the topic structure, the occurrence of the *regula* is an even more interesting issue for this study. The phrase itself ("*Ubi eadem ratio, ibi est eadem ius*" or "*iuris dispositio*") does not feature in Gammarus' topic of analogy; however, the word "*ratio*" appears there on several occasions (in *de loco a simili*). One can find it as "*rationis convenientia*", which could be rendered roughly as "a concordance of rationale". To exemplify this, Gammarus mentioned Iulianus' text concerning the absence of written law (D. 1.3.32)[37] and the commentary thereto written by Baldus. Broadly speaking, that Roman legal text spoke of the sequential order of legal application of rules such as ancient mores and customs, then dis-

35 Mack, *History of Renaissance*, 278.

36 The analysis of the following passages is based on Gammarus' edition dated 1524, due to more precise page numbering than the 1507 edition. See: Petrus Andreas Gammarus, *Legalis dialectica ab auctore suo recognita et multis additionibus ornata noviter impressa* (Bologna: in Aedibus Heredum Benedicti Hectoris de Faellis, 1524), fo. 30r–30v: "Libet [...] nonnullos hic singulariter casus annectere: in quibus ab uno ad aliud similitudinis ducitur argumentum".

37 *Iulianus libro 84 digestorum.* pr. De quibus causis scriptis legibus non utimur, id custodiri oportet, quod moribus et consuetudine inductum est: et si qua in re hoc deficeret, tunc quod proximum et consequens ei est: si nec id quidem appareat, tunc ius, quo urbs Roma utitur, servari oportet. 1. Inveterata consuetudo pro lege non immerito custoditur, et hoc est ius quod dicitur moribus constitutum. Nam cum ipsae leges nulla alia ex causa nos teneant, quam quod iudicio populi receptae sunt, merito et ea, quae sine ullo scripto populus probavit, tenebunt omnes: nam quid interest suffragio populus voluntatem suam declaret an rebus ipsis et factis? Quare rectissime etiam illud receptum est, ut leges non solum suffragio legis latoris, sed etiam tacito consensu omnium per desuetudinem abrogentur.

cussed their analogical procedures and, finally, the law used in the city of Rome.[38] Those circumstances gave rise to analogical argumentation, or, in other words, to applying a certain procedure of interpretation based on similarity.[39]

Besides, Gammarus wrote that concordance of rationale is not required in all cases, but only in those where a question arises, otherwise there would never have been such a similarity, unless a greater dissimilarity appeared.[40] Furthermore, it should be extended to similar cases where said concordance is present.[41] Although, the author drew on another rule, i.e. "*ratio enim est anima legis*" ("rationale is the soul of legal acts"), it seems that he did not apply it equally articulately to the *regula* "*Ubi eadem ratio ...*".

As underlined previously, my principal goal is to find the literal wording of the *regula* in *loci a simili*. If the literal wording is lacking, the goal is to determine whether any elements of the *regula* appear, and subsequently establish the nature of related source references. Not only did I search in vain for the *regula* itself ("*Ubi eadem ratio, ibi eadem iuris dispositio*") in Gammarus' work, but also found no reference to its origin, i.e. the *Æstimari* gloss. Admittedly, the direct extract from the Digest of Justinian regarding *lex Aquilia* (D. 9.2.32pr) is mentioned, but as a tangible instance of analogies, which is *a furto ad iniuriam et damnum*. It would seem that the *regula* as an expression is missing in Gammarus' *de loco a simili*, though the subject of *ratio* is present and relatively broadly shown.

7 Nicolaus Everardus (Nicolaas Everaerts)

Among authors engaging with argumentation, the one who played a vital role, given the perspective of this study, was Nicolaus Everardus (1462–1532). His first version of *Topicorum* was published in 1516 in Leuven. The revised edition

---

38 Filippo Gallo, *L'officium del pretore nella produzione e applicazione del diritto. Corso di diritto romano* (Torino: Giappichelli, 1997), 162, 165; Pietro Cerami, "Breviter su Iul. D. 1,3,32 (Riflessioni sul trinomio lex, mos, consuetudo)," in *Nozione formazione e interpretazione del diritto dall'età romana alle esperienze moderne* (Napoli: Jovene, 1997), 1: 135–137.

39 Baldus de Ubaldis, *In primam Digesti Veteris partem Commentaria* (Lyon, 1585), fo. 27va: "[...] tamen proceditur in ea de similibus ad similia in defectu iuris scripti [...]".

40 Gammarus, *Legalis dialectica*, fo. 29r: "Istam autem rationis convenientiam requirit hec argumentatio, non in omnibus sed in hiis tantum de quibus exoritur questio, alias nunquam tanta esset similitudo quin maior appareret dissimilitudo".

41 Gammarus, *Legalis dialectica*, fo. 29v.

of 1552 (where the number of *loci* was increased from 100 to 131) "became the best-selling book in its field".[42]

Nicolaus Everardus studied at the university of Leuven, where he obtained his *doctor utriusque iuris* title in 1493, held the position of law professor, became a judge at the Great Council of Mechlin (Mechelen), then was appointed president of the Court of Holland and finally president of the Great Council of Mechlin.[43] Next to the significant career, his books (especially the volume concerned with *topica*) also kept him relevant for over a century. There were around thirty editions of his treatise on *loci*, printed between 1516 and 1662 in various European cities, and held today in many libraries around the world. His work was one of systematic attempts to find a paradigm to organise legal arguments, combining previous legal experience with the ability to adapt legal sources of *ius commune*. In this fashion, Everardus followed in the footsteps of the medieval jurists, retracing a path marked by "places" (*loci*).[44]

Everardus introduced his *locus a simili* by presenting components that constitute the argument by analogy.[45] If there is the same reason or equity, the same legal solution should be applied, hence, it is possible to go beyond, as long as equal reason can be provided. At the outset, Everardus quoted both antique and medieval legal texts which explained such a concept. To enhance analogical reasoning, Everardus cited a Roman legal source pertaining to the validity of a stipulation (D. 45.1.108).[46] Taken Iavolenus' text in the broadest

42 Otto Vervaart, "Argumentation in Practice: Nicolaus Everardi (1462–1532) on Canon Law and Custom in the Low Countries," in *Proceedings of the Tenth International Congress of Medieval Canon Law. Syracuse, New York, 13–18 August 1996*, ed. Kenneth Pennington, Stanley Chodorow, and Keith H. Kendall (Città del Vaticano: Biblioteca Apostolica Vaticana, 2001), 635.

43 See on Everardus: Vervaart, *Studies*; Jan Hallebeek, "Nicolaas Everaerts (Nicolaus Everardi)," in *Juristas universales. Vol. II: Juristas modernos*, 50–51; Alain Wijffels, "Everardus, A Book on Topics," in *The Formation and Transmission of Western Legal Culture. 150 Books that Made the Law in the Age of Printing*, ed. Serge Dauchy et al. (Cham: Springer, 2016), 65–67.

44 Feenstra, "Everaerts," 194.

45 Nicolaus Everardus, *Topicorum seu de locis legalibus liber* (Leuven: in aedibus Theodorici Martini Alustensis, 1516), fo. 22vb: "ubicunque est eadem ratio vel aequitas ibi debet esse eadem iuris dispositio […] illa enim quae in radice et causa conveniunt, conveniunt etiam in effectu".

46 *Iavolenus libro decimo epistularum.* A Titio ita stipulatus sum: 'si qua mihi nupserit, decem dotis eius nomine dare spondes?' quaerebatur, an consistat talis stipulatio. respondit: si stipulanti mihi dos ita promissa est: 'quamcumque uxorem duxero, dotis eius nomine decem dare spondes?', nihil in causa est, quare ea pecunia condicione expleta non debeatur: nam cum condicio etiam ex incertae personae facto parere obli-

terms, the question arose as to determinacy (the degree of precision) of a condition for the validity of a conditional stipulation. A compelling phrase is a conclusion to the contrary (*ratio reddi non potest*), which underlines that there is no reason why the same answer should not be given in a similar case (as in Iavolenus: "where a dowry was promised"). Everardus also sought concordance for the similarity of cases, since what is consistent in the root and cause (*in radice et causa*), should also be consistent in the effects.[47] It is a direct reference to Angelus de Ubaldi's commentary on Iulian's text about the procedure applicable should written law be absent (D. 1.3.32pr).[48] The excerpted passage from Angelus provides a motive to formulate a mode of creating an argument by analogy.

In addition to *ratio*, Everardus' formula of analogy was linguistically enhanced by the term of equity. The word itself is absent in the above-mentioned texts (D. 9.2.32pr and D. 45.1.108), but it appears in the subsequent Everardus' observations on glosses to ancient Roman legal sources containing the words "*eadem ratio*" and "*aequitas*".[49] In the first gloss to *Authenticum*, Everardus pointed out the phrase "*item eadem est aequitas argumentatio*".[50] Additionally, the Accursian Gloss to a text from the Digest of Justinian highlights the issue of combining reason and equity, i.e. "*quia eadem ratio aequitatis intervenit*" (gl. s.v. '*Mariti*' ad D. 24.3.24pr).[51] Besides, Everardus noted a commentary written by Johannes de Platea (c. 1380 – after 1427) to a text concerning hog dealers who could be exempted from performing ignoble services (C. 11.17.1).[52] Johannes de Platea stated that, in view of the immunity granted to that group of people, it should be also granted to

---

gationem possit, veluti 'si quis in Capitolium ascenderit, decem dare spondes?' 'si quis a me decem petierit, tot dare spondes?', cur non idem et in dote promissa respondeatur, ratio reddi non potest.

47 Everardus, *Topicorum*, fo. 23ra.

48 Angelus de Ubaldis, *Lectura super prima Digesti veteris* (Lyon: per Joannem Moulin, 1534), fo. 9vb.

49 Gloss to C. 5.35 *Auth. 'Matri & Aviae', sv. 'Tutelam'*; Gloss to C. 5.34 *Auth. 'Minoris debitor'*.

50 *Codicis Dn. Iustiniani Sacratissimi Imp. Augusti, Repetitae Praelectionis Libri Duodecim* (Lyon: sumptibus Claudii Landry, 1627), col. 1294.

51 *Infortiatum, seu Pandectarum Iuris Civilis*, vol. 2 (Lyon: Sumptibus Claudii Landry, 1627), col. 34.

52 *Imperatores Valentinianus, Theodosius, Arcadius.* Porcinarii urbis aeternae cum pervilegem laborem populi Romani commodis exhibeant, sordidis semper muneribus liberentur. Valentin. Theodos. Et Arcad. Aaa. Ad Albinum Pu. ‹A 389 D. VIII K.Sept.Romae Timasio Et Promoto Conss.›

merchants on the same basis (*ubi est eadem ratio immunitatis concedende ibi idem ius esse debet*).[53]

In summary, two factors are noticeable, i.e. reason and equity. Both are components of Everardus' *locus a simili* and seem to be necessary conditions. The word "*aequitas*" was integrated into *locus a simili* within the discussed *regula*. However, it should be mentioned that a reference to equity may originally be found among the legal sources attached to the *Aestimari* gloss (specifically in the previously cited text of the *Institutes* IV.7.2a).[54]

Everardus provided several specific examples of the rejection of argument by analogy, among which there is one relying on *ratio*: if there is no *ratio*, there is no analogy ("*non procedit quando lex vel statutum non habet in se aliquam rationem* …").[55] In conclusion, Everardus enriched that part of the description of analogy by making the term of equity a cumulative element accompanying the *ratio*. Thus, the originality of his approach consisted in advancing a new arrangement of legal arguments and using earlier experience of *ius commune* in topical thinking.

8 Claudius Cantiuncula (Claude Chansonnette)

According to the chronology of the first editions of books on *loci*, Claudius Cantiuncula's *Topica* should be described next, having been published in 1520.[56] It was printed in Basel, where Cantiuncula arrived in 1517 and later obtained a doctorate in law, and where he was also appointed to the office of rector of the university.[57] He was associated with other universities, such as

53 Johannes de Platea, *Lectura super tribus libris Iustiniani Codicis. Liber 10–12* (Lyon: Johann Siber, c. 1498), fo. 86va.

54 Inst.Just. IV.7.2a: Istas tamen duas actiones praetor reddit et si liberum quis hominem aut alienum servum navi aut tabernae aut cuilibet negotiationi praeposuerit, scilicet quia eadem aequitatis ratio etiam eo casu interveniebat.

55 Everardus, *Topicorum*, fo. 24vb.

56 Claudius Cantiuncula, *Topica* (Basel: apud A. Cartandrum, 1520).

57 Hans-Peter Ferslev, *Claudius Cantiuncula: Die didaktischen Schriften* (Cologne, 1967), 3–4; Guido Kisch, *Claudius Cantiuncula. Ein Basler Jurist u. Humanist d. 16. Jahrhunderts* (Basel: Verlag von Helbing & Lichtenhahn, 1970), 26; Javier Fajardo, "Claude Chansonnette (Claudius Cantiuncula)," in *Juristas universales. Volumen II: Juristas modernos* (Madrid: Marcial Pons, 2004), 83–85; Herbert Jaumann, *Handbuch Gelehrtenkultur der Frühen Neuzeit. Biobibliographisches Repertorium. Band I* (Berlin: Gruyter, 2004), 1: 163; Alain Wijffels, "Chansonnette (Cantiuncula) Claude," in *Dictionnaire historique des juristes français, XIIe–XXe siècle*, ed. Jean-Louis Halpérin et al. (Paris: Presses Universitaires de France, 2007), 178–179.

Leuven where he studied law, consequently it can be assumed that his book is likely to have been inspired by Everardus' seminal work.[58] Not only because "he may have been at Leuven around the time of its publication",[59] but also in view of a direct reference in his *Topica*, which recalls Everardus' 100 legal arguments.[60] Moreover, Cantiuncula's overview of analogy seems too similar to Everardus' collection of *loci* not to merit reflection. Just as the instances of analogy in Gammarus' argument, the internal division of Cantiuncula's *locus a simili* seems even more akin. However, he went well beyond a mere list, providing a more extensive and in-depth description.

Cantiuncula distinguished dozens of types of analogy, stressing that an argument can be derived in different ways. The author started with a rather extensive introduction, then went into a detailed characterisation (which is beyond the scope of this study, however) and elucidated particular arguments, quoting ancient and medieval authors ones. His selection within *locus a simili* is very broad, spanning 37 examples, e.g. *a feudo ad emphiteosim et contra*, *a legatis ad fideicommissa*, *a contractibus ad ultimas voluntates*, *a contractibus ad quasi contractus*, *a matrimonio carnali ad spirituale*, *persona ad tempus*, *a persona ad res ipsas* and *a re ad tempus*. Those instances constitute separate arguments in Everardus, which demonstrates the different approaches to organising topics. Nonetheless, they are not particularly relevant to this study, as information related to the *regula* is noticeable already in the first part of Cantiuncula's *locus a simili*.

Argument by analogy could be used in a large number of cases where similarity in applies in one way or another, as long as "equality of reason shines on both sides", and *ratio* is "a purpose, root and anchor of this argument".[61] Cantiuncula directly invoked the *Æstimari* Gloss to D. 9.2.32pr, recalling the *regula* as "*in quibus propositis eadem ratio similiter intervenit, idem iuris debet*", which could be translated as "where the same reason occurs, the same law must follow".[62] Cantiuncula followed previous authors, relying on the same texts (D. 1.3.32 and D. 45.1.108) and mentioning the compatibility of roots and effects.[63]

---

58 Ferslev, *Claudius Cantiuncula*, 62–63; Wijffels, "Chansonnette," 179.

59 Wijffels, "Everardus," 67.

60 Cantiuncula, *Topica*, 3.

61 Cantiuncula, *Topica*, 51: "modo rationis paritas utrobique similiter reluceat: iste enim est scopus, radix et ancora huius loci a simili".

62 Cantiuncula, *Topica*, 52.

63 Cantiuncula, *Topica*, 53: "similibus rebus eadem convenire, quae enim in radice et causa conveniunt, conveniunt etiam in effectu".

Cantiuncula's shape of the *regula* is evidently reflected in the phrase "*in quibus propositis eadem ratio similiter intervenit, idem iuris debet*" and in the direct reference to the gloss to D. 9.2.32pr. The Roman legal references are consistent with Everardus' examples. One can also notice that the argument is enhanced to some degree by virtue of the solution suggested in Iavolenus' text on a stipulation (D. 45.1.108), given that Cantiuncula referred to a moment when a reason for difference cannot be given.

9 Iohannes de Arnono (Giovanni d'Arnono)

Yet another work devoted to legal argumentation in the first half of the 16th century is *Topica ex divino, et humano iure excerpta*, written by the jurist Iohannes de Arnono. He was a professor of civil law in Salerno and seems to have been quite a prolific author, as evidenced by writings such as *Singularia, Tractatus cautelarum, Soliloquia centum, Epitomata centum, Problemata centum, Dialogi centum, Commentarii ducenti*.[64] *Topica* was published at least fourfold in Venice (1535, 1536, 1542, 1571).[65] However, it is a relatively modest work and topics are described using only a few phrases. Among the 88 arguments (arranged as *capites*), there are both repeated examples of *loci* (after Gammarus, Everardus, Cantiuncula) and a number of new ones. The first group contains e.g. *ab ordine, a legatis a fideicommissa, a matrimonio carnali ad spirituale, a positione specie* and *a destructione consequentis*. The second one includes new topics, such as *a matre ad aviam et ab avia ad matrem, de usufructuario ad bonae fidei possessorem* and *a lege correcta*.

The problem of analogy is the most extensively explained *locus* in de Arnono's *Topica*,[66] yet it seems less insightful than any account by other jurists who analysed it. The description includes *ius commune* texts, as well as the aforementioned *lex Aquilia* (D. 9.2.32pr). De Arnono spoke of the resemblance of

64 Iacopo Morelli, *Nuovo dizionario istorico*, vol. II (Bassano: A spese Remondini di Venezia, 1796), 185a.

65 Lorenzo Gustiniani, *Memorie istoriche degli scrittori legali del regno di Napoli* (Napoli: Nella Stamperia Simoniana, 1787), I: 88; Lipenius, *Bibliotheca*, 528. One can find also editions in online sources, e.g. in *Catalogo del Servizio Bibliotecario Nazionale, Institutio per i beni artistici culturali*, as well as in Library of Congress.

66 Iohannes de Arnono, "*Topica ex divino, et humano iure excerpta*," in *id., Hoc in volumine hæc continentur. Soliloquia centum. Epitomata centum. Problemata centum. Dyalogi centum. Commentarii ducenti. Ex diuino et humano iure excerpta* (Venetia: Hieronymi de Maria de Salerno, 1535), fo. 147v.

reason (*similis ratio*), whereby he drew on Baldus' commentary to a Roman legal text (C. 6.2.21) where the argument from analogy (*a simili*) was compared to the argument from the contrary (*a contrario*).[67] In essence, argument *a contrario* would be used in an unlike case, since where the same or greater rationale is present, the argument *a simili* should be applied. Also, extending the concept of *similium*, de Arnono added the element of necessary equity, which he derived from Baldus' commentary to *Libri Feudorum*, where it was formulated as follows: "argument by analogy desires equity as it bonds similar cases".[68] All the more, while reading the quote from Baldus, it is not possible to omit an adjacent phrase from his commentary, namely that equity is "the mind and reason" of the acts of law.[69]

In the context of this study, Iohannes de Arnono may be said to have confined himself to a rather brief explanation. He failed to clarify the *regula* or the word *ratio* itself, but the direct mention of equity seems a distinctive element in the analysed context. Apart from the latter author, that factor had hitherto been employed only by Everardus. Furthermore, Iohannes de Arnono made a direct reference to Baldus' text concerning *Libri Feudorum*, which had not been quoted in the other analysed works.

10 Joannes à Reberteria (Jean de La Reberterie)

Probably one of the last of 16th-century jurists interested in *loci* was the Parisian law professor Joannes à Reberteria (1517–1590). His *Topicώn iuris libri quatuor*[70] was published at least four times in Paris and Wittenberg (1575, 1580, 1581, 1590).[71] His idea to develop a manual of legal arguments anchored in the study of rhetoric is most likely the closing proposal of that time.

Argument *a simili* was placed in the first of the four books of *Topicώn*. Reberteria's description of analogy seems to reiterate previous legal experi-

67 Baldus de Ubaldis, *In sextum Codicis Librum Commentaria* (Venice: apud Iuntas 1615), fo. 18rb: "Hoc est verum, si in casu contrario est ratio contraria, sed si est eadem, vel maior ratio, tunc sumitur argumentum a simili, vel ab aequipollentibus, non a contrario".

68 Baldus de Ubaldis, *Opus aureum super feudis* (Lyon: per Joannem Moulin, 1536), fo. 73ra: "[...] argumentum a simili desiderat equitatem que similes casus iungit [...]".

69 Baldus, *Opus aureum*, fo. 73ra: "equitas ipsa mens et ratio legis".

70 Jean de La Reberterie, *Topicώn juris libri quatuor: quibus ad civilis philosophiae studium facilis patet aditus, in hisque lectos juris studiosus plerosque locos corruptos in Topicis Ciceronianis suae integritali restitutos inveniet* (Paris: apud Ioannem Richerium, 1575).

71 Mack, *History of Renaissance*, 280.

ence to some extent, e.g. following Gammarus or Everardus. Of the dozens of examples emerging from *ius commune* texts, only a few legal sources on analogy are new in comparison with the topics discussed by earlier scholars. Among the passages describing analogy, one can find information on examples of arguments (such as *de matrimonio carnali ad spirituale* or *de contractibus ad ultimas voluntates*), as well as on the scope of arbitrator's activity set against the competence of a judge. Reberteria stated the *regula* quite clearly: *ubi est eadem ratio vel aequitas, ibi debet esse eadem iuris dispositio*, which seems reminiscent of Everardus' explanation, both as to the wording and the legal sources (D. 9.2.32pr and D. 45.1.108).

Reberteria neither reflects on the *regula* in detail nor does he describe the word *ratio*. It may be argued to have gone no further than duplicating Everaert's point of view (in this narrow, specific section of *locus a simili*). Reberteria's description corroborates the enduring presence of *ratio*, and leads to the conclusion that the shape of the *regula* had been slightly linguistically altered, at least regarding the addition of "equity".

11 Conclusions: *regula "ubi eadem ratio ibi eadem iuris dispositio"* among *loci a simili*

The main goal of my research was to answer the question of how the *regula* "*Ubi eadem ratio* ..." was pressed into topical reasoning. Authors of *loci a simili* presented the *regula* as a part of the argument by analogy and elucidated its "behavior" in action based on the *ius commune* texts. Their intention was to strengthen the authority and value of argumentation.[72] As well as aspires, among other things, was to find a solution through topics which would lead to a fair and convincing answer. It seems that topics were intended to tip the scales in favor of a just outcome. Hence, the strength of the argument had to be determined by the existence of *ratio*.

One may conclude that the *regula* was indeed present in 16th-century books on topics and became an inherent element of legal argumentation by analogy.[73] With the collections of *loci* as the axis of my interest, and particular

72 On the topic of the search for objective and systematic ways of legal argumentation in the early modern period, see also Adolfo Giuliani's contribution to this volume.

73 It is worth noting that the subject of the *regula* and its *ratio* appears in other *loci* related to *extensio legis*. It is not only present in *locus a simili* but additionally in *locus a ratione legis larga ampla seu generali ad extensionem ipsius legis* – *cf.* Everardus, *Topicorum*, fo. 54vb.

focus on one to those – *a simili* – I examined whether the *regula* was included in analogical argumentation, being aware of many other themes surrounding the *regula* before the 16th century (e.g. *brocarda*), as well as other literary genres (e.g. *consilia*) at that time.

Having carried out such an inquiry, I attempted to approach the *regula* as a premise of analogy. Its amplitude was measured by *ratio* and legal sources which accompanied it as part of *loci a simili*. Thus, one could observe that an assortment of texts marked the paths for the *regula*, starting with the *Æstimari* gloss and further legal sources added later. It would appear that the most extended form of the *regula* was elaborated by Everardus. A new linguistic component of *locus a simili* was equity, which (albeit not unknown to earlier jurists), was added as another weight on the scale of argument by analogy.

Even if all comparisons fall short of the mark, explicitly "are limping" and any resemblance is somehow "invalid" (*omnis similitudo claudicat*), *ratio* must at least be one of its mainstays. It was an indispensable root of legal topics relating to analogy in the 16th century.

Acknowledgements

I would like to express my gratitude to Prof. Wojciech Dajczak, Prof. Nils Jansen and Prof. Alain Wijffels for their invaluable feedback and support.

This article is an abbreviated excerpt from part of my Ph.D. dissertation which will be submitted at my home institution in 2025.

Bibliography

Literature

Beekes, Robert S.P., and Lucien van Beek. *Etymological Dictionary of Greek*. 2 vols. Leiden: Brill, 2010.

Burczak, Krzysztof, Antoni Dębiński, and Maciej Jońca. *Łacińskie sentencje i powiedzenia prawnicze*. Warszawa: C.H. Beck, 2013.

Cerami, Pietro. "Breviter su Iul. D. 1,3,32 (Riflessioni sul trinomio lex, mos, consuetudo)." In *Nozione formazione e interpretazione del diritto dall'età romana alle esperienze moderne*, IV: 117–137. Napoli: Jovene, 1997.

Chantraine, Pierre. *Dictionnaire étymologique de la langue grecque. Histoire des mots. Λ–Ω*. Paris: Librairie C. Klincksieck, 1984.

Curtius, Ernst Robert. *Europäische Literatur und lateinisches Mittelalter*. München: A. Francke Verlag, 1954.

Dallari, Umberto. *I Rotuli dei lettori legisti e artisti dello Studio bolognese dal 1384 al 1799*. 4 vols. Bologna, Regia Tipografia dei Fratelli Merlani: 1888–1924.

Fajardo, Javier. "Claude Chansonnette (Claudius Cantiuncula)." In *Juristas universales. Volumen II: Juristas modernos*, edited by Rafael Domingo, 83–85. Madrid: Marcial Pons, 2004.

Feenstra, Robert. „Everaerts (Everardi), Nicolaas." In *Juristen. Ein biographisches Lexikon. Von der Antike bis zum 20 Jahrhundert*, edited by Michael Stolleis. München: C.H. Beck, 2001.

Ferslev, Hans-Peter. *Claudius Cantiuncula: Die didaktischen Schriften*. Cologne: 1967.

Fitzpatrick, Richard. *Euclid's Elements of Geometry*. Austin: University of Texas at Austin, 2008.

Gallo, Filippo. *L'officium del pretore nella produzione e applicazione del diritto. Corso di diritto romano*. Torino: Giappichelli, 1997.

Gustiniani, Lorenzo. *Memorie istoriche degli scrittori legali del regno di Napoli*. 3 vols. Napoli: Nella Stamperia Simoniana, 1787.

Hallebeek, Jan. "Nicolaas Everaerts (Nicolaus Everardi)." In *Juristas universales. Vol. II: Juristas modernos*, edited by Rafael Domingo. Madrid: Marcial Pons, 2004.

Herbut, Józef. "Kilka uwag o definicji analogii." *Roczniki Filozoficzne* 14, no. 1 (1966): 115–125.

Jaumann, Herbert, *Handbuch Gelehrtenkultur der Frühen Neuzeit. Biobibliographisches Repertorium, Band I*. Berlin: Gruyter, 2004.

Kisch, Guido. *Claudius Cantiuncula. Ein Basler Jurist u. Humanist d. 16. Jahrhunderts*. Basel: Verlag von Helbing & Lichtenhahn, 1970.

Krąpiec, Mieczysław Albert. *Teoria analogii bytu*. Lublin: Redakcja Wydawnictw Katolickiego Uniwersytetu Lubleskiego, 1993.

Liebs, Detlef. *Lateinische Rechtsregeln und Rechtssprichwörter*. München: C.H. Beck, 2007.

Lipenius, Martinus. *Bibliotheca Realis Iuridica*. Frankfurt am Main: Cura et sumptibus Johannis Friderici, 1679.

Mack, Peter. *A History of Renaissance Rhetoric 1380 – 1620*. Oxford: Oxford University Press, 2011.

Morelli, Iacopo. *Nuovo dizionario istorico*. Vol. II. Bassano: a spese Remondini di Venezia, 1796.

Padovani, Andrea. "Gammaro, Pietro Andrea." In *Dizionario biografico dei giuristi italiani (XII–XX secolo)*, edited by Italo Birocchi, Ennio Cortese, Antonello Mattone, and Marco Nicola Miletti, 941–942. Bologna: Il Mulino, 2013.

Piano Mortari, Vincenzo. *Dialettica e giurisprudenza. Studio sui trattati di dialettica legale del sec. 16*. Milano: Giuffrè, 1955.

Scattola, Merio. "Scientia Iuris and Ius Naturae: The Jurisprudence of the Holy Roman Empire in the Seventeenth and Eighteenth Centuries." In *A Treatise of Legal Philosophy and General Jurisprudence. Vol. 9. A History of the Philosophy of Law in the Civil Law World, 1600–1900.* Edited by Damiano Canale et al. Dordrecht: Springer, 2009.

Schröder, Jan. „Juristische Methode." In *Handwörterbuch zur deutschen Rechtsgeschichte. Band 2. Geistliche Gerichtsbarkeit – Konfiskation*, edited by Albrecht Cordes et al., col. 1449–1456. Berlin: Erich Schmidt Verlag, 2012.

Schröder, Jan. *Recht als Wissenschaft. Geschichte der Juristischen Methodenlehre in der Neuzeit (1500–1933)*. München: C.H. Beck, 2020.

Steinwenter, Artur. "Analoge Rechtsanwendung im römischen Recht." In *Studi in memoria di Emilio Albertario*, II: 105–127. Milano: Giuffrè, 1953.

Steinwenter, Artur. "Prolegomena zu einer Geschichte der Analogie." In *Festschrift Fritz Schulz*, II: 345–363. Weimar: Hermann Böhlaus Nachfolger, 1951.

Stintzing, Roderich von. *Geschichte der deutschen Rechtswissenschaft*. München, Leipzig: R. Oldenbourg, 1880.

Vacca, Letizia. "L'interpretazione analogica nella giurisprudenza classica." In *Fides humanitas ius. Studi in onore di Luigi Labruna*, edited by Cosimo Cascione and Carla Masi Doria, VIII: 5727–5746. Napoli: Editoriale scientifica, 2007.

Vervaart, Otto Maria Dominicus Franciscus. *Studies over Nicolaas Everaerts (1462–1532) en zijn Topica*. Arnhem: Gouda Quint, 1994.

Vervaart, Otto. "Argumentation in Practice: Nicolaus Everardi (1462–1532) on Canon Law and Custom in the Low Countries." In *Proceedings of the Tenth International Congress of Medieval Canon Law. Syracuse, New York, 13–18 August 1996*, edited by Kenneth Pennington, Stanley Chodorow, and Keith H. Kendall, 635–650. Città del Vaticano: Biblioteca Apostolica Vaticana, 2001.

Vogenauer, Stefan. *Die Auslegung von Gesetzen in England und auf dem Kontinent*. 2 vols. Tübingen: Mohr Siebeck, 2001.

Watson, Alan. *The Evolution of Western Private Law*. Baltimore: Johns Hopkins University Press, 1985.

Wijffels, Alain. "Chansonnette (Cantiuncula) Claude." In *Dictionnaire historique des juristes français, XIIe–XXe siècle*, edited by Jean-Louis Halpérin, Jacques Krynen, Patrick Arabeyre, 178–179. Paris: Presses Universitaires de France, 2007.

Wijffels, Alain. "Everardus, *A Book on Topics*." In *The Formation and Transmission of Western Legal Culture. 150 Books that Made the Law in the Age of Printing*, edited by Serge Dauchy, Georges Martyn, Anthony Musson, Heikki Pihlajamäki, and Alain Wijffels, 65–67. Cham: Springer, 2016.

Printed Editions

Angelus de Ubaldis. *Lectura super prima Digesti veteris*. Lyon: per Joannem Moulin, 1534.

Baldus de Ubaldis. *In primam Digesti Veteris partem Commentaria*. Lyon, 1585.

Baldus de Ubaldis. *In sextum Codicis Librum Commentaria*. Venice: apud Iuntas, 1615.

Baldus de Ubaldis. *Opus aureum super feudis*. Lyon: per Joannem Moulin, 1536.

Claudius Cantiuncula. *Topica*. Basel: apud A. Cartandrum, 1520.

Codicis Dn. Iustiniani Sacratissimi Imp. Augusti, Repetitae Praelectionis Libri Duodecim. Lyon: sumptibus Claudii Landry, 1627.

Infortiatum, seu Pandectarum Iuris Civilis, vol. 2. Lyon: Sumptibus Claudii Landry, 1627.

Iohannes de Arnono. "*Topica ex divino, et humano iure excerpta.*" In *Hoc in volumine hæc continentur. Soliloquia centum. Epitomata centum. Problemata centum. Dyalogi centum. Commentarii ducenti. Ex diuino et humano iure excerpta*, 147r–154r. Venice: per Hieronymi de Maria de Salerno, 1535.

Johannes de Platea. *Lectura super tribus libris Iustiniani Codicis. Liber 10–12*. Lyon: Johann Siber, c. 1498.

Nicolaus Everardus. *Topicorum seu de locis legalibus liber*. Leuven: in aedibus Theodorici Martini Alustensis, 1516.

Pellegrino Antonio Orlandi. *Notizie degli scrittori Bolognesi e dell'opere loro stampate e manoscritte*. Bologna: per Costantino Pisarri, 1714.

Petrus Andreas Gammarus. *Legalis dialectica ab auctore suo recognita et multis additionibus ornata noviter impressa*. Bologna: in Aedibus Heredum Benedicti Hectoris de Faellis, 1524.

Petrus Andreas Gammarus. *Legalis dialectica, in qua de modo argumentandi et locis argumentorum legaliter disputatur*. Bologna: per Benedictum Hectori, 1507.

CHAPTER 4

The *Regulae Iuris* as a Key Instrument of the Systematics of Law: The Example of French Legal Doctrine (before and after 1804)

David Deroussin

This paper is an attempt to analyse how a part of the French legal doctrine, from the *Ancien Régime* to the first half of the 19th century, sought to use the concept of *regulae iuris* to identify the general rules of French law.[1] The choice of this period may seem surprising, given that it steps over one of the most important events in the history of French private law: the enactment of the French Civil Code in 1804. However, not to choose 1804 as the *dies a quo* or the *dies ad quem* of this study is neither a whim nor an absurdity, but the result of an observation: the promulgation of the Civil Code did not have a significant impact on the way in which the French legal doctrine conceived its *raison d'être* and its own mission within the legal system. In support for this contention, special attention will be paid to Jean Domat[2] (described by his contemporary Nicolas Boileau as "*le restaurateur de la raison dans la jurisprudence*")[3] and André M.J.J. Dupin (commonly called Dupin the Elder).

Although it is not necessary to introduce Domat, who published *Les Lois civiles dans leur ordre naturel* in 1689 (including a preliminary book devoted to the "*règles du droit*"), a few words about Dupin will make us fully aware of the influence he was able to exert on his contemporaries and on generations of French jurists. Lawyer at the Paris bar, Dupin the elder is best known for having been attorney general at the French *Cour de cassation* from 1830 to 1852, then from 1857 to his death in 1865. He also had a political career, as a deputy and as the President of the Chamber of Deputies (1832–1840), then of the National Assembly (1849–1851). Though he was never appointed Profes-

1 For an overview of the French doctrine of the *Ancien Régime*, see: David Deroussin, "Remarques sur les *regulae iuris* et les principes en droit (Temps Modernes)," *Revue historique de droit français et étranger* 90, no. 2 (April–June 2012): 195–236.

2 See: David Deroussin, "Domat, principes, règles du droit," in *Mélanges en l'honneur du Professeur Nicole Dockès,* coll. Maxime Blachon (Paris: La Mémoire du droit, 2018), 313–350.

3 In a letter from Boileau to Brossette quoted by G. Boileau: Gustave Lanson, *Boileau* (*Paris: Hanchette,* 1919), 10.

 | DOI:10.1163/9789004736092_006

sor, he was very interested in the teaching of Law and, thanks to the legal training he received from his father (completed by the courses he followed at the Academy of Legislation at the start of the Revolution), he had a thorough knowledge of previous legal literature. In addition to the eminent role he played in the evolution of French law as a magistrate, he developed a serious interest in the concept of *regula iuris*, in relation with his conception of the legal order as a set of legal rules organised and structured around principles. This conception is particularly prevalent in his *Notions élémentaires sur la justice, le droit et les lois* and his *Réflexions sur l'enseignement et l'étude du droit.* As for the *regulae iuris*, they are especially the object of two of his books: his *Prolegomena iuris ad usum scholae et fori*, whose second part, *De regulis juris generalibus*, contains a chapter entitled "*Regulae generales, tam naturalis quàm civilis juris*", in which Dupin enumerates a number of statements to which he gives the status of *regulae iuris*, and his annotated edition of Francis Bacon's *Tractatus de fontibus iuris* (already translated and edited in France in 1646),[4] published under the title "*Legum leges*",[5] a title he chose because he considers that, through his aphorisms, Bacon gave *laws to laws* (*des lois aux lois*).[6]

Focusing on these two authors is based on several reasons: they both took the trouble to draw up and propose their own list of *regulae iuris* with the conviction that such rules were useful both in the interests of the science of Law (didactics as well as dogmatics) and for the practical implementation of the laws (by the judge). They were also both convinced that the existence of these special rules has something to do with the fact that the Law can be put into order in a rational way. The idea that the various branches of Law can be organised in a way that conforms to reason is, of course, not new. It went back quite far in time (to Cicero's "*ius in artem redigendo*")[7] and would be adopted

4 Francis Bacon, *Les Aphorismes du droit, traduits du latin,* trans. Jean Baudoin (Paris: s.l., 1646).

5 See: Andre Dupin, *Manuel des étudians en droit et des jeunes avocats, recueil d'opuscules de jurisprudence* (Paris: Joubert, 1835), 219 and following.

6 Dupin, *Manuel*, VII.

7 Cicero's treatise *De iure civili in artem redigendo* is lost, but we can get an idea of the aims it was meant to achieve and the method employed by Cicero from some clues: 1) composing a "*perfecta ars iuris civilis*" presupposes the use of the dialectical method (*De oratore*, 1.190: "*ut primum omne ius civile in genera digerat, quae perpauca sunt; deinde eorum generum quasi quaedam membra dispertiat; tum propriam cuiusque vim definitione declaret; perfectam artem iuris civilis habebitis*"); 2) "*iuris disciplina*" is not to be drawn from the praetor's edict or the xii Tables, but from philosophy (*De legibus*, 1.17). See: Deon H. van Zyl, *Cicero's Legal Philosophy* (Roodeport: Digma Publications, 1986), and James Gordley, *The Jurists: A Critical History* (Oxford: Oxford University Press, 2013), 111–127.

in France by the legal doctrine after 1804. The particularity of these two authors lies in the fact that they intend to respond to this concern for coherence by means of what they continue to call *regulae iuris*. Despite the novelty introduced by codification, they share similar views on how to draw up these *regulae iuris* and on the function they are supposed to play within the French legal order; and this similarity can be seen as the manifestation of a common legal culture, a common way of thinking, which, in a way, goes back in France to the 16th century and the maxims collected by Antoine Loisel in his *Institutes coutumières* (1607),[8] and which is also embodied by other French jurists, like, for instance, Claude Pocquet de Livonnière, Professor of French law at the Faculty of Law at Angers.[9] This common way of thinking could be summarised as follows: the resolution of a case requires the application of logically prior rules that have been previously identified by the legal doctrine in the legal system and that "normatively range over an indefinite spectrum of future cases".[10]

1 How to Identify and Shape the *Regulae Iuris* in France?

Domat and Dupin are both connoisseurs of Roman law, which they consider to be an impassable horizon, but which provides them with tools that they do not hesitate to use, in particular the famous *regulae iuris* of the Digest.[11] How-

8 The maxims listed in Loisel's *Institutes* may be considered the equivalent of *regulae iuris*, with the difference that Loisel himself did not explicitly refer to the technical concept of *regulae iuris*, which he did not attempt to define.

9 Claude Pocquet de Livonnière, *Règles du droit français* (Paris: J.-B. Coignard, 1730). Pocquet de Livonnière placed his work in the wake of the collections of "règles" made by Roman jurists and Canonists, with the difference that, just as Loisel before him, he does not use the expression "*regula iuris*", and that these "*maximes*" are based on Roman law but also on the French case law, the French royal ordinances and the local customs (pref., VI).

10 These words are borrowed from: Shivprasad Swaminathan, "*Mos Geometricus* and the Common Law Mind: Interrogating Contract Theory," *The Modern Law Review* 82–1 (Jan 2019): 46–70.

11 See: Peter Stein, *Regulae iuris. From Juristic Rules to Legal Maxims* (Edinburgh: Edinburgh University Press, 1966) and *id.*, "The Digest Title *De diversis regulis iuris antiqui* and the General Principles of Law," in *Essays in Jurisprudence in Honour of Roscoe Pound*, ed. Ralph A. Newman (New York: Bobbs-Merrill Co, 1962): 1–20; Bruno Schmidlin, *Die römischen Rechtsregeln* (Cologne: Böhlau, 1970); *id.*, "Horoi, pithana und regulae. Zum Einfluß der Rhetorik une Dialektik auf die juristiche Regelbildung," *Aufstieg und Niedergang der römischen Welt* 2.15 (1976): 101; Dieter Nörr, "Spruchregel und Generalisierung," *Zeitschrift der Savigny-Stiftung für Rechtsgeschichte* 89 (1972): 18; Laurens C. Winkel, "A

ever, this does not mean for them copying the Roman *regulae iuris* (as they were recorded in the Digest), but performing once again the gesture that the Roman jurists had made in their time, in order to give birth, in a new context, to the *regulae iuris* that the French Law needs. To this end, they endorse Paulus' assertion[12] according to which a *regula iuris* is characterised first and foremost by its appearance. Domat refers to D. 50.17.1 and defines the "*règles du Droit*" as short and clear statements.[13] Dupin also defines the *regulae iuris* in an apparently rather classical way. Relying on D. 50.17.1,[14] he equates the *regulae iuris* with short-form statements, this brief form being considered the best way of highlighting the general dimension of the rule thus stated.

The *regulae iuris* are indeed characterised by their generality, even though some are more general than others (as was the case in Rome: some of the *regulae iuris* of D. 50.17 applied to all matters, others were limited to a particular matter).[15] Domat's *Loix civiles* (preliminary Book) distinguish between *regulae iuris* according to whether they are genuinely general (because they are intended to operate across the whole legal domain), common to several areas of the law or specific to a particular area. In particular, the *regulae iuris* reflecting the requirements of natural equity and whose content replicates that of the *praecepta iuris* of Jutinian's *Institutes* (*alterum non laedere*; *suum cuique tribuere*), are general *regulae iuris*.[16] A century and a half after Domat, Dupin repeats that, formally, a *regula iuris* is a statement characterised by its brevity.

Note on Regulae Iuris in Roman Law and on Dworkin's Distinction between Rules and Principles," in *Critical Studies in Ancient Law, Comparative Law and Legal History: Essays in Honour of Alan Watson,* ed. John W. Cairns and Olivia F. Robinson (London: Hart, 2001): 413 and f.

12 D. 50.17.1.

13 Jean Domat, *Les loix civiles dans leur ordre naturel* (Paris: J.-B. Coignard, 1697), liv. prélim., I, I, I: "Les regles du Droit sont des expressions courtes & claires de ce que demande la justice dans les divers cas".

14 Dupin, *Prolegomena iuris ad usum scholae et for* (in *Manuel*, 290). See also: Jean-Simon Loiseau and Andre Dupin, *Dictionnaire des arrêts modernes en matière civile et criminelle, de procédure et de commerce* (Paris: Nève, 1814), I: x: "Ce n'est pas de la règle que vient le droit; c'est, au contraire, du droit que la règle tient son origine et sa force".

15 For example, D. 50.17.96 did not apply to all contracts. The distinction drawn by Domat with regard to the greater or lesser generality of the scope of application of these rules is not new. It was already that, for instance, of Hubert Van Giffen's *Tractatus de diversis regulis iuris antiqui* (Strasbourg: Zetzner, 1607), 6, where the *regulae iuris* were divided into general (or common) *regulae* and particular (*propriae*) *regulae*, the former being those relating to one of the three *genus* which served as a plan for Gaius and Justinian's *Institutes*, while the *propriae regulae* are those *quae ad unum juris locum pertinent* (for instance: marriage or wills).

16 See: Domat, *Loix civiles*, liv. prél., I, I, V.

Out of respect for the tradition (embodied in particular by Bacon)[17] and because he is convinced that Latin is better able than French to formulate a proposition compendiously, he even decides to formulate his proposed list of *regulae iuris* in Latin.[18]

So far, there is nothing very original: it is simply a matter of saying that French law, like Roman law in its time, must be understood and implemented in the light of rules whose brief form reflects their generality. But our two authors are much more original when they list these rules. Until then, at least in France, the jurists who had been interested in the *regulae iuris* had contented themselves with commenting on D. 50.17 by following the order of the *leges* chosen by Justinian[19] (with the notable exception of Donellus). Domat takes a radically different approach. He identifies some legal rules that he calls *règles du droit en general* and makes them the subject matter of Title I of the preliminary book of his *Loix civiles*, in which they are distinguished from the ordinary legal rules with which the judge accomplishes his daily task (which he calls: *règles*). Far from simply reproducing D. 50.17 (he is even quite critical of the work accomplished by Justinian's compilers)[20], he intends to propose his own list of *règles du droit*, sometimes by taking over some of the *regulae iuris* which had been gathered in D. 50.17, but also by drawing on other sources.[21] So did Dupin, who also distinguishes *regulae iuris* from ordinary rules (which is the reason why all the provisions of the Napoleonic codes do not necessarily have the status of *regulae iuris*).[22] Such an attitude is revealing: it shows that formulating *regulae iuris* is at the heart of doctrinal activity, precisely because the legal doctrine, more than the judge or

17 I voluntarily leave aside, for the moment, the criteria of definition that Dupin borrows directly from Bacon, because they relate more to the question of the content of the *regulae iuris*.

18 On Bacon and the use of Latin, see: Stein, *Regulae iuris*, 172.

19 In France, R.-J. Pothier distinguished himself from the usual commentaries on D. 50.17, insofar as, in accordance with the general method of his edition of the *Digest*, he did not comment on the *leges* by slavishly following the order in which they are exposed: he presented them following an order he found more rational and suitable. But the very content of the *regulae iuris* was not modified.

20 In the preface to *Les Loix civiles*, Domat underlines the absence of organisation, the lack of an orderly presentation of the different rules: "les règles mêmes qu'on a mises sous un dernier titre des règles du Droit, comme pour rassembler ce qu'il est plus nécessaire de retenir, y ont si peu d'ordre, qu'on auroit peine à y en retrouver deux de suite sur une matière".

21 See: Deroussin, "Domat," 313 and following.

22 André Dupin, "*Aphorismes de Bacon*," in: Dupin, *Manuel*, 259: "*Singuli articuli Codicis civilis nostri, non sunt regulae juris, quamvis omnes sint juris scita*".

the legislator, is the authority best able to say what the *regulae iuris* are. To carry out this mission, the legal doctrine implements reasoning based on induction and abstraction.

1.1 *The Legal Doctrine as the Authority Best Able to Formulate the* Regulae Iuris

Because Domat considers the jurisconsult as the expert on social relations and the most qualified to say what equity and natural reason require, it is up to the legal doctrine to set the *regulae iuris* by identifying the reasons underlying the resolution of all the particular cases, and to bring them together to build a genuine science of law whose purpose is to govern social relations. Dupin shares the same view. Commenting on D. 50.17.1 (*non ex regula ius sumatur, sed ex iure quod est regula fiat*), he claims that what Paulus called *ius* refers to the specific content of the laws (*les lois*). The *regulae iuris* are therefore to be learnt and extracted from the laws (*les lois*).[23] Such a rapprochement between *les lois* and the *regulae iuris* is, for instance, perceptible in his *Réflexions sur l'enseignement et l'étude du droit*, where he explains that the *regulae iuris* must be proven by laws ("*doivent se prouver par les lois*")[24] and that the familiarity with the *regulae iuris* has something to do with the knowledge of the spirit of the laws, in which precisely the legal science consists (assuming that penetrating the spirit of the laws is a much more valuable advantage than the mere technical knowledge of the content of laws).[25] Does this reference to *les lois* have anything to do with the fact that the French legal order is now codified? Certainly not. The point here is to make it clear that the *regulae iuris* are not the product of an *ex nihilo* reflection, and that they must be based on objective elements (in the same way that legal provisions must be based on general and objective factors), so as not to appear arbitrary. Dupin is deeply convinced that the *regulae iuris* (or this is the same: a principle likely to be applicable to all and each cases) are not to be built on the basis of subjective or too

---

23 Loiseau and Dupin, *Dictionnaire des arrêts*, I: XII: "Ainsi le Jurisconsulte fera bien de ne jamais chercher hors de la Loi de prétendues maximes générales uniquement fondées sur des préjugés peut-être mal interprétés ou mal entendus". This was already Fr. Hotman's idea (François Hotman, *Observationum in ius civile libri IX* (Paris: Vignon, 1589), 41: the *regulae iuris* express, in addition to the laws, the common idea that the doctrine derives from the study of laws), and also that of the 16th-century humanistic school. Let's note in passing that, on this point, Dupin distances himself from Bacon, insofar as Bacon defined the maxims of law as general principles deduced, by induction, from the constant jurisprudence of courts (see: Stein, *Regulae iuris*, 171).

24 Dupin, *Manuel*, 71.

25 Dupin, *Manuel*, 72.

specific data, because the correct way of reasoning in Law is to move from the general to the particular, and not, in an upward movement, to draw general lessons (applicable to other specific cases) from what is particular. In this respect, he does not consider judges' decisions, for example, as relevant objective considerations, insofar as a court decision is nothing more than the specific solution given to a singular case (distinguished from others by its own peculiarities).[26] As a consequence, he shares with Portalis the conviction that the act of formulating *regulae iuris* cannot fall within the competence of the judge, which consists only in the law's enforcement. It could, on the contrary, enter into the missions of the Legislator: it is up to the Legislator, writes Dupin, to fix by broad views the general maxims of laws, and thus to establish principles fruitful in consequences.[27] However, the Legislator cannot provide for all the needs that social life is likely to create. It is therefore especially to the *Jurisprudence* (in the Roman meaning of the term) that this mission falls,[28] which amounts to saying that the *regulae iuris* are statements whose particularity is that they belong to the register of doctrinal statements, although some of them may have taken the form of legislation (when enshrined by the legislator in statute law). It is even likely that, in the eyes of Dupin, this particularity prevails over the formal and external criteria likely to characterise the *regulae iuris.* Such a point of view is not original. As early as the beginning of the 18th century, Chancellor Daguesseau already compared the *regulae iuris* to *oracles of jurisprudence*, which was a way to emphasise

26 Loiseau and Dupin, *Dictionnaire des arrêts*, XII: "on ne peut argumenter du particulier au général; par conséquent, on ne doit point ériger en principe absolu, applicable à toutes les hypothèses, la décision intervenue sur une hypothèse particulière". A little later, Dupin reiterates his condemnation of the so called "arrêts de principe" (which he also calls "arrêts doctrinaires") and explains that "il ne faut pas, en jugeant un seul cas, les préjuger tous" (Andre Dupin, *Réquisitoires, plaidoyers et discours de rentrée* ... (Paris: Videcoq, 1836), III: 12, quoted by Frank Brami, *Dupin Aîné (1783–1865), procureur général près la Cour de cassation et jurisconsulte* (Paris: Dalloz, 2013), 298).

27 Jean-Etienne-Marie Portalis, "Discours préliminaire prononcé lors de la presentation du projet de la Commission du Gouvernement," in *Recueil complet des travaux préparatoires du Code civil*, ed. P. Antoine Fenet (Paris: Videcoq, 1836), I: 470: "L'office de la Loi est de fixer par de grandes vues les maximes générales du Droit, d'établir des principes féconds en conséquences, et non de descendre dans le détail des questions qui peuvent naître sur chaque matière".

28 In the 19th century, many of French jurists still use the word "jurisprudence" as a synonym for Legal science (see: Charles Aubry and Charles Rau, *Cours de droit civil français* (Strasbourg: Lagier, 1839), I, § 1, for instance), although nowadays the word is used more and more to designate the judicial activity.

their doctrinal dimension.[29] But it raises an important issue: what authority can a doctrinal statement have in a legal system dominated by written laws enacted by a public authority? Domat and Dupin do not answer this question, but give a few clues. First: in France, both before and after 1804, the legal doctrine's opinions are not considered binding on the courts, because they are no *official* sources of French law. No doubt alluding to the famous constitution of Valentinian III of 426 (C.Th. 1.4.3), Dupin points out that, in France, doctrinal opinions are not counted, they are weighed:

> chez nous, les docteurs n'ont jamais joui d'un tel crédit: on ne les compte pas, on les pèse; on estime leurs raisons ce qu'elles valent, et personne n'est ténu d'y déférer. Mais les jurisconsultes réellement dignes de ce nom, n'en exercent pas moins une grande influence sur la décision des procès, par l'ascendant naturel qu'obtiennent les esprits supérieurs sur ceux qui leur sont subordonnés.[30]

Their only strength is persuasion, because they do not enjoy any public authority. As a result, a professor has to explain how he manages to formulate a rule. He must explain the general notions he uses, he has to go back to the causes, to make explicit the reasons behind these precepts, to show the connection that they have with each other in order to convince of their veracity and their certainty. Dupin frequently insists on the fact that teaching Law should be based on a method comparable to that of a scientist, because scholars must reveal the secrets of the demonstration by which they justify the principles they formulate: "*Personne n'a droit d'exiger qu'on l'en croie sur parole*".[31]

Second clue: some *regulae iuris* can be taken for granted, as long as they are agreed upon by consensus. A *regula iuris* formulated and validated by most of the scholars becomes an axiom, and it is precisely the role of the legal doctrine to identify the rules whose content is the subject of consensus and therefore no longer needs to be discussed and justified.[32] In this sense, the *regulae iuris*

---

29 Francois-Henri Daguesseau, *Œuvres complètes du Chancelier Daguesseau* (Paris: Fantin, 1819), I: 279, *Première Instruction à son fils*: "On ne saurait trop se remplir l'esprit de ces notions communes qui sont comme autant d'oracles de la jurisprudence, et comme le précis de toutes les réflexions des jurisconsultes". Dupin endorses this view and quotes Daguesseau in the preface to his *Prolegomena* (Dupin, *Manuel*, 272).

30 Dupin, *Manuel*, 416.

31 Dupin, *Manuel*, 61.

32 For example: "*Libertas inaestimabilis res est*" (D. 50.17.106), quoted by Dupin in his *Manuel*, 70.

are the doctrinal assertions which have acquired such a high level of objectivity that they must be considered indisputable, it being understood that this degree of objectivity may result from the fact that the rule is not specific to one legal system, but is adopted by several, as Dupin points out in commenting on Bacon's aphorism 83, which is a way to take up the medieval distinction between *notabilia, generalia* and *regulae* without explicitly referring to it.[33] There is, however, an ambiguity here, which Dupin does not resolve: the *regulae iuris* are indisputable propositions, but no technical procedure can guarantee their respect.

1.2 *How to Design a* Regula Iuris*?*

Before the French Revolution, the status of Roman law in France gave rise to much debate,[34] but even those who did not elevate Roman Law to the rank of the *droit commun du royaume* admitted that it could be applied in France as *ratio scripta*. To use Domat's words: everyone considered Roman law as the most perfect manifestation of equity in History (the equity's "*unique dépôt*"), thanks to which the Romans managed to develop a "*science du droit naturel*".[35] Since the *regulae iuris* of D. 50.17 were supposed to be the best expression of equity and natural reason, it would have been possible to stick to them, without adding anything or changing them. Domat takes, however, a different route. He agrees that it is from the material provided by Roman law that it is possible to design axioms and general rules[36] (which amounts to saying that legal history is of great help to those who try to design *regulae iuris*, since this particular category of rules was already known by Roman Law), but he chooses to move away from the framework provided by D. 50.17. Rather than slavishly taking over all the *regulae* listed in D. 50.17, he makes a selection and chooses only those that meet two criteria: (1) a formal criterion, which selects only the fragments characterised by their brief form and (2) a substantial criterion, which leads to select only the fragments whose function is to describe the way the ordinary legal rules should be implemented or interpreted. In

33 *Notabilia* and *Generalia*, alongside the words *Summae* or *Distinctiones*, were terms that designated particular types of literary forms. *Generalia* referred to short sentences illustrating and summarising a text, while *notabilia* rather referred to a series of remarks made on issues chosen because of their importance or difficulty. It is difficult to say whether Dupin had these distinctions in mind, but what is certain is that, for him, they express the idea of a progression from the least general (*notabilia*) to the most general (*regulae*). See I.A. Kotlyar's contribution to this volume.

34 See, on this point, the numerous works of J. Krynen.

35 Domat, *Loix civiles*, pref.

36 The idea is shared by H.-Fr. Daguesseau (Daguesseau, *Œuvres completes*, 15:104).

other words: the *regulae* gathered in D. 50.17 are of interest only to the extent that they allow him to produce useful general rules for the good understanding and application of the laws in France. As a consequence, of the twenty-nine rules mentioned in title 1 of the preliminary book of *Les loix civiles*, nearly fourteen are based on a *regula iuris* listed in D. 50.17, which shows that Domat authorises himself to create new *regulae iuris*. Even when he quotes a fragment from D. 50.17 in support of the *regula* he proposes, that *regula* may have a different meaning than it had in Roman Law. For example, the rule relating to the interpretation of the laws is based on a reference to D. 50.17.90, but while the Roman *regula iuris* required an interpretation consistent with equity, Domat's *regula iuris* requires an interpretation consistent with the will of the Legislator.[37] Thus, Domat does not seek to rearrange D. 50.17 to make it a bit more coherent (a mission to which Pothier will dedicate himself),[38] nor to comment on D. 50.17. The *regulae* gathered in D. 50.17 serves for reflection, but it is not the object of Domat's reflection.

After 1804, the debate relating to the authority of Roman law in France obviously arises in different terms, to the disadvantage of Roman law. In a codified system which does not give the *leges* the status of positive law, the function of Roman law can no longer be to provide ready-to-use technical solutions for judgement (incidentally, that explains why, in his activity as a magistrate, Dupin actually makes little reference to the provisions of Roman law).[39] Roman *leges*, including the *regulae iuris*, do no longer have any binding force. However, it is not in the Civil Code that Dupin searches the *regulae iuris*, but in the very content of the Roman *leges*, which he still considers the best expressions of human wisdom and natural reason. As such (and under the condition, of course, that they do not conflict with what he calls the French national genius, "*notre génie national*"),[40] they are always the most useful and appropriate material for setting out the guidelines that are likely to structure any other legal order, including French law, which is now codified.

In this regard, Dupin[41] behaves in exactly the same way as French jurists did before the codification, as if the codification did not imply that the legal system was closed in on itself. He keeps on treating Roman Law in a pragmatic

37 Domat, *Loix civiles*, Liv. prélim., I, II, I.

38 See: Robert J. Pothier, *Pandectae Iustinianae* (Paris: Saugrain, Desaint & C, 1752), vol. III.

39 On this point, see: Brami, *Dupin Aîné*, 346.

40 André Dupin, ed., *Œuvres de Pothier* (Paris: Bechet, 1823–35), I: LXXVI.

41 See, for instance: André Dupin, *Principia juris civilis tum romani, legum romanorum ex corpore Justinianeo depromptarum …* (Paris: Marchant 1806) – where the Roman law is considered a set of statements to be synthesised in order to design useful rules.

and instrumental manner. There seems to be a paradox here, but this paradox is easily dispelled if we bear in mind the influence that Daguesseau exerted on Dupin. Daguesseau (just as Domat) was indeed convinced that Roman Law offers a better playing field than French Law for those who want to embark on a quest for the principles of Law. But if such an attitude was conceivable in the 18th century (when, despite the royal ordinances, French positive Law was still largely made up of customs and special provisions), it is more surprising that Dupin does not undertake to look for the existence of general rules in the codes promulgated by Napoleon. Anyway, among the one hundred and fifteen *regulae* he proposes, only forty-nine are simple copies of the *regulae* listed in D. 50.17. The process that leads Dupin to the creation of new *regulae iuris* can be observed, one might say, *in vivo* in his *Prolegomena iuris*,[42] a book which is to be read in connection with his *Principia iuris civilis cum romani tum gallici* (Paris, 1806). In that book, Dupin does not only engage in a work of commentary on a selection of fragments hitherto identified as *regulae iuris*. He himself recomposes a *corpus* of rules to which he gives the status of *regulae iuris*. For the most part, they are the result of a personal work of drafting based on many Roman sources (here, too, Dupin follows Domat and Daguesseau's footsteps).[43] For example, *Regula* 56 (*plerumque sub auctoritate iuris scientiae perniciose erratur*) is elaborated on the basis of Paulus' longer discussions devoted to the perpetuation of the obligation in case of *mora debitoris* (D. 45.1.91.3): Dupin extracts from Paulus' technical discussions the only general reflection contained therein, which consists in warning against too much deference to the legal science. *Regula* 62 (*Beneficio adfici hominem interest hominis*)[44] is drawn from D. 18.7.7,[45] a rather long fragment dealing with the sale of

42 Dupin, *Manuel*, 272 and following.

43 Daguesseau, *Œuvres completes*, 15:649, 4è instruction: "c'est dans l'étude de tout le droit romain qu'il faut être attentif à remarquer tout ce qui peut former un axiome ou une règles générale de droit, soit dans la décision même, soit dans la raison de la decision".

44 Editor's note: In the FWO.OPR.2020.005001 database, this *regula* is registered under No. 1131.

45 D. 18.7.7, Papinianus: "servus ea lege veniit, ne in italia esset: quod si aliter factum esset, convenit citra stipulationem, ut poenam praestaret emptor. Vix est, ut eo nomine vindictae ratione venditor agere possit, acturus utiliter, si non servata lege in poenam quam alii promisit inciderit. Huic consequens erit, ut hactenus agere possit, quatenus alii praestare cogitur: quidquid enim excedit, poena, non rei persecutio est. Quod si, ne poenae causa exportaretur, convenit, etiam affectionis ratione recte agetur. Nec videntur haec inter se contraria esse, cum beneficio adfici hominem intersit hominis: enimvero poenae non irrogatae indignatio solam duritiam continet".

a slave under the condition that the slave will work outside Italy, under pain of a financial penalty, (but not in the form of a stipulation). In this fragment, Papinianus took care to specify that (1) the seller could legitimately claim this penalty if he had a personal pecuniary interest to claim (for example, if he had to pay a sum to the one to whom he himself promised that this slave would be remote from Italy); (2) on the contrary, the seller's request should not be favourably received by the judge when the penalty was claimed only *vindictae ratione*; (3) the seller could also claim this penalty *ratione affectionis*. All this does not enter into contradiction. The first affirmation is based on the fact that revenge is not a legitimate reason to take legal action, while the possibility of claiming *ratione affectionis* is based on the idea that everyone may have an interest in another man being treated favourably: "*cum beneficio adfici hominem, intersit hominis*". From this long passage of the *Digest*, it is these last words that Dupin isolates to transform them into a *regula iuris*, because they express the reason for the solutions recommended.

There are many other examples showing that Dupin seeks in all the Roman jurists' writings the elements capable of serving as justifications for the solutions they proposed, in order to present these justifications under the guise of a *regula iuris*, after having freed them from their former casuistic dimension. He thus proceeds exactly as Labeo had done before him, or as Domat. For instance, and according to *Regula* 64, it is not forbidden to seek one's own profit, unless this involves harming others. This rule finds its origin not in one of the fragments of D. 50.17, but in one of Ulpian's assertions collected by the compilers of Justinian in D. 39.3.1.11, according to which the owner of a land can lawfully keep for himself, on his own land, the rainwater (under the condition it is not the result of works carried out on his neighbours' lands), because the owners are not prohibited to benefit from what is theirs. In Ulpian's text, the words "*prodesse enim sibi unusquisque, dum alii non nocet, non prohibetur*" appeared in parentheses, but they basically unveiled the decision's *ratio*. Adopting Labeo's method,[46] Dupin makes this *ratio*, expressed in a few words, a *regula iuris* by disconnecting it from the specific case Ulpian was dealing with. By only retaining these few words from the whole fragment, he gives them a character of generality and abstraction which they perhaps

46 See: Rafael Domingo, "The Roman Jurists and the Legal Science," *University of Navarra*, 30 June 2017, https://dx.doi.org/10.2139/ssrn.2994130; Matthijs Wibier, "Marcus Antistius Labeo and the Idea of Legal Literature," in *Roman Law and Latin Literature*, ed. Ioannis Ziogas and Erica Bexley (London: Bloomsbury, 2022), 125–144.

did not have in Ulpian's mind and finally makes them the expression of a general principle in line with the needs of a society whose economy is based on private initiative.[47] For this purpose, and like the Glossators, he uses "indefinite" or "indeterminate" terms.[48]

So, it is not as historians seeing in the Roman *regulae iuris* a vestige of the past to be understood with regard to their historical context that Domat and Dupin focus on the concept of *regulae iuris.* They do not treat the Roman *regulae iuris* as objects that should be studied in accordance with the historical method. However, that does not mean that they do not make legal history an essential element in the training of the jurists. Dupin, for instance, even takes up Montesquieu's famous formula: "*comprendre les lois par l'histoire, et l'histoire par les lois*".[49] But, contrary to Savigny, he does not claim that the creation of the Law is intrinsically a historical process (in his opinion, Roman law is nothing but dead legislation and cannot be anything else in the codified legal system established by Napoleon I). Neither is he interested in History as a science. What he calls "History" is only a certain knowledge or perception of the past inspired by the reading of selected historical sources, such as for example the speeches or harangues of the great magistrates or the writings of the former jurisconsults who can be praised for the solidity, firmness and correctness of the principles they formulated.[50] Referring to the past is relevant only under the condition that it provides lessons for the present. Studying Roman law is useful and necessary only insofar as it makes it possible to discover general maxims based on natural law or common sense, or legal reasoning patterns characterised by their simplicity.[51] Domat's (whose aim is not to implement the historical method of the humanists) and Dupin's (who stays away from the movement of revival of historical studies noticeable in France

47 *Regulae* 62 and 64 perfectly illustrate the phenomenon of abstraction-generalisation which leads to the formulation of a *regula iuris* designed as a general directive. Moreover, their respective places in Dupin's list suggest that they are to be read and understood together: *Regula* 62 provides a very general directive, the meaning of which is specified by *Regula* 64.

48 See: Ilya A. Kotlyar, "Medieval juristic *regulae*: unity or disunity?," *Tijdschrift voor Rechtsgeschiedenis* 89 (2021): 425.

49 Charles L. Montesquieu, *De l'esprit des lois*, XXXI, 2. On this issue, see: Celine Spector, "'Il faut éclairer l'histoire par les lois et les lois par l'histoire': statut de la romanité et rationalité des coutumes dans *L'Esprit des lois de Montesquieu*," in *Généalogie des savoirs juridiques: le carrefour des Lumières*, ed. Mikhail Xifaras (Bruxelles: Bruylant, 2007), 15–41.

50 Dupin, *Manuel*, 5.

51 Dupin, "*Dissertation sur la vie et les ouvrages de Pothier*", in *Œuvres de Pothier*, I: LXXVI.

from the years 1830)[52] conception of History is clearly utilitarian: they find in the writings of classical Roman jurists a method, that of Labeo, and a tool (*Pythana*, *regula*), which they reactivate because they seem both relevant and useful for the French Law. In their project of organisation of the Law, the concept of *regula iuris* is an abstract and a-historical form in the sense that the rules gathered in D. 50.17 are only a particular concrete and historical manifestation of this concept, the particularity of which lies in the fact that it can give rise to other new concrete realisations in other historical contexts. If we had to attempt a comparison, we could say that this concept[53] operates in the same way as the ideal type of Weberian sociology: as used by Domat and Dupin, it is a category which corresponds to a set of real phenomena which can be studied empirically. In this view, Domat and Dupin do not help us understand the content of all the Roman *regulae iuris*, but the way in which Roman jurists were able to understand the legal category they called *regulae iuris*.

2 What Are the *Regulae Iuris*'s Possible Functions in France?

The *regulae iuris* are not characterised only by their external form. Substantively, they are also statements giving an account of legal solutions already implemented. A *regula* is, as Peter Stein pointed out, "a brief statement of the subject-matter, that is, the existing law".[54] But what exactly is behind the word "law" (or "*ius*", to speak like Paulus: "*non ex regula ius sumatur, sed ex iure quod est regula fiat*")? To answer this question, it is now necessary to examine the function our two authors assigned to the *regulae iuris*, which is both simple and complex: to give laws to laws.

The importance of such a function is particularly evident in the context of legal pluralism in which Domat still operated at the end of the 17th century. But this importance does not decline after the Napoleonic codifications: despite the fact that none of the legal rules which henceforth constitute the French legal order is legally defined or classified as *regulae iuris*, Dupin pursues the same goal as Domat and still intends to take advantage of all the

52 See: Brami, *Dupin aîné*, 311.

53 There is, in what Domat and Dupin write about the *regulae iuris*, everything that is usually used to define a concept: a name (which designates the thing itself), attributes (the essential characteristics of the concept), and finally examples or concrete cases, which are designated by that name and which illustrate these attributes.

54 Stein, *Regulae iuris*, 69.

potentialities that the concept of *regula iuris* can offer, which remain numerous even in a codified legal order, especially since the Civil Code does not contain a general part whose purpose would be to set out the most general legal rules likely to be applied generally in several branches of law. In particular, they expect the *regulae iuris* they identify to perform three functions: to provide a rational structure for the law, to guide the interpretation of the laws (these two functions have something important in common: they ensure the proper and effective functioning of the legal order by introducing the logic necessary for its correct operation), and to promote the social and ethical values that the legal order should consider as essential. In other words, the *regulae iuris* are a key tool for framing a scientific approach to the law and underlying its implementation, but they are also the means to ensure the influence of an ideology, without concern for any axiological neutrality of the law, which, again, is very "Roman", since such a project corresponds perfectly to the idea that law is nothing else that the *ars boni et aequi.*

2.1 Regulae Iuris *as a Key to Organising the Legal Order*

The importance of the concept of *regula iuris* in the structuring of the legal universe can be explained in two ways. On the one hand, it follows from the fact that the elements of a system which originate in the human reason and which have therefore a great degree of universality and generality should be considered prior by nature, *prius natura*. They then deserve the first place, as if all the other elements of the system could be deduced from them. In Domat's *Loix civiles* architecture, which reflects the *mos geometricus*,[55] these *first elements* are called *les premiers principes des lois*. They consist of the two fundamental commandments identified by Domat as necessary for the perpetuation of mankind and society: the love of God and the mutual love between people.[56] A *principe* is not a *regula iuris*,[57] but a *regula iuris* is what is derived from a *principe*. In other words, either a *principe* can be trans-

55 The same *mos geometricus* which is at work in the philosophy of Descartes at the same time, see: Olivier Duboulcez, "L'ordre géométrique et le dispositif argumentatif des Méditations métaphysiques de René Descartes," *Revue d'histoire des sciences* 2 (2016): 311–334. See also: James Gordley, *The Jurists*, 165–194.

56 On these two principles, see: Yves-Charles Zarka, *Philosophie et politique à l'âge classique* (Paris: Hermann, 2016), 289. See also: Simone Goyard-Fabre, "La philosophie du droit de Jean Domat ou la convergence de l'ordre naturel et de l'ordre rationnel," in *Justice et Force: Politiques au temps de Pascal*, ed. Gerard Ferreyrolles (Paris: Klincksieck, 1996), 187–207; Marie-France Renoux-Zagamé, "Domat, le salut, le droit," *Revue d'histoire des facultés de droit et de la science juridique* 8 (1989): 69–111.

57 I take the liberty to translate Domat's words "règles du droit en général" as "*regulae iuris*".

formed into a *regula iuris*, but it is then the *regula* that is applied in practice by the judge;[58] or it does not lend itself to such an enunciation in the form of a *regula iuris*, and the judge must then deliver judgement according to both his interpretation of the meaning of this principle and the common sense. The terms "*principe*" and "*regula iuris*" are therefore not synonymous (and this is certainly the reason why Domat uses the word "*principe*" in his *Traité des loix*, but not in the section of the preliminary book of the *Loix civiles* devoted to the *règles du droit en général*). In the legal universe drawn up by Domat, *les principes* are in the first place, just before the *regulae iuris*, which themselves precede the ordinary legal rules. The *regulae iuris* are thus distinguished both from what he calls "*principes*" in the strict sense and from what may be called "ordinary legal rules": they fall somewhere in between. Domat no longer reduces a *regula iuris* to being a mere expression of specific *rationes decidendi*, as Bulgarus did ("*quasi quaedam singulorum coniunctio disposita*"),[59] which would amount to deny the *regulae iuris'* normative autonomy vis-à-vis the cases on which they are founded. On the contrary, he embraces the humanist tradition (Decius, Hotman, Coraius, Peckius, J. Gothofredus, E. Bronchorst),[60] insofar as, in turn, he considers the *regulae iuris* as legal rules from which the jurist can reason by analogy.

On the other hand, it stems from the very function of the legal science as Domat conceives it, which is to show the way in which legal rules depend on each other, the relations of connection ("*suites*") between them, not for the sake of aesthetics, but because legal science is nothing else than the method by which the meaning of legal rules is revealed and unveiled (the application of a *regula* to a concrete case presupposing knowledge of the "*liaison*" between this *regula* and the principle it is intended to transpose, because this link makes it possible to identify its meaning).[61] More generally, it must be under-

58 For instance, the principle according to which arbitrary laws (which Domat opposes to immutable laws, which are immutable because they give concrete expression to the precepts of natural law) are "facts", and that they can therefore be ignored by the litigants, can be reduced to a fixed rule: an arbitrary law binds only from the moment of its publication.

59 Quoted by Stein, *Regulae iuris*, 133.

60 However, Accursius already regarded the *regulae iuris* as legal norms and agreed to apply a *regula* to a case which had not yet been decided, if that case fell under the same *ratio* as that which justified the existence of the *regula* (see: Stein, *Regulae iuris*, 146).

61 Jean Domat, «*Le droit public*,» II, IV, I, III (in *Les Loix civiles dans leur ordre naturel, le Droit public et Legum delectus* (Paris: Le Gras, 1723), vol. II). In this sense, the intellectual operation by which legal rules are put in order is both an operation of exposition of the rules and a method of interpreting those rules (see: Marie-France Renouz-Zagamé, "Domat: du jugement de Dieu à l'esprit des lois," *Le Débat* 74–2 (1993): 49).

lined that the rules that Domat refers to as "règles du droit en général" are those which have as their object the nature, the use and the interpretation of laws. To put it another way, and using the distinction popularised by Herbert L.A. Hart,[62] it is not a question of so-called primary rules, that is to say, those whose object is to determine the behaviour of individuals.[63] They are more similar to what Hart will call secondary rules, insofar as they are rules whose function is to identify the primary rules and ensure their proper application.

Like Domat, Dupin believes that the mission of legal science is to methodically classify legal institutions and legal rules and to present them in a rational order. Such a point of view is not very original: it was already held by the partisans of the *mos geometricus*, whose merits are praised by Dupin in his introduction to his edition of Pothier's treatises: every idea must find its rightful place in a whole made up of parts which must fit together in a logical manner.[64] Regarding our issue, this has two consequences. First, professors are supposed to base their teaching on principles they have to explain. It is their duty to show their students the logical connection between each of their statements and these principles.[65] The solution to a particular case and the teachings of a professor must flow from the correct application of the principles, of which they are only a consequence, like water flowing from its font. Speaking of *principles*, Dupin, however, does not refer to "*what is capable of producing consequences*", but to "*what serves to put knowledge in order*" (just as Newton used the term "*principle*" in the physical sciences). A principle is therefore defined as such because of the particular function it performs: it is a tool designed to organise and to explain. In Dupin's mind, this is precisely also what the *regulae iuris* are made for, since they are nothing else than the form in which principles are to be expressed. In the same way that the constitution (here, the 1814 Charter) is at the top of the hierarchy of norms,[66] the *regulae iuris* shall serve as keystone to the presentation and the organisation of all legal matters. That is why Dupin sometimes describes them as axioms:

62 Herbert L. A. Hart, *The Concept of Law*, 2nd ed. (Oxford: Oxford University Press, 1994).

63 Massimo La Torre, "The Hierarchical Model and H. L. A. Hart's Concept of Law," *Revus* 21 (2013): 141–161.

64 Dupin, *Œuvres de Pothier*, 1:VIII.

65 Dupin, *Manuel*, 59.

66 The hierarchy of norms proposed by Dupin is not very original: at the top are the fundamental laws ("*lois fondamentales*", that give shape to the social contract); below them, the laws he calls secondary laws ("*lois secondaires*", which must be consistent with the fundamental laws), and the regulations (*les règlements*, provided that they are consistent with the laws), see: Dupin, "*Notions élémentaires*", in: *Manuel*, 330).

regulae iuris are similar to scientific truths, and it is up to the scholars to convince their students of the truth of these axioms, so as to leave no doubt in mind about their certainty.[67]

Second, Dupin's approach to the *regulae iuris* implies a synonymy between *regula iuris* and *definitio*.[68] It is clear indeed that the function of some of the *regulae iuris* listed by Dupin is to briefly define some general legal notions. This is especially the case of those gathered in the first part of the *Prolegomena*, entitled *De Justitia and Jure*, which really looks like a lexicon of legal terms, insofar as it gives, on the basis of fragments taken from the *Corpus iuris civilis*, the definition of some words or expressions used to draw the outlines of certain elementary legal notions, such as *iustitia, ius, iurisprudentia, ius naturale / ius gentium / ius civile* and *ius publicum*.[69] For example, *Regula* 73 defines good faith as follows: *Fides bona contraria est fraudi et dolo*. Moreover, the intellectual process by which a word is defined is comparable to the one by which a *regula iuris* is created. In both cases it is a question of reducing all characteristics of a notion or a legal institution to its "first principles"[70] (in this respect, Dupin follows a tradition that dates back to the *Rhetorica ad Herennium*, 4.24.35, according to which a definition must briefly and completely embrace the particular qualities of an object: *definition est quae rei alicuius proprias amplectitur breviter et absolute*). Commenting on *Regula* 56.1 (*Omnis definitio in iure civili periculosa est*), which is simply a copy of D. 50.17.202, Dupin even asserts that the word *regula* can be taken as a syno-

67 Andre Dupin, "Réflexions sur l'enseignement et l'étude du droit," in *Manuel*, 59: "les convaincre de la vérité de ces préceptes, de manière à ne laisser dans leur esprit aucun cloute sur leur certitude".

68 "To define is nothing else than making known the meaning of a word by means of other expressions which are not synonyms" (Dupin, "*Réflexions*," in *Manuel*, 65: "Définir, n'est autre chose que faire connaître le sens d'un mot par le moyen d'autres expressions qui ne soient pas synonymes").

69 The first part of the *Prolegomena* also mentions basic notions on the different strata that make up a legal order: written Law (*droit écrit*, which leads Dupin to talk about the laws – "*les lois*": what the laws are, how they must be interpreted, how they can be repealed) and unwritten Law (*droit non écrit*, in which he includes the legal doctrine, as well as customary laws, but also the decisions of the courts, though they are, from a formal point of view, written). The inference to be drawn from this is that, paradoxically, the distinction made by Dupin between written and unwritten law is not really based on a formal criterion, but it serves to highlight the difference between the laws, *i.e.* legal rules, that have the force of law and the rules that do not have the same force.

70 Dupin, "*Réflexions*," in *Manuel*, 65: "Les définitions se trouvent par l'analyse, lorsque nous examinons soigneusement une chose dans toutes ses parties, et que nous la réduisons à ses premiers principes".

nym for *definitio*. To the question: "*What is, in Law, a definition*?" – he answers: "*Definitio, id est regula, sententia*".[71] Such an answer is, actually, self-evident, given that (1) *regulae iuris* and *definitions* have in common to be set out in a synthetic manner;[72] (2) they both must be used carefully and with discernment,[73] because (a) definitions can easily be criticised, or even overturned and (b) the slightest modification in the specific circumstances of a case to which a *regula* is intended to apply can lead to the greatest consequences;[74] (3) definitions, like *regulae iuris*, are normative because they are stipulative: they state the meaning that *must be given* to a word or an expression.

Finally, Domat and Dupin use the concept of *regula iuris* in relation with the work of rationalising the law (*droit*) which falls to the doctrine; a work intended to guarantee better intelligibility of the law both in terms of the training of the legal mind[75] and in terms of the implementation of the law.

2.2 Regulae Iuris *as Guidelines for the Interpreter*

Domat clearly sees the *regulae iuris* as a guide for the interpreters, mainly the judge. In his systematics, the concept of *regulae iuris* is linked to the "*iuris dictio*": *regulae iuris* are directives offered to the judge for the implementation of the laws. They have the same function as, in mathematics, the elements of a demonstration: they are signs capable of being understood by every judge in the same way, because they are endowed with a fixed meaning, accessible to all. They therefore make it possible for the judge to reason on the basis of impersonal and uncontested rules. It is, in this respect, not insignificant that the *Loix civiles*' chapter titled "*Des règles du droit en général*" contains a section (section II) entirely dedicated to the question of the interpretation of laws by

71 Dupin, "*Prolegomena*," in *Manuel*, 291.

72 Dupin, "*Prolegomena*," in *Manuel*, 290–291.

73 Sometimes, the application of one *regula iuris* presupposes taking into account another *regula*, which delimits its scope. For example, the courts are asked to take account of reality rather than opinion (*Regula* 96: "*Plus valet quod in veritate est, quàm quod in opinione*", formulated by Dupin on the basis of Inst.Just. II.20.11, dealing with the issue of *incertae personae*), but also to draw all the consequences of the error made by an individual, when this error takes on all the characteristics of an *error communis*, as stated by *Regula* 97.1: "*error communis facit ius*".

74 Dupin, "*Prolegomena*," in *Manuel*, 291: "*modica enim circumstantiae varietas totum plerumque ius immutat*".

75 According to Domat, teaching law requires a method intended to facilitate learning and memorisation, which requires a clear and precise system, because order is much more necessary to bring into the mind the infinite detail of the truths that make up a science.

the judge, in which, using general rules, he tries to objectify judicial interpretation while recalling that it must conform to the requirements of equity and that the judge must exercise discernment.[76]

In accordance with its commonly accepted etymology, Dupin in his turn is convinced that the *regulae iuris* are instruments (just like the square used by the architect), more precisely guidelines allowing an individual to decide correctly, *i.e.* rationally (knowing the *regulae iuris*, and knowing how to use them, is therefore the very condition of any good decision: *quod recte ducit*).[77] As suggested by the title of the *Prolegomena* (*Prolegomena iuris ad usum scholae et fori*), these guidelines are specifically designed for judges and students. As regards the judges, Dupin insists that the best way for them to fulfil their task is to implement the laws with caution (in the sense of the Roman word "*prudentia*"). This prudence requires them to search outside of themselves and their sole consciousness the elements on which they shall base their interpretation of the laws. The *regulae iuris' raison d'être* precisely lies in the fact that they make it possible to objectify the interpretative work, therefore framing the way courts interpret the laws[78] and the facts.

For example, the *regula* according to which every individual shall live honestly allows the judge to reject any behaviour contrary to morality, even though this behaviour is not expressly prohibited by law: "*Honeste vivere. Hoc praecepto vetantur omnia quae pugnant cum bonis moribus et publicâ honestate, etiamsi non expressè prohibita*".[79] In the same vein, the *regula* according to which it is necessary to consider what equity demands[80] amounts to inciting the judge to prefer equity to the rigor of the law, because he must always look for the solution deemed the fairest, which is the one that the Legislator is supposed to call for,[81] not only in cases where the laws does not give an explicit solution ("*In omnibus scilicet, quae lege palàm non sunt definita*").[82]

---

76 Domat, *Loix civiles*, I, I, II, XXIX.

77 Dupin, "*Prolegomena*," in *Manuel*, 290.

78 Dupin, "*Notions*" (in *Manuel*, 414), regarding unwritten Law: "Lors même que la loi nous manque et nous abandonne aux seules inspirations de notre conscience et de notre raison, la prudence veut encore qu'on ne s'en rapporte pas entièrement à soi-même, et que l'on cherche à s'environner, au moins à titre de conseil, de tout ce qui peut éclairer notre jugement".

79 Dupin, "*Prolegomena*," in *Manuel*, 292.

80 "In omnibus quidem, maxime tamen in jure, aequitas spectanda sit" (Paulus, D. 50.17.90).

81 Inspired by Cicero (*De Legibus*, I, 42), Dupin states: "ius semper quoerendum est aequabile; neque enim aliter jus esset".

82 Dupin, "*Prolegomena*", in *Manuel*, 292. Dupin, in a not very original way, sees in equity the expression of natural reason.

More generally, the *regulae iuris* are a means to promoting good faith in legal relations (which implies, in particular, the sanction of unjust enrichment), it being understood that good faith only condemns what is fraudulent (behaviour or acts that intentionally cause harm to other individuals' interests), which excludes acts which are merely the consequence of the exercise of a subjective right, according to *Regula* 94 ("*Nullus videtur dolo facere, qui suo jure utitur*", formulated from D. 50.17.55). Moreover, the judge is not expected to make a personal moral judgment and to sanction any behaviour that appears to him to be contrary to his personal morality, because he must know that *Non omne quod licet honestum est*,[83] which means that legal norms, whose implementation he is in charge of, are narrower and less demanding than moral ones.[84] Interpreting his mission this way, he works towards the implementation of what Dupin calls "*le gouvernement du droit*" – the rule of law; a *gouvernement du droit* that, in Dupin's mind, merges with what he calls "*constitutional government*" – *le gouvernement constitutionnel*.[85]

No doubt this supervisory function appears even more visibly when a *regula iuris* is formulated in such a way that it is clear that it orders the judge to do or not to do something. For example, to consider as a *regula iuris* the statement "*Bona fides non patitur ut bis idem exigatur*" (*Regula* 73.2)[86] is to ask the judge to reject any new request relating to the same subject matter. The same could be said about such *regulae iuris* as: "*Expressa nocent, non expressa non nocent*" (*Regula* 84; D. 50.17.195);[87] "*Non videntur qui errant consentire*" (*Regula* 81; D. 50.17.116); "*In toto et pars continetur*" (*Regula* 87;

83 Paulus, D. 50.17.144.

84 More generally, true and authentic jurisconsults must possess two essential qualities: have the greatest knowledge of the Law and demonstrate the most perfect impartiality (they must be the implacable enemies of arbitrariness: "amis de la règle, et par là-même ennemis irréconciliables de l'arbitraire", Dupin, *Manuel*, 15). Like the perfect orator described by Cicero (*De oratore*, II, VI), the jurisconsult must possess in mind all the greatest ideas and values the human intelligence has designed (*omnium rerum magnarum atque artium scientiam*), as Dupin writes in *Notices historiques, critiques et bibliographiques* ... (Paris: Warée, 1820), I. As a consequence, he is expected to get used to the general rules and to the terminology of the legal order. That is the reason why Dupin's *Manuel des étudiants* ends with a lexicon of legal terms (*Vocabulaire des termes de droit*), in which he repeats the famous formula of the Digest: *ominis definitio in iure civili periculosa est.*

85 Dupin, *Manuel*, 15: "Un gouvernement constitutionnel est éminemment le gouvernement du droit".

86 Editor's note: In the FWO.OPR.2020.005001 database, this *regula* is registered under No. 253.

87 Editor's note: In the FWO.OPR.2020.005001 database, this *regula* is registered under No. 1028.

D. 50.17.113);[88] "*In ambiguo sermone, non utrumque dicimus, sed id duntaxat quod volumus*" (*Regula* 88). Other examples of this type of directives are provided by *Regula* 62.2 ("*adversus periculum naturalis ratio permittit se defendere*"), *Regula* 64 ("*prodesse unusquisque sibi, dùm alii non nocet, non prohibetur*"),[89] which is formulated by Dupin on the basis of D. 39.3.1.11 (Ulpian)[90] and outlines the reasonable limits within which each individual can legitimately carry out his activities, leaving to the courts the care of deciding on the fate of acts performed outside these limits. All these *regulae* are binding on the courts when it comes to interpreting the legal acts of individuals and their conduct.[91]

2.3 Regulae Iuris *as a Vehicle for Ethical and Social Values*

It is likely that the Roman jurists of the classical period considered the *regulae iuris* (like the rules of contract interpretation for example) as mere elements of rhetoric, that is, as *ad hoc* arguments available to lawyers to win a case. This is not the case of Domat and Dupin, who characterise the *regulae iuris* by their content, which they determine in contemplation of some specific values.

In this respect, Domat's definition of a *regula iuris* that can be found in the preliminary book of the *Loix civiles* closely resembles Paulus' definition as collected in the Digest, with one difference: the word *justice* has replaced the word *ius* ("*les règles du Droit sont des expressions courtes et claires de ce que demande la justice dans les divers cas*": short and clear formulations of what justice requires in various cases).[92] This substitution is basically the result of

88 Editor's note: In the FWO.OPR.2020.005001 database, this *regula* is registered under No. 41.

89 Dupin, "*Prolegomena,*" in *Manuel*, 296. According to this *regula*, people are not prohibited to optimise their profits as long as no harm or no damage is done to another. This *regula* is to be understood and applied in conjunction with *Regula* 70.1 ("*Ubi periculum, ibi et lucrum collocetur*"), which states that those who derive benefits from their activity must assume the risks caused by their activity.

90 D. 39.3.1.11: "*Idem aiunt aquam pluviam in suo retinere vel superficientem ex vicini in suum derivare, dum opus in alieno non fiat, omnibus ius esse* (*prodesse enim sibi unusquisque, dum alii non nocet, non prohibetur*) *nec quemquam hoc nomine teneri*".

91 This *regula*, built on a commentary from Gaius on the *lex Aquilia* (D. 9.2.4, Gaius: "*Itaque si servum tuum latronem insidiantem mihi occidero, securus ero: nam adversus periculum naturalis ratio permittit se defendere*"), is an invitation to the courts to take into account self-defence as a cause of exemption from liability.

92 Domat, *Loix civiles*, Liv. prélim., I, I, I. Likewise, Daguesseau, a few years after Domat, will describe the general principles of French law as "conséquences directement tirées des règles de la justice naturelle" (consequences directly derived from the rules of natural justice). See: Daguesseau, *Œuvres de Pothier*, 1ère instruction.

the rejection of legalistic positivism, and it opens up the possibility of looking for *regulae iuris* well beyond the repository constituted by D. 50.17, since a *regula* deserves to be identified as such less because of its historical origin than by virtue of its conformity to reason and justice. It matters little in this respect that *Les loix civiles*, in the chapter *Des règles du droit en général*, classify the "*règle du droit en général*" into two categories, whether they are natural or civil/positive according to their origin. The first one, like all natural laws, are given by God and characterised by the fact that they are the expression of immutable justice.[93] The latter are also not totally disconnected from the spirit of justice, since, although arbitrary (in the sense that Domat gives to this word: arbitrary rules are those which are decreed by a Legislator or those to which a social group has recognised the status of customs), they have their basis in equity.[94]

Dupin takes an identical approach. He does not see the *regulae iuris* only as a means to serve the legal order. He also uses them as a means in the service of the higher values that the legal order should promote. Only philosophy can give a clear idea of the Truth and prevent from basing a reasoning on false ideas or drawing erroneous consequences from a true principle.[95] But when he claims that philosophy is intended to feed *Iurisprudentia*,[96] he does not have in mind what he pejoratively calls *la nouvelle philosophie*,[97] especially that of Kant.[98] He rather refers to the *ancient philosophy* (that of the Greeks and Romans, like Cicero, but also Ulpian)[99] reinvigorated by Christianity,[100] and also Francis Bacon and the representatives of the science of natural law. Anyway, such a reference to philosophy and values proves that the concept of *regulae iuris* cannot be defined only by its operative dimension in the legal

93 Domat, *Loix civiles*, I, I, I, III: "ce sont ces loix qui ont une justice immuable, et qui est la même toujours et par tout".

94 Domat, *Loix civiles*, I, I, II.

95 Loiseau and Dupin, *Dictionnaire des arrêts*, XXIX.

96 Dupin, *Manuel*, 2.

97 Dupin, "*Réflexions*," 27.

98 See: Brami, *Dupin aîné*, 252.

99 D. 1.1.1.1.

100 Dupin, *Manuel*, 3–4: "Etudiez la philosophie; non celte scolastique obscure et futile qui, se comprenant à peine elle-même, ne peut que bien difficilement se communiquer à ses adeptes; mais cette philosophie morale et pratique qu'anime et que rehausse le sentiment religieux, qui est fondée sur la nature et l'organisation de l'homme, sa dignité propre, la connaissance éclairée de ses droits, et la conscience intime de ses devoirs, envers Dieu, envers la patrie, envers les autres hommes; cette philosophie que nous irions chercher encore à l'école de Platon et de Socrate, ou dans les Offices de Cicéron, si elle n'avait pas trouvé son complément et sa sanction dans un livre plus parfait".

order: it also includes a *substantial* dimension, which gives the content of these rules a very high importance. To put it in a more positive way: this content is not axiologically neutral, since both the creation and the implementation of Law are placed under the seal of equity (understood as a higher principle of justice),[101] as recalled by *Regula* 56, that warns against too much deference to the legal science, when such deference is likely to unfairly divert from equity ("*plerumque sub auctoritate iuris scientiae perniciose erratur*").[102]

In order to appreciate the importance of such a substantial criterion, it is worth going back to Dupin's definition of a *regula iuris* developed on the basis of Bacon's *Aphorisms*, especially *Aphorism* 83, in which Bacon claimed that a rule can be referred to as a *regula iuris* under two conditions: (1) if its content is in conformity with Justice ("*quae in forma ipsa justitiae haeret*") and (2) if the existence of this rule is attested in several legal orders. Adopting these two criteria, Dupin distinguishes between the *regulae iuris* themselves and all the other legal rules that can be found in statutes or codes. These two criteria are met, for example, by Article 2 of the French Civil Code, which provides that laws have no retroactive effect (so that Article 2 is both a *loi* and a *regula iuris*). It is however of little importance whether a rule has been transcribed by the legislator into a *loi*, or even a code, or not. Conversely, the fact that the legislator has taken on a *regula iuris* to make it the provision of a *loi* does not change its nature: it is an accidental quality, not an essential one. In sum, it can be said that each article of the French civil code is *une loi*, but only those that concisely ("*breviter concinnata*") formulate righteous and universal truths deserve to be called *regulae iuris*, because they are neither more nor less than the axioms of French law.[103]

---

101 In this regard, we must keep in mind the way Dupin describes the attitude of what he calls a "*good professor of laws*": "qu'un bon professeur[…] ait toujours l'équité devant les yeux; qu'il ne sépare point le Droit de la justice, et qu'il abandonne l'esprit de chicane à l'esprit d'intérêt" (Dupin, *Manuel*, 74). This view is consistant with the definition of Law as the art of distinguishing what is good and fair from what is not (Dupin, "*Notions élémentaires*," in *Manuel*, 323), which is not without recalling the words of Celsus: *ius est ars boni et aequi* (D. 1.1.1).

102 Dupin ties together *Regula* 56 and D. 50.17.202 (*Omnis definitio in iure civili periculosa est: parum est enim, ut non subverti posset*) (Dupin, "*Prolegomena*," in *Manuel*, 291).

103 Dupin, "*Aphorismes de Bacon*," in *Manuel*, 259: "*Sed regularum numero adscribi debet arliculus 2, in quo legimus*: les lois n'ont point d'effet rétroactif: (*non placet Janus in legibus*). *Tale axioma, in forma ipsa justitiae haeret, et apud omnes gentes peraequè custoditur. – Regula igitur haberi polest, omnis propositio generalis quae justa et vera in se est, et breviter concinnata*".

On several occasions,[104] Dupin insists on the fact that these righteous and universal truths are to be extracted from Natural Law, which he regards as constituting the primitive and universal Law, and, as a consequence, as the necessary and indelible part of any legislations. Accordingly, the notions of Good and Evil, Fair and Unfair are not mere social conventions, arbitrary and changeable. They are immanent ideas, whose content is revealed by God.[105] In this respect, the drafting of a catalogue of *regulae iuris* is an opportunity to point out the importance of Natural Law. This importance explains why Dupin distinguishes between the *regulae iuris* drawn directly from the precepts of Natural law (which are brought together in the category he calls: *regulae generales ex Jure naturali deductae*) and the *regulae iuris* that are derived from the *ius civile*. All these *regulae* fulfil the same function in the legal order, only their origin differs, and this difference is sufficient to distinguish them. Dupin does not even bother to justify this distinction, perhaps because it is rather traditional: the method of defining and then classifying the *regulae iuris* according to whether they derive from equity/Natural law or civil law, was already Pothier's method when he undertook to publish a new version of the Digest,[106] and also Domat's method, as mentioned above.

---

104 Dupin, *Manuel*, 4: it is "dans l'étude de la nature que vous irez chercher les grandes pensées".

105 In his comments on *Regula* 74.1 (*civilis ratio naturalia jura corrumpere non potest*), Dupin writes: "*Etenim distinctio boni et mali, justi et iniqui, non verborum est, non conventionis, non sortis, sed Dei ejusque providentiae: substantiae rerum ipsarum inhaeret: praecedit legem humanam quae eam tantùm declarat; adhuc viveret, etiamsi omnia lex humana vertens, injustum justum, malumque bonum vocaret*" (Dupin, "*Prolegomena*", in *Manuel*, 300). Such statements distance him from legal positivism and constructivism.

106 Pothier, *Pandectae Iustinianae*. After Daguesseau (*Œuvres de Pothier*, 463, 1ère instruction), who pointed out the two major defects of D. 50.17 (its incompleteness and the lack of a logical order), Pothier endeavoured not only to arrange D. 50.17 in an order he found more logical to him, but to add new *regulae iuris* to those that Justinian had placed in D. 50.17. He proposed to study these *regulae iuris* according to a specific plan, starting with an approach that could be qualified as *general*, which leads him, first, to distinguish the *regulae* drawn from natural law (which he divided into two categories, depending on whether they arise *ex ipsa rerum natura*, such as the rule "*nemo plus iuris*", or from natural equity, such as, for example, the famous *praecepta iuris* of the *Institutes*) from those based on civil law. As for the second category of *regulae iuris* (*regulae* based on civil law, e.g., "What is vitiated *ab initio* cannot be confirmed by the sole effect of time"), they were listed one after the other, starting with those which are of legislative origin, then continuing with those which are of customary origin, and finally ending with those which consist of privileges and result from particular decisions (like the Roman *rescripta*).

Anyway, the *regulae iuris ex iure naturali deductae* put in legal words the precepts inherent to human nature ("*insitae et quasi consignatae in animis nostris*" notions).[107] In the list of these specific *regulae iuris*, D. 1.1.10.1 (Ulpian: "*Iuris praecepta sunt haec: honeste vivere, alterum non laedere,*[108] *suum cuique tribuere*")[109] occupies the first place, undoubtedly because it is a very general statement likely to serve as support for many other rules. This rule is followed by other *regulae*, whose content is precisely intended to safeguard the provisions of the Natural Law. For instance, Dupin raises to the rank of a *regula iuris* (*Regula* 74.1) Gaius' affirmation, according to which *civilis ratio naturalia iura corrumpere non potest.*[110] He also endorses Celsus' affirmation,[111] according to which what is naturally prohibited cannot be confirmed by positive law ("*Quae rerum natura prohibentur, nulla lege confirmata sunt*").[112]

107 This formulation is borrowed from Arnold Vinnius, *In quattuor libros Institutionum Imperialium Commentatius academicus et forensis* (Lyon: de Tournes, 1767), 9, sur *iuris praecepta*: "*ita non tres regulae, sed una tantum proponeretur praeceptorum iuris distributio. Rectius praecepta hic accipiemus generalia quaedam dictata ac praescripta iuris illius communis, quod semper aequum et bonum est, sive notiones quasdam a natura insitas et quasi consignatas in animis nostris*".

108 "*Alterum non laedere*" means, according to Dupin, that the first task of Justice is that no one harms anyone: "*Justitiae primùm munus est, ut ne cui quis noceat*" (Dupin, "*Prolegoma*", in *Manuel*, 292).

109 On the Platonic foundations of Ulpian's *praecepta iuris*, see: Marko Petrak, "Plato and Ulpian's *praecepta iuris*," *Fundamina* 20/2 (2014): 694–701; Wolfgang Waldstein, "Zu Ulpians Definition der Gerechtigkeit (D. 1,1,10 pr.)," in *Festschrift für Werner Flume zum 70. Geburstag*, ed. Horst H. Jakobs, Brigitte Knobbe-Keuk, Eduard Picker, and Jan Wilhelm (Koln: Schmidt, 1978), 213–232; Malte Diesselhorst, "Die Gerechtigkeitsdefinition Ulpians in D. 1,1,10 pr. und die *Praecepta iuris* nach D. 1,1,10,1 sowie ihre Rezeption bei Leibniz und Kant," in *Romisches Recht in der europaischen Tradition*, ed. Okko Behrends, Malte Diesselhorst, and Wulf E. Voss (Ebelsbach: Rolf Gremer, 1985), 185–211; Franco Gallo, "Diritto e giustizia nel titolo primo del Digesto," *Studia et documenta historiae et iuris* 54 (1988): 1–36; Laurens C. Winkel, "Die stoische *οικείωσις-Lehre* und Ulpians Definition der Gerechtigkeit," *Zeitschrift der Savigny-Stiftung für Rechtsgeschichte, romanistische Abteilung* 105 (1988): 669–679; Ulrich Manthe, "Beitrage zur Entwicklung des antiken Gerechtigkeitsbegriffes II: Stoische Würdigkeit und die *iuris praecepta* Ulpians," *Zeitschrift der Savigny-Stiftung* ... 114 (1997): 1–26.

110 D. 4.5.8, where Gaius explains that *capitis deminutio* does not extinguish natural obligations.

111 D. 50.17.188.1.

112 Other examples can be given, such as *Regula* 74.2 (*Legum subtilitate*[...] *rei veritas deleta vel confusa non est*), built on the basis of C. 5.12.30, where Justinian explained that, although the positive laws consider that the dowry goods are in the husband's *dominium* during the marriage – what Justinian called "a subtlety of the laws" – these goods continue *in truth* to belong to the woman.

That being said, Dupin reiterates the distinction already made by the Glossators in the Middle Ages between *aequitas scripta* and *aequitas non scripta*,[113] and he gives his preference to the former.[114] Commenting on Paulus, D. 50.17.90 ("*In omnibus quidem, maxime tamen in iure aequitas spectanda est*"), he explains that the equity referred to in this fragment is "civil equity", the requirements of which are precisely shaped by means of the *regulae iuris*.[115] In doing so, Dupin fits perfectly in the doctrinal tradition (embodied

113 On this distinction, see: Eduard M. Meijers, "Le conflit entre l'équité et la loi chez les premiers glossateurs," *Tijdschrift voor Rechtsgeschiedenis* 17 (1941): 117–141; Marguerite Boulet-Sautel, "Equité, Justice et Droit chez les glossateurs du XIIe siècle," *Recueils de Memoires et Travaux de l'Université de Montpellier* 2 (1951): 1–8; Ennio Cortese, *La Norma Giuridica* (Milano: Giuffré, 1964), 322; Philippe Godding, "L'interprétation de la "loi" dans le droit savant médiéval et dans le droit des Pays-Bas méridionaux," in: *L'interprétation en droit*, ed. Michel van de Kerchove (Bruxelles: Presses universitaires Saint-Louis, 1978), 445.

114 Dupin does not hesitate to criticise the "*équité naturelle*", which he compares to a *glimmer of reason* –"*lueur de raison*"– spread by Nature in all human minds, but always likely to degenerate into illusion or arbitrariness, insofar as it always ends up identifying with the whims or interests of those who invoke it. He relies in that respect on the authority of the ancient French jurisconsults (Dargentré, Daguesseau, Dumoulin, Bouhier ...), which, incidentally, shows that the Napoleonic codification did not introduce a break in the way of reasoning. See: Loiseau and Dupin, *Dictionnaire des arrêts*, XXVIII: "Il y a des Arrêts qu'on appelle d'équité. Rien, en apparence, d'aussi louable et d'aussi bon: *Nam aequitas in omnibus quidem rebus, maxime tamen in jure spectanda est.* L. 90, ff. *de reg. jur.* Mais il n'y a rien où l'on soit si sujet à se tromper, et c'est ce qui m'engage à entrer sur cela dans quelques éclaircissemens". Dupin bases his analysis on Jean Bouhier (*Observations sur la Coutume de Bourgogne* (Paris: Augé, 1742)) and goes on to write: "Communément on entend par équité cette lueur de raison que la nature a répandue dans tous les esprits; et l'on ne peut nier, en effet, qu'elle ne soit le fond de la saine Jurisprudence. Cependant, comme cette lueur pourrait dégénérer en illusion, et souvent même devenir arbitraire, suivant le caprice ou l'intérêt des hommes, les Législateurs ont senti le besoin d'en fixer les règles par des décisions réfléchies et méditées, qu'ils ont appelées équité civile" (with a quotation to Quintilian, *Declam.* 264: "*Credo fuisse tempora aliquando quae solam et nudam justitiae haberent aestimationem ...*".

115 Civil equity is natural equity contained within its just and reasonable limits. To make understand the difference between civil equity and natural equity and the need to restrict natural equity by civil equity, Dupin takes as an example the person who holds someone else's property: according to natural equity, he is always under the obligation to return what does not belong to him; according to civil equity, the owner can no longer claim the thing after a too long delay, because acquisitive prescription is a legal mechanism contrary to natural equity, but necessary to protect the possessor and all those who have, in good faith, acquired rights over the thing thanks to him (Loiseau and Dupin, *Dictionnaire des arrêts*, I:XXVII–XXVIII: "Ce qui prouve que quand on nous ordonne de suivre l'équité, ce n'est pas toujours celle que nous inspire la nature et qui pourrait quelquefois nous abuser, mais, avant tout, celle qui est dirigée par les Lois",

in particular by Donellus) which tends to regard these *praecepta* not just as philosophical or moral guidelines, but as legal standards.[116] But, whereas Domat expressly qualifies them as general rules of law ("*règles du droit générales*")[117] and claims that there is no gap between the special legal rules of positive law and the *regulae iuris/praecepta iuris* on which they are based,[118] it seems that, in Dupin's eyes (and this is undoubtedly a consequence of the codification), these rules have more the nature of what we would today call soft law. Indeed, as standard-setting instruments, directives, whose function is to shape the social and economic behaviours and patterns of conduct of the individuals, they are authentic normative rules: (1) their normativity is a legal normativity and not only a moral one, if by *normativity* we designate all the techniques by which the Law, without necessarily resorting to a jurisdictional constraint, seeks to guide human behaviour; (2) however, they are not prescriptive rules, insofar as Dupin does not say a word about the practical consequences that could result from not following these rules.

3 Conclusion

A number of conclusions can be drawn from the foregoing, both with regard to Domat's and Dupin's legal conceptions and with regard to the concept of *regulae iuris* itself. There are several reasons for the interest that Domat and Dupin and, through them, the French legal doctrine of the time, took in *regulae iuris* (both as a concept and as a tool). Firstly, it is a way for them to emphasise the place and role of doctrine. At a time when the *ius publice*

where Dupin justifies this assertion on the basis of the authority of Roman Law and Cujas (*de Feudis*, in tit. 1, lib. 2).

116 In Rome, these *praecepta iuris* were rather meta-legal principles, statements which were not strictly speaking considered legal norms of positive Law, but which rather served to clarify the ends that positive Law was supposed to achieve. Perhaps the gradual integration of these *praecepta* into the legal sphere began with some medieval commentators. Pierre de Belleperche, for example, did not hesitate to link these *praecepta* directly to precise legal rules of positive Law. He thus made the obligation to repair the damage caused the immediate consequence of the *praeceptum* "*alterum non laedere*", explaining that whoever harms the interests of others is in fact acting in direct contravention of this *praeceptum* ("*qui laedit alterum contra iuris praecepta facit*", Pierre de Belleperche, *In libros Institutionum* … (Lyon: Vincenti, 1536), 53).

117 Domat, *Loix civiles*, Liv. prélim., I, I, V.

118 In Domat's view, the *règles du droit générales* are fully integrated into the legal sphere, of which they are the elementary rules in the sense that, from them and by means of a logical-deductive reasoning, other legal rules, the more special ones, can be deduced.

respondendi[119] no longer exists, the French legal doctrine continues to assert that it is up to them to reveal the general principles of French Law likely to provide a framework for the courts' job. Secondly, placing French law under the patronage of these *regulae iuris* makes it possible to affirm the permanence of what might be called the "spirit" of French law, to link the present to the past (Rome), insofar as Domat and Dupin share the same legal culture,[120] strongly imbued with Roman law and references to an immutable natural law. Even if they create new *regulae*, they do so on the basis of natural law and equity conceived in a traditional way and therefore stable over time. As far as Dupin is concerned, this has two advantages: on the one hand, it reconnects French law with the past by stepping over the French Revolution and the Civil Code;[121] on the other hand, it responds to Savigny's criticism of the French Civil Code, according to which the Civil Code created the Law *ex nihilo* and in contempt of the past. Against what has been called the "German impulse",[122] the message is clear: France is still the homeland of the legal science, French law has its *rules of rules*, in line with the French national genius. More broadly, Dupin is convinced that the elementary language of the law, which the *regulae iuris* are designed to specify, was fixed by the great

119 See: Fernand de Visscher and Mathieu Nicolau, "Le 'IUS PUBLICE RESPONDENDI'," *Revue historique de droit français et étranger* 15 (1936): 615–650; Andre Magdelain, "Jus respondendi," in *id, Jus imperium auctoritas. Études de droit romain* (Rome: Ecole française de Rome, 1990), 103–152; Kaius Tuori, "The ius respondendi and the Freedom of Roman Jurisprudence," *Revue Internationale des droits de l'Antiquité* 51 (2004): 295–337; Aldo Schiavone, "L'auctoritas des juristes et le ius publice respondendi ex auctoritate principis," in *L'auctoritas à Rome: une notion constitutive de la culture politique*, ed. Jean-Michel David and Frederic Hurlet (Bordeaux: Ausonius, 2020), 315–322.

120 This expression is not taken here in its sociological sense (legal culture as a set of mechanisms for acculturation to the law), but in its ordinary sense, to designate the values and ways of representing what the law is. On the different meanings of this expression, see: Frédéric Audren, Jean-Louis Halpérin, *La culture juridique française, Entre mythes et réalités XIXe–XXe siècles* (Paris: CNRS, 2013), https://doi.org/10.7202/1028145ar.

121 For instance, Dupin, about D. 50.17.32 (*omnes homines aequales sunt*), claims that the principle of equality before law, which prevailed in the ancient republics, has also and always been adopted in France, both before and since the Revolution (which amounts to passing over the silence the legal inequalities induced by the existence of privileges in Ancient France!). See: Dupin, *Manuel*, 76: "Notre professeur enseignera que ces maximes ne sont pas seulement celles des républiques, qu'elles sont aussi celles de la vieille comme de la nouvelle France; qu'on les retrouve dans les anciennes ordonnances de nos rois aussi bien que dans la Charte constitutionnelle".

122 See: Donald R. Kelley, *Historians and the Law in Post Revolutionary France* (Princeton: Princeton U.P., 1984).

jurists of the past centuries, in particular by Cujas, Heineccius, Domat, or Pothier,[123] and he is also convinced that this language, collected in the *regulae iuris*, should be enough for the needs of modern jurists, which is a way of saying that they do not have to formulate a new language based on the Civil Code.

Regarding the very concept of *regula iuris*, another conclusion may be that, according to the French legal doctrine (from the Modern Age till the early 19th century), the existence of a *regula iuris* presupposes the conjunction of three criteria: (1) a formal one: a *regula iuris* must be stated briefly, in a few words, not only because this brevity is the result of the effort of synthesis carried out by its author, but because this *brevitas* makes it easier to learn and to memorise it;[124] (2) a functional one, insofar as it is because of its role within the legal order, that is to say its usefulness, that a statement deserves to be set up as a *regula iuris*; and (3) a substantial one, since it's about promoting some values (in this regard, referring to *regulae iuris* is a way of perpetuating the presence, in a codified system, of certain precepts and of certain values, which are intended to guide the education of jurists, the drafting of legislation and the judicial implementation of law, since they are aimed at both students, legislators and judges). Of these three criteria, only the first two were foreseen by Roman jurists, while the third originates in the junction made by some medieval commentators of the *Corpus iuris civilis* and then by the modern judicial science of the natural law between the concept of *regulae iuris* and the concept of *praecepta iuris*. Anyway, this third criterion sheds light on an important point: shaping *regulae iuris* is perceived as an opportunity to tie in an inextricable way two facets of legal science, didactics and dogmatic, insofar as the role of these rules also consists in directing the operation of the Law towards a certain purpose: Justice and Truth, or at least what an authentic jurist should consider as Justice and Truth. Presenting the Law as a body organised by means of general rules that are themselves no more than the logical consequence drawn by the intellect from the demands of human nature puts the legal doctrine in a comfortable position and gives scholars a considerable advantage: they can put forward their vision as if it were self-evident, a necessity even, the result of a knowledge/expertise itself presented as neutral.

The fact remains that, after Domat and Dupin, French legal doctrine stopped using this concept in favour of what are now called "*les principles généraux du droit*", for the identification and formulation of which they no

---

123 Dupin, *Manuel*, 64.

124 Dupin, "*Prolegomena*," in *Manuel*, 274.

longer seek inspiration in Roman law, because the Civil Code itself is now expected to provide the materials necessary for the construction of a "*théorie générale du droit civil*".[125] Talking of *principes* rather than *regulae iuris* is not just a change of terminology, but reveals a paradigm shift: it reflects the victory of legalistic positivism. The consequence of this positivist tendency would be that, henceforth, the distinction between principles and rules would take on a different aspect: a principle is a general statement which is not formulated by the positive law, whose axiological content is manifest and whose implementation assumes that it is combined with other competing principles, while the rules consist of provisions of positive law, whose scope of application is not limited to a single type of case and whose application excludes the application of any other rule (a rule applies, or it does not apply, but it does not apply more or less, unlike a principle).

Bibliography

Sources

Aubry, Charles, and Charles Rau, *Cours de droit civil français*. Strasbourg: Lagier, 1839.

Bacon, Francis. *Les Aphorismes du droit, traduits du latin*. Translated by Jean Baudoin. Paris: s.l., 1646.

Belleperche, Pierre de. *In libros Institutionum ... Commentarii longe acutissimi*. Lyon: Vincenti, 1536.

Bouhier, Jean. *Observations sur la Coutume de Bourgogne*. Paris: Augé, 1742.

Daguesseau, Francois-Henri. *Œuvres complètes du Chancelier Daguesseau*. 16 vols. Paris: Fantin, 1819.

Domat, Jean. *Les loix civiles dans leur ordre naturel*. 5 vols. Paris: J.-B. Coignard, 1697.

Dupin, André M.J.J. *Manuel des étudians en droit et des jeunes avocats, recueil d'opuscules de jurisprudence*. Paris: Joubert, 1835.

Dupin, André M.J.J. *Notices historiques, critiques et bibliographiques*. Paris: Warée, 1820.

Dupin, André M.J.J. *Oeuvres de Pothier: contenant les traités du droit français*. 11 vols. Paris: Béchet, 1823–35.

Dupin, André M.J.J. *Principia juris civilis tum romani, legum romanorum ex corpore Justinianeo depromptarum*. Paris: Marchant, 1806.

Dupin, André M.J.J. *Réquisitoires, plaidoyers et discours de rentrée*. 14 vols. Paris: Videcoq, 1836.

125 Aubry and Rau, *Cours de droit civil*, I, § 7.

Hotman, François. *Observationum in ius civile libri IX*. Paris: Vignon, 1589.

Lanson, Gustave. *Boileau*. Paris: Hanchette, 1919.

Loiseau, Jean-Simon, and André M.J.J. Dupin, *Dictionnaire des arrêts modernes en matière civile et criminelle, de procédure et de commerce*. 2 vols. Paris: Nève, 1814.

Pocquet de Livonnière, Claude. *Règles du droit français*. Paris: J.-B. Coignard, 1730.

Portalis, Jean-Etienne-Marie. *"Discours préliminaire prononcé lors de la presentation du projet de la Commission du Gouvernement."* In *Recueil complet des travaux préparatoires du Code civil*, edited by P. Antoine Fenet, vol. I. Paris: Videcoq, 1836.

Pothier, Robert J. *Pandectae Iustinianae, in novum ordinem digestae*. 24 vols. Paris: Saugrain, Desaint & C, 1752.

Vinnius, Arnold. *In quattuor libros Institutionum Imperialium Commentatius academicus et forensis* (Lyon: de Tournes, 1767)

Literature

Audren, Frederic, and Jean-Louis Halpérin. *La culture juridique française, Entre mythes et réalités XIXe–XXe siècles*. Paris: CNRS, 2013. https://doi.org/10.7202/1028145ar.

Boulet-Sautel, Marguerite. "Equité, Justice et Droit chez les glossateurs du XIIe siècle," *Recueils de Memoires et Travaux de l'Université de Montpellier* 2 (1951): 1–8.

Brami, Frank. *Dupin Aîné (1783–1865), procureur général près la Cour de cassation et jurisconsulte*. Paris: Dalloz, 2013.

Cortese, Ennio. *La Norma Giuridica*. 2 vols. Milano: Giuffré, 1962–64.

Deroussin, David. "Remarques sur les *regulae iuris* et les principes en droit (Temps Modernes)," *Revue historique de droit français et étranger* 90, no. 2 (April–June 2012): 195–235.

Deroussin, David. "Domat, principes, règles du droit." In *Mélanges en l'honneur du Professeur Nicole Dockès*, collected by Maxime Blachon, 313–350. Paris: La Mémoire du droit, 2018.

Diesselhorst, Malte. "Die Gerechtigkeitsdefinition Ulpians in D. 1,1,10 pr. und die *Praecepta iuris* nach D. 1,1,10,1 sowie ihre Rezeption bei Leibniz und Kant." In *Romisches Recht in der europaischen Tradition*, edited by Okko Behrends, Malte Diesselhorst, and Wulf E. Voss, 185–211. Ebelsbach: Rolf Gremer, 1985.

Domingo, Rafael. "The Roman Jurists and the Legal Science." *University of Navarra*. Uploaded 30 June 2017. https://dx.doi.org/10.2139/ssrn.2994130.

Duboulcez, Olivier. "L'ordre géométrique et le dispositif argumentatif des Méditations métaphysiques de René Descartes." *Revue d'histoire des sciences* 2 (2016): 311–334.

Gallo, Franco. "Diritto e giustizia nel titolo primo del Digesto." *Studia et documenta historiae et iuris* 54 (1988): 1–36

Godding, Philippe. "L'interprétation de la "loi" dans le droit savant médiéval et dans le droit des Pays-Bas méridionaux." In *L'interprétation en droit*, edited by Michel van de Kerchove, 443–483. Bruxelles: Presses universitaires Saint-Louis, 1978.

Gordley, James. *The Jurists: A Critical History*. Oxford: Oxford University Press, 2013.

Goyard-Fabre, Simone. "La philosophie du droit de Jean Domat ou la convergence de l'ordre naturel et de l'ordre rationnel." In *Justice et Force: Politiques au temps de Pascal*, edited by Gerard Ferreyrolles, 187–207. Paris: Klincksieck, 1996.

Hart, Herbert L. A. *The Concept of Law*. 2nd ed. Oxford: Oxford University Press, 1994.

Kelley, Donald R. *Historians and the Law in Post Revolutionary France*. Princeton: Princeton University Press, 1984.

Kotlyar, Ilya A. "Medieval juristic regulae: unity or disunity?" *Tijdschrift voor Rechtsgeschiedenis* 89 (2021): 409–438

La Torre, Massimo. "The Hierarchical Model and H. L. A. Hart's Concept of Law," *Revus* 21 (2013): 141–161

Magdelain, André. "Jus respondendi." In *id, Jus imperium auctoritas. Études de droit romain* (Rome: Ecole française de Rome, 1990): 103–152.

Manthe, Ulrich. "Beitrage zur Entwicklung des antiken Gerechtigkeitsbegriffes II: Stoische Würdigkeit und die *iuris praecepta* Ulpians." *Zeitschrift der Savigny-Stiftung für Rechtsgeschichte, romanistische Abteilung* 114 (1997): 1–26.

Meijers, Eduard M. "Le conflit entre l'équité et la loi chez les premiers glossateurs," *Tijdschrift voor Rechtsgeschiedenis* 17 (1941): 117–141.

Nörr, Dieter. "Spruchregel und Generalisierung," *Zeitschrift der Savigny-Stiftung für Rechtsgeschichte, romanistische Abteilung* 89 (1972): 18–93.

Renoux-Zagamé, Marie-France. "Domat, le salut, le droit," *Revue d'histoire des facultés de droit et de la science juridique* 8 (1989): 69–111.

Schiavone, Aldo. "L'auctoritas des juristes et le ius publice respondendi ex auctoritate principis." In *L'auctoritas à Rome: une notion constitutive de la culture politique*, edited by Jean-Michel David and Frederic Hurlet, 315–322. Bordeaux: Ausonius, 2020.

Schmidlin, Bruno. "Horoi, pithana und regulae. Zum Einfluß der Rhetorik une Dialektik auf die juristiche Regelbildung." *Aufstieg und Niedergang der römischen Welt* 2.15 (1976): 101–130.

Schmidlin, Bruno. *Die römischen Rechtsregeln*. Cologne: Böhlau, 1970.

Spector, Celine. "'Il faut éclairer l'histoire par les lois et les lois par l'histoire': statut de la romanité et rationalité des coutumes dans *L'Esprit des lois de Montesquieu*." In *Généalogie des savoirs juridiques: le carrefour des Lumières*, edited by Mikhail Xifaras, 15–41. Bruxelles: Bruylant, 2007.

Stein, Peter. "The Digest Title de *diversis regulis iuris antiqui* and the General Principles of Law." In *Essays in Jurisprudence in Honour of Roscoe Pound*, edited by Ralph A. Newman, 1–20. New York: Bobbs-Merrill Co, 1962.

Stein, Peter. *Regulae iuris. From Juristic Rules to Legal Maxims*. Edinburgh: Edinburgh University Press, 1966.

Swaminathan, Shivprasad. "*Mos Geometricus* and the Common Law Mind: Interrogating Contract Theory." *The Modern Law Review* 82–1 (Jan 2019): 46–70.

Tuori, Kaius. "The ius respondendi and the Freedom of Roman Jurisprudence." *Revue Internationale des droits de l'Antiquité* 51 (2004): 295–337.

Visscher, Fernand de, and Nicolau, Mathieu. "Le 'IUS PUBLICE RESPONDENDI'," *Revue historique de droit français et étranger* 15 (1936): 615–650.

Waldstein, Wolfgang. "Zu Ulpians Definition der Gerechtigkeit (D. 1,1,10 pr.)." In *Festschrift für Werner Flume zum 70. Geburstag*, edited by Horst H. Jakobs, Brigitte Knobbe-Keuk, Eduard Picker, and Jan Wilhelm, 213–232. Koln: Schmidt, 1978.

Wibier, Matthijs. "Marcus Antistius Labeo and the Idea of Legal Literature." In *Roman Law and Latin Literature*, edited by Ioannis Ziogas and Erica Bexley, 125–144. London: Bloomsbury, 2022.

Winkel, Laurens C. "Die stoische *οικείωσις* und Ulpians Definition der Gerechtigkeit." *Zeitschrift der Savigny-Stiftung für Rechtsgeschichte, romanistische Abteilung* 105 (1988): 669–679.

Winkel, Laurens C. "A Note on Regulae Iuris in Roman Law and on Dworkin's Distinction between Rules and Principles." In *Critical Studies in Ancient Law, Comparative Law and Legal History: Essays in Honour of Alan Watson*, edited by John W. Cairns and Olivia F. Robinson, 413–418. London: Hart, 2001.

Zarka, Yves-Charles. *Philosophie et politique à l'âge classique*. Paris: Hermann, 2016.

Zyl, Deon H. van. *Cicero's Legal Philosophy*. Roodeport: Digma Publications, 1986.

CHAPTER 5

Does Truth Fear No Scandal? On the *Regulae Iuris* and the Legal Commentaries in Canon Law (12th–17th Centuries)

Piotr Alexandrowicz

1 Introduction

The *regulae iuris* in medieval Canon law were listed in several compilations of papal letters and ancient laws such as *Compilatio prima* by Bernard of Pavia (1 Comp 5.37), the Decretals by Gregory IX (*Liber extra*; X 5.41) and the Sext (*Liber Sextus*; VI 5.13).[1] While the latter is without doubt the best-known of these and has received the broadest recognition in legal science, this paper focuses on the former two. All eleven *regulae iuris* from *Liber extra* were inspired by the rules from *Compilatio prima*. One of these was the rule excerpted from the homily of Bede, stating that it is more useful to allow scandal than to abandon the truth – c. *Qui scandalizaverit*: "Utilius scandalum nasci permittitur, quam veritas relinquatur" (1 Comp 5.37.9; X 5.41.3).[2] The broad scholarship dedicated to the notion of *scandalum* in medieval Canon law makes it possible to better understand the role of this *regula iuris* in the Canon law approach to *scandalum*.[3] Therefore, I will not present the complex and detailed history of *scandalum* as such; I have two other main objectives.

1 For an introduction on *regulae iuris* in Canon law, see Andrea Zuffellato, "Il *Tractatus de regulis juris* di Anacleto Reiffenstuel: spunti critici per una traduzione ragionata" (Ph.D. diss., Universitá degli Studi di Padova, 2014), 9–19; Fernando Jesús González, "Significación de las Palabras y Reglas del Derecho (DCH)" *Max Planck Institute for Legal History and Legal Theory Research Paper Series*, No 2025-01, 1–9.

2 For a general survey on the role concept of truth in medieval Canon law, see Corinne Leveleux-Teixeira, "Droit et verité: Le point de vue de la doctrine médiévale (XIIè–XVè)," *Bien dire et bien aprandre – Revue de médiévistique* 23 (2005): 333–49.

3 See i.a. Capucine Nemo-Pekelman, "Scandale et vérité dans la doctrine canonique médiévale (XIIe–XIIIe siècles)", *Revue historique de droit français et étranger* 85, no 4 (2007): 491–504; Arnaud-Vivien Fossier, "*Propter vitandum scandalum*: Histoire d'une catégorie juridique (XIIe–XVe siècles)", *Mélanges de l'École française de Rome – Moyen Âge* 121, no 2 (2009): 317–48; Corinne Leveleux-Teixeira, "Le droit canonique médiéval et l'horreur du scandale", *Cahiers de recherches médiévales et humanistes* 25 (2013): 193–211; Wouter Druwé, *Scandalum in the Early Bolognese Decretistic and in Papal Decretals (ca.1140–1234)* (Leuven: Peeters, 2018); Raffaella Bianchi Riva, "Il giudice e la misericordia. Riflessioni sull'amminis-

 | DOI:10.1163/9789004736092_007

First, to illustrate the evolving relationship between the *regula* and the legal text as well as the evolving meaning of the *regula* under the influence of its textual context (on the example of c. *Qui scandalizaverit*). Second, to show the evolution of the genre of legal commentary on the basis of this case study dedicated to c. *Qui scandalizaverit* from the rise of this form of legal communication in the 12th century, through its most renowned 15th-century examples, up to the decline and exhaustion of this genre in the 17th-century Canon law.[4]

Additionally, this investigation will seek three further clarifications. Firstly, it will highlight the role of c. *Qui scandalizaverit* for the category of *scandalum* in Canon law and the evolution of the meaning and relevance of *scandalum*. Secondly, it will help us to understand the different role of *De regulis iuris* in *Liber extra* and *Liber Sextus*, as to the former the commentaries of the canonists were very concise or even non-existent, while to the latter the canonists dedicated even separate volumes focusing only on legal rules. And thirdly, it will explain the role of the *summarium* to X 5.41.3 as it shaped the understanding of the core *ratio* of this chapter but was only later added to the printed source editions of *Liber extra*.

All of this will be achieved through the investigation of the commentaries to c. *Qui scandalizaverit* between the 12th and 17th centuries. I will apply a broad definition of commentary and I will focus here on these sources which were printed in the early modern period and which, therefore, may provisionally be considered as the most relevant.

2 The Origins and Interpretation of c. *Qui scandalizaverit* up to 1234

The content of c. *Qui scandalizaverit* was not coined by the medieval canonists. As was the case for many *regulae*, it was rooted in the ancient Christian writings. Even though I will focus here on the history of this saying as a *regula iuris*, it should be briefly outlined how this rule was integrated into the corpus of legal texts.

---

trazione della giustizia nel diritto canonico classico," *Vergentis* 5 (2017): 185–219; Raffaella Bianchi Riva, *Lo scandalo tra alto medioevo e prima età moderna: Itinerari tra dimensione giuridica, politica e sociale* (Torino: Giappichelli, 2022).

4 On the genre of legal commentary in Canon law, see i.a. Peter Erdö, *Storia della scienza del diritto canonico: Una introduzione* (Roma: Editrice Pontificia Università Gregoriana, 1999), 93–97; 113–16, 145–46; Andreas Thier, "Zwischen Exegesesammlung und Ordnungsentwurf: Zur Kommentarliteratur des gelehrten Rechts in der Frühen Neuzeit," in *Kommentare in Recht und Religion*, ed. David Kästle and Niels Jansen (Tübingen: Mohr Siebeck, 2014), 235–246.

From the inscription to 1 Comp 5.37.9 as well as to X 5.41.3, we can learn that this sentence was excerpted from the homily of Bede the Venerable (672/673–735) from the passage starting with the words "*qui scandalizaverit etc*". It referred to Bede's homily, which comments on one of the most well-known passages in the Gospels about scandal, where Jesus said: "But he that shall scandalize one of these little ones that believe in me, it were better for him that a millstone should be hanged about his neck, and that he should be drowned in the depth of the sea" (Matthew 18,6 in Douay–Rheims translation; cf. Mark 9,41). In the homily in the passage beginning with "*Et quisquis scandalizaverit*", we find the relevant words: "*Utilius scandalum nasci permittitur, quam veritas relinquatur*".[5] Also in the literature, the origins of this canon are sometimes simply linked with Bede's homily.[6] It seems, however, that Bede's phrase was a quotation from even older writings of Gregory the Great (c. 540–604).[7] In his commentary to Ezechiel, he used exactly the same wording: "*Si autem de veritate scandalum sumitur, utilius permittitur nasci scandalum quam veritas relinquatur*".[8] This approach to *scandalum* was, therefore, firmly established in the ancient Christian teaching, and it was also recorded in medieval theology at the latest in the writings of Bernard of Clairvaux (1090–1053).[9] Bernard of Pavia (?–1213) found this passage relevant and excerpted it from Bede's homily to include it in the final title of his *Breviarium extravagantium* (*Compilatio prima*) around 1191.[10]

5 If not indicated otherwise, all quotations from the *Corpus iuris canonici* are taken from Friedberg's edition. The 67th Homily of Bede containing this phrase can be found in PL 94 442C.

6 See Ulrich Bubenheimer, "*Scandalum et ius divinum*: Theologische und rechtstheologische Probleme der ersten reformatorischen Innovationen in Wittenberg 1521/22", in *Wittenberg 1517–1522: Diskussions-, Aktionsgemeinschaft und Stadtreformation*, ed. Thomas Kaufmann and Alejandro Zorzin (Tübingen: Mohr Siebeck, 2023), 208.

7 Marie-Anselme Dimier, "A propos du Congrès Bernardin," *Revue d'histoire ecclésiastique* 50 (1955): 547; Nemo-Pekelman, "Scandale," 498–99.

8 Gregory the Great, *Sancti Gregorii Magni Homiliae in Hiezechielem prophetam*, ed. Marc Adriaen (Turnhout: Brepols, 1971), 85, lib. 1, hom. 7, num. 5 (cf. PL 76 842C). Gregory used the same phrase two times, see Matthias Schmoeckel, *Die Jugend der Justitia. Archäologie der Gerechtigkeit im Prozessrecht der Patristik* (Tübingen: Mohr Siebeck, 2013), 70, n. 55 and 56.

9 Dimier, "A propos," 547; Schmoeckel, *Die Jugend*, 70, n. 56; for an overview on the legal notion of *scandalum* in antiquity and beyond, see Ulrich Hilp, *"Den bösen Schein vermeiden". Zu Ethos und Recht des Amtes in Kirche und Staat* (Berlin: Duncker & Humblot, 2004), 32–38; Schmoeckel, *Die Jugend*, 67–73.

10 We may note that, in the early modern edition of *Compilatio prima*, c. *Qui scandalizaverit* was phrased only with minor changes in comparison to Bede's homily: "Qui scandalizatur etc. utilius scandalum nasci permittatur, quam veritas relinquatur". See Bernard of

However, it was not the first time these words had attracted the attention of medieval canonists.[11] This very same passage was also cited by Simon of Bisignano (fl. 1174–1179) with direct mention of Gregory the Great as the original author. In his *Summa* to the *Decretum*, he commented on C. 11, q.3, c. 22, saying:

> Non faciatis malum unde homines scandalizentur. Bonum vero propter scandalum non est dimittendum, nam teste Gregorio utilius scandalum nasci permittitur quam ut veritas relinquatur.[12]

Whether Bernard found this passage and decided to include it in his *Breviarium* via Simon's *Summa* is not known, but, as Bernard attributed it to Bede and not to Gregory (as did Simon), it is not very likely.[13]

Interestingly, Corinne Leveleux-Teixeira (possibly inspired by Capucine Nemo-Pekelman) indicated that c. *Qui scandalizaverit* in *Compilatio prima* contained the longer passage from Bede's homily, starting with the words "*qui scandalizaverit*"[14] and closing with "*relinquatur*".[15] This would mean that Bernard intended to include as *regula iuris* a much longer passage from Bede (longer even than the one translated by Leveleux-Teixeira in her article). This might not be the case as she referred at this point to Friedberg's edition of *Compilatio prima* where this canon is not quoted *in extenso*. Three consulted manuscripts, as well as the early modern edition of *Compilatio prima*,[16] do not include the full reference to Bede, only the first words with "etc" (as cited above), and that rather means that these first two words were used only to indicate where the sentence quoted from the Homily should be found.

As part of *Compilatio prima*, c. *Qui scandalizaverit* was commented on by the early decretalists; however, as these early glosses fall outside the main

---

Pavia, "*Breviarium extra*", in *Antiquae collectiones Decretalium*, ed. Antonio Agustín (Lérida: apud Petrum Rob. et Ioannem a Villanova, 1576), fo. 85rb.

11 Contrary to what Nemo-Pekelman, "Scandale,", 498–500, indicated in his study, as noted by Druwé, *Scandalum*, 49, n. 74.

12 Cited after Druwé, *Scandalum*, 49, n. 74.

13 Cf. Bernard of Pavia, *Breviarium decretalium Bernardi Papiensis*, Archiwum i Biblioteka Krakowskiej Kapituły Katedralnej, Ms 89, fo. 62ra; Bernard of Pavia, *Decretalium Compilatio prima cum apparatu Tancredi, et glossulis*, BAV, Vat. lat. 1377, fo. 98va; Bernard of Pavia, *Decretalium Compilatio prima cum Glossa ordinaria Tancredi Bononiensis*, BAV, Borgh. 264, fol. 74va.

14 Or rather "Et quisquis scandalizaverit", as this was verbatim the phrase in Bede's homily.

15 Leveleux-Teixeira, "Le droit canonique", 204. See also Nemo-Pekelman, "Scandale", 498.

16 For the manuscripts, see above n. 13. For the early modern edition, see Bernard of Pavia, "Breviarium extra", fo. 85rb.

scope of this investigation, I will only mention three examples of accounts inspired by this canon before the promulgation of the Decretals. First, there were three rather short glosses to this canon in the apparatus by Tancred of Bologna (c. 1185–1236), some of which were linked to the earlier canonists. Second, in a gloss attributed to Laurentius Hispanus (fl. 1200–1248), a division of three types of truth to which this canon referred had been introduced into the Canon law science.[17] This division was most likely rooted in the works of Jerome (c. 342–420). Laurentius wrote about "the truth of good life" (*veritas bonae vitae*), applicable to everyone, "the truth of justice" (*veritas iustitiae*), applicable to the judge, and "the truth of discipline" (*veritas disciplinae*), applicable to the prelate. The first one should always go before *scandalum*, i.e. in cases involving the threat of a mortal sin one should not refrain from inciting *scandalum*. The remaining two may sometimes be abandoned in order to avoid *scandalum*.[18] Third, the contents of this canon were mentioned by Raymond of Peñafort (c. 1180–1275) in his *Summa de poenitentia*, where he added "*Veritas scilicet vitae, doctrinae, iustitiae*".[19] This division was taken from Peter de Chanter's (?–1197) *Summa de sacramentis et animae consiliis*[20] and was a different version than the one offered by Laurentius. It was also explained in more detail by Raymond.[21]

It is not easy to determine in what sense c. *Qui scandalizaverit* was offered by Bernard as a *regula iuris* and when it started to be treated as such by his fellow canonists. The meaning of the title *De regulis iuris* in *Breviarium extravagantium* did not indicate that Bernard, in his *Compilatio prima*, listed some general legal provisions. He rather understood this term as *constitutio canonica*, i.e. the statutes relevant to the clergy.[22] In light of the research findings of Wouter Druwé, it seems unlikely that Bernard had any clear and sharp concept of *scandalum* in mind while he was editing his work in the late 1180s as there was no established definition or theory of *scandalum* at this time.[23] The canon *Qui scandalizaverit* was rather an interesting passage pointing at the main challenge of all regulations related to *scandalum*, namely the tension

17 Cited after Nemo-Pekelman, "Scandale," 500, n. 46: "Triplex est veritas. Bonae vitae haec numquam omittenda est propter scandalum et ad quaelibet pertinent. Alia iustitiae haec pertinet ad iudicem, alia diciplinae haec ad praelatum, haec quandoque propter scandalum omittitur".

18 Nemo-Pekelman, "Scandale," 500.

19 Druwé, *Scandalum*, 88, n. 18.

20 Leveleux-Teixeira, "Le droit canonique," 206.

21 Leveleux-Teixeira, "Le droit canonique," 206–07.

22 Nemo-Pekelman, "Scandale," 498.

23 Druwé, *Scandalum*, 91.

between *scandalum* and truth. This had already been noted by Simon and later highlighted in the gloss to this canon by Laurentius. We may speculate that originally this *regula iuris* was meant to remind the clerics of the main challenge related to *scandalum* in the ecclesiastical reality. The earliest commentators of this canon provided some interesting conceptualisations and linked it with many other sources through various references (especially in the gloss of Tancred).[24]

3 The Earliest Commentaries to c. *Qui Scandalizaverit* in *Liber extra*

The canon *Qui scandalizaverit* was reiterated by Raymond in the Decretals, again in the final title of the compilation dedicated to *regulae iuris*.[25] Leveleux-Teixeira rightly pointed out that this was a "double canonisation of the primacy of truth before scandal". First, because it was reiterated as a *regula iuris*. Second, because it was part of an authoritative legal text. There was a certain paradox in this as the truth was seen as a rule and avoiding the scandal was an exception, consequently all laws concerning *scandalum* would not always have had a possibility of application for the sake of public order within the Church.[26] Only when there was no competition between truth and scandal.

As the whole *Liber extra*, this canon quickly attracted the attention of canonists. Geoffrey of Trani (Goffredus, d. 1245) authored a *summa titulorum* but he did include some specific comments on the particular chapters from each title of the Decretals. He started his commentary on *De regulis iuris* with a short presentation of the concept of *regula iuris* based on the references to the two bodies of law, and he followed with some general observations concerning the challenges of providing definitions in law (as, in the first place, he

24 Cf. on *scandalum* in the decretals of Innocent III, Hilp, *"Den bösen Schein vermeiden,"* 42–47.

25 Leveleux-Teixeira, "Le droit canonique", 204, indicated that the rule was expressed here "de façon plus lapidaire", but for the reasons explained above I think that Raymond simply reiterated this canon without any alterations or abbreviations. She also included *summarium* in her quotation of X 5.41.3 while *summaria* were not part of the Decretals promulgated in 1234. More on this issue see below.

26 Leveleux-Teixeira, "Le droit canonique," 205: "On notera donc que le primat donné à la vérité sur le scandale est doublement canonisé: par sa qualification comme «règle de droit», d'une part; par son inscription dans le recueil officiel du droit pontifical, enseigné dans toutes les universités d'Occident, d'autre part. D'autre part, ce primat de la vérité est exprimé sous une forme paradoxale, qui fait du respect de la vérité la règle et de l'évitement du scandale l'exception, les impératifs d'ordre public étant minorés par rapport à la fin surnaturelle poursuivie par le droit canonique".

equated *regulae iuris* with *diffinitiones iuris*).[27] In his explanation of c. *Qui scandalizaverit*, Geoffrey focused on the meaning of *veritas*. He firstly noted that it could be understood as *veritas fidei* or *veritas bonae vitae*, and, immediately after that, he indicated that there are three types of *veritas*, reiterating the division already indicated by Laurentius. Geoffrey dedicated slightly more attention to the first type of truth, stating that this one should never give precedence to *scandalum* as this would lead to the commission of a mortal sin.[28] He also added references to other relevant legal texts: c. *Quum ex iniuncto* (X 5.32.2) and c. *Non potest* (C. 23, q. 4, c. 32), the latter being the example showing that also in the case of two other types of truth, sometimes the truth should prevail over scandal. After this, he also noted other possible divisions of truth to *veritas vitae*, *veritas doctrinae*, and *veritas iustitiae*: the first should always be saved, while the remaining two were to be forsaken in confrontation with scandal.[29] This latter part of Geoffrey's commentary was an epitomised reiteration of the division introduced and explained more broadly by Raymond in his *Summa* (after Peter de Chanter).

The *Glossa ordinaria* of Bernard of Parma (c. 1200–1266) included two glosses to c. *Qui scandalizaverit*. The first, to the initial words of the canon, provided only a couple of references to the cases relevant for the subject matter.[30] The second gloss began with the division of truth into three, following Laurentius' scheme (and with the addition of a reference to c. *Ut constitueretur* – D. 50, c. 25). More importantly, this teaching, which we may consider as an established one at this point, was supplemented with additional explanations. Bernard stated that this division refers to those issues which are not dispensable and that, in such cases, the universal indispensable law (*ius commune*) is also called "truth". *Veritas iustitiae* should be understood according to what has been said in c. *Sane* (X 1.11.2). In the gloss to this canon, Bernard merged these two divisions of truth and equated *veritas doctrinae* with *veritas disciplinae*. In the discussed canon, there were multiple clergymen who committed delicts as they were led by local customs contrary to the universal

27 Geoffrey of Trani, *Summa super titulis Decretalium* (Lyon: impensis Romani Morin, 1519), fo. 249vab, X 5.41, ad rubricam and nos. 1–2.

28 Geoffrey of Trani, *Summa*, fo. 250rab, X 5.41.3, no. 5.

29 Geoffrey of Trani, *Summa*, fo. 250rb, X 5.41.3, no. 5.

30 Bernard of Parma, "Glossa ordinaria" in *Decretales Dominii Gregorii Papae IX suae integritati una cum glossis restitutae* (Rome: in aedibus populi Romani, 1582), col. 1962–3, X 5.41.3, sv. '*Qui scandalizaverit*': "Collige casum 11 q. 3, inter verba [C. 11, q. 3, c. 55]; et 22 q. 2, primum, in principo [C. 22, q. 2, c. 8]; et 30 q. 5, ita ne [C. 32, q. 5, c. 3]; et supra, de his quae vi metusve causa fiunt, sacris [X 1.40.5]".

law.[31] Bernard noted that solely the number of the clerics involved constituted the core of the delict and was not a cause for impunity. However, this was exactly the case when the truth of justice and doctrine (or discipline) should concede to scandal due to the number of people involved in the delict.[32] Similar reference was also made in a gloss to another relevant canon concerning *scandalum*, i.e. X 1.9.10. There was, however, a certain contradiction within the Gloss, as in the note to the latter canon also *veritas iustitiae* was said to be impossible to abandon for the sake of avoiding scandal.[33]

If we merge these considerations from various passages of the Gloss, we see clearly that there were instances in which *veritas iustitiae,* or *ius commune,* should concede to the threat of a great scandal.[34] Bernard complemented this explanation with the note that sometimes universal law is not dispensable (and never concedes to the scandal), while sometimes it is dispensable and due to the threat of scandal should be waived.[35] The main achievement of

---

31 On *scandalum* and *multitudo*, see Bianchi Riva, *Lo scandalo*, 116–18.

32 Bernard of Parma, "Glossa ordinaria", col. 250, X 1.11.2, sv. *'Multitudo'*: "In multitudine tamen illis non parcitur, quod magis causam delicti esse constiterit, infra, clerico excommunicato, latores [X 5.27.4]. Et ita propter scandalum aliquid omittitur impunitum, cum alias non esset omittendum, quod fieri potest si veritas non offenditur, quae triplex est, scilicet iustitiae, infra, de regulis iuris, qui scandalizaverit [X 5.41.3]; veritas doctrinae suae disciplinae, 11 q. 3, quando ergo [C. 11, q. 3, c. 23]; veritas bonae vitae, 22 q. 2, primum, in principio [C. 22, q. 2, c. 8]; et 32 q. 5, ita ne [C. 32, q. 5, c. 3]. Haec numquam dimittenda est propter scandalum, 11 q. 3, inter verba [C. 11, q. 3, c. 55], sed veritas iustitiae et veritas doctrinae sive disciplinae quandoque omittitur propter scandalum, puta quando multitudo est in causa, ut hic dicitur. De hoc dicitur supra, de renuntiatione, nisi § pro gravi quoque (X 1.9.10). Veritas iustitiae ad iudicem, doctrinae sive disciplinae ad praelatum, bonae vitae ad quemlibet pertinet. Unde versus: est verum vitae doctrinae iustitiaeque. Primum semper habe, duo propter scandala linque".

33 See Bernard of Parma, "Glossa ordinaria," col. 235, X 1.9.10, sv. *'Distinguendum'*: "Veritas enim bonae vitae vel iustitiae numquam deserenda est, veritas disciplinae quandoque. Tunc autem debet deseri veritas disciplinae quando multitudo peccantium est in causa". See Bianchi Riva, *Lo scandalo*, 137–39.

34 On the tension between *ius dispensabile* and *ius indispensabile*, see Bianchi Riva, *Lo scandalo*, 140–43.

35 Bernard of Parma, "Glossa ordinaria," col. 1963, X 5.41.3, s.v. *'Veritas'*: "Quae triplex est, scilicet bonae vitae: haec nunquam omittenda est propter scandalum, et ad quemlibet pertinet. Alia iustitiae: haec ad iudicem pertinet. Alia disciplinae: haec pertinet ad praelatum. In his duabus quandoque aliqua omittuntur propter scandalum, 50. distinctio, ut constitueretur [D. 50, c. 25]. Et intellige quod hic dicitur de his quae indispensabilia sunt: et tale ius commune, quod indispensabile est, veritas appellatur. De hoc dictum fuit supra, de temporibus ordinationum, sane [X 1.11.2]. Et quod dicitur ibi, veritas iustitiae, intellige secundum quod hic dicitur. Ius commune quandoque indispensabile est, 1 q. ultima, et si illa [C. 1, q. 7, c. 23]. Et de tali hic loquitur: tale ius pro nullo scandalo relaxandum est. Sed quando ius commune dispensabile est propter scandalum receditur

Bernard's gloss was, therefore, a successful merger of two differing divisions of *veritas* and a more or less coherent application of the *regula iuris* concerning *scandalum* in various parts of his work. Clearly, at the latest from this moment on, we can talk about c. *Qui scandalizaverit* as a *regula iuris*: it was supplemented with a sort of definition and thanks to this, it was much more easily applicable to various instances.

The next author whose work should be analysed here was Innocent IV (Sinibaldo Fieschi, born before 1200, died 1254).[36] His *Apparatus* is a testimony to the poor development of the commentaries to *regulae iuris*: the entire volume of his commentary to the last title of *Liber extra* is only slightly in excess of one page of two-column print. To some canons, there was no commentary at all. The apparatus to c. *Qui scandalizaverit* consisted only of a couple of references, the most important of which was the first one, to c. *Nisi* (X 1.9.10).[37] Therein, Innocent IV provided the divisions of truth but he assessed them differently: *veritas bonae vitae* (or *veritas iustitiae*) should never be abolished, while *veritas disciplinae* could concede to *scandalum* in cases of numerous sinners. Interestingly, this was only accurate if there was no risk of a common error: if the numerous sinners actively defend or excuse themselves, one should not have fear of *scandalum* and strive for truth.[38] Innocentius IV, through the invocation of the threat of common error, in this case, established the utility, or social risk, as the relevant criteria for solving the tension between truth and scandal.[39] Indeed, we can add these *rationes* into the guidelines for the application of the *regula iuris* concerning *scandalum*.[40]

In the *Summa aurea* of Henry of Susa (Hostiensis; c. 1200–1271), there was no discussion of any particular *regulae iuris* in the final part of his work.[41] The presentation of *scandalum* by Hostiensis was included in the title dedi-

a iure communi, 50. distinctio, ut constitueretur [D. 50, c. 25]; et 1 q. ultima, dispensationes [C. 1, q. 7, c. 16]; et capitulum exigunt [C. 1, q. 7, c. 18]". See Nemo-Pekelman, "Scandale," 502.

36 On the understanding of *scandalum* by Innocent IV, see Hilp, *"Den bösen Schein vermeiden,"* 49–51.

37 Innocent IV, *Apparatus super quinque libris Decretalium* (Frankfurt am Main: Feierabendt Sigismundus, 1570), fo. 574rb, X 5.41.3.

38 Innocent IV, *Apparatus*, fo. 93va, X 1.9.10, no. 6, sv. '*Distinguendum*'.

39 Leveleux-Teixeira, "Le droit canonique," 207.

40 On the various *rationes* behind legal framework of *scandalum*, see Bianchi Riva, *Lo scandalo*, 177–209.

41 On the understanding of *scandalum* by Hostiensis, see Hilp, *"Den bösen Schein vermeiden,"* 51–54.

cated to *renuntiatio* (X 1.9) and was supported by three references to c. *Qui scandalizaverit*.[42] To this may be given two coherent explanations. First, that each legal concept was discussed simply in the earliest important place within the scope of *Summa* and later only briefly referred to (so he discussed *scandalum* in the chapter from the beginning of his work and not in the very last chapter of *Summa*). Second, that the *regulae iuris* were not treated as separate *sedes materiae* and were only supplementary material; they were useful for legal reasoning, but they did not constitute an autonomous set of laws. The three references to c. *Qui scandalizaverit* may suggest that Hostiensis used this canon as an argumentative resource. In all three instances when Hostiensis pointed at this canon, he presented the more radical opinion that no type of truth could be abandoned in order to avoid scandal. It seems, therefore, that for him c. *Qui scandalizaverit* constituted a general rule that the truth should always prevail: when there was a threat of scandal and the risk of abandoning the truth, the legal rule stated that one should always stick to the truth.

Hostiensis also contributed to the development of the doctrine of *scandalum* within his *Lectura* or *Commentaria*. The commentary to c. *Qui scandalizaverit* was a short compilation of various texts with very small additions by Hostiensis. It consisted of the reference to Mt 18, the list of related cases (as in *Glossa ordinaria*), a clarification that this canon had been excerpted from Bede, and a longer note on *veritas*. In this last part, Hostiensis reiterated verbatim the gloss of Bernard of Parma and only at the very end added that he wrote more about this topic in his commentary to c. *Nisi* and to c. *Sane*.[43] In the commentary to the latter, there was only a passing mention of *scandalum* and no reference to c. *Qui scandalizaverit*.[44] In the passage directly indicated in a longer commentary to c. *Nisi*, we can find observations similar to those given in *Summa aurea*. On two occasions, Hostiensis referred directly to c. *Qui scandalizaverit* in a context similar to the one described above;[45] in one instance, this reference supported Hostiensis' observation that, to avoid scandal, the truth should not be abandoned, as it is also one of the titles of Jesus,

42 Henry of Susa, *Summa aurea* (Venice: apud Iacobum Vitalem, 1574), col. 165–66, X 1.9, nos. 8–9.

43 Henry of Susa, *In quintum Decretalium librum commentaria* (Venice: apud Iuntas, 1581), fo 134ra, X 5.41.3.

44 Henry of Susa, *In primum Decretalium librum commentaria* (Venice: apud Iuntas, 1581), fo. 98va, X 1.11.2, no. 3.

45 Henry of Susa, *In primum*, fo. 92va, X 1.9.10, nos. 63–67.

who called himself "the Truth, the Way, and the Life" and had already been abandoned through sin.[46]

Interestingly, in the earlier part of his commentary to c. *Nisi* (not indicated in the commentary to c. *Qui scandalizaverit*), Hostiensis added a subtle distinction within "the truth of justice". There was the truth of justice of natural law (*veritas iustitiae iuris naturalis*), originating in the divine law and the Gospel, and the truth of justice stemming from positive law (*veritas iustitiae iuris positivi*). The former could never be abandoned to avoid scandal, while the latter was subjected to Canon law and could have been altered, mitigated or even rejected.[47] It was another step towards the sophistication of the concept of *scandalum*: now not only the truth of life should always be given precedence over threat of scandal but also one type of truth of justice, namely the one rooted in divine law. This development may be interpreted as the "instrumentalisation of truth as a concept"[48] – *veritas* was still a major and key value, but in many instances could or even should be negotiated with other values relevant to the ecclesiastical community. This was also a way to reconcile the internal contradictions within the Gloss indicated above.

The last author to comment on c. *Qui scandalizaverit* within the first half-century after its promulgation was Bernard of Montmirat (Abbas Antiquus, c. 1225–1296).[49] In his commentary, he focused on interpreting this canon in light of a case provided by c. *Magnae* (X 3.34.7). The latter decretal addressed the threat of scandal incited by a bishop who pledged to go on a crusade for the sake of his diocese, but, as circumstances changed, the key reason for his vow ceased to exist. Bernard highlighted that the key factor influencing the pope's decision to release the bishop from the vow, despite the threat of scan-

46 Henry of Susa, *In primum*, fo. 92va, X 1.9.10, no. 65, sv. '*Distinguendum*': "non est propter scandalum relinquenda veritas id est filius Dei, qui est via, veritas et vita, et qui relinquitur per peccatum"; cf. Bubenheimer, "*Scandalum*," 209, n. 261.

47 Henry of Susa, *In primum*, fo. 91rb, X 1.9.10, no. 25.

48 Leveleux-Teixeira, "Le droit canonique," 208.

49 Bernard of Montmirat, "Super quinque libris Decretalium lectura aurea certe ac brevi resolutione iuris ambagens enodans," in *Perillustrium doctorum tam veterum quam recentiorum in libros Decretalium aurei commentarii* (Venice: apud Iuntas, 1588), fo. 152ra, X 5.41.3: "Pone casum per decretalem de voto et voti redemptione, c. magnae [X 3.34.7]. Sic. Scandalizantur aliqui, quia Papa cum se ne episcopo dispensavit in voto: quod sine magno periculo non poterat adimplere. Dicit Papa quod non est curandum, quia utilius etc. Ad glossam, quae triplex est, etc. ubi dicit, quod veritas bonae vitae omittenda est propter scandalum. Adde, nisi esset talis bona vita, sine qua salus non habetur, supra de novi operis nuntiatione, c. 2 [X 5.32.2]. Versus: Est verum vitae, doctrinae, iustitieaque: Primum semper habe, duo propter scandala linque. Intelligitur tamen, ut dixi".

dal, was utility and the fact that the bishop would only keep his vow at great risk. Abbas Antiquus added the tripartite division of truth and warned that the truth of life should only be abandoned when there was no risk to salvation, citing the same verses as Hostiensis.

The canonists interpreting and commenting on the *regula iuris* expressed in c. *Qui scandalizaverit* within the first fifty years after the promulgation of *Liber extra* clearly focused on the tension between the truth and scandal. This tension was explained and nuanced by the development of divisions of truth which opened up the path to assess various occurrences of scandals differently. In all of this, they followed in the footsteps of their predecessors and did not create brand-new concepts or interpretations. While the discussion about *scandalum* was mainly conducted on the margin of c. *Nisi*, the actual relevance of c. *Qui scandalizaverit* is not clear. It certainly was of relevance and was referred to in order to protect the truth and combat the potential threat of scandal in clashing with the necessity of truth. At the same time, after Geoffrey and Bernard established the key elements of the framework for the interpretation of *scandalum* and *regula iuris* in c. *Qui scandalizaverit*, the later authors, Innocentius IV and Hostiensis, centred their attention on c. *Nisi* and did not elaborate on the meaning, application, or limitations of this *regula iuris*. On the other hand, this may be interpreted as reflecting the impact of this *regula iuris*, as the tension between truth and scandal formed a relevant part of the discourse on *scandalum* in general.

We also see a certain development of the legal genre here. At the earliest stage of the history of commentary, there were only short glosses directly linked to the selected words of the legal text. After the promulgation of *Liber extra*, forms were developed that still followed the structure of the source but were too elaborate to fit within its margins. Alongside the increase in the volume of commentaries, we can also see an increase in the internal frameworks within them, based on the references to other passages of the text. Of course, this was also a natural part of the earliest glosses and apparatuses, however, it seems that within the works of Innocentius IV and Hostiensis, this kind of internal referencing system was more advanced.

4 Later Medieval Commentaries

The 14th- and 15th-century canonists also commented on c. *Qui scandalizaverit*. As regards these later commentaries, I will solely focus on that canon to highlight how it was perceived as one of the *regulae iuris*. This may be justified by the fact that with the promulgation of *Liber Sextus* in 1298, the *regulae iuris* became much more relevant for Canon law: this very last title of *Liber Sextus* contained 88 *regulae iuris*. It was certainly the most relevant collection of legal rules drafted within medieval Canon law. With the rise in relevance of this concept in papal law and in the science of Canon law, the earlier *regulae iuris*, i.e. those listed in *Liber extra*, also received more attention. Therefore, I will report on how c. *Qui scandalizaverit* was commented on by late medieval authors.

Giovanni d'Andrea (Johannes Andreae, c. 1270–1348) is best known for his *Novella* to *Liber Sextus*, but among his many works he authored also *Novella*, i.e. the commentary, to *Liber extra*.[50] He wrote about c. *Qui scandalizaverit* very briefly but his comment is quite complicated as it consists of a series of references to *Glossa ordinaria*. He started with the references to the Gospel of Matthew and to c. *Magnae* (X 3.34.7) and noted that Bede's words were an adverbial expression of the Gospel's message. He noted the contents of the second gloss to c. *Qui scandalizaverit* which he labelled as "the double truth". He also added references to the Johannes Teutonicus' (c. 1170–1245) gloss to the *Decretum*[51] and to c. *Nisi*. It seems that "the double truth" was a more general division of the truth: one was to be abandoned due to the threat of scandal, while the other was not. Finally, Giovanni noted that he had written about it in his own gloss to c. *Nisi* and stressed the contradiction expressed already in *Glossa ordinaria*. There was, on the one hand, a clear directive to avoid scandal if there was a doubt whether the sin occurred. And on the other hand, there was the general rule that it was always more useful to allow scandal than to abandon the truth.[52] He also referred in his gloss to c. *Nisi*[53] to Hostiensis' works and seemed to agree with him, that the directive to avoid scandal in

50 On the understanding of *scandalum* by Giovanni d'Andrea, see Hilp, *"Den bösen Schein vermeiden,"* 66–67.

51 Johannes Teutonicus, "Glossa ordinaria", in *Decretum Gratiani emendatum et notationibus illustratum una cum glossis* (Rome: in aedibus populi Romani, 1582), col. 280, D. 44, c. 1, s.v. '*Cum multitudine*'.

52 Giovanni d'Andrea, *In quintum Decretalium librum novella commentaria* (Venice: apud Franciscum Franciscium, 1581) fo. 158vb, X 5.41.3, no. 1: "[utilius] Glossa Bedae et hic fac punctum, ut ponatur adverbialiter. Glossa ii tractat de duplici veritate. In glossa ii [ibi sane] et per Ioannem 44 commessationes [D. 44, c. 1] de hoc de renuntiatione nisi cum pridem § pro gravi [X 1.9.10] et vide, quod ibi dixi super glossam prout Gregorius quae huic est contraria in veritate iustitiae".

53 Giovanni d'Andrea, *In primum Decretalium librum novella commentaria* (Venice: apud Franciscum Franciscium, 1581), fo. 149vb, X 1.9.10, sv. '*Prout Gregorius*', no. 51: "si vero dubitatur, an sit peccatum, videtur scandalum vitandum [...] nam si dubitatur de peccato, et certum sit de scandalo, dicemus cum Augustino: tene certum et dimitte incertum [...]. Sed de veritate iustitiae contrarium nota [...]. Unde hic Hostiensis fatetur de

case of dubious sin was not applicable to the situations involving *veritas vitae*. Giovanni did not hesitate to stress the contradiction between c. *Nisi* and c. *Qui scandalizaverit*. The clash of these rules provided him with the opportunity to clarify the scope of application of each canon. The former was applicable to cases involving *veritas iustitiae*, while the latter was adequate for dealing with cases of *veritas vitae*. Giovanni's account is at the same time very short and quite complicated. It is mostly a conjunction of references to other laws and glosses, demonstrating that, at the latest in the early 14th century, Canon law commentaries were mature and sophisticated, and that possibly some issues were treated as being sufficiently discussed in the scholarship. Also, he very clearly defined the boundaries of application of this *regula iuris*, which proves that the concept had already been established in the doctrine.

Henri Bohic (Henricus Bohicus, c. 1310–1350) offered a broad presentation of distinctions relevant for each chapter of *Liber extra*.[54] In his notes to c. *Qui scandalizaverit*, he included numerous references to other relevant laws and indicated many more authors than his predecessors (apart from *Glossa ordinaria*, he listed Hostiensis, Geoffrey, Giovanni d'Andrea, and a certain Gulielmus, often referring to parts of their commentaries that were not earlier linked to c. *Qui scandalizaverit*). He provided a clear rule, based on many authorities, that scandal should be avoided when there is no offence against God Himself, as Jesus called himself the Truth.[55] Afterwards, following Gulielmus, he described in detail the division of *veritas iustitiae* into three categories (*veritas iustitiae iuris naturalis, veritas iuris positivi, disciplina iuris correctionis et doctrinae*). While the first two had already been introduced by Hostiensis, the third type was modelled on the basis of the well-established *veritas disciplinae*, and so the divisions of truth were only differently organised. In the last part of his commentary, Bohic noticed that these divisions of truth were applicable to the discussion of *scandalum*, but there was also *veritas poenarum*, in case of which scandalum was not relevant at all. In his account, we should acknowledge the evolving doctrinal sophistication of the concept of *scandalum* and the addition of new topics not present in the earlier commentaries to c. *Qui scandalizaverit*.

---

veritate vitae: sed de veritate iustitiae non, dicens illam propter scandalum dissimulandam, vel differendam […]".

54 Briefly on the understanding of *scandalum* by Innocent IV, see Hilp, *"Den bösen Schein vermeiden,"* 67.

55 Henri Bohic, *In quinque Decretalium libros commentaria* (Venice: apud haeredem Hieronymi Scoti, 1576), 312, X 5.41.3, no. 1: "ubi dicunt quod scandalum vitandum est dummodo Deus non offendatur. Nam Christus sapientia est, iustitia, veritas, sanctitas, fortitudo".

Francesco Zabarella (1360–1417) followed closely Giovanni d'Andrea in his short commentary.[56] He stressed that in some cases the truth might be omitted and highlighted the contradiction within *Glossa ordinaria*: the gloss to c. *Qui scandalizaverit* and the glosses to c. *Nisi* and c. *Sane* offered different approaches to the relevance of *veritas iusititae*.[57] Zabarella was in favour of the Gloss to *regula iuris* and explained his account in another place of his commentary.[58]

Antonio da Budrio (c. 1360–1408) in his notes to c. *Qui scandalizaverit* included the reference to Matthew 18, to c. *Magnae,* and a summary of the canon in only one sentence.[59]

The most celebrated canonist of the 15th century was Niccolò Tedeschi (de Tudeschis, Abbas Panormitanus, 1386–1445). In many instances in his vast *Commentaria* medieval Canon law reached its apex. Alas, also in this case the commentary on the *regulae iuris* in *Liber extra* was not very broad. In his discussion of c. *Qui scandalizaverit,* Panormitanus started as usual with a summary (on this see below) and the internal division of this canon (into the words from the Gospel and the words of Bede). Then he quoted the *casus* after Bernard of Parma. Panormitanus' personal notes on this canon were short. He only noted that the canon implied that, in order to avoid scandal, one should not commit any wrong or tell any lie – even the purpose of protecting one's relative before the greater evil of scandal did not justify committing a sin.[60] In other words, no sin can be justified so that scandal is avoided. This short commentary is made from a completely different perspective and is

56 On the understanding of *scandalum* by Zabarella, see Hilp, *"Den bösen Schein vermeiden,"* 67–68.

57 Francesco Zabarella, *In quartum et quintum librum Decretalium* (Lyon: excudebat Claudius Seruanius, 1558), fo. 148ra, X 5.41.3: "Oppono primo quod veritas possit omitti propter scandalum l distinctio ut constitueretur [D. 50, c. 25]. Solutio ut in glossa. Et in ea ibi sane et de hoc per glossam 44 distinctio commessationes [D. 44, c. 1] et de renuntiatione nisi § pro gravi [X 1.9.10] et de temporibus ordinationum sane [X 1.11.2] in quibus duobus canones glossa tenet contrarium eius quod hic dicit de veritate iustitiae: sed haec verior quod dixi in dicto § pro gravi [X 1.9.10]".

58 Francesco Zabarella, *In primum librum Decretalium* (Lyon: excudebat Claudius Seruanius, 1558), fo. 183vb, X 1.9.10, § pro gravi.

59 Antonio da Budrio, *In librum quintum Decretalium commentarii* (Venice: apud Iuntas, 1578), fo. 146rb, X 5.41.3.

60 Niccolò Tedeschi, *Commentaria in quartum et quintum Decretalium librum* (Venice, 1581), fo. 245vb, X 5.41.3, no. 1: "Nota 1: ex textus quod propter scandalum evitandum non debet quis committere malum, et ideo non debet quis dicere mendacium etiam ad finem, ut proximus evitet iniuriam suam [...] nec debet quis committere malum, quantumcunque parvum, ut proximus evitet maius malum et scandalum [...]".

a very fresh perception of the meaning and relevance of this *regula iuris*. Moreover, the sources included within Panormitanus' commentary were not exactly the same as usual. After more than two hundred years of interpretation of this rule, he managed to find yet another interpretation of the words of Bede. It is difficult not to see this commentary as a breakaway from the earlier doctrine, especially in contrast with the accumulation of earlier doctrinal accounts on this canon.

Pietro d'Ancarano (c. 1333–1416) and Felino Sandeo (1444–1503) did not comment on the last title of *Liber extra*, but they also omitted other parts of the compilation. Still, one could expect that this title may be among the more relevant concerning the general nature of *regulae iuris*, but it seems that it was not the case.

For the late medieval canonists, c. *Qui scandalizaverit* was rather not seen as a major point of reference for the discussion of *scandalum*. On the contrary, their commentaries were not broad and did not hesitate to mark the inner tensions within the *Glossa ordinaria* concerning the policy against scandal. They also did not repeat the notes of the Gloss on the universal law added to this canon. Still, the late medieval authors offered at least several new insights or new links to other relevant laws from *Corpus iuris canonici*.

5 Early Modern Commentaries

As the "early modern" commentaries I understand here the works whose structure was closely following the structure of *Liber extra* and for this reason we can extend this period up to the second half of the 17th century. At this point, *Liber extra* lost its status as the central point of reference for scholars, the new method of commenting on Canon law sources was developed by Ehrenreich Pirhing, and a new period was initiated in the history of Canon law, sometimes labelled as the "golden age" of Canon law.[61]

61 Willibald Maria Plöchl, *Geschichte des Kirchenrechts*, vol. 5.3 (Wien: Herold, 1969), 349; Charles Lefebvre, Marcel Pacaut and Laurent Chevailler, *L'Époque moderne (1563–1789): Les sources du droit et la seconde centralisation romaine* (Paris: Editions Cujas, 1976), 64–66; Constant Van de Wiel, *History of Canon law* (Louvain: Peeters, 1991), 157; Charles Lefebvre, Marcel Pacaut and Laurent Chevailler, *L'Époque moderne (1563–1789): Les sources du droit et la seconde centralisation romaine* (Paris: Editions Cujas, 1976), 64–66; Constant Van de Wiel, *History of Canon law* (Leuven: Peeters, 1991), 157; Matthias Schmoeckel, *Kanonisches Recht. Geschichte und Inhalt des* Corpus iuris canonici. *Ein Studienbuch* (München: C. H. Beck, 2020), 328.

Overall, the *regulae iuris* in *Liber extra* were not eagerly commented on by the authors of the late commentaries. Before the presentation of three accounts which at least noticed c. *Qui scandalizaverit,* we can make a few brief general notes. In many cases, the early modern *commentaria* to *Liber extra* were not written with the aim of commenting on all books, titles and chapters. Moreover, the method and form of commentaries differed to some extent as most of them were not the works similar to the long late medieval *commentaria* or *lectura* but applied only a selected approach to sources (an exegetical one) or provided a summarised and concise presentation of the contents of *Liber extra.* There are several works which discussed only parts of the compilation and, for some reason, omitted i.a. the last book of the Decretals. Sometimes, there was no discussion of the title *De regulis iuris,* e.g. Filippo Decius (1454–1536) and Prospero Fagnani (1588–1678) did not comment on any canon from the last title of the Decretals. Hendrik Zoesius (c. 1561–1627) and André Delvaulx (1569–1636) in their works included only a brief description of the title *De regulis iuris,* without any detailed analysis of the selected *regulae,* but their works may be seen as the predecessors of the new type of commentary.[62]

We should also note that there were commentaries dedicated solely to *regulae iuris.* Nevertheless, they usually focused on the lists of *regulae iuris* in the Digest or in the Sext. Only occasionally did they address the less known *regulae iuris* from *Liber extra.* Marco Mantua Benavidio (1489–1582) primarily listed references to relevant passages from other learned authors.[63] Johann Strein (1584–1662) defined two types of scandal (active and passive), three types of truth and two types of goods (spiritual and material). Based on the latter, he explained when scandal should be avoided or not and then he presented a case illustrating the application of this rule (the dispute between Thomas Becket and King Henry II).[64] Anaklet Reiffenstuel (1642–1703) described various types of *veritas* relevant for the proper understanding of c. *Qui scandalizaverit* and then presented the normative scope of the *regula*

62 Hendrik Zoesius, *Commentarius ad Decretales epistolas Gregorii IX* (Leuven: typis ac sumptibus Hieronymi Nempaei, 1647), 656, X 5.41; André Delvaulx, *Paratitla sive summaria et methodica explicatio Decretalium Domini Gregorii Papae IX* (Leuven: apud Cornelium Coenestenium, 1649), 892–93, X 5.41.

63 Marco Mantua Benavidio, *Epitoma sive commentariolus in omnes fere leges et capita Digestorum, Decretalium et Sextii de regulis iuris* (Padova: sumptibus Iohanni Georgii Werdenstein, 1555), 153r–153v, X 5.41.3.

64 Johann Strein, *Summa iuris canonici, Pars 4, Commentarius in regulas iuris pontificii, quae in libro Quinto, et Sexto Decretalium continentur* (Köln: curavit Iodocus Kalcovius Bibliopola, 1659), 9–11, X 5.41.3.

in the form of answers to two questions: what is the scope of the rule for the respective types of *veritas* and what exceptions apply to the rule.[65] As these works were of different nature, i.e. they purposedly focused on *regulae iuris*, I will not investigate them closer. They were not part of the genre which I aim to discuss here. However, three general *commentaria* to *Liber extra* require our attention.

Agostinho Barbosa (1589–1649) wrote an untypical commentary to *Liber extra*. Barbosa's objective was to recollect the various opinions of learned authors on the respective canons from the papal compilation. In the first paragraph on c. *Qui scandalizaverit,* Barbosa listed numerous (mostly recent) authors for the reader interested in definition, division and content of *scandalum*. In the second paragraph he recalled briefly the accepted division of truth applicable for the discussion of *scandalum* and referred to two writers. In the third one, he noted another accepted view that in order to avoid scandal many deeds, which otherwise would not be, are conceded and he similarly pointed at other canonists discussing this issue.[66]

Emanuel González Téllez (?–1649) wrote an enormous commentary to *Liber extra*. For each canon there were separate sections: *notae* – discussing the origin and transmission of the text, and *commentarium*. To c. *Qui scandalizaverit* there was no *commentarium*. In *notae* Téllez listed the other appearances of the same or very similar quote (Gregory the Great, Bede, Bernard of Clairvaux, Thomas Aquinas). He also referred to a couple of other relevant canons from *Corpus iuris canonici*. He added that these laws about passive scandal (*scandalum passivum*) for which the truth should never be abandoned were correctly accepted by a couple of early modern authors.[67] Finally, he indicated two other authors for further reading.

Heinrich Wangnereck (1595–1664)[68] authored probably the longest account on c. *Qui scandalizaverit* in the early modern *commentaria*. Interestingly, the

65 Anaklet Reiffenstuel, *Tractatus de regulis iuris* (Ingolstadt: sumptibus Ioannis Andreae de la Haye, 1733), 8–9, X 5.41.3.

66 Agostinho Barbosa, *Collectanea doctorum tam veterum quam recentiorum in ius pontificium universum* (Lyon: sumptibus Laurentii Durand, 1637), 3: 351, X 5.41.3: "Notatur ad hoc quod ad scandala vitanda multa sunt concedenda, quae alias non concederentur".

67 Emanuel González Téllez, *Commentaria perpetua in singulos textus quinque librorum Decretalium Gregorii IX* (Venice: apud Nicolaum Pezzana, 1699) 1: 475–76, X 5.41.3: "et recte ea iura de scandalo passive, pro quo veritas numquam deserenda est, acceperunt [...]".

68 Heinrich Wangnereck, *Commentarius exegeticus sacrosanctum canonum seu expositio brevis et clara omnium pontificiarum Decretalium* (Dilingen: apud Ioannem Federle, 1672), 978, X 5.41.3: "Glossa triplicem hanc veritatem ita explicat, ut prima veritas bonae vitae, quae ad quemlibet pertinet, nunquam sit dimittenda propter scandalum,

author was more of a theologian than a jurist and it was not without impact on his reading of the discussed *regula iuris*. In his *exegesis* he started with a series of standard references to the origins of this canon and then he focused on the coherence between the theological account of *scandalum* and the legal one. For the former, the key authority for Wangnereck was Thomas Aquinas (c. 1225–1274) and, for the latter, it was *Glossa ordinaria* to *Liber extra*. He stressed that Aquinas rightly said that one should not measure the threat of scandal only against the truth necessary for salvation, but also against the truth which more perfectly leads to salvation.[69] He presented examples, partly inspired by Aquinas, of virtuous deeds which could and should be omitted with the purpose of avoiding the scandal, i.e. the threat of sin of others. This brought Wangnereck to the observation that no scandal which leads to sin against any precept could be permitted. He openly declared that the *regula iuris* from c. *Qui scandalizaverit* should more adequately be phrased in a contrary way, as it is more damnable to offend God by abandoning the truth than to allow this kind of scandal ("*Damnabilius veritas cum offensa Dei relinquitur, quam tale scandalum permittatur*"). Finally, he discussed to what extent it was

veritas autem iustitiae est, quae pertinet ad iudicem, et veritas diciplinae, quae pertinet ad praelatum; in his ait glossa quandoque aliqua praetermitti propter scandalum. Sed rectius Summa theologiae l.c. ad 4 docet, in triplici hanc veritate quamlibet comprehendi non tantum id, quod est de necessitate salutis, sed etiam, per quod perfectius pervenitur ad salutem, ut per consilia, quae sunt aliquando dissimulanda vel dimittenda propter scandalum, vel charitatem, sic charitas violat ieiunium, et viri perfecti admittunt relaxationes corporis, ne videantur contemnere imperfectos aut peccatores etc. Similiter iudices et praelati differunt et mitigant ac donant poenas, disciplinaeque rigorem temperant, maxime erga illos qui ipsos laeserunt, item erga pauperes, vel quos vident clementiam iuvandos, ne cum scandalo putentur se vindicare, parcere divitibus, nimio rigore illos frangere, quos possent flectere.

Nunquam tamen utiliter sed damnabiliter scandalum permittitur, quando praeceptum aliquod sub peccato obligans sive in veritate vitae privatae, sive officii iudicialis, sive praelationis cuiuscunquae violandum est, tunc enim regula haec sic e contrario formari debet: 'Damnabilius veritas cum offensa Dei relinquitur, quam tale scandalum permittatur'. Dixerunt quidem aliqui ait Summa Theologiae 'l.c. ad 5 peccatum veniale esse committendum propter vitandum scandalum'. Sed hoc implicat contraria. Si enim faciendum est, iam non est malum, neque peccatum; nam peccatum non est eligibile. Contingit tamen aliquid propter circumstantiam aliquam non esse peccatum veniale, quod illam circumstantiam sublatam peccatum veniale esset. Sicut verbum iocosum est veniale, quando sine utilitate dicitur, si autem ex causam rationabili profertur, non est peccatum, neque otiosum. Quae S.D. doctrina utrum extendi queat ad peccatum officiosum, praesertim boni publici causam, disputari posset".

69 On the understanding of *scandalum* by Aquinas, see e.g. Hilp, *"Den bösen Schein vermeiden,"* 55–64.

allowed to sin venially in order to avoid scandal and wondered whether this doctrine of Aquinas may be applied also to the sin committed in official acts. What we see in the account of Wangnereck is staggering: in the very last source discussed here there is more discontinuity with the earlier commenting tradition than standard repetition typical for the genre. Wangnereck, similarly to the first authors commenting on this *regula iuris*, reached for valuable insights into the theological works. This approach led him to openly contest the very core of c. *Qui scandalizaverit* to the point where he suggested a completely different *regula iuris* as a more adequate one. This tells us a lot as about the very limited relevance of this canon for the overall doctrine of *scandalum* and of the significance of *regulae iuris* in *Liber extra*. This set of general legal provisions was certainly not considered as the unquestionable source of guidelines for handling the inner tensions within Canon law.

6 *Summarium* to c. *Qui scandalizaverit*

Before closing this investigation there is one more point that requires our attention: *summarium* to c. *Qui scandalizaverit*. There was no consistent pattern of adding short summaries to each canon in the *Liber Extra* in handwritten sources. It was only 250 years after the promulgation of the Decretals that these summaries were included in the printed editions of the papal collection of laws.[70] They were meant to grasp the core *ratio* of the respective legal provision.[71] In case of c. *Qui scandalizaverit,* the history of its *summarium* is not very complicated. As was the case for numerous canons this *summarium* was firstly included in *Commentaria* of Panormitanus.[72] He usually started his comment with the summary marked by the letters "h.d." (*hoc dicit*) and it was also the case for c. *Qui scandalizaverit*: "*Propter scandalum evitandum veritas non est omittenda. Hoc dicit*". We can find this *summarium* both in printed

70 Piotr Alexandrowicz, "The history and normative significance of *summaria* in the *Liber extra*," *Tijdschrift voor Rechtsgeschiedenis* 90, no. 1–2 (2022): 148–76.

71 Andrea Errera, "Alle origini della scuola del commento: le *additiones* all'apparato accursiano," in *Studi di storia del diritto medioevale e moderno*, ed. Filippo Liotta, vol. 2 (Bologna: Monduzzi Editoriale, 2007), 93–102; Andrea Padovani, "'*Tenebo hunc ordinem*': Metodo e struttura della lezione nei giuristi medievali (secoli XII–XIV)," *Tijdschrift voor Rechtsgeschiedenis* 79, no. 3–4 (2011), 381.

72 For a more complicated case, see Piotr Alexandrowicz, "*Pacta sunt servanda*: Canon Law and the Birth and Dissemination of the Legal Maxim," *Bulletin of Medieval Canon Law* 38 (2021): 193–210.

editions of *Commentaria* and in manuscripts.[73] There had been no other variants of summary offered to this canon in the earlier glosses and commentaries (at least those that were printed afterwards) and, for this reason, it was the only summary which was then incorporated into the printed editions of *Liber extra*. We can find it in one of the first editions with summaries from 1491 (GW 11482), in an edition with additional summaries from 1499 (GW 11497), in Jean Chappuis' edition from 1507 and in *editio Romana* from 1582. The only unclear point in this story is the *additio* in printed *Commentaria* by Bernard of Montmirat which includes this *summarium* (with the change of "omittenda" into "amittenda" and a reference to Thomas Aquinas).[74] However, the author of the *additiones* was obviously not Bernard – in this case it was Sebastiano Medici (c. 1545–1595). As we do not find this phrase in *Summa theologiae* by Aquinas in *quaestio* dedicated to *scandalum* (as indicated in *additio*) and Medici wrote his *additiones* much later than Panormitanus had written his *Commentaria*, it seems justified to give credits for coining this adage to Panormitanus. This summary was a successful one, as it is sometimes referred to as a part of the very law promulgated by Gregory IX or even substituting the very contents of c. *Qui scandalizaverit*.[75] If we recall that Panormitanus had a very different approach to c. *Qui scandalizaverit*, the success of his *summarium* can be seen as an effective way to impose this unconventional reading of the canon and its interpretation.

7 Conclusions: c. *Qui scandalizaverit* and *regulae iuris* in Canon Law

The *regulae iuris* from *Liber extra* were certainly not the focal set of legal provisions for medieval Canon law. Contrary to the *regulae iuris* from *Liber Sextus*, the earlier legal rules were not broadly commented on or were even omitted by many authors across the ages. These rules were not without relevance, but served only subsidiary purposes. They were viewed primarily

73 Niccolò Tedeschi, *Commentaria*, fo. 245vb, X 5.41.3, no. 1. See e.g. Niccolò Tedeschi, *Commentaria in Decretales Gregorii IX*, BAV, Vat. lat. 2253, fo. 260va.

74 Bernard of Montmirat, "Super quinque," fo. 152rb, X 5.41.3, additio: "Propter scandalum evitandum veritas non est amittenda (S. Thom. 2 2 q. 43 art. 7 et sequentes)".

75 See Delvaulx, *Paratitla sive summaria*, 893, X 5.41; Leveleux-Teixeira, "Le droit canonique," 205, n. 34; Bubenheimer, "*Scandalum*," 208; see examples of motto on *scandalum*: Michał Kokowski, "Odkrycie grobu Mikołaja Kopernika: fakt medialny czy naukowy?," *Komunikaty Mazursko-Warmińskie* 4 (2014): 567; James T. O'Reilly and Margaret S.P. Chalmers, *The Clergy Sex Abuse Crisis and the Legal Responses* (New York: Oxford University Press, 2014), 193.

as hermeneutical tools rather than as typical norms to be applied when necessary.

As the canonists noted the contradiction within *Glossa ordinaria* concerning the *regula iuris* from c. *Qui scandalizaverit*, it held only marginal relevance for the doctrine of *scandalum*. Certainly, more significant for the overall approach of Canon law and for the ecclesiastical policy on *scandalum* was the simple *ratio scandali vitandi* than the words "*utilius scandalum nasci permittitur, quam veritas relinquatur*". Nevertheless, the discussion on the margins of c. *Qui scandalizaverit* provides us with some interesting observations on how theological issues permeated Canon law.

The penetration of Canon law with theological concepts was one of the outcomes of the development of the *regulae iuris* in Canon law and the history of c. *Qui scandalizaverit* is a good example of this impact.[76] This *regula iuris* was also a typical case of a rule not understood as a general and abstract legal provision coined on the basis of a series of similar legal cases.[77] This might have been one of the reasons for the very limited success of this *regula iuris* – it was not created to encapsulate the best way for handling the cases involving the threat of scandal, but it was a simple yet far-reaching statement transmitted from theology to Canon law. For this reason the most atypical interpretations of c. *Qui scandalizaverit*, by Panormitanus and Wangnereck, may also be the most appealing to the modern scholars, although they do not easily fit into the broader doctrine of *scandalum* within Canon law.

Finally, this study showcases the varying form of legal commentary. It seems that the most prolific period of the development of this legal genre within the science of Canon law was the period between approximately 1234 (the promulgation of *Liber extra*) and 1445 (the death of Panormitanus). Before this period, the glosses and *apparata* had not been as consistent, broad and internally coherent. After this period, the commentaries were usually not as complex, exhaustive, and innovative. For obvious reasons these preliminary observations on the changing form of commentary deserve further studies and clarifications.

---

76 Zuffellato, "Il *Tractatus*", 13–14. Interestingly, this seems to align with the claims of Hilp, who, in his study on *scandalum* in canon law, argued that the originally moral-theological concept of *scandalum* was effectively transformed into a solely legal provision protecting the internal integrity of the Church and canon law. See Hilp, *"Den bösen Schein vermeiden,"* 68–72.

77 Zuffellato, "Il *Tractatus*", 12–13.

Acknowledgements

This work has been supported by the National Science Centre, Poland (project no. 2022/47/D/HS5/00076).

I am grateful to those who have read this piece and shared their comments: Raffaella Bianchi Riva, Wouter Druwé, Ilya Kotlyar, and Corinne Leveleux-Teixeira. Any remaining errors are my own.

Bibliography

Manuscripts

Bernard of Pavia. *Breviarium decretalium Bernardi Papiensis*. Archiwum i Biblioteka Krakowskiej Kapituły Katedralnej. Ms 89.

Bernard of Pavia. *Decretalium Compilatio prima cum apparatu Tancredi, et glossulis*. BAV. Vat. lat. 1377.

Bernard of Pavia. *Decretalium Compilatio prima cum Glossa ordinaria Tancredi Bononiensis*. BAV. Borgh. 264.

Tedeschi, Niccolò (de Tudeschis, Abbas Panormitanus). *Commentaria in Decretales Gregorii IX*. BAV. Vat. lat. 2253.

Printed Editions

Antonio da Budrio (Butrio). *In librum quintum Decretalium commentarii*. Venice: apud Iuntas, 1578.

Barbosa, Agostinho. *Collectanea doctorum tam veterum quam recentiorum in ius pontificium universum*. Lyon: sumptibus Laurentii Durand, 1637.

Benavidio, Marco Mantua. *Epitoma sive commentariolus in omnes fere leges et capita Digestorum, Decretalium et Sextii de regulis iuris*. Padova: sumptibus Iohanni Georgii Werdenstein, 1555.

Bernard of Montmirat. "Super quinque libris Decretalium lectura aurea certe ac brevi resolutione iuris ambagens enodans". In *Perillustrium doctorum tam veterum quam recentiorum in libros Decretalium aurei commentarii*. Venice: apud Iuntas, 1588.

Bernard of Parma. "Glossa ordinaria." In *Decretales Dominii Gregorii Papae IX suae integritati una cum glossis restitutae*. Rome: in aedibus populi Romani, 1582.

Bernard of Pavia. "*Breviarium extra*." In *Antiquae collectiones Decretalium*. Edited by Antonio Agustín. Lérida: apud Petrum Rob. et Ioannem a Villanova, 1576.

Bohic, Henri. *In quinque Decretalium libros commentaria*. Venice: apud haeredem Hieronymi Scoti, 1576.

D'Andrea, Giovanni (Johannes Andreae). *In primum Decretalium librum novella commentaria.* Venice: apud Franciscum Franciscium, 1581.

D'Andrea, Giovanni (Johannes Andreae). *In quintum Decretalium librum novella commentaria.* Venice: apud Franciscum Franciscium, 1581.

Delvaulx, André. *Paratitla sive summaria et methodica explicatio Decretalium Domini Gregorii Papae IX.* Leuven: apud Cornelium Coenestenium, 1649.

Friedberg, Emil A., ed. *Corpus Iuris Canonici.* 2 vols. Leipzig: Tauchnitz, 1879–81.

Geoffrey of Trani. *Summa super titulis Decretalium.* Lyon: impensis Romani Morin, 1519.

Gregory the Great. *Sancti Gregorii Magni Homiliae in Hiezechielem prophetam.* Edited by Marc Adriaen. Turnhout: Brepols, 1971.

Henry of Susa. *In primum Decretalium librum commentaria.* Venice: apud Iuntas, 1581.

Henry of Susa. *In quintum Decretalium librum commentaria.* Venice: apud Iuntas, 1581.

Henry of Susa. *Summa aurea.* Venice: apud Iacobum Vitalem, 1574.

Innocent IV (Sinibaldo Fieschi). *Apparatus super quinque libris Decretalium.* Frankfurt am Main: Feierabendt Sigismundus, 1570.

Johannes Teutonicus. "Glossa ordinaria." In *Decretum Gratiani emendatum et notationibus illustratum una cum glossis.* Rome: in aedibus populi Romani, 1582.

Strein, Johann. *Summa iuris canonici, Pars 4, Commentarius in regulas iuris pontificii, quae in libro Quinto, et Sexto Decretalium continentur.* Köln: curavit Iodocus Kalcovius Bibliopola, 1659.

Tedeschi, Niccolò (de Tudeschis, Abbas Panormitanus). *Commentaria in quartum et quintum Decretalium librum.* Venice, 1581.

Téllez, Emanuel González. *Commentaria perpetua in singulos textus quinque librorum Decretalium Gregorii IX.* Venice: apud Nicolaum Pezzana, 1699.

Wangnereck, Heinrich. *Commentarius exegeticus sacrosanctum canonum seu expositio brevis et clara omnium pontificiarum Decretalium.* Dilingen: apud Ioannem Federle, 1672.

Zabarella, Francesco. *In primum librum Decretalium.* Lyon: excudebat Claudius Seruanius, 1558.

Zabarella, Francesco. *In quartum et quintum librum Decretalium.* Lyon: excudebat Claudius Seruanius, 1558.

Zoesius, Hendrik. *Commentarius ad Decretales epistolas Gregorii IX.* Leuven: typis ac sumptibus Hieronymi Nempaei, 1647.

Secondary Literature

Alexandrowicz, Piotr. "*Pacta sunt servanda*: Canon Law and the Birth and Dissemination of the Legal Maxim," *Bulletin of Medieval Canon Law* 38 (2021): 193–210.

Alexandrowicz, Piotr. "The history and normative significance of *summaria* in the *Liber extra.*" *Tijdschrift voor Rechtsgeschiedenis* 90, no. 1–2 (2022): 148–76.

Bianchi Riva, Raffaella. "Il giudice e la misericordia. Riflessioni sull'amministrazione della giustizia nel diritto canonico classico." *Vergentis* 5 (2017): 185–219.

Bianchi Riva, Raffaella. *Lo scandalo tra alto medioevo e prima età moderna: Itinerari tra dimensione giuridica, politica e sociale*. Torino: Giappichelli, 2022.

Bubenheimer, Ulrich. "*Scandalum et ius divinum*: Theologische und rechtstheologische Probleme der ersten reformatorischen Innovationen in Wittenberg 1521/22." In *Wittenberg 1517–1522: Diskussions-, Aktionsgemeinschaft und Stadtreformation*, edited by Thomas Kaufmann and Alejandro Zorzin, 159–225. Tübingen: Mohr Siebeck, 2023.

Dimier, Marie-Anselme. "A propos du Congrès Bernardin." *Revue d'histoire ecclésiastique* 50 (1955): 543–56.

Druwé, Wouter. *Scandalum in the Early Bolognese Decretistic and in Papal Decretals (ca. 1140–1234)*. Leuven: Peeters, 2018.

Erdö, Peter. *Storia della scienza del diritto canonico: Una introduzione*. Roma: Editrice Pontificia Università Gregoriana, 1999.

Errera, Andrea. "Alle origini della scuola del commento: le *additiones* all'apparato accursiano." In *Studi di storia del diritto medioevale e moderno*, edited by Filippo Liotta, 2: 41–137. Bologna: Monduzzi Editoriale, 2007.

Fossier, Arnaud-Vivien. "*Propter vitandum scandalum*: Histoire d'une catégorie juridique (XIIe–XVe siècles)." *Mélanges de l'École française de Rome – Moyen Âge* 121, no 2 (2009): 317–48.

González, Fernando Jesús. "Significación de las Palabras y Reglas del Derecho (DCH)." *Max Planck Institute for Legal History and Legal Theory Research Paper Series*, No 2025-01: 1–32.

Hilp, Ulrich. *"Den bösen Schein vermeiden." Zu Ethos und Recht des Amtes in Kirche und Staat*. Berlin: Duncker & Humblot, 2004.

Kokowski, Michał. "Odkrycie grobu Mikołaja Kopernika: fakt medialny czy naukowy?" *Komunikaty Mazursko-Warmińskie* 4 (2014): 567–600.

Lefebvre, Charles, Marcel Pacaut, and Laurent Chevailler. *L'Époque moderne (1563–1789): Les sources du droit et la seconde centralisation romaine*. Paris: Éditions Cujas, 1976.

Leveleux-Teixeira, Corinne. "Droit et verité: Le point de vue de la doctrine médiévale (XIIè–XVè)." *Bien dire et bien aprandre – Revue de médiévistique* 23 (2005): 333–49.

Leveleux-Teixeira, Corinne. "Le droit canonique médiéval et l'horreur du scandale." *Cahiers de recherches médiévales et humanistes* 25 (2013): 193–211.

Nemo-Pekelman, Capucine. "Scandale et vérité dans la doctrine canonique médiévale (XIIe–XIIIe siècles)." *Revue historique de droit français et étranger* 85, no 4 (2007): 491–504.

O'Reilly, James T., and Margaret S.P. Chalmers. *The Clergy Sex Abuse Crisis and the Legal Responses*. New York: Oxford University Press, 2014.

Padovani, Andrea. "'*Tenebo hunc ordinem*': Metodo e struttura della lezione nei giuristi medievali (secoli XII–XIV)." *Tijdschrift voor Rechtsgeschiedenis* 79, no. 3–4 (2011): 353–89.

Plöchl Willibald, Maria. *Geschichte des Kirchenrechts*. Vol. 5.3. Wien: Herold, 1969.

Schmoeckel, Matthias. *Die Jugend der Justitia. Archäologie der Gerechtigkeit im Prozessrecht der Patristik*. Tübingen: Mohr Siebeck, 2013.

Schmoeckel, Matthias. *Kanonisches Recht. Geschichte und Inhalt des* Corpus iuris canonici. *Ein Studienbuch*. München: C. H. Beck, 2020.

Thier, Andreas. "Zwischen Exegesesammlung und Ordnungsentwurf: Zur Kommentarliteratur des gelehrten Rechts in der Frühen Neuzeit." In *Kommentare in Recht und Religion*, edited by David Kästle and Niels Jansen, 207–47. Tübingen: Mohr Siebeck, 2014.

Van de Wiel, Constant. *History of Canon law*. Leuven: Peeters, 1991.

Zuffellato, Andrea. "Il *Tractatus de regulis juris* di Anacleto Reiffenstuel: spunti critici per una traduzione ragionata." Ph.D. diss, Universitá degli Studi di Padova, 2014.

CHAPTER 6

Landmarks in the Historical Development of the Double Jeopardy Principle

Ger Coffey

1 Introduction

The Civil law "*ne bis in idem*" *regula*[1] and its Common law counterpart "double jeopardy" proscribes multiple criminal trials and punishments for the same offence, which is predicated on a final verdict of acquittal (*autrefois acquit*) or conviction (*autrefois convict*) by a court of competent criminal jurisdiction.[2] The principle is entrenched in legal systems concerned with safeguarding civil liberties and is fundamental to balancing individual rights of accused persons commensurate with the powers and resources available to states and restricting prosecutorial discretion. The incremental development of the principle in historical perspective reflects the diverse social, political, and legal climates delimiting the contours of the procedural defence.

This chapter provides a historical account of the *ne bis in idem* principle in continental Civil law, and Canon law derivative, which influenced the evolution of the Common law double jeopardy principle that incrementally developed a particularly unique interpretation of the concept from the late medieval period.

2 Raison d'être

The injustice of repeated ordeals of trials and punishments necessitated the development of the principle as a limitation on the authority of the state and prosecutorial discretion. The adverse standing of accused persons in criminal

1 Editor's note: The principle *ne bis in idem* is included into the FWO.OPR.2020.005001 database as "Aliquis non debet duplici poena ex eodem delicto puniri" under No. 819. It is notable, however, that this *regula* was not found in some of the most popular early modern collections of *regulae*, such as those of Thomasetis and Socini. This suggests that its status as a *regula* was not firmly established.

2 Carl-Friedrich Stuckenberg, "Double Jeopardy and *Ne Bis in Idem* in Common Law and Civil Law Jurisdictions," in *The Oxford Handbook of Criminal Process*, ed. Darryl K. Brown, Jenia Iontcheva Turner, and Bettina Weisser (Oxford: Oxford University Press, 2019), 457–475.

 | DOI:10.1163/9789004736092_008

trials necessitated the development of a double jeopardy principle against the ordeal of multiple trials and punishments for the same offence.[3] The principle is based on the universal law of reason, justice, and conscience, the development of which is based on deontological precepts from its inception in classical antiquity as a primitive form of *res judicata*. Multiple criminal trials and punishments for the same offence are intrinsically unlawful from a deontological perspective.[4] Deontological ethics, including the nature of duty and state obligations concerning individual rights in criminal trials, impacted on the prescriptive ethical theory that morality of conduct should be constructed based on whether impugned conduct is right or wrong according to a series of rules of law, rather than based on the consequences of prohibited conduct. Reconciling power imbalances and disproportionate resource allocation vis-à-vis states and accused persons necessitated a formal limitation on state powers and prosecutorial discretion.[5]

3 Genesis of the Principle

Ancient laws prohibiting variations to judgments can be traced to the Babylonian Code of Hammurabi (c. 1754 BCE),[6] conceivably the first written legal code that was not a new law but rather a codification of preceding laws. The Code does not include specific laws against multiple criminal trials and punishments for the same offence. Nonetheless, an effective yet gruesome procedure for preventing a second trial by the same prosecutor following an acquittal is evident from a reading of Law 1, which stipulated:

> If anyone ensnare another, putting a ban upon him, but he can not prove it, then he that ensnared him shall be put to death.

3 Martin L. Friedland, *Double Jeopardy* (Oxford: Clarendon Press, 1969), 4; *Green v United States* (1957) 355 US 184, 187–188, Black J.

4 Heidi M. Hurd and Michael S. Moore, "The Ethical Implications of Proportioning Punishment to Deontological Desert," *Criminal Law and Philosophy* 15 (2021): 495–514; Guyora Binder, "Punishment Theory: Moral or Political?," *Buffalo Criminal Law Review* 5 (2002): 321–371.

5 Daniel Epps, "Checks and Balances in the Criminal Law," *Vanderbilt Law Review* 74 (2021): 1–84; *Cf.* Carissa Byrne Hessick, "Separation of Powers Versus Checks and Balances in the Criminal Justice System: A Response to Professor Epps," *Vanderbilt Law Review* 74 (2021): 159–185.

6 *The Code of Hammurabi,* trans. Leonard William King, Yale Law School, The Avalon Project, https://avalon.law.yale.edu/ancient/hamframe.asp.

An interpretative analysis of Law 5 (binding judges to a verdict) also suggests the recognition of the principle:

> If a judge try a case, reach a decision, and present his judgment in writing; if later error shall appear in his decision, and it be through his own fault, then he shall pay twelve times the fine set by him in the case, and he shall be publicly removed from the judge's bench, and never again shall he sit there to render judgement.

This edict from one of the earliest written legal codes illustrates the importance of finality of the verdict, or judicial decision, which is encapsulated in the doctrine of *res judicata* that has broader application than the *ne bis in idem* principle.

4 Classical Antiquity

A prohibition on multiple criminal trials based on the same offence was recognised in the ancient law of Athens,[7] which stipulated that a "man could not be tried twice for the same offense".[8] The prohibition against double jeopardy in classical antiquity was however susceptible to restrictions by legal technicalities depending on the nuances of the triers of fact. Referring to the practice in the late 5th century BCE, Jones writes:

> The main concern of a man brought into court was to win a verdict by one means or another, for once tried he could not be prosecuted again on the same charge, the rule *ne bis in eadem* being accepted in Athens if not in Sparta, though in this matter again the pleaders were not slow to find loopholes in the law and to employ various devices, including charges of false witnesses, for reopening questions which had apparently already been disposed of by the courts.[9]

In 355 BCE, Demosthenes (384–322 BCE), Athenian statesman, orator and law pleader in courts, in a speech against Leptines proclaimed "the laws forbid the

7 *Cf.* David Phillips, *The Law of Ancient Athens* (Michigan: University of Michigan Press, 2013).
8 Robert J. Bonner, *Lawyers and Litigants in Ancient Athens: The Genesis of the Legal Profession* (Chicago: University of Chicago Press, 1927), 195.
9 John Walter Jones, *The Law and Legal Theory of the Greeks* (Oxford: Clarendon Press, 1977), 148–149.

same man to be tried twice on the same issue, be it a civil action, a scrutiny, a contested claim, or anything else of the sort".[10] By the same token, Demosthenes, in a speech to be given by Diodorus against Timocrates, opined that "the legislator does not permit any question once decided by judgement of the court to be put a second time",[11] which bound prosecutors and judges to the original verdict.

Republican and imperial periods of ancient Rome recognised a legal protection against double jeopardy. Under the Republic, a verdict of acquittal was final,[12] whereas a conviction could be appealed to the People.[13] The implication was that, while the prosecutor and judge could err in law, the people were sovereign and ultimate arbitrators correcting those errors. Following the demise of the Roman Republic and the ascendency of the emperors the sovereignty of the people diminished. The Opinions of Julius Paulus (222–235 CE) one of the most influential and distinguished Roman jurists in the early 3rd century proclaimed that "[a]fter a public acquittal a defendant can again be prosecuted by his informer within thirty days, but after that time this cannot be done".[14] The public prosecutor could appeal an acquittal to the imperial appeal courts.[15] This procedure was gradually altered and, by the time of the Digest of Justinian (a collection and abridgement of classical jurists' writings on law and justice on then-existing Roman law, compiled and published under the Byzantine emperor Justinian I in 533 CE), Roman law prohibited a second trial following an acquittal,[16] although a conviction could be appealed.[17] While the Digest is silent regarding whether

10 James Herbert Vince (translation), *Demosthenes I: Olynthiacs, Philippics, Minor Public Speeches, Speech Against Leptines* (Cambridge Massachusetts: Harvard University Press, 1962), 589.

11 Demosthenes, "Against Timocrates", in Demosthenes, *Against Meidias, Against Androtion, Against Aristocrates, Against Timocrates, Against Aristogeiton,* trans. James Herbert Vince (Cambridge Massachusetts: Harvard University Press, 1935), 407.

12 James Leigh Strachan-Davidson, *Problems of the Roman Criminal Law* (Oxford: Clarendon Press, 1912), I: 155 and II: 177.

13 Strachan-Davidson, *Problems of the Roman Criminal Law*, I: 127; Herbert Felix Jolowicz, *Historical Introduction to Roman Law*, 2nd edn (Cambridge: Cambridge University Press, 1954), 322 ff.; Pandias Michael Schisas, *Offences against the State in Roman Law* (London: University of London Press, 1926), 172 ff.

14 *The Opinions of Paulus*, trans. Samuel P. Scott, Book V, Title XVII Concerning Aquittals, https://droitromain.univ-grenoble-alpes.fr/Anglica/Paul5_Scott.htm.

15 Strachan-Davidson, *Problems of the Roman Criminal Law*, II: 177; Schisas, *Offences against the State,* 190, 221–222, 232.

16 D. 48.7.2.

17 D. 49.6.

the state could appeal an acquittal, there are copious references to appeals against convictions.[18]

An acquittal by a magistrate during the Roman Republic proscribed subsequent proceedings whatsoever against the accused.[19] The Roman Empire recognised the principle based on the rule "there was no appeal and no chance of reviewing the verdict of a jury".[20] During the reign of Tiberius (42 BCE–37 CE), a jury acquitted the accused whom Tiberius believed should have been convicted. Tiberius was unable to overturn an acquittal rendered by a jury. Tiberius admonished the jury and charged the accused with another offence; however, he could not change the verdict already given.[21] Subsequently, Roman law provided alternatives to trial by jury[22] and the accuser could pursue a review of an acquittal in the imperial appeal courts.[23]

Ancient Roman law recognised an entrenched precursor of the contemporary *ne bis in idem* principle. The pervasive nature of Roman law expressed in the Digest of Justinian stipulated that "the Governor should not permit the same person to be again accused of crime of which he has been acquitted"[24] and "the Senate decreed that no one can be accused of the same crime under several laws",[25] which incorporated the maxim *nemo debet bis puniri pro uno delicto*. However, the text of Ulpian, included in the Digest, qualifies:

> Where a case has been decided so far as certain persons are concerned, this does not prejudice others, if he who now appears as an accuser prosecutes on account of some injury of his own, and proves that he did not know that the accusation had been brought by another, ... there is good reason that he should be permitted to make the accusation.[26]

18 D. 49.1.6; 49.1.15; 49.1.18; 49.4.1; 49.4.2.3; 49.5.2; 49.7.1.2; 49.7.1.3; 49.7.1.5; and 49.9.1.

19 Jolowicz, *Historical Introduction to Roman Law*, 325; Strachan-Davidson, *Problems of the Roman Criminal Law*, I: 155.

20 Strachan-Davidson, *Problems of the Roman Criminal Law*, II: 157.

21 Schisas, in *Offences against the State*, 190, writes that Tiberius had "no right to revise" the jury's decision.

22 Strachan-Davidson, *Problems of the Roman Criminal Law* (Oxford: Clarendon Press, 1912), vol. II, 157.

23 Strachan-Davidson, *Problems of the Roman Criminal Law*, II: 177; Schisas, *Offences against the State*, 221–222, 232.

24 Samuel Parsons Scott, *The Civil Law* (Cincinnati: Central Trust Company, 1932), II: 17, D. 48.2.7, D. 48.2.7.2.

25 D. 48.2.14.

26 D. 48.2.7.2.

An acquittal could not be appealed in the Roman Republic; nevertheless, the laws of ancient Rome recognised an exception to the principle, in that judgements upon an action between an accused and his accuser did not bind against a second accuser who was not a party to the first action, or at least was not aware of the first trial.[27] This exception provided a second accuser with standing to initiate a second trial for the same offence (presumably based on the existence of more conclusive evidence against the accused).

The principle differed significantly from the application of double jeopardy in contemporary criminal trials because criminal prosecutions were not always proffered by public prosecutors.[28] Ancient Athens was a stable and prosperous society without having developed an extensively centralised rule of law institutions.[29] As there was no professional police force or public prosecutor, the legal process largely depended on private citizens initiating criminal trials.[30] Victims of crime or any Roman citizen could instigate proceedings against the accused.[31] A person injured by the wrongful conduct of another could elect[32] to bring a prosecution against the accused or, alternatively, bring a private (delictual) action for a penalty (other than an award of compensation) from the accused.[33]

The Code of Justinian (534 CE) recorded the laws of the empire, citing imperial constitutions, legislation and pronouncements, which includes a decree promulgated by Emperors Diocletian (284–305 CE) and Maximian (250–310 CE) in the year 289 CE:

> Anyone who has been charged with a public crime, cannot again be accused of the same crime by another person. If, however, several offences arise from the same act, and complaint is only made of one of

---

27 Scott, *The Civil Law*, II: 17–18.

28 Charles Phineas Sherman, in *Roman Law in the Modern World*, 2nd edn. (New Haven: New Haven Law Book, 1922), II: 486, writes that, in the Republic, "[a]ny Roman citizen or subject, desiring to cause anybody to be prosecuted criminally, could apply to the presiding judge of the appropriate court for permission to make an accusation against the alleged offender."

29 Federica Carugati, Gillian K. Hadfield, and Barry R. Weingas, "Building Legal Order in Ancient Athens," *Journal of Legal Analysis* 7 (2015): 291–324.

30 Adriaan Lanni, *Law and Order in Ancient Athens* (Cambridge: Cambridge University Press, 2016).

31 Jolowicz, *Historical Introduction to Roman Law*, 331; Max Radin, *Handbook of Roman Law* (St. Paul, Minnesota: West Publishing, 1927), 469.

32 Radin, *Handbook of Roman Law*, 468.

33 Radin, *Handbook of Roman Law*, 127–128.

> them, it is not forbidden for an accusation of another to be filed by some other individual.[34]

This edict acknowledged the possibility of prohibited conduct constituting an offence against several victims, and each victim would be entitled to instigate proceedings for the harm caused to them individually.

5 Late Antiquity

Legal developments from the end of classical antiquity to the early medieval reign of the Anglo-Saxons from the 5th to 11th centuries is generally referred to as the "Dark Middle Ages" mainly because written sources for this period are scarce.[35] The double jeopardy principle does not appear to have been extant during the Anglo-Saxon period (410–1066 CE), which did not employ abstract and general principles of law. Prior to the Norman Conquest a primitive form of criminal procedure operated during the reign of the Anglo-Saxons.[36] Compensating victims of crime was the underlying principle of sentencing, which avoided nonlegal violence in the form of vengeance or feud.[37]

Punishment imposed upon a second conviction for every offence was death or mutilation, albeit there were few capital offences in existence at this time, such as murder and treason. In Ethelred II's (978–1016) laws, it was said of the accused that when convicted "let him be smitten so that his neck break".[38] Cnut's (1016–1035) reign did not improve the situation of accused persons. Capital punishment was common after Cnut's reign, notwithstanding his cautions against the abuse of such punishments, as William the Conqueror found

34 Scott, *The Civil Law*, C. 9.2.9, https://droitromain.univ-grenoble-alpes.fr/Anglica/CJ9_Scott.gr.htm.

35 Contemporary historians refer to this period as "early middle ages' or "early medieval period"; Janet N. Nelson, "The Dark Ages", *History Workshop Journal* 63 (2004): 191–201; Nick Higham, "From sub-Roman Britain to Anglo-Saxon England: Debating the Insular Dark Ages," *History Compass* 2 (2004): 1–29; Craig Kallendorf, "The Historical Petrarch," *American Historical Review* 101 (1996): 130–141; Theodore E. Mommsen, "Petrarch's Conception of the 'Dark Ages'," *Speculum: A Journal of Medieval Studies* 17 (1942): 226–242.

36 William Searle Holdsworth, *A History of English Law* (London: Methuen, 1926), II: 108–110.

37 Andrew Rabin, *Crime and Punishment in Anglo-Saxon England* (Cambridge: Cambridge University Press, 2020), 51.

38 James Fitzjames Stephen, *A History of English Criminal Law* (London: Macmillan, 1883) I: 58.

it necessary to proscribe such punishments.[39] Trials for criminal offences were by ordeal in pre-Conquest criminal laws, and habitual criminals were subjected to the "triple ordeal". Assumptions of guilt following a second ordeal resulted in amputation of the hands, feet, or both, and following a third ordeal punishments included blinding, excision of the nose, ears and upper lip, or scalping.[40]

While the general consensus is that individual rights and liberties came to the centre of legal theory in the era of liberalism, from the 18th century on, it does not mean there were no rights and liberties before then. Nevertheless, before the 18th century, there was no notion that the state was bound to protect such rights and liberties, at the expense of political and social considerations. The absence of the double jeopardy principle during the Anglo-Saxon period was (presumably) not a lacuna but possibly a natural feature of societies at a certain stage of social development.

6 Canon Law

Roman law antecedents influenced the development of the Canon law exposition of the principle. The 11th-century rediscovery of the Digest of Justinian in Europe is significant where it was widely applied until the 18th century.[41] Combined with the teaching of Roman law at the University of Oxford and the University of Cambridge since the 12th century,[42] the Digest influenced the medieval Catholic Church and canonists to refer to this code of laws as a legal source to explicate canonical rules.[43] Thereafter the Civil law *ne bis in idem* principle migrated into continental legal systems and subsequently influenced the development of the Common law principle.

Since the fall of Rome (476 CE), the development of Canon law opposed subjecting Christian clerks to the jurisdiction of temporal courts. Medieval

39 Stephen, *A History of English Criminal Law*, I: 59.

40 Benjamin Thorpe, *Ancient Laws and Institutes of England: Comprising Laws Enacted under the Anglo-Saxon Kings from Aethelbirht to Cnut* (London: Commissioners of the Public Records, 1840), 393–395.

41 George Mousourakis, *A Legal History of Rome* (London: Routledge, 2007); Charles Radding and Antonio Ciaralli, *The Corpus Iuris Civilis in the Middle Ages* (Leiden: Brill, 2006), 35–65.

42 Francis De Zulueta and Peter Stein, *The Teaching of Roman Law in England Around 1200* (London: Selden Society, 1990).

43 Peter De Cruz, *Comparative Law in a Changing World* (London: Routledge, 2007), 56–57.

scholars and canonists found biblical support for the claim that no person should be twice judged for the same offence.[44] The ecclesiastical principle based on natural law, reason and justice is attributed to an interpretation by St. Jerome in 391 CE on a passage from the Old Testament from the prophet Nahum (Book of Nahum 1:9) "For God judges not twice for the same offence" (Douay Rheims version: "there shall not rise a double affliction"; King James' version: "affliction shall not rise up the second time") that was subsequently included in Gratian's *Decretum*[45] and in canonist procedural sources.[46]

7 *Privilegium Clericale* in 12th to 13th-Century England

During the 12th century, clerks asserted their immunity from the jurisdiction of the king's court when accused of felony: they would be prosecuted and, if convicted, punished by the ecclesiastical courts. The ecclesiastical courts claimed exclusive jurisdiction over offences committed by clerk and jurisdiction over offences committed by laypeople against clerks. The claim that criminous clerks should not be tried in temporal courts and that all disputes between laypeople and clerks should be settled by ecclesiastical courts was controversial. The "benefit of clergy" developed as an immunity from prosecution in temporal courts based on the high regard in which the Church and its officials were held by secular rulers. Notably, in 355 CE, Roman Emperor Constantius (317–361 CE) decreed that bishops could be tried only by bishops. Justinian I (482–565 CE) allowed the clergy the right to have episcopal judges, though he carefully reserved the power of disregarding the exemption.[47]

The ecclesiastical courts claimed jurisdiction over civil and criminal matters concerning clerks. Punishment was degradation in the ecclesiastical courts; there was no forfeiture of the offender's property to the king. In 1164, the Constitutions of Clarendon restricted ecclesiastical privileges and curbed the power of the ecclesiastical courts, restrained the authority of ecclesiastical courts, and curtailed the extent of papal authority in England. Henry II declared that clerks who had been acquitted in the ecclesiastical courts would also be subject to the jurisdiction of the king's court for trial and pun-

44 Heikki Pihlajamaki and Mia Korpiola, "Medieval Canon Law: The Origins of Modern Criminal Law," in *The Oxford Handbook of Criminal Law,* ed. Markus D. Dubber and Tatjana Hörnle (Oxford: Oxford University Press, 2014), 201–224, 215.

45 C. 23, q. 5 c. 6.

46 Pihlajamaki and Korpiola, "Medieval Canon Law," 215.

47 Henry Charles Lea, *Studies in Church History* (Philadelphia: Collins, 1883), 177, 182.

ishment. The Church had extended the jurisdiction of the ecclesiastical courts bolstered by the growth of Canon law and had usurped many secular judicial prerogatives by taking advantage of the weakness of royal authority during the chaotic reign of Stephen (1135–1154), Henry II's predecessor. Ecclesiastical courts were notoriously lenient to criminous clerks. The purpose of the Constitutions was to restore the law and customs of the realm extant during the reign of Henry I (1100–1135). Clause 3 was the most controversial provision in that it exposed clerks to secular punishment. The bishops, led by Becket, reluctantly promised to observe the Constitutions; however, within a year, Becket repudiated his oath and was forced into six years of exile in France by Henry II.

The benefit of clergy was controversial and many offences committed against victims and the community remained unpunished. While clerks had immunity from secular law, they were still capable of committing secular offences. Clerks were treated more favourably by the ecclesiastical courts owing to the fraternal allegiance, and ecclesiastical judges were inclined to be lenient toward clerks accused of wrongdoing.[48] Nonetheless, the benefit of clergy existed throughout the medieval period and was not formally abolished until 1827.[49]

The influence of Roman law was significant on the early development of the Common law on this issue, especially following the posthumous victory of Thomas Becket, the Archbishop of Canterbury, after the power struggle between the Church and Henry II.[50] The principle that clerks should not be punished by the king's court after a trial in the ecclesiastical courts was a major source of the dispute between Becket and Henry II. The full extent of the claim was that not merely every criminal charge but every personal action against a clerk remained outside the competence of the temporal courts.[51] While the controversy over clerical immunity was not the only contentious issue in the medieval power struggle between Church and state,[52]

48 Charles Henry Pearson, *History of England During the Early and Middle Ages* (London: Bell and Daldy, 1867), II: 487.

49 7 & 8 Geo. IV, c. 27, s. 6 (1827).

50 Friedland, *Double Jeopardy*, 328, and chapter 1.

51 Frederick Pollock and Frederick William Maitland, *The History of English Law: Before the Time of Edward I*, 2nd edn. (Cambridge: Cambridge University Press, 1928), I: 446.

52 Brett Edward Whalen, *The Two Powers: The Papacy, the Empire, and the Struggle for Sovereignty in the Thirteenth Century* (Pennsylvania: University of Pennsylvania Press, 2019).

the controversy was the single aspect around which the dispute was waged most bitterly.[53]

Becket's main argument was that any further punishment of clerks in the king's court would violate the maxim *nemo bis in idipsum*: no man ought to be punished twice for the same offence.[54] Becket objected firstly to the summoning of clerks before a secular justice at the initial stage of the King's procedure; secondly, that no secular punishment should follow the deposition of a guilty clerk, since secular judges had no jurisdiction over clerks (who were under the jurisdiction of the ecclesiastical courts); thirdly, that deposition was itself the penalty for the offence in question, to which no secular punishment could be legitimately added, for this would involve the imposition of a double punishment.[55] This approach underscores the rationale for the inception of the concept in classical antiquity based on the universal law of reason, justice, and conscience. This development is the earliest intimation in the Common law of the inequity of the imposition of double punishment and multiple trials for the same criminal offence, influenced by ecclesiastical law.

Becket's successor, Archbishop Richard, was not opposed to dual punishment and wanted laypeople who murdered clerks to be handed over to the temporal courts for punishment, who could impose more severe forms of punishment on the basis that "there is no duplication where what is begun by one is completed by another". This was Henry II's position concerning offences committed by clerks.[56]

Becket prevailed albeit posthumously in 1176.[57] The king's court thereafter applied the principle. The compromise between the State and the Church meant that criminous clerks were exempt from trial and punishment in the king's court, with the result that ecclesiastical courts would henceforth bring justice to criminous clerks.[58] The punishment for all felonies was the death penalty which was unlikely to be commuted. However, for the clerks who could avail themselves of the benefit of clergy[59] this operated as a "structured

53 Charles Duggan, "The Becket Dispute and the Criminous Clerks," *Bulletin of the Institute of Historical Research* 35 (1962): 1–28, esp. 2.

54 James Craigie Robertson, *Materials for the History of Thomas Becket* (London: Longman, 1875), I: 28.

55 Duggan, "The Becket Dispute", 1–28, esp. 4.

56 Friedland, *Double Jeopardy*, 7.

57 Pollock and Maitland, *The History of English Law*, I: 448–449.

58 Jill Hunter, "The Development of the Rule against Double Jeopardy," *Journal of Legal History* 5 (1984): 3–19, esp. 6.

59 John De Morgan, "Executions and Executioners," *Green Bag* 12 (1900): 125–134.

bargain", somewhat analogous to the scale of tariffs extant in Anglo-Saxon laws, whereby accused clerks received the benefit of the prearranged "bargain" of being confined to the jurisdiction of ecclesiastic courts in exchange for his plea.[60] The benefit of clergy applied only to the first offence, and offences committed thereafter would subject the clerk to the jurisdiction of the king's court, without placing the accused twice in peril of conviction and punishment for the same offence.

Towards the end of the reign of Henry III (1216–1272), the king's courts were conducting their own trial before handing the clerk over to the spiritual courts. The purpose of this trial was to determine whether the offender's goods should be forfeited to the Crown. Although the Church protested reiterating Becket's argument based on *non bis in idipsum*, the king's court did not desist.[61]

8 Medieval English Criminal Procedure

Criminal trials during the medieval period were initiated by a procedure known as the appeal of felony by the victim or the victim's next of kin. Prosecution by the crown through a new procedure known as the king's indictment was subsequently introduced, the rationale of which was to permit the King to proceed with a prosecution within the prescribed period, a year and a day, to ensure that persons accused of committing felonies were duly prosecuted and punished, and the convicted person's property was then forfeit to the Crown.

If the appeal of felony did not succeed at the pleading stage, or the complaint was withdrawn before the trial concluded, the accused (appellee) would not be permitted to plead this in bar of a subsequent appeal for the same offence. While the appellor could not bring a second appeal of felony, this legal impediment did not operate to prevent another person from initiating an appeal against the same accused for the same offence provided that the person had standing.[62] Medieval procedure facilitating a second accusation by the appeal of felony may have placed the accused in double jeopardy of conviction and punishment, depending on whether the initial appeal of felony concluded with a criminal trial.

---

60 Jay Wishingrad, "The Plea Bargain in Historical Perspective," *Buffalo Law Review* 23 (1974): 499–528, esp. 511.

61 Friedland, *Double Jeopardy*, 7.

62 *Seler v Limoges* (1321) 85 Selden Society, Eyre of London 14 Ed. II 87, 89.

During the 13th century, an acquittal or conviction following a criminal trial commenced by an appellor prevented a second suit by the appellor, and a judgement in a criminal trial initiated by the king's indictment prevented a further suit by the King. Conceivably, the posthumous victory by Becket in the 12th century might have influenced the king's court to acknowledge an embryonic principle against double jeopardy. Towards the end of the thirteenth and for part of the 14th century, a criminal trial initiated by an appellor would not bar a suit by the king and *vice versa*,[63] especially true if the appellor's trial involved trial by battle.[64] This procedure permitting two criminal trials for the same offence, by the appeal of felony or king's indictment, witnesses against the recognition of a principle against double jeopardy during this period. With that being said, an obvious motive for the king's involvement in criminal trials during this period was not necessarily to vindicate the harm caused to victims of crime but rather to ensure that the convicted offender's property was forfeit to the crown in cases where the felony was punishable by death.[65]

Both Kirk[66] and Friedland[67] have suggested that the retention of the appeal of felony with the king's indictment facilitated the possibility of a dual process for instigating criminal trials that militated against any notion of the principle being recognised during this period. Conversely, it could be argued that the retention of this dual procedure ensured that the felonies were brought to the attention of the King who could then initiate a criminal trial without necessarily depriving the victim of subsequently proceeding with the appeal of felony.

The established criminal procedure required the King to wait a year and a day before initiating a prosecution, the interim period allowing for the appeal of felony to be commenced. The difficulty in prosecuting after a year and a day meant that many offences went unpunished, principally due to the time lapse in prosecuting resulting in witnesses having vague recollections of the alleged criminal episode, not to mention the fact that such witnesses may have since died or could not be located.

63 Friedland, *Double Jeopardy*, 8–9; Marion S. Kirk, "Jeopardy During the Period of the Books," *University of Pennsylvania Law Review* 82 (1934): 602–617, esp. 607.

64 *Bartkus v Illinois* (1958) 359 US 121, 151–152, Black J.

65 Krista J. Kesselring, "Felony Forfeiture in England, c.1170–1870," *Journal of Legal History* 30 (2009): 201–226; *Cf.* Arie Freiberg and Richard Fox, "Fighting Crime with Forfeiture: Lessons from History," *Australian Journal of Legal History* 6 (2000): 1–50.

66 Kirk, "Jeopardy During the Period of the Books," 602–617, esp. 605.

67 Friedland, *Double Jeopardy*, 8–9.

In the late 15th century, legislative intervention permitted the king's indictment to be brought within the prescribed period (a year and a day) in the case of homicide only, and an acquittal would not prevent a second trial being initiated by the victim through the appeal of felony.[68] This dual procedure was incompatible with a recognition of legal protection against double jeopardy. Prior to this legislative intervention, an acquittal following an appeal after a trial by jury operated as a bar to a prosecution for the same offence by king's indictment and an acquittal on an indictment was a bar to a prosecution for the same offence by an appeal. However, the effect of this enactment was that neither a conviction nor an acquittal on an indictment could be raised as a bar to a subsequent prosecution for the same offence by an appeal, if the appeal was brought within the year and a day.[69] This dual procedure was followed until the late 17th century when in *Armstrong v Lisle*[70] Chief Justice Holt opined:

> The statute of 3 H. 7 is severe in overthrowing a fundamental point of law, in subjecting a man that is acquitted, to another trial, which is putting his life twice in danger for the same crime; therefore the purview of 3 H. 7 ought to be taken strictly, and the exception favourably.

This judicial declaration indicates the recognition of an embryonic notion of legal protection against double jeopardy. The jeopardy of the accused person's life had a literal meaning during the medieval period because of the harsh punishments that were imposed on conviction for felony offences.

Protection was qualified in *Young v Slaughterford*,[71] wherein Chief Justice Holt ordered an appeal to be brought against the accused for the same offence following an acquittal on indictment for murder. The accused was convicted and sentenced to death.[72] This judgment illustrates the enhanced prospects for placing the same accused in double jeopardy of multiple trials and consequential life in jeopardy owing to the dual procedure.

A subsequent statutory intervention in the early 16th century also hindered the embryonic development of the principle.[73] Provision was made to permit

---

68 3 Hen. VII, c. 1 (1487).

69 Kirk, "Jeopardy During the Period of the Books," 607, n. 26; Jay A. Sigler, "A History of Double Jeopardy," *American Journal of Legal History* 7 (1963): 285–311, esp. 289.

70 (1697) 84 ER 1096 at 1101.

71 (1709) 88 ER 999.

72 (1709) 88 ER 1007.

73 26 Hen. VIII, c. 6 (1534).

a criminal trial in England of persons accused of committing felony offences in Wales, presumably following an acquittal or conviction for the same offence in that jurisdiction. This procedure was seemingly a legislative response to the less rigorous criminal trial procedure and punishments in Welsh courts, which, once again, was an obstacle to the recognition of the principle as a cornerstone of criminal procedure during this period.[74]

Medieval criminal trial procedure did not provide accused persons with basic due process and fair trial guarantees, and procedural ambiguities were resolved in favour of the prosecution. These inherent deficiencies in the medieval criminal trial are vividly illustrated in *Lisle's Case*,[75] as Stephen commented that "[i]t was cruel, but legal, to sentence a woman to be burnt alive for harbouring two rebels for a night. The conviction was illegal on the grounds that Hicks, whom she harboured, had not been convicted before the trial".[76] Accused persons on trial for treason or felonies were denied the assistance of defence counsel and were also denied the opportunity to examine the indictment against them. The prosecution was permitted to call witnesses, but this privilege was not accorded to the accused. There was also some doubt as to the admissibility of evidence and the general conduct of the trial, but, once again, these uncertainties were resolved in favour of the prosecution.[77] These procedural deficiencies to the disadvantage of accused persons suggest that the prohibition on double jeopardy was not seen as important enough to be recognised as an essential principle of criminal procedure during this period.

9 The Absence of the Principle against Double Jeopardy in the Sources of Common Law

The incremental development of the concept was in consequence the adverse standing of accused persons during the medieval period and procedural anomalies that undermined fair trial rights of accused persons. The development of the principle was necessitated at a time when criminal procedure did not resolve disputes on the merits but according to the powers and resources available to the prosecution as opposed to the adverse position of the accused. If an embryonic double jeopardy principle had existed during this period, then the prohibition on retrials and multiple punishments would (presumably)

74 Friedland, *Double Jeopardy*, 10.

75 (1697) 84 ER 1095.

76 Stephen, *A History of English Criminal Law* (London: Macmillan, 1883), I: 413.

77 Holdsworth, *A History of English Law*, IX: 224.

have carried over from the Norman Conquest and the inception of the Common law.

The existence of the principle deeply rooted in English legal history cannot be demonstrated with a sufficient degree of certainty, notwithstanding the fact that there have been numerous judicial statements[78] and academic commentaries[79] asserting that the concept is as old as the Common law itself, which (presumably) stems from the beginning of legal memory in 1189 as with other customs and practices.[80]

In 1166, Henry II enacted in the Assize of Clarendon (remodelling of criminal procedure) that even though the accused was acquitted by the ordeal he must abjure the realm if he was of bad character.[81] While this enactment may have been in response to the high volume of acquittals by the ordeal, it was nonetheless anathema to an embryonic principle against double jeopardy.

A prohibition on double jeopardy is conspicuously absent from Magna Carta of 1215 and cannot be inferred from the most famous repository of liberties in the annals of the Common law.[82] This lacuna suggests the principle was not recognised as a fundamental right of accused persons during the formative period of the Common law.

Owing to the absence of plea rolls, the extent to which the courts prevented double jeopardy from evolving before the 12th century is difficult to ascertain. The earliest recording of court decisions began with the Year Books (1290–1535) under the authority of the Norman Kings. Written in the Anglo-Norman language these were the earliest series of reported cases of the Common law courts, which include eleven mentions of the word "jeopardy". Embryonic criminal trial procedure extant during the period of the Year Books further evinces that the double jeopardy principle was not an established principle of liberty since the inception of the Common law, but

78 *The People* (DPP) *v Quilligan* (*No. 2*) [1989] IR 46, 54 Henchy J; *United States v Jenkins* (1973) 490 F 2d 868, 870 Friendly J; *Bartkus v Illinois* (1958) 359 US 121, 151–152, Black J. (dissenting); *Green v United States* (1957) 355 US 184, 200 Frankfurter J (dissenting); *Stout v State* (1913) 36 Okl 744, 756 Ames J; *R* (*Hastings*) *v Justices of Galway* [1906] 2 IR 499, 505 Palles CB.

79 Walter T. Fisher, "Double Jeopardy, Two Sovereignties and the Intruding Constitution," *University of Chicago Law Review* 28 (1961): 591–613, esp. 603.

80 *Cf.* Alan Wharam, "The 1189 Rule: Fact, Fiction, or Fraud?," *Anglo-American Law Review* 1 (1972): 262–278.

81 Friedland, *Double Jeopardy*, 6.

82 Roscoe Pound, *Interpretations of Legal History* (Cambridge Massachusetts: Harvard University Press, 1923), 8–9.

that the principle gradually evolved throughout the post-medieval development of the Common law as a procedural defence.

The English Bill of Rights (1689) did not incorporate a double jeopardy provision. Furthermore, the principle does not appear to have been enshrined in a statute prior to its inclusion in the Fifth Amendment to the United States Constitution 1787. This suggests the political climate militated against the recognition of the importance of the concept as the administration of criminal law during the medieval period was more concerned with dealing with offenders as opposed to respecting individual rights of accused persons.

10 Treatises, Commentaries, and Institutes

The courts will typically have recourse to the writings of recognised and authoritative legal commentators where there is a lacuna of formal legal sources. Such commentaries were accorded a status akin to that of judicial decisions. A survey of medieval English commentators reveals an incremental development of the principle, which suggests that the concept was not a pre-existing Common law principle.[83]

Glanville was Chief Justiciar during the reign of Henry II (1154–1189). The treatise written in 1187 was the first book on medieval English Common law and is attributed to Glanville; written at the behest of Henry II as the culmination of his long-term endeavours to restore peace and prosperity following years of anarchy under Stephen I. The treatise which mostly deals with explaining the proper use of royal writs in actions is a complete statement of the law since the fall of Rome. This record of the proceedings of the king's court does not refer to a prohibition on double jeopardy, which suggests the principle was not carried over as an established principle of law from the Anglo-Saxon period.

Glanville's Treatise was followed by a treatise composed by Henry de Bracton (c. 1210–c. 1268), which owes much of its heritage to the Glanville. Bracton (writing in the 1220s and 1230s, soon after the promulgation of *Magna Carta*) does not make any reference to the principle. While Coke identified tenets of the principle in Bracton's writings, this is a personal interpretation and not indicative of an embryonic principle extant during that period.[84] Judicial pronouncements suggest that Bracton did recognise the

83 Frank M. Wilson, "Pillars of Anglo-American Law," *Baylor Law Review* 12 (1960): 251–260.

84 Sigler, "A History of Double Jeopardy," *American Journal of Legal History* 7 (1963): 291.

necessity of a legal principle against multiple prosecutions for the same offence.[85] This uncertainty among leading Common law writers and jurists suggests the prohibition on multiple trials and punishments was not an important principle of the Common law during this period.

The influence of Roman law on the development of the Common law principle could have been introduced by the influx of Roman law scholars in the 12th, 13th, and 14th centuries,[86] or, alternatively, that the Conquest strengthened the influx of continental Canon law texts and ideas. This immigration influenced the writer and jurist Bracton and others who were enthusiastic to supplement the relatively unsophisticated Common law with the doctrinal refinements of Roman jurisprudence.[87]

Britton[88] is the earliest work (first printed around 1530) on the Common law of England at the behest of Edward I (1272–1307) written in the French language which declared a former judgement barrier during that period.[89] Significantly, the Norman-French terminology of the pleas in bar, *autrefois acquit* and *autrefois convict*, might be attributable to this work and suggests that the incremental development of the Common law principle might have been influenced by, and migrated from, continental Civil law.

Jurisprudence emanating from the King's Court from the 14th to 16th centuries demonstrates the existence of an embryonic principle that developed incrementally.[90] In the 17th century, Lord Chief Justice Coke[91] constructed the evolution of the principle on the basis of late medieval legal practice, which is reflected in the judicial decisions of the King's Court, especially from the post-medieval period (discussed in the next section).[92] By the 18th century, Blackstone described the principle as follows:

85 George Edward Woodbine, ed., *Bracton On the Laws and Customs of England*, trans. Samuel E. Thorne (Cambridge, Mass: Belknap Press, 1968), II: 391.

86 Ralph V. Turner, "Roman Law in England Before the Time of Bracton," *Journal of British Studies* 15 (1975): 1–25; Edward D. Re, "The Roman Contribution to the Common Law," *Fordham Law Review* 29 (1961): 447–494.

87 Hunter, "The Development of the Rule against Double Jeopardy," 4.

88 Francis Morgan Nichols, ed., *Britton: An English Translation and Notes* (Washington: John Byrne & Co., 1901).

89 Sigler, "A History of Double Jeopardy," 292.

90 Discussed in text accompanying footnotes 98 to 123.

91 Edward Coke, *The Third Pard of the Institutes of the Laws of England (Concerning High Treason, and other Pleas of the Crown, and Criminal Causes)* (London: Forgotten Books, 2018).

92 Ian Williams, "The Tudor Genesis of Edward Coke's Immemorial Common Law," *Sixteenth Century Journal* 43 (2012): 103–123, esp. 116–117.

> [T]he plea of *autrefois acquit*, or a former acquittal, is grounded on this universal maxim of the common law of England, that no man is to be brought into jeopardy of his life or limb more than once for the same offence .... The plea of *autrefois convict*, or a former conviction for the same identical crime ... is a good plea in bar to an indictment. And this depends upon the same principle as the former that no man ought to be twice brought in danger of his life for one and the same crime.[93]

Notably, the Restoration of Charles II who returned from exile in continental Europe (where he spent time in France, the Dutch Republic, and the Spanish Netherlands) following the Interregnum (1649–1660) witnessed the reinstatement of the old forms of law.[94] Continental law and procedure might have impressed Charles II to the extent that those principles of law were adopted in the Common law of England, which in turn might have augmented the Norman-French terminology of the pleas in bar. Likewise, Becket was exiled in France for six years (1164–1170) and conceivably might have been impressed by the Civil law concept.

Although the word "jeopardy" began to have some significance during the earlier periods of the development of the Common law, it was not originally concerned with the principle that a man's life should not be twice placed in jeopardy of conviction with imposition of punishment, for the same offence.[95] It appears that the contemporary term "double jeopardy" was unknown during the earlier periods of English legal history. The principle as expressed by the pleas in bar *autrefois acquit* and *autrefois convict*, which are still referred to in contemporary criminal justice systems, are probably attributable to Blackstone, although the concepts existed before his time;[96] being referred to by Britton in the 16th century.

The Common law has a rich Christian heritage, a tradition that was embodied in the drafting of *Magna Carta*. Eminent jurists, including Blackstone and Coke, frequently invoked their devout Christian faith when

93 William Blackstone, *Commentaries on the Laws of England*, Book IV: Of Public Wrongs, Chapter 26, Yale Law School, The Avalon Project, https://avalon.law.yale.edu/18th_century/blackstone_bk4ch26.asp.

94 John Baker, *An Introduction to English Legal History*, 5th edn (Oxford: Oxford University Press, 2019), 228.

95 Baker, *An Introduction to English Legal History*, 84.

96 Jay A. Sigler, *Double Jeopardy: The Development of a Legal and Social Policy* (New York: Cornell University Press, 1969), 222.

expounding and developing legal principles.[97] It is conceivable that Canon law expositions directly influenced the development of the Common law principle (notwithstanding the omission of the principle in the Great Charter).

11 Post-medieval Developments

Jurisprudence emanating from the king's court from the late 16th century illustrates the emerging judicial recognition of the principle after a criminal trial on the merits. In *Vaux's Case*,[98] the Court of King's Bench ruled that a new trial could proceed following an acquittal based on a defective indictment, charging an offence unknown to the law. Since the acquittal was founded on an error of law, the plea *autrefois acquit* was not available to the accused. An acquittal based on a defective indictment meant that the accused was not formerly in jeopardy of conviction and punishment on the first criminal trial. The *autrefois acquit* plea in bar to a subsequent trial would be available to the accused following an acquittal on the merits. In *Wrote v Wigges*,[99] a conviction for the lesser-included offence of manslaughter was pleaded in bar to a subsequent trial for the greater (compound) offence of murder. The Court of King's Bench ruled that "*auterfoits convict* of manslaughter, and clergy thereupon allowed, is a good bar in an appeal of murder".[100] The Court further ruled that "such bar is good at the Common law, and not restrained by Stat. 3 H. 7, c. 1, and is also a good bar to an indictment for murder".[101]

In *R v Read*,[102] the Court of King's Bench ruled that that earlier cases which had permitted the prosecution to seek a new trial after an acquittal were no longer to be followed: "new trials may be in criminal cases at the prayer of the defendant, where he is convicted (but) not at the suit of the King where he is acquitted".[103] The courts grappled with the problem of re-indictment for a different offence in *R v James Turner and William Turner*.[104] The accused

97 Augusto Zimmermann, "Christianity and the Common Law: Rediscovering the Christian Roots of the English Legal System," *University of Notre Dame Australia Law Review* 16 (2014): 145–177.
98 (1591) 76 ER 992 at 993.
99 (1591) 76 ER 994.
100 (1591) 76 ER 994 at 994.
101 (1591) 76 ER 994 at 994.
102 (1660) 83 ER 271.
103 (1660) 83 ER 271 at 271.
104 *R v Turner* (1664) 84 ER 1068.

were indicted for burglary resulting in the conviction of the first named accused and the acquittal of the second. The prosecution sought to re-indict the second accused of the burglary with the additional charge of stealing money from a servant of the person whose property had been burgled. The Court of King's Bench ruled that having once been acquitted of the burglary he could not be re-indicted for that offence, but he could be indicted for a different offence, in this case the offence of stealing. Likewise in *R v Jones and Bever*,[105] two accused were acquitted on a charge of burglary and were subsequently indicted for the same burglary with the additional count of stealing goods. The Court of King's Bench ruled that they could not be re-indicted for the same burglary but could be indicted on the count of stealing for which they had not previously been tried upon.

In *Sir Henry Vane's Case*,[106] the Court of King's Bench refused to accept a bill of exceptions, which Friedland[107] suggests "would have substantially widened the scope for the appeal by writ of error and would have had the effect of permitting further trials in cases of felony". *Vane* was indicted for high treason and, after the indictment had been read out in open court, he requested that it be read a second time, and this was done. He then requested that the indictment be read out a third time, but this time to be read in Latin, however, the court refused this request. The accused was convicted, to which he entered a bill of exceptions, however the trial court refused to accept this, ruling that a bill of exceptions does not lie in criminal cases, but only in civil cases. *Vane* was executed by beheading. This is an early intimation of the increasing consciousness by the courts of the inherent injustice in permitting more than one criminal trial for the same offence.

In *Sir John Jackson's Case*,[108] the Court of King's Bench extended the application of the embryonic principle to misdemeanours, ruling that a retrial should be prevented following a conviction for perjury. Likewise, in *R v Lewin*,[109] the Court of King's Bench refused an indictment of the accused who had already been convicted of perjury, while in *R v Marchant*[110] the Court of King's Bench refused a trial *de novo* for perjury where the accused had already been convicted of that same perjury. In a similar vein, the Court

105 (1665) 84 ER 1078.
106 (1662) 83 ER 300.
107 Friedland, *Double Jeopardy*, 11–12.
108 (1663) 83 ER 1157.
109 (1668) 84 ER 248.
110 (1668) 2 Keble 403.

of King's Bench in *R v Hannis*[111] refused to order retrial after a conviction on the charge of perjury.

In cases where a verdict of guilty has been set aside by the trial judge because of procedural irregularities, this would not prevent a retrial of the accused as there was no formal verdict of either acquittal or conviction recorded by the court. The pleas in bar, *autrefois acquit* and *autrefois convict*, are predicated on a final acquittal or conviction for the same criminal offence as in a subsequent indictment. In *R v Smith*,[112] the accused was convicted of perjury by an "obstinate jury" against the direction of the trial Judge. The Court of King's Bench set aside this verdict and a new trial was ordered. The double jeopardy principle could only be raised as a plea in bar when the first trial of the accused was concluded following a lawful adjudication of the case.

Criminal trial procedure during the medieval period developed in a manner detrimental to the accused in that the Crown possessed all the advantages such as knowledge of the charges in the indictment so as to inform prosecution strategies, the prosecution alone could call witnesses and related procedural issues also advantaged the Crown.[113] The blatant discharge of the jury when it appeared that an acquittal was likely allowed the prosecution to bring a further charge on more compelling evidence, a practice that continued up until the end of the 17th century and resulted in the courts affording greater recognition to the emerging principle against double jeopardy. In *R v Roberts*,[114] the accused was indicted as a principal on a count of burglary, but from the evidence he was only an accessory in that he received the principals and the goods stolen but did not take any part in the actual burglary. The prosecution was unsure of, if the jury acquitted him, as they were most likely to do, whether he would be subsequently indicted and convicted as an accessory. The Court of King's Bench discharged the jury and indicted him as an accessory to the burglary. This blatant discharge of the jury with the purpose of seeking a new trial can also be evidenced in the infamous treason case of *R v Whitebread and Fenwick*[115] where the jury was discharged after evidence had been given and concluded by the prosecution, which was insufficient to convict the accused. This practice illustrated the role of the king's court in safeguarding the accused against multiple criminal trials, a practice that could be

111 (1671) 84 ER 483.

112 (1681) 84 ER 1197.

113 Holdsworth, *A History of English Law*, IX: 224.

114 (1662) 84 ER 1066.

115 (1679) 7 How. St. Tr. 311.

found in subsequent cases,[116] including *R v Perkins*,[117] wherein Chief Justice Holt strenuously disapproved of the practice of discharging the jury early in a criminal trial with the objective of seeking a new trial and improving prosecution strategies to enhance the prospects of a conviction. Notwithstanding, this procedure prevailed throughout the 18th century. In *R v Kinloch*,[118] the Court of Crown Cases discharged the jury to allow the accused to enter a different plea and ruled that such discharge did not constitute an acquittal.

The most important expansion in the recognition and application of the double jeopardy principle occurred during the late 17th century when the Court of King's bench began to recognise judgements in other jurisdictions that would prohibit a subsequent trial proceeding in England for the same offence. In *R v Thomas*,[119] the Court of King's Bench ruled that an acquittal in Wales on a charge of murder could be raised as a plea in bar to a second trial in England. Likewise, in *R v Hutchinson*,[120] the Court of King's Bench ruled that an acquittal on a charge of murder committed in Portugal prevented a subsequent trial for the same murder in England.[121] The procedure whereby an acquittal by a foreign court would form the basis of an *autrefois acquit* plea in bar to a subsequent trial for the same offence was firmly established in *R v Aughet*.[122] The accused was a Belgian military officer stationed in London, where he shot a Belgian soldier, and was surrendered to the Belgian authorities. The accused was acquitted in Belgium, and upon his arrival back in England, a criminal trial was instigated. Notwithstanding the offences under Belgian law and English law were not the same, the accused was permitted to raise the plea in bar, *autrefois acquit*.

Legal protection was not absolute during the 17th century, when judges habitually discharged juries to enable prosecutors to present a stronger case on a retrial. In murder cases, a private person could appeal after the accused had been acquitted following a trial on indictment. Nevertheless, it was during the 17th century that defendants were gradually afforded broader rights to appeal from a conviction. The latter half of the 17th century was a period of increasing consciousness by the courts of the importance of the emerging

116 *R v Jackson* (1661) 83 ER 330; *R v Fenwick and Holt* (1663) 82 ER 1025.

117 (1698) 90 ER 1122.

118 (1746) 168 ER 9.

119 (1664) 83 ER 1180, see also (1664) 83 ER 1147, (1664) 83 ER 1172.

120 (1677) 84 ER 1011.

121 *Cf.* Ann Mumford and Peter Alldridge, "The History of Double Jeopardy and Criminal Jurisdiction: *US v Gamble* (2019) and *R v Hutchinson* (1677)," *Law Quarterly Review* 139 (2023): 390–411.

122 (1918) 13 Cr App R 101.

double jeopardy jurisprudence. This was partly due to the writings of Lord Chief Justice Coke and partly as a reaction against the lawlessness in the first half of that century.

By the 18th century, Justice Hawkins declared that judgements given by other criminal courts in England formed the basis of the pleas in bar:

> Notwithstanding the opinion of the Book of Assizes (9 Assize 15), that no acquittal in any other court can be any bar to a prosecution in the Court of King's Bench, because that is the highest court, I take it to be settled at this day, that an acquittal in any court whatsoever, which has a jurisdiction of the cause, is as good a bar of any subsequent prosecution for the same crime, as an acquittal in the highest court.[123]

By the late 18th century in the *Duchess of Kingston's Case*[124] defence counsel authoritatively opined "whenever, and by whatever means, there is an acquittal in a criminal prosecution, the scene is closed and the curtain drops".

12 Analysis

The origins of the rule of law theory can be traced back to ancient Roman laws during the formation of the first republic. While Albert V. Dicey's theory of the rule of law focuses on the form of law and the process by which laws are made and applied, other theories expand on this and encompass the substance or content of laws respecting fundamental rights.[125] Coke's imperatives on the absence of arbitrary power on the part of government and that no person is punishable except for a distinct breach of law established in the ordinary legal manner before courts of criminal justice is pivotal to the post-medieval recognition of the principle.

Safeguarding individual rights against unwarranted harassment through multiple criminal trials and punishments is fundamental to the rule of law which is a critical constitutional concept delimiting the exercise of arbitrary power in criminal trials. The application of the rule of law to the double jeopardy principle in historical contexts reflects the diverse social, political, and

123 Cited by Friedland, *Double Jeopardy*, 12.

124 (1776) 20 How St Tr 355, 528.

125 Mark D. Walters, "The Spirit of Legality: A.V. Dicey and the Rule of Law," in *The Cambridge Companion to the Rule of Law,* ed. Jens Meierhenrich and Martin Loughlin (Cambridge: Cambridge University Press, 2021), 153–170.

legal climates underpinning state and prosecutorial discretion and the temporal courts to the enforcement of criminal law and procedure. This is compounded by the adverse standing of accused persons throughout the historical development of the principle. In the context of criminal law enforcement philosophies from the post-medieval period, the development of the Common law principle forms the rationale for the status of the principle in contemporary trials, namely, to redress the imbalance between the power and resources available to states and public prosecutors, as opposed to the adverse standing of accused persons. Nonetheless, legal philosophical rationales for the incremental development of the principle through post-medieval jurisprudence relate to outdated perceptions of the standing of accused persons and the purpose of the contemporary criminal process. Statutory modifications to the application of the principle in many Common law jurisdictions empower public prosecutors to apply to the appellate courts to quash an acquittal based on new and compelling evidence against the acquitted person, which, if granted, paves the way for a post-acquittal retrial for the same offence.[126]

The pervasive nature of Roman law from 753 BCE to the fall of the Western Empire in 476 continued in the Eastern Empire until 1453 CE and formed the basis for the legal systems of most continental European Civil law inquisitorial states. There is a close analogy between the way Roman law and the Common law of England evolved,[127] which might suggest the Civil law *ne bis in idem* principle influenced the incremental development of the Common law double jeopardy principle. In the same vein, the Canon law of the church being derived in large measure from Roman law was also a considerable influence on the development of the Common law principle. While developments of the Common law principle are the focus of this chapter, it is notable that the Common law of England was transported and transplanted to other countries;[128] therefore, the discussion and analysis presented herein may be of interest to readers from cognate jurisdictions.

---

126 England, Wales and Northern Ireland (Criminal Justice Act 2003, Part 10); Scotland (Double Jeopardy (Scotland) Act 2011); Western Australia (Criminal Appeals Amendment (Double Jeopardy) Act 2012); Victoria (Criminal Procedure Amendment (Double Jeopardy and Other Matters) Act 2011); South Australia (Criminal Law Consolidation (Double Jeopardy) Amendment Act 2008); Queensland (Criminal Code (Double Jeopardy) Amendment Act 2007); New South Wales (Crimes (Appeal and Review) Amendment (Double Jeopardy) Act 2006); New Zealand (Criminal Procedure Act 2011); Ireland (Criminal Procedure Act 2010, Part 3).

127 Stephen, *A History of English Criminal Law*, 1: 49.

128 Arthur Lehman Goodhart, *The Migration of the Common Law* (London: Stevens & Sons, 1960).

13 Conclusion

Contemporary interpretations of the double jeopardy principle should consider the historical context wherein the procedural defence originated. The basis of double jeopardy jurisprudence can be traced to the formative periods in the development of the Common law and the policies it espouses have progressively evolved as a procedural defence through the decisions of the Common law courts in response to the adverse standing of the accused in medieval criminal trials. The development of the Common law principle against double jeopardy was influenced by the continental Civil law, which may have been transmitted through the Canon law of the Church, and perhaps notions of the Civil law concept migrated back to England with the return of Becket and Charles II from exile. The incremental procedural development of the common law principle especially from the post-medieval period was conceivably influenced by the extant Civil law *ne bis in idem* principle and Canon law exposition.

Contemporary interpretations of the double jeopardy principle should consider the historical context wherein the procedural defence originated. The basis of double jeopardy jurisprudence may be traced to the formative periods in the development of the Common law and the policies it espouses have progressively evolved through the decisions of the Common law courts in response to the adverse standing of the accused in medieval criminal trials. The development of the Common law principle against double jeopardy was influenced by the continental Civil law, which may have been transmitted through the Canon law of the Church. It is unlikely that the principle was native to the Common law of England, particularly in consideration of the former Anglo-Saxon rudimentary legal system and the absence of reported decisions of the Common law courts during the formative periods in the development of the Common law legal system.

Bibliography

Baker, John. *An Introduction to English Legal History*. 5th edn. Oxford: Oxford University Press, 2019.

Binder, Guyora. "Punishment Theory: Moral or Political?" *Buffalo Criminal Law Review* 5 (2002): 321–371.

Blackstone, William. *Commentaries on the Laws of England*. Book IV: Of Public Wrongs, Chapter 26. Yale Law School. The Avalon Project. https://avalon.law.yale.edu/18th_century/blackstone_bk4ch26.asp.

Bonner, Robert J. *Lawyers and Litigants in Ancient Athens: The Genesis of the Legal Profession.* Chicago: University of Chicago Press, 1927.

Brooke, Zachary Nugent. *The English Church and the Papacy.* Cambridge: Cambridge University Press, 1931.

Carugati, Federica, Gillian K. Hadfield, and Barry R. Weingas. "Building Legal Order in Ancient Athens." *Journal of Legal Analysis* 7 (2015): 291–324.

Coke, Edward. *The Third Pard of the Institutes of the Laws of England (Concerning High Treason, and other Pleas of the Crown, and Criminal Causes).* London: Forgotten Books, 2018.

De Cruz, Peter. *Comparative Law in a Changing World.* London: Routledge, 2007.

De Morgan, John. "Executions and Executioners." *Green Bag* 12 (1900): 125–134.

De Zulueta, Francis, and Peter Stein. *The Teaching of Roman Law in England Around 1200.* London: Selden Society, 1990.

Demosthenes. *Against Meidias, Against Androtion, Against Aristocrates, Against Timocrates, Against Aristogeiton.* Translated by James Herbert Vince. Cambridge Massachusetts: Harvard University Press, 1935.

Demosthenes. *Olynthiacs, Philippics, Minor Public Speeches, Speech Against Leptines, I–XVII, XX.* Translated by James Herbert Vince. Cambridge MA: Harvard University Press, 1930. Reprint, 1962.

Duggan, Charles. "The Becket Dispute and the Criminous Clerks." *Bulletin of the Institute of Historical Research* 35 (1962): 1–28.

Epps, Daniel. "Checks and Balances in the Criminal Law." *Vanderbilt Law Review* 74 (2021): 1–84.

Fisher, Walter T. "Double Jeopardy, Two Sovereignties and the Intruding Constitution." *University of Chicago Law Review* 28 (1961): 591–613.

Freiberg, Arie, and Richard Fox. "Fighting Crime with Forfeiture: Lessons from History." *Australian Journal of Legal History* 6 (2000): 1–50.

Friedland, Martin L. *Double Jeopardy.* Oxford: Clarendon Press, 1969.

Goodhart, Arthur Lehman. *The Migration of the Common Law.* London: Stevens & Sons, 1960.

Hessick, Carissa Byrne. "Separation of Powers Versus Checks and Balances in the Criminal Justice System: A Response to Professor Epps." *Vanderbilt Law Review* 74 (2021): 159–185.

Higham, Nick. "From sub-Roman Britain to Anglo-Saxon England: Debating the Insular Dark Ages." *History Compass* 2 (2004): 1–29.

Holdsworth, William Searle. *A History of English Law.* London: Methuen, 1926.

Hunter, Jill. "The Development of the Rule against Double Jeopardy." *Journal of Legal History* 5 (1984): 3–19.

Hurd, Heidi M., and Michael S. Moore. "The Ethical Implications of Proportioning Punishment to Deontological Desert." *Criminal Law and Philosophy* 15 (2021): 495–514.

Jolowicz, Herbert Felix. *Historical Introduction to Roman Law*. 2nd edn. Cambridge: Cambridge University Press, 1954.

Jones, John Walter. *The Law and Legal Theory of the Greeks*. Oxford: Clarendon Press, 1977.

Kallendorf, Craig. "The Historical Petrarch." *American Historical Review* 101 (1996): 130–141.

Kesselring, Krista J. "Felony Forfeiture in England, c.1170–1870." *Journal of Legal History* 30 (2009): 201–226.

Kirk, Marion S. "Jeopardy During the Period of the Books." *University of Pennsylvania Law Review* 82 (1934): 602–617.

Lanni, Adriaan. *Law and Order in Ancient Athens*. Cambridge: Cambridge University Press, 2016.

Lea, Henry Charles. *Studies in Church History*. Philadelphia: Collins, 1883.

Maitland, Frederic William. "Henry II and the Criminous Clerks." In *The Collected Papers of Frederic William Maitland*, edited by Herbert Albert Laurens Fisher, II: 239. Cambridge: Cambridge University Press, 1911.

Mommsen, Theodore E. "Petrarch's Conception of the 'Dark Ages'." *Speculum: A Journal of Medieval Studies* 17 (1942): 226–242.

Mousourakis, George. *A Legal History of Rome*. London: Routledge, 2007.

Mumford, Ann, and Peter Alldridge. "The History of Double Jeopardy and Criminal Jurisdiction: *US v Gamble* (2019) and *R v Hutchinson* (1677)." *Law Quarterly Review* 139 (2023): 390–411.

Nelson, Janet N. "The Dark Ages." *History Workshop Journal* 63 (2004): 191–201.

Nichols, Francis Morgan, ed. *Britton: An English Translation and Notes*. Washington: John Byrne & Co., 1901.

Pearson, Charles Henry. *History of England During the Early and Middle Ages*. London: Bell and Daldy, 1867.

Phillips, David. *The Law of Ancient Athens*. Michigan: University of Michigan Press, 2013.

Pihlajamaki, Heikki, and Mia Korpiola. "Medieval Canon Law: The Origins of Modern Criminal Law." In *The Oxford Handbook of Criminal Law*, edited by Markus D. Dubber and Tatjana Hörnle, 201–224. Oxford: Oxford University Press, 2014.

Pollock, Frederick, and Frederick William Maitland. *The History of English Law: Before the Time of Edward I*. 2nd edn. 2 vols. Cambridge: Cambridge University Press, 1928.

Poole, Austin Lane. *From Domesday Book to Magna Carta, 1087–1216*. 2nd edn. Oxford: Clarendon Press, 1955.

Pound, Roscoe. *Interpretations of Legal History*. Cambridge Massachusetts: Harvard University Press, 1923.

Rabin, Andrew. *Crime and Punishment in Anglo-Saxon England*. Cambridge: Cambridge University Press, 2020.

Radding, Charles, and Antonio Ciaralli. *The Corpus Iuris Civilis in the Middle Ages*. Leiden: Brill, 2006.

Radin, Max. *Handbook of Roman Law*. St. Paul, Minnesota: West Publishing, 1927.

Re, Edward D. "The Roman Contribution to the Common Law." *Fordham Law Review* 29 (1961): 447–494.

Robertson, James Craigie. *Materials for the History of Thomas Becket*. London: Longman, 1875.

Schisas, Pandias Michael. *Offences against the State in Roman Law*. London: University of London Press, 1926.

Scott, Samuel Parsons. *The Civil Law*. Cincinnati: Central Trust Company, 1932.

Sherman, Charles Phineas. *Roman Law in the Modern World*. 2nd edn. New Haven: New Haven Law Book, 1922.

Sigler, Jay A. "A History of Double Jeopardy." *American Journal of Legal History* 7 (1963): 285–311.

Sigler, Jay A. *Double Jeopardy: The Development of a Legal and Social Policy*. New York: Cornell University Press, 1969.

Stephen, James Fitzjames. *A History of English Criminal Law*. London: Macmillan, 1883.

Stephen, James Fitzjames. *A History of English Criminal Law*. London: Macmillan, 1883.

Strachan-Davidson, James Leigh. *Problems of the Roman Criminal Law*. Oxford: Clarendon Press, 1912.

Stuckenberg, Carl-Friedrich. "Double Jeopardy and *Ne Bis in Idem* in Common Law and Civil Law Jurisdictions." In *The Oxford Handbook of Criminal Process*, edited by Darryl K. Brown, Jenia Iontcheva Turner, and Bettina Weisser, 457–475. Oxford: Oxford University Press, 2019.

The Code of Hammurabi. Translated by Leonard William King. Yale Law School. The Avalon Project. https://avalon.law.yale.edu/ancient/hamframe.asp.

The Opinions of Paulus. Book v, Title xvii Concerning acquittals. Translated by Samuel P. Scotts. https://droitromain.univ-grenoble-alpes.fr/Anglica/Paul5_Scott.htm.

Thorpe, Benjamin. *Ancient Laws and Institutes of England: Comprising Laws Enacted under the Anglo-Saxon Kings from Aethelbirht to Cnut*. London: Commissioners of the Public Records, 1840.

Turner, Ralph V. "Roman Law in England Before the Time of Bracton." *Journal of British Studies* 15 (1975): 1–25.

Walters, Mark D. "The Spirit of Legality: A.V. Dicey and the Rule of Law." In *The Cambridge Companion to the Rule of Law*, edited by Jens Meierhenrich and Martin Loughlin, 153–170. Cambridge: Cambridge University Press, 2021.

Whalen, Brett Edward. *The Two Powers: The Papacy, the Empire, and the Struggle for Sovereignty in the Thirteenth Century*. Pennsylvania: University of Pennsylvania Press, 2019.

Wharam, Alan. "The 1189 Rule: Fact, Fiction, or Fraud?" *Anglo-American Law Review* 1 (1972): 262–278.

Williams, Ian. "The Tudor Genesis of Edward Coke's Immemorial Common Law." *Sixteenth Century Journal* 43 (2012): 103–123.

Wilson, Frank M. "Pillars of Anglo-American Law." *Baylor Law Review* 12 (1960): 251–260.

Wishingrad, Jay. "The Plea Bargain in Historical Perspective." *Buffalo Law Review* 23 (1974): 499–528.

Woodbine, George Edward, ed. *Bracton On the Laws and Customs of England*. Translated by Samuel E. Thorne. Cambridge, Mass: Belknap Press, 1968.

Zimmermann, Augusto. "Christianity and the Common Law: Rediscovering the Christian Roots of the English Legal System." *University of Notre Dame Australia Law Review* 16 (2014): 145–177.

CHAPTER 7

Duorum in solidum dominium esse non potest

Harry Dondorp

1 Introduction

"Ownership in entirety cannot be in two persons" is a *regula* taken from Ulp. D. 13.6.5.15: "(Celsus the Younger) says that ownership and possession in entirety cannot be in two persons, nor ownership of a part of the thing, but ownership of the whole thing in an undivided share".[1] The *regula* occurs in French, German, Dutch, and Italian collections of legal maxims[2]; Common law dictionaries quote the Digest fragment.[3]

The German phenomenologist Adolf Reinach (1883–1917) considered the principle an "*a priori* truth grounded on the essence of owning".[4] In so many words he rebuked the assertion of Friedrich Endemann (1857–1935), professor of civil law at Heidelberg, that the maxim is an inference of the way ownership

1 D. 13.6.5.15: "Et ait duorum quidem in solidum dominium vel possessionem esse non posse et nec quemquam partis corporis dominum esse, sed totius corporis pro indiviso pro parte dominium habere" (my translation). Birks translates: "And he says that it is impossible for two people each to own or possess the entirety of something". See *The Digest of Justinian*, English language translation, ed. Alan Watson (Philadelphia: University of Pennsylvania Press, 1998), vol. 1, 403.

2 See e.g. Auguste Jouanneau, *Recueil de maximes et citations latines à l'usage du monde judiciaire* (Paris: Administration et librarie des Annales de justices de paix, 1912), 112: "Une propriété ne peut appartenir à deux personnes pour le tout". Detlef Liebs, *Lateinische Rechtsregeln und Rechtssprichwörter* (Darmstadt: Wissenschaftliche Buchgesellschaft, 1982), 69: "Das Eigentum kann nicht bei zweien ganz sein". Editor's note: in the FWO. OPR.2020.005001 database, this *regula,* under a formulation "Domini in solidum plures eiusdem rei vel iuris esse non possunt", is registered under No. 405.

3 Cf. e.g. Seymour S. Peloubet, *A collection of legal maxims in law and equity* (New York: George Diossy, 1880), 61: "Ownership or possession in entirety cannot be in two of the same thing"; James A. Ballentine, *A Law Dictionary* (Indianapolis: The Bobbs-Merill Co, 1916), 138: "Sole ownership or possession cannot be in two persons".

4 Cf. Adolf B.P. Reinach, "Die apriorischen Grundlagen des bürgerlichen Rechts," *Jahrbuch für Philosophie und phänomenologische Forschung* 1 (1913), 685–847 at 751 note 1: "Der Satz «duorum in solidum dominium esse non posse» ist keineswegs eine «Folgerung aus der Definition des geltenden Eigentumrechtes» (Endemann), sondern eine im Wesen des Gehörens gründende apriorische Wahrheit".

 | DOI:10.1163/9789004736092_009

is defined in the German codification,[5] which in its turn is based upon the notion of ownership in Justinian's *Corpus iuris*.

Before Justinian, as Endemann recounted,[6] two persons could own the same thing, one protected by the law of the Roman people (*dominium ex iure Quiritium*), the other by the praetorian edict.[7] In classical Roman law this was e.g. the case, when the prescribed formal mode of conveyance was not used: If a Roman transferred possession of his slave because of a sale, donation or barter, he remained owner according to the law of the Roman people, but the praetor protected the good-faith acquirer.[8] Justinian abolished the formal modes of conveyance of slaves and Italic land (C. 7.31.1.5) and, consequently, the transferor's *nudum dominium ex iure Quiritium* after a mere delivery (C. 7.25.1). He considered "*ex iure Quiritium*" an empty and superfluous addition, which needlessly terrified the minds of students who came to their first lecture on law.

Robert Pothier (1699–1777) listed the statement of D. 13.6.5.15 as one of the *regulae* in his treatise on Digest-title 50.17 *De diversis regulis iuris antiqui*.[9] The compilers of the Digest had not included this rule in this title, but early-modern writers regularly referred to a *regula* that ownership in entirety cannot be in two persons. Thus, for instance, the Leuven law professor Antonio Perez (1583–1672), while discussing the ownership of pictures painted on

---

5 See the addition to note 1 in the 1905 revised edition of Friedrich Endemann, *Lehrbuch des bürgerlichen Rechts* (Berlin: Heymans, 1905), vol. II.1, 442: "Der Satz: *dominium plurium in solidum esse non potest*, vergl. D. 13.6.5.15, enthält [als Folgerung aus der Definition des geltenden Eigentumrechtes *add 1905*] eine allgemeingültige Rechtswahrheit". Compared with the 1900 edn., 269.

6 Endemann continues: "Auf den Gegensatz zweier Rechtssysteme beruht es, dass neben dem *dominium ex iure Quiritium* sich ein prätorisches Eigenthum entwickelte, das jenes bestehen liess, im Erfolge aber nahezu entwerthete".

7 Gaius (Inst. I.54, II.40) spoke of a duplex dominium, of which one was "Quiritian" ownership, the other 'in bonis meam esse'. Theofilus (Paraphrase Inst. 1.5.4) termed the latter "natural ownership" and such an owner a "bonitary owner". Cf. Mike MacNair, "The Case of the Careless Purchaser, or Bonitary Ownership and Ownership," in *Principle and Pragmatism in Roman Law*, ed. Benjamin Spagnolo and Joe Sampson (Oxford: Hart Publishing, 2020), 37–55. See also Dorothy Gruyaert, *De exclusiviteit van het eigendomsrecht* (Ph.D. diss., KU Leuven, Antwerpen: Interscientia, 2016), 76–81, and the literature cited.

8 Such a case is described in Gaius II.41 and in a collection of fragments from Ulpian's commentary to the Edict (Fragm Ulp. I.16), published in Paris in 1549. Cf. *Domitii Ulpiani Fragmenta*, ed. Eduard Böcking (Bonn: Adolfus Marcus, 1831), 4.

9 Robert Pothier, *Pandectae Justinianeae in novum ordinem digestae*, vol. 3 (Paris: Saugrain, Desaint & C, 1752), 711.

another's panel,[10] the Franeker law professor Ulric Huber (1636–1694) deliberating the ownership of the building material with which someone else has built his house,[11] the Paduan law professor Marcaurelio Galvani (1595–1659) writing about dotal property,[12] and Charles Dumoulin (1500–1566) discussing subinfeudation.[13] Sixteenth-century collections – though not all[14] – of *loci communes* and *axiomata* include that ownership in entirety cannot be in two persons.[15]

In 1510, the maxim first[16] appeared in print in a popular collection of 445 legal rules, compiled by the Italian jurist Bartolomeo Socini (1436–1507) and published posthumously by Benedetto Vadi under the title "*Regulae fere super toto corpore iuris cum omnibus fallentiis suis*".[17] It lists eight exceptions (in fact, only seven)[18] to the rule "*Domini in solidum plures eiusdem rei uel iuris esse non*

10 Antonio Perez, *Institutiones ... ex ipsis principiis regulisque iuris passim insertis explicate* (Amsterdam, 1654), 112: "Nec obstat regula iuris quod duorum in solidum dominium esse non possit, nam intelliguntur domini duarum rerum, unus tabulae et picturae, alter aestimationis".

11 Ulric Huber, *Praelectiones iuris civilis* (Franeker: Amama & Taedama, 1687), 127 (ad Inst. Just. II.1.29). Johannes Bilsten and Joachim Mynsinger a Frundeck also refer to the *regula*, while discussing Inst.Just. II.1.29. Cf. Johannes Bilsten, *Iustiniani Institutionum* (Hannover: Apud Guilielmum Antonium, 1596), 189; Joachim Mynsinger a Frundeck, *Apotelesma* (Basel: apud Nicolaum Episcopum, 1563), 121.

12 Marcaurelio Galvani, *Dissertationes variae de usufructu* (Geneve, 1626), 271: "Desumitur autem ex vulgata regula quod duos dominos in solidum iurisprudentia non admittit. l. Si ut certo § Si duobus ff. commod (D. 13.6.5.15) [...] Fallit superior regula vbi ex duobus dominis alter est cum administratione, alter sine administratione".

13 Charles Dumoulin, *Prima Pars Commentariorum in Consuetudines Parisiensis* (Paris, 1536), fo. 43rb.

14 Cf. *Brocartica iuris* (Paris, 1495; Paris, 1505, Paris, 1562). This collection contains the rule that possession in entirety cannot be in two persons. The first edition is prior to Socini's *regulae*.

15 *Brocardica iuris* (Paris, 1515; Paris, 1541), sub littera d; *Axiomata legum* (Lyon, 1547), 8; *Loci communes iuris civilis* (Lyon: Gryphius, 1545), 113; *Sententiae sive loci communes utriusque iuris* (Cologne: Baumius, 1585) 119; Giovanno Donato Fina, *Enchiridion conclusionum et regularum utriusque iuris* (Frankfurt, 1574), 20 refers to Socini, regula 99.

16 The maxim cannot be found in the medieval brochard collections compiled by Pilius, Azo, and Damasus. Cf. Pilius, *Libellus disputatorius* in Ms. Wien ÖNB 2157, fo. 89r–100v at 90va–91ra (littera d); Azo, *Brocarda* (Naples: apud Ioannem Boium, 1568; repr. Turin: Ex Officina Erasmiana, 1967), col. 76–77 (rubr. 31); Damasus, *Burchardica siue regulae canonicae* (Cologne: Birckmann, 1564).

17 See the appendix to this article. The text is based upon the Pavia 1510 edition, and Paris 1514. The editions Venice 1514 and 1524 follow Pavia 1510, and so do Lyon 1541, 1543 and Cologne 1626. Paris 1515 follows Paris 1514, and so do Lyon 1519, 1524, 1533, and 1540.

18 As the eighth exception Socini mentioned that a legatee must respect existing servitudes on the bequeathed land as owner by legal fiction from the moment of the testator's

possunt", found in D. 13.6.5.15 and D. 41.2.3.5. Socini used the contemporary, broad concept of *dominium*, comprising ownership of corporeal things and having a right.[19] His first exception to the rule provides an example thereof: A father has given his perpetual lease of municipal land as dowry for his daughter under paternal power. In such a case, the dowry is said to belong to him and his daughter (D. 24.3.2.1).[20]

Four of the other exceptions derive from texts in Justinian's *Corpus iuris*: children under paternal control are during his lifetime thought of as in some sense owners of their father's estate (D. 28.2.11),[21] of the property a wife has given as dowry she remains natural owner, even though it passes to the husband (C. 5.12.30),[22] when someone builds on his own land with another's building material, he is the owner of the building, but the owner of the material does not thereby lose his ownership of it (D. 41.1.7.10),[23] if someone ransoms a slave, which was captured by the enemy, the slave is thenceforth his; but the price he paid being offered to the ransomer, the slave is to be regarded as having returned (to his master) by *postliminium* (D. 49.15.12.7).[24]

There are more texts in Justinian's *Corpus iuris* which suggest double ownership. The artist who painted a picture on another's panel, for instance, is said to have the owner's action for recovery against the owner of the panel (D. 41.1.9.2).[25] If a testator bequeathed the same thing twice and made it clear

---

death, but the heir (as owner) in truth from the moment he accepts the inheritance. This coincides with the example he gave of the fourth exception to the rule, of one person being owner *habitu* (a legatee), the other *actu* (the heir).

19 Cf. e.g. Bartolus ad D. 45.1.58: "omnis enim qui habet aliquod ius in re potest recte dicere ego habeo dominium illius iuris", – quoted in Helmut Coing, "Zum Eigentumslehre des Bartolus," *Savigny Zeitschrift für Rechtsgeschichte, Romanistische Abteilung* 70 (1953), 348–371; on the broad concept of *dominium* see also Robert Feenstra, "Der Eigentumsbegriff bei Hugo Grotius im Licht einiger mittelalterlicher und spätscholastiker Quellen," in *Festschrift für Franz Wieacker*, ed. Okko Behrends, Malte Diesselhorst, H Hermann Lange e.a. (Göttingen: Vandenhoeck und Ruprecht, 1978), 209–234.

20 Cf D. 24.3.2.1: "si in patris potestate est et dos ab eo profecta sit, ipsius et filiae dos est".

21 Cf D. 28.2.11: "qui etiam vivo patre quodammodo domini existimantur".

22 See infra note 32.

23 Cf. D. 41.1.7.10: "Cum in suo loco aliquis aliena materia aedificaverit, ipse dominus intellegitur aedificii, quia omne quod inaedificatur solo cedit. Nec tamen ideo is qui materiae dominus fuit desiit eius dominus esse".

24 Cf. D. 49.15.12.7: "Si quis servum captum ab hostibus redemerit, protinus est redimentis, quamvis scientis alienum fuisse: sed oblato ei pretio quod dedit postliminio redisse aut receptus esse servus credetur".

25 Cf. D. 41.1.9.2: "Adversus dominum vero tabularum ei qui pinxerit rectam vindicationem competere dicimus".

that each legatee is to receive the whole legacy, the legatee who first joined issue (i.e. performed *litis contestatio* in the court) has the choice of the thing itself or its value being adjudicated to him (D. 30.33),[26] which implies that both legatees are capable of bringing the owner's action for recovery of the legacy.

Bartolomeo Socini was the first to include the maxim in D. 13.6.5.15 in a collection of *regulae* and exceptions to the rules. It is, however, a statement which has been discussed from about 1150 on. This paper aims at describing the way the Glossators and Commentators up to Socini interpreted and applied the principle expressed in D. 13.6.5.15. How the early glossators first limited it to ownership under the same set of law (par. 2), how Azo and Accursius then applied the principle without restriction (par. 3), while Odofredus limited the maxim to ownership of the same nature (par. 4) and excluded sovereign rights (par. 5), how the Commentators interpreted the texts that conflict with D. 13.6.5.15 (par. 6) and Socini used them as basis for his exceptions to the rule (par. 7).

2 Under the Same Law Ownership in Entirety Cannot Be in Two Persons

The Digest fragment (Ulp. D. 13.6.5.15) from which the *regula* is taken, deals with the case of two people together hiring or borrowing a vehicle. It quotes Celsus the Younger as having said that, in contrast to use, ownership and possession in entirety cannot be in two persons.[27] The earliest glosses on D. 13.6.5.15, dating back to the times of the *Quatuor doctores*, list similar and conflicting texts, e.g. Paul. D. 41.2.3.5 (several persons cannot possess the same thing *in solidum*),[28] Ulp. D. 43.17.3.pr (both you and I are possessors *in*

26 Cf. D. 30.33 "tunc enim uni pretium, alii ipsa res adsignatur electione rei vel pretii servanda ei, qui prior de legato sive fideicommisso litem contestatus est".

27 See above, footnote 1. Rüfner, following Peter Birks' translation, phrases the maxim differently: "no two persons can own the entirety of a thing". Cf. Thomas Rüfner, "The Roman Concept of Ownership and the Medieval Doctrine of *dominium utile*," in *The Creation of the Ius commune, From Casus to Regula*, ed. John W. Cairns and Paul J. du Plessis (Edinburgh: Edinburgh University Press, 2010), 127–142, at 131.

28 On this issue see Lucien Masmejan, *La Protection possessoire en droit romano-canonique médiéval: (XIIIe–XVe siècles)* (Ph.D. Diss., University of Lausanne, Montpellier: Société d'Histoire du Droit et des Institutions des Anciens Pays de Droit Écrit, 1990), 66 – 67.

solidum), and Tryphon. D. 49.17.19.3 (ownership *pro solido* cannot belong to two persons), and Gai D. 41.1.1.pr (of some things we acquire ownership *iure gentium,* of others *iure civili*).[29]

A gloss of Henricus de Bayla, who taught in Bologna in the 1160s, limits the rule expressed in D. 13.6.5.15 to ownership and possession based upon the same set of law. Ownership and possession in entirety, he said, can be in two persons, when each grounds his or her ownership on a different set of law, like husband and wife.[30] In support, Henricus cited two texts: D. 2.8.15.3 and C. 5.12.30. The first expresses with regard to land given as dowry, that the wife is understood to be as much possessor as her husband. The other (C. 5.12.30) regards ownership. It is constitution of Emperor Justinian, which states that a woman's property she gives as dowry[31] to her husband "naturally remains hers, for the truth of the matter is not obscured, because – owing to the contrivance of the laws – it seems to have passed into the estate of the husband".[32]

Henricus' line of thought, viz. that ownership in entirety can be in two persons under different sets of laws, as in the case of husband and wife, is in line with the early glossators' reading of C. 5.12.30. Martinus and Bulgarus[33]

---

29 See e.g. the *allegationes* in Mss. Paris, BN lat. 4450, fo. 139r: "infra de adquir. poss. Possideri [D. 41.2.3.5], infra de castr. pec. l. Hereditate [D. 49.17.19.3], infra uti pos. l. Si duo [D. 43.17.3.pr], infra locati Item queritur § Duo [D. 19.2.13.9: in a lease, there can be two debtors *in solidum*]". Ms. Bamberg Jur 12 lists D. 31.66.2 instead of D. 43.17.3.pr. Ms. Stockholm, KB, Ms. 680, fo. 144v lists D. 31.66.2 and D. 41.1.1.pr instead of D. 41.2.3.5. On the dating of the glosses, see: Gero Dolezalek, *Manuscripta Iuridica*, https://manuscripts.rg.mpg.de.

30 Cf. gloss s.v. '*Dominium et possessio*' ad D. 13.6.5.15 in Ms. Stockholm, KB 680, fo. 144r: "Eodem iure. Diuerso enim iure potest, ut in uiro et uxore. ut supra qui satisdat. l. Sciendum [D. 2.8.15.3] et C. de iure dot. In rebus [C. 5.12.30]. yr."

31 In case of a dowry given by the *pater familias* of a woman under paternal power, he needs his daughter's consent to recover the dowry after the dissolution of the marriage (D. 24.3.2.1). The text prompted the first of Socini's exceptions.

32 Cf. C. 5.12.30: "[...] cum eaedem res et ab initio uxoris fuerant et naturaliter in eius permanserunt dominio. Non enim quod legum subtilitate transitus earum in mariti patrimonium videtur fieri, ideo rei veritas deleta vel confusa est". On ownership of dotal property in Justinianic law, see: Ernst Levy, *West Roman vulgar law: the law of property* (Philadelphia: American Philosophical Society, 1951), 82–83. Levy argued that Justinian considered the wife to be the true owner, stigmatizing the husband's ownership as *legum subtilitas,* without abolishing it.

33 Accursius (gloss s.v. '*Naturali iure*' ad C. 5.12.30) and Odofredus (lectura super C. 5.12.30) ascribed this view to Martinus, but Bulgarus most likely held the same position. See Wilhelmus de Cabriano, *Casus Codicis*, ed. Tammo Wallinga (Frankfurt a.M: Klostermann, 2005), 377 (C. 5.12.30): "Si autem inestimate fuerunt tunc iuris civilis artificio mariti fuerit, de iure naturali, id est gentium, remanent in dominio uxoris". On Martinus'

read in this constitution that the husband was the civil-law owner and his wife the natural-law owner of dotal property. They must have considered each of them an owner in entirety, but Henricus was the first glossator who used C. 5.12.30 to limit the ruling in D. 13.6.15.5.

Rogerius, who taught in Montpellier in the 1150s, used this concept (of ownership according to different sets of laws) in case of a picture painted on someone else's wooden panel. The paint does not accede to the panel and the artist becomes owner of the painting, but the owner of the panel may nonetheless recover the picture from the artist if he pays the cost of painting (Inst. Just II.1.34 and D. 41.1.9.2). To explain the action for recovery of the owner of the panel, Rogerius considered him a "natural-law owner" of the picture.[34]

In the 1160s, Jacobus, the youngest of the *Quatuor* Doctores in Bologna, and Placentinus, who in Montpellier completed and revised Rogerius' summa, applied the above-mentioned concept to prescription. At Roman law, good-faith purchasers acquired ownership of movables in three years (Inst.Just. II.6. pr and C. 2.3.20). In regard to land, the *Corpus iuris* was less clear, because even after the completion of the prescription term the old owner had an action for recovery (C. 7.39.8.1a). Whether good-faith purchasers of land acquired ownership with the passage of time, thus became the subject of a *dissensio dominorum* among the *Quatuor doctores*.[35] Martinus said that they did, which Bulgarus denied. Jacobus, and in his footsteps Placentinus, reasoned, in analogy to dotal property, that the good-faith purchaser of land

---

and Bulgarus view, see Manlio Bellomo, *Ricerche sui rapporti patrimoniali tra coniugi, Contributo alla storia delta famiglia medievale* (Milan: Giuffrè, 1961), 76–77. In his lecture on C. 5.12.30, Azo did not specify who held this view. Cf. Azo, *Lectura super Codice* (Paris, 1577; repr. Turin, Bottega d'Erasmo, 1966), 593 (super C. 5.12.30 s.v. '*Et naturaliter in eius remanserunt dominio*').

34 *Rogerii summa codicis*, ed. Giovanni B. Palmieri (*Scripta Anecdota Glossatorum*, vol. I.4) (Bologna: In aedibus Societatis Azzoguidianae, 1913), 46 (C. 3.32): "Si autem dominus sit iure naturali tantum cum alius sit dominus iure gentium uel ciuili, habet utilem, ut dicitur de eo qui pinxit tabulam. Nam dominus tabule remanet dominus iure naturali, is qui pinxit est dominus iure gentium, domino iure naturali datur utilis, domino iure gentium datur directa". Quoted in Ennio Cortese, *La norma giuridica* (Milan: Giuffrè, 1964), I: 88. Paola Maffei only refers to a similar line of thought in the *Lectura Vindobonensis*, because she only made use of Rogerius' Institutes. Cf. Paola Maffei, *Tabula picta. Pittura e scrittura nel pensiero dei glossatori* (Milan: Giuffrè, 1988), 29. Marta Madero does not discuss the issue in her *Tabula Picta*, trans. Monique D. Inciarte and Roland D. Valayre (Philadelphia: University of Pennsylvania Press, 2009).

35 Listed in the early collections. Cf. *Dissensiones dominorum*, ed. Gustav Hänel (Leipzig: Hinrich, 1834; repr. Aalen: Scientia, 1964), 18 (Vetus collectio, 27), 89 (Collectio Rogerii, 27).

became a second owner upon completion of the prescription period.[36] The land still belonged *naturaliter* to the older owner, while the good-faith purchaser now owned the land *civiliter*.[37] In other words, each is owner in entirety of the land by virtue of a different set of law.

The teaching of the early Glossators that two persons could be the owners in entirety under different sets of law became implausible about 1200, because Johannes Bassianus (fl. 1180–1185) argued convincingly that the common interpretation of C. 5.12.30 was flawed.[38] He claimed that the husband is both the civil-law and the natural-law owner of the property which the wife had transferred to him as dowry, because *traditio* is a natural-law mode of acquisition.[39] Johannes interpreted "remain naturally hers" in C. 5.12.30 as remaining for her to enjoy and use in virtue of the primaeval natural law, when all things were

36 Jacobus' teaching is described in *Dissensiones dominorum*, 90, note 1 (Collectio Hugolini, 327), and more lucidly in a 12th-century collection of *dissensiones dominorum* in a manuscript of Admont Abbey. Cf. Ms. Admont SB 88, fo. 60rb: "Ia[cobus] dicit praescriptiones praedictas esse inuentas ad dominium adquirendum et ad hoc ut quis se ualeat tueri, nam dicit utrosque dominium habere, sicut uxor et maritus rerum dotalium".

37 Cf. Placentinus, *Summa Codicis* (Mainz: Schoeffer, 1536, repr. Turin: Bottega d'Erasmo, 1962), 334 (C. 7.33): "Sed [ut aestimo] si praescriptor intendere noluit, uetustior dominus directo uindicabit, ergo uterque dominus est, ut et alias, puta in dote reperitur. Praescriptor ciuiliter dominus, uetustior naturaliter. Praescriptori datur utilis uindicatio, [nempe competit ei exceptio contra actionem sicque si uetustiori domino, tantum naturaliter domino, competit et adhuc directa uindicatio]". Collated with Mss. Admont SB 188, Düsseldorf ULB 9A, and Grenoble BM 391.1. [] *om. ed.* (*homoiotel*).

38 Johannes Bassianus' argumentation is reported in the lectures of Azo, his pupil, and in Collectio Ottobonianae 1298, a collection of dissensiones dominorum preserved in a Vatican manuscript (BAV Ottobat. 1298). The author of the collectio Hugolini combined this dissensio dominorum (no. 75 at fo. 32v–33r) with another one (no. 70) changing the opening words "Dicunt quidam" into "Alii dicunt" (uxorem dominam fore de iure naturali). Cf. *Dissensiones dominorum*, 436 (Collectio Hugolini, 266 from line 11). It provides a slightly abridged version, adding references to Azo and a few extra arguments.

39 Cf. Azo, *Lectura*, 393 (super C. 5.12.30 s.v. '*Et naturaliter*'): "Sed Io. dixit mulierem non esse dominam, immo de iure ciuili et naturali; et pro se induxit contra alios [quod] lex dicit marito de iure naturali dominium acquiri. ut inst. de rerum diu. § Per traditionem [Inst.Just. II.1.40]; ergo mulier non de iure naturali erit domina ...".

Collectio Ottobonianae 1298, nr 75 (fo. 33ra): "Iob. contra tam in re extimata quam in inextimata; nec enim iure ciuili seu naturali mulier est domina. Cum enim per traditionem iure etiam naturali res nobis acquiruntur. ut in inst. de rerum di. § Et per trationem [Inst.Just. II.1.40], constat manifeste uxorem etiam naturaliter non esse dominam. Si quidem ex causa dotis aut qualibet ex causa res nobis tradantur, sine dubio iure naturali transferuntur. ut inst. eod. [Et] si quidem [Inst.Just. II.1.41]. ..." The author of Collectio Hugolini, 266 added after Iob. 'et dominus Azo'.

communal property.[40] It is a description of use not of ownership. One should not be surprised, argued Johannes, that the wife nevertheless has an action for recovery (*vindicatio*) of the dotal property, for even someone who is neither owner nor has been may have this remedy, as in C. 7.39.8.[41]

Johannes' pupil Azo copied the above-mentioned gloss of Henricus de Bayla (which limited the rule expressed in D. 13.6.5.15 to ownership and possession based upon the same set of laws) into his apparatus to the Digest. But he added that he disagreed.[42]

Roffredus Beneventanus (c. 1177–1244), a pupil of Azo, limited the maxim – as the early Glossators had done – to ownership under the same set of laws. But he reasoned differently, not taking dotal property as his starting point, but superficiary property. In his compendium of civil procedure, completed in the 1220s, Roffredus gave the correct wording of legal actions, among them the superficiary's claim for recovery, termed *rei uendicatio utilis*[43], where the superficiary asserted to have *dominium utile*. The objection that two persons cannot be the owners in entirety of the same thing did not hold according to Roffredus, because this applies only to persons who claim ownership under the same set of laws and on the same legal ground. The owner of the land and

40 See Azo, gloss s.v. '*Naturaliter*' ad C. 5.12.30: "Non dicit 'naturaliter', id est iure gentium, quo cuique adiudicatur, sed iure naturali, id est, primaeuo, quo omnia erant communia. nam in omni re ita habebat unus ut alter dominium: dicebatur autem tunc aliquid meum, scilicet quo utebar et fruebar, et hoc modo dicitur uxor domina; ipsa enim et omnia sua onera de dote sustebantur. Hoc ergo ueritas non est deleta uel confusa relatione facta super ad primaeuum ius et naturale sic enim concedimus. De iure uero gentium ipsa nullo modo est domina az".

Consulted Mss. Bamberg SB Jur. 21, fo. 94vb; Bamberg SB Jur. 22, fo. 96va. Melk 73 fo. 98r; Paris BN 4536, fo. 95v. BAV Vat.lat 11152, fo. 96vb.

41 A fragment of the constitution rules, that even bad faith possessors have an action for recovery against the owner who forcefully regains possession after more than thirty years. See C. 7.39.8.2: "Nam si quis violenter eam abstulit, omnimodo licebit priori possessori sine ulla distinctione eam vindicare".

42 See Azo, gloss s.v. '*Dominium uel possessionem*' ad D. 13.6.5.15, published by Rüfner, "The Roman Concept of Ownership," 135.

43 It was disputed among the Glossators, if the superficiary's *actio in rem*, described in D. 13.7.16.2 as an "*actio utilis*", was in fact a variant of the owner's *rei uindicatio*. See *Libellus de preparatoriis litium*, ed. Giovanni B. Palmieri (*Scripta Anecdota Glossatorum*, vol. III.2) (Bologna: In aedibus successori Monti, 1901), 66. This small tract, written about 1220, reported that some allowed a phrasing based upon ownership: "peto dictam rem mihi restitui quam dico ad me pertinere iure dominii uel quasi".

It is debated among legal historians whether in the *Corpus Iuris* the superficiary owns the building. See Eduardo C. Silveira Marchi, "La proprietà per piani nel diritto romano," *Index* 18 (1990), 265–274; Ana Zaera García, *La superficies en derecho romano* (Madrid: Dykinson, 2017), 243–267.

the superficiary are not owners of the building and its surface under the same law, because the owner of the land is an owner by virtue of the laws (*ius civile*), the superficiary by virtue of the praetorian edict (*ius praetorium*).[44] Roffredus said the same of the phrasing of the action of a long-term lessee (e.g. under an *emphyteusis*),[45] who was also believed to have a *dominium utile*.[46]

3 Ownership in the Entirety of the Same Thing Cannot Be in Two Persons

Accursius (c. 1182–1263), while glossing the statement in D. 13.6.5.15, confined himself to the remark that it was clear that ownership in entirety cannot be in two persons.[47] The brevity of his gloss indicates that Accursius adopted the view of his teacher Azo that one should not distinguish between natural-law and civil-law owners. This is also apparent in the way Accursius interpreted those texts in Justinian's legislation that suggested that ownership in entirety could be in two persons, each of them being a full owner.

D. 24.3.2.1 suggests that not only the *pater familas* is the owner of his assets, but a son or daughter under paternal power too; similarly, C. 5.12.30 indicates that not only the husband owns the property his wife has transferred to him as dowry, but she as well. Accursius considered the *pater familias* a sole owner, also of the dotal property. If she would be an owner as well, he said, there are two persons being owners in entirety, which is impossible.[48] Consequently, where it is stated in the Digest that children under paternal control are in some sense owners of the estate during their father's lifetime (D. 24.3.2.1), and in the Codex that the property his wife has transferred as dowry remains

44 Cf. Roffredus Beneventanus, *De libellis et ordine iudiciorum* (Avignon, 1500; repr. Turin, Bottega d'Erasmo, 1968), fo. 12v: "nec obstat quod opponis duo in solidum domini esse non possunt. Verum est eodem iure et eadem causa. duo ergo non sunt domini de iure ciuili, sed diuerso iure sunt domini, et ex diuersis causis. Nam unus est dominus de iure ciuili, et habet rei uendicationem directam, ut dominus soli, alius est de iure praetorio, ut superficiarius et habet utilem rei uendicationem".

45 Cf. Roffredus Beneventanus, fo. 13rb: "Item unus de iure ciuili alter de iure praetorio possunt esse domini, ut in superiori actione notaui".

46 In the medieval version of the Codex, the long-term lessee is described as the "owner" in C. 11.62.12.1. The manuscripts read "cum fundorum sint domini" instead of "cum fundorum sunt domini" (as if they were owner of the land). See Laurent L.J.M. Waelkens, *Amne adverso, Roman legal heritage in European Legal Culture* (Leuven: Leuven University Press, 2015), 292.

47 Cf. Accursius, gloss s.v. '*Domininum et possessionem*' ad D. 13.6.5.15.

48 Cf. Accursius, gloss s.v. '*Naturaliter*' ad C. 5.12.30.

naturally hers (C. 5.12.30), ownership is not meant, but use[49] – as Azo had already taught.[50]

Inst.Just. II.1.34 and D. 41.1.9.2 suggest that there are two owners in entirety when an artist has painted a picture on another's panel. In Accursius' opinion, there is one owner: the artist, if he possessed the panel in good faith;[51] otherwise, the owner of the panel. If someone builds on his own land with another's material, he owns the building, while the owner of the material remains the owner thereof, as Inst.Just. II.1.29 and D. 47.1.7.10 state.

Accursius deduced from D. 49.15.30, that a Roman is restored in his rights over a slave, who has been captured by the enemy, at the moment he returns in his power (*potestas*).[52] In this line of thought there are two consecutive owners when he finds his slave serving someone else and offers him the purchase price. For when he does, the slave is to be regarded as having returned by *postliminium* (D. 49.15.12.7).

Where it is said, in case a testator bequeathed the same thing twice and made it clear that each legatee is to receive the thing in entirety, that the legatee who first joined issue has the choice of the thing itself or its value (D. 30.33), the thing is due only from that moment on, Accursius said, otherwise two persons would have an action and ownership in entirety of the same thing, which is impossible.[53]

---

49 Cf. Accursius, gloss s.v. '*Quodammodo*' ad D. 28.3.11: "Et consistit hoc in nudo intellectu et puro, uel eo quod inde sustentantur, sicut uxor dicitur domina et possidere dotem suam eodem respectu". Accursius, gloss s.v. '*Rei ueritas*' ad C. 5.12.30: "Vel quae est ut uideatur esse domina quantum ad sustentationem ...".

50 Cf. Azo, gloss s.v. '*Naturaliter*' ad C. 5.12.30: "Hoc modo filii rerum paternarum et uxor rerum mariti dicitur domina, id est, propter usum promiscuum. ut infra de furt. Quamuis etiam [C. 6.2.17] et ff. de rerum amotarum l.i [D. 25.2.1] et in inst. de her. qualitate et differ. [Inst.Just. II.19.2] et ff. de li. et post. In suis [D. 28.2.11]. az".

Consulted Mss. Bamberg SB Jur. 21, fo. 94vb; Bamberg SB Jur. 22, fo. 96va. Melk 73 fo. 98r; Paris BN 4536, fo. 95v. BAV Vat.lat 11152, fo. 96vb.

51 Cf. Accursius, gloss s.v. '*Directam uindicationem*' ad D. 49.1.9.2. In which case, the owner of the panel loses ownership. See Accursius, gloss s.v. '*Utilis actio*' ad Inst.Just. II.1.34: "in rem, non directa, quia desinit dominus esse et sic est mirabile quod non dominus a domino uindicat".

52 Cf. Accursius, gloss s.v. '*Sic serui*' ad C. 8.50.10: "Item in seruis intellige, si tamen in potestate domini uel intra domini praesidia sint, licet in liberis statim cum sunt intra limina imperii. ut ff. eod. l. fi. [D. 49.15.30] et l. In bello § Manumittendo [D. 49.15.12.9]".

53 Cf. Accursius, gloss s.v. '*Litem contestatus*' ad D. 30.33: "Et nota quod hic dicit Jo. quod ante litem contestatam nulli debetur et tunc demum lite contestata incipit deberi, alioquin et duo haberent actionem et dominium insolidum, quod est impossibile ..."

4 The Ownership of the Same Nature Cannot Be in Two Persons

In his lectures, Odofredus (c. 1200–1265) returned to what Azo had said. Azo's gloss (in fact, the one by Henricus) prompted him to spend more time explaining the maxim than otherwise would be warranted. Apparently, it was not as obvious as Accursius thought that ownership in entirety could not be in two persons.

In his analysis of the concept of ownership in medieval jurisprudence, Thomas Rüfner discusses in detail Odofredus' lecture on D. 13.6.5.15.[54] Odofredus expounded that, in conflict with the principle that ownership in entirety cannot be in two persons, dotal property is both said to belong to the husband (C. 3.32.9) and to the wife (C. 5.12.30). Some Glossators (in fact, Henricus de Bayla), he said, solved the contradiction by saying that two persons cannot be owners in entirety *eodem iure*, on the basis of the same set of law, but they can be, if each is the owner in entirety *alio iure*, on the basis of a different set of laws, after the example of husband and wife in C. 5.12.30.[55] Johannes Bassianus and Azo had countered this solution of the contradiction, arguing that the husband is the sole owner, the wife not an owner but the "owner *in spe*".

Unfortunately, in his lecture on D. 13.6.5.15 Odofredus – or, perhaps, the *reportator* of his lecture[56] – confused their argumentation with that of the early Glossators, which they countered.[57] His lecture on C. 5.12.30 reports Johannes Bassianus' and Azo's argumentation correctly.[58] There, Odofredus

54 Rüfner, "The Roman Concept of Ownership," 132–136.

55 His report of their view in his lecture on D. 13.6.5.15 (*dicunt quod maritus est dominus iure gentium et non civili*) is flawed. In his lecture on C. 5.12.30, Odofredus reported correctly that they (he ascribed this view to Martinus) considered the husband owner *iure civili*, the wife *iure naturali or iure gentium*. Cf. Odofredus, *Lectura super Codice*, vol. 1 (Lyon: Marchant, 1550, repr. Bologna: Forni, 1968), fo. 277vb.

56 The lecture notes reflect an orally presented lecture and could have been made by a student (lectura reportata).

57 Having said that some Glossators (*quidam*) limited the maxim to owners under the same set of law, based upon an incorrect interpretation of C. 5.12.30, Odofredus continued his lecture on D. 13.6.15.5 (as quoted by Rüfner, "The Roman Concept of Ownership," 132, note 1): "Et ad legem illam In rebus [C. 5.12.30] respondent (*adde* Johannes Bassianus et Azo), licet maritus in ueritate sit dominus et uxor sit domina, uerum est quod non re sed spe, quia soluto matrimonio reddenda est dos". Without the reference to Johannes Bassianus and Azo, it seems as if the early Glossators (*quidam*) interpreted C. 5.12.30 as stating that the husband was the owner *in re* and the wife *in spe*, as Rüfner, *ibid.*, 134, reads.

58 Compare Odofredus, *Lectura super Codice*, fo. 277v–278r (super C. 5.12.30 no. 6) with Azo, *Lectura*, 394 no. 7 (super C. 5.12.30): "Item solus uir uendicare potest rem dotalem, ut supra de rei uend. Dote [C. 3.32.9], quia tamen maritus obligatur ad rem dotalem red-

considered the husband the sole owner during the marriage, arguing that ownership in entirety cannot be in two persons.[59]

Nevertheless, in his lecture on D. 13.6.5.15, Odofredus agreed with the early Glossators that the same thing can be owned in entirety by two persons *alio et alio iure*, but not after the example of dotal property. He argued that two persons can be owners in entirety after the example of superficiary property, the superficiary having *dominium utile* of the building and its surface, and the owner of the land having *dominium directum* of what is built on it.[60] In contrast to Roffredus Beneventanus, Odofredus does not argue that both own the building under different sets of law, viz. *ius civile* and *ius honorarium*. His phrasing suggests that they have different rights. In this respect, his lecture is more akin to a gloss of Hugolinus (1185–1235) on D. 13.6.5.15, which simply said that two persons cannot have undivided ownership of the same thing, but one may have a *dominium utile* (for instance, a long-term lessee) and the other, "the true owner", a *dominium directum*.[61] Accursius also hinted that ownership may be divided in such a way in a gloss to D. 1.1.5.[62]

Odofredus cited D. 6.3.1.1 in support of his thesis, that two persons can be owner in entirety after the example of superficiary property.[63] This fragment

dandam, tenetur de dolo et culpa quasi pro rebus alienis, ut dicit lex Si constante [D. 24.3.24.5]. Et quod dicit 'de alienis' bene glosat ibidem 'id est dotalibus' et ita spe non re sunt aliena, sed post matrimonium redeunt ad mulierem".

59 Ibid.: "Ecce, si mulier que mecum contraxit dat mihi fundum inestimatum in dotem, ut inst. de rerum diuisione Per traditionem [Inst.Just. II.1.40], desinit esse domina et ego dominus efficior; igitur ego habeo [rei] uendicationem, non ipsa, quia duo eiusdem rei dominium habere non possunt in solidum".

60 Cf. Odofredus (Rüfner, "The Roman Concept of Ownership," 132 note 1): "Sed uos ponatis ita exempla, quod duo possunt habere dominium eiusdem rei et alio iure, puta ut unus potest habere directum dominium, sicut ille qui habet directam proprietatem, alius potest habere utile dominium, ut superficiarius, ut supra si ager vect.vel emph. petatur l.ii. [D. 6.3.1.1]. Sed duo non possunt habere dominium eiusdem rei in solidum, ita ut ambo directi domini sint in solidum uel utiliter".

61 Cf. Hugolinus, gloss s.v. '*Dominium*' ad D. 13.6.5.15: "scilicet directum et utile, nam utile unus, puta emphyteota, eiusdem rei, directum uerus dominus habet, nam primus utilem, secundus directam intendit rei uendicationem. H."

Consulted Mss. London British Library, Royal 11.C.III (fo. 133rb), Paris BN lat 4461 (fo. 138r), Seu d'Urgell, BdC 2063 (no fol).

62 Cf. Accursius, gloss s.v. '*Dominia*' ad D. 1.1.5: "uel dic dominia distincta, scilicet directa ab utilibus et econtra".

63 He could instead have cited D. 6.1.75, which said the same about a superficiary. Cf. Odofredus, *Lectura super Digesto Veteri*, vol. I (Lyon: Marchant, 1550; repr. Bologna: Forni, 1967), fo. 244v (super D. 6.1.75 s.v. 'In rem'): "utilem rei uendicationem contra omnem et contra dominum soli".

concerns not a superficiary but a long-term lessee. It states that the lessee of municipal land, even though he is not the owner, has an *actio in rem* against everyone who gains possession of the land, even if this would be the grantor[64] – an action which Odofredus termed *"rei uendicatio utilis"*.[65] In his opinion, ownership in entirety of the same thing can be in two persons, each *alio iure*, the bare owner having *dominium directum*, the superficiary or long-term lessee *dominium utile*; similarly, in the case of prescription, the old owner has *dominium directum*, the new *utile*.[66] Rüfner translates *alio iure* as "under different sets of law",[67] but this seems to be a slip of the pen, because he claims that Odofredus' *alio iure* must be taken as referring to *dominium utile*, which co-exists with the *dominium directum* of another person.[68] In other words: ownership in entirety can be in two persons, if their right differs in nature.[69]

The very notion of *dominium utile* was disputed at that time: Jacobus Balduini (c. 1186–1235) called it a *"chimaera"*, something illusory.[70] About 1350, Bartolus (1313–1357) reported in his lecture that an Orléans law professor – probably, Jean Nicot[71] – acknowledged but one type of ownership. About a

64 D. 6.3.1.1: "Qui in perpetuum fundum fruendum conduxerunt a municipibus, quamvis non efficiantur domini, tamen placuit competere eis in rem actionem adversus quemvis possessorem, sed et adversus ipsos municipes".

65 Cf. Odofredus, *Lectura super Digesto Veteri,* fo. 248v (super D. 6.3.1): "Vnum sciatis: qui conducit predium in perpetuum habet utilem rei uendicationem".

66 As Odofredus said in his lecture on D. 41.2.3.5. Cf. Odofredus, *Lectura super Digesto Novo* (Lyon: Marchant, 1550; repr. Bologna: Forni, 1968), fo 56ra (super D. 41.2.3.5): "Duo non possunt habere dominium eodem iure sed alio et alio iure sic, quia dominus habet directum dominium, emphyteuta autem utile; item qui prescribit habet utile dominium, sed dominus directum ut infra de praescr. xxx uel xxxx ann. l. Si quis emptionis [C. 7.39.8]".

67 Cf. Rüfner, "The Roman Concept of Ownership," 132: "Two people can have ownership of the same thing under different sets of laws, for example one person can have the superior ownership, like one who owns property directly, and the other can have the inferior ownership, like a superficiary, as seen above *si ager vectigalis vel emphyteuticarius petatur* l. ii. [D 6.3.2].

68 Cf. Rüfner, "The Roman Concept of Ownership," 135–136.

69 On the issue of whether Odofredus may have used the word "ius" in the sense of "right", cf. Harry Dondorp, "Rights in civil law: the glossators," in *The Cambridge History of Rights, Volume II: The Middle Ages*, ed. Lidia Lanze and Marco Toste (Cambridge: Cambridge University Press) (forthcoming).

70 Cf. Robert Feenstra, "Dominium utile est chimaera; nouvelles réflexions sur le concept de propriété dans le droit savant," *Tijdschrift voor Rechtsgeschiedenis* 66 (1998), 381–397.

71 Cf. Ennio Cortese, "Controversiae medievali sul dominium utile: Bartolo e il quidam doctor de Aurelianis," in *Amicitiae pignus: studi in ricordo de Adriano Cavanna*, ed. Antonio Padoa Schioppa e.a. (Milan: Giuffrè, 2003), 1: 613 – 635 at 619.

century later, Paulus de Castro (c. 1360–1441) said the same of the law school in Orléans in general.[72] But in Italy, the notion of *duplex dominium* survived.

Odofredus' thesis, that ownership can be in two persons when their right differs in nature, returns in the commentaries of Bartolus and Albericus de Rosate (1290–1359). *Dominium utile* is a different type of ownership, Bartolus wrote, because the same ownership cannot be in two persons.[73] In his lecture on C. 5.12.30,[74] Baldus (1327–1400) distinguished between rights, such as easements, which do not diminish when they concur, and others which do, such as ownership.[75] Several neighbours can each[76] have a right of way over one's land, but the ownership cannot be in two persons, unless their type of ownership differs, as in land given in a long-term lease. The lessor has *dominium directum*, the lessee *dominium utile*, which Baldus considered a subordinate ownership.[77] According to Paulus de Castro, one should add "*respectu eiusdem dominii*" to what is said in D. 13.6.5.15, because of the same thing one person may have *dominium directum*, the other *utile*, as, for instance, a long-term lessee.[78]

5 Ownership in Entirety Cannot Be in Two Private Persons

Odofredus also quoted "Ownership in entirety cannot be in two persons" in his lecture on Justinian's constitution *Omnem*, one of the introductory constitu-

72 Cf. Cortese, "Controversiae," 626.

73 Cf. Bartolus, ad D. 42.2.17.1 (as cited in Rüfner, "The Roman Concept of Ownership", 139 note 42): "diuersa dominia sunt quia non potest idem dominium esse apud duos, ut l. Si ut certo § Si duobus uehiculum supra com. [D. 13.6.5.15]". On Albericus' view, see Rüfner, "The Roman Concept of Ownership," 138.

74 Discussed in Jacques A. Pluss, "Baldus de Ubaldis of Perugia on dominium over dotal property," *Tijdschrift voor Rechtsgeschiedenis* 52 (1984), 399–411 at 408. In his lecture on D. 13.6.5.15, Baldus only discussed if possession could be in two persons. His lectures on the Digestum Novum do not contain D. 49.17.19.3, for they end at D. 46.8.

75 Cf. Baldus, ad C. 5.12.30 no. 6 as quoted in Pluss, "Baldus," 408 note 34.

76 Jacques A. Pluss erroneously speaks of "rights that can be shared by many people jointly". Cf. Pluss, "Baldus," 408.

77 Cf. Pluss, "Baldus", 409 note 37.

78 Cf. Paulus de Castro, *In secundam Digesti veteris partem commentaria* (Venice: Giunti, 1575), fo. 76va (ad D. 13.6.5.15) no. 2: "Ex prima parte no(ta) illud vulgare, ad quod semper allegatur, et non est melior textus quod duo non possunt esse domini in solidum respectu eiusdem rei, supple et respectu eiusdem dominii, nam diuersorum sic, nam unus potest esse dominus in solidum respectu directi dominii et alter in solidum respectu utilis ut fructuarius uel emphyteuta".

tions to the Digest.[79] The emperor claiming "the Commonwealth" (*res publica*) as his own, prompted him to discuss a view ascribed to Martinus,[80] that the prince is not only the owner of imperial goods but of the private properties as well.[81] Several authoritative texts supported this view,[82] among them C. 7.39.3, which argues that "*omnia principis esse intelliguntur*".[83] Taken out of context – Justinian referred to all imperial goods, comprising those of the treasury, the crown domain and the emperor and his wife[84] – the phrase suggests that the emperor owns everything in the world, private property included. If that were true, as the Tuscan judge and notary Rolando di Lucca had already written in 1195/7, no one of his subjects would have a *rei uendicatio directa* of an owner.[85]

79 The maxim is not quoted by Accursius in his gloss s.v. '*Sanctionem*' ad const. *Omnem* as Willem Zwalve suggests in his "Text and Commentary: The Legal Middle Ages and the Roman Law Tradition, Justinian's Const. *Omnem* and its Medieval Commentators," in *Neo Latin Commentaries and the Management of Knowledge in the Late Middle Ages and the Early Modern Period (1400–1700)*, ed. Karl Enenkel and Henk Nellen (Leuven: Leuven University Press, 2013), 349–386, at 368.

80 Ascribed to Martinus in a story which circled orally until c. 1220. Emperor Frederick, while riding with Bulgarus and Martinus, asked them whether he was "*dominus mundi*". Bulgarus said he was Lord (*dominus*) of the world, but the world was not his own (*non quo ad proprietatem*). Martinus simply said he was *dominus*. See Kenneth Pennington, *The Prince and the Law, 1200 – 1600, Sovereignty and Rights in the Western Legal Tradition* (Berkeley: University of California Press, 1993), 16.

81 Cf. Odofredus, *Lectura super Digesto veteri*, fo. 3a (super const. Omnem): "Sed quare dicit litera "totius nostre reipublice"? Dicit dominus Martinus quod imperator non solum est dominus eorum que sunt imperii, immo est dominus proprietatis omnium rerum singulorum hominum". Similarly, Accursius gloss s.v. '*Omnia principis*' ad C. 7.37.3.

82 Kings 1:8.11 and D. 6.1.5.2, D. 21.2.11, D. 14.2.9, D. 40.11.3, C. 10.4.1, and C. 7.39.3.

83 In C. 7.37.3.1a Justinian states that Zeno's constitution (C. 7.37.2) is applied to things alienated by the treasury, but not to dispositions from the imperial Privy Purse. This was irrational, he said, since all are thought of as to belong to the emperor.

84 This is the prevailing interpretation among the Glossators. Thus, for instance, Otto Papiensis, a pupil of Placentinus (see Pennington, *The Prince*, 22, note 60) and Rolandus de Lucca. See Emanuele Conte, "Defensa. Resistance against unjust power in the medieval learned law (12th–13th centuries)," in *Revolten und politische Verbrechen zwischen dem 12. und 19. Jahrhundert: Rechtliche Reaktionen und juristisch-politische Diskurse*, ed. Angela de Benedictis and Karl Härter (Frankfurt aM: Klostermann, 2013), 21–134, at 126, note 22. Azo discussed the issue in his lecture, but a similar gloss at C. 7.37.3.1a fails. See Azo, *Lectura*, 574 (super C. 7.37.3): "id est tam fiscalia quam patrimonalia, non intellige quod res alicuius priuati sit sua, nisi quo ad protectionem"; similarly Hugolinus, gloss s.v. '*Principis*' ad C. 7.37.3.1a: "scilicet fiscalia et quae sunt in patrimonio caesaris, nam subdiuit postea; vel dic omnia quantum ad iurisdictionem. h", consulted Mss. Berlin SB 408, fo. 133r, Brussels KB 125, fo 146rb, Vienna ÖNB 2268, fo. 199vb.

85 In the first version of his summa the *Tres Libri* (Codex 10–12) in Ms. Madrid BN 1876; See Rolando da Lucca, *Summa trium librorum* (1195–1197), ed. Emanuele Conte and Sara

Odofredus added the silent premise in Rolando's argumentation: ownership in entirety cannot be in two persons.[86]

This reasoning was questioned by the Orléans law professor Jacques de Révigny (1230/1240–1296), who in his lecture on const. *Omnem* discussed whether everything in the world belonged to the prince.[87] He argued that Justinian's constitution (C. 7.37.3) extended an enactment of Emperor Zeno on alienations by the treasury to all conveyances by officers of the imperial household (C. 7.37.2). Hence, not only those who acquire from the treasury are safe from any claim whatsoever. Justinian said the same in his Institutes: the acquirers are at once secure, while those who think that they have a cause of action as owners or hypothecary creditors of the things alienated by the emperor, may bring an action[88] against the treasury within four years (Inst. Just. II.6.14). Accursius gave the following example: someone bought from the treasury the estate of Titius who had died without heirs,[89] but among the goods were some that belonged to someone else.[90] In such a case, the pur-

Menzinger (Rome: Viella, 2012), 32: "Si enim omnia essent principis, iam rei vendicatio directa nulli subiectorum competeret". Accursius expressed the same view in the gloss s. v. *'Omnia principis'* ad C. 7.37.3: "Vnde codex meus non est principis, sed mihi pro eo datur rei uendicatio directa, non principis".

86 Cf. Odofredus, Lectura super C. 7.37.3, as quoted by Pennington, *The Prince,* 24, note 73, and Odofredus, fo. 3a (super const. Omnem): "Vnde si priuato competit rei uendicatio pro sua re quia est dominus rei sue, ergo non competit imperatori, cum duo non possunt dominium eiusdem rei habere insolidum".

87 Published by Cortese, *La norma giuridica,* II: 452–453.

88 Azo and Accursius reported that Placentin and Johannes Bassianus differed of opinion with regard to the action brought. Placentin said, that the former owner had an *actio in rem,* Johannes Bassianus a *condictio ex lege.* Cf. Azo, gloss s.v. *'Aerariam'* ad Inst.Just. II.6.14 in Mss. Bamberg. SB Jur 4, fo. 21rb and Florence BML 392, fo. 11rb: "actio in rem uel hypothecaria. Vnde speciale est ut datur non domino aduersus dominum ut dicit p. Secundum i.b. datur condictio ex lege."; Acccursius, gloss s.v. *'Actiones'* ad Inst.Just. II.6.14.

89 D. 5.3.13.9 states that an estate (*hereditas*) could be recovered from the buyer, if the treasury had sold the estate of someone who had seemingly died without heirs. Johannnes Bassianus and Azo, therefore, had distinguished between actions for individual goods and for estates. See Johannes Bassianus, *Lectura Institutionum,* ad Inst.Just. IV.6.14 in Ms. Admont SB 88, fo. 72vb; Leiden UB d'Ablaing 3, fo. 7vb; Leipzig UB 921, fo. 159vb: "[...] Item hoc uerum est si uendat rem singularem secus enim est si uendat hereditatem. ut ff. de pet. hered. l. Etiam § Item [D. 5.3.13.9]". Azo, Lectura, 5744 (super C. 7.37.2), Azo, gloss s.v. *'Accipiunt'* ad Inst.Just. II.6.14 in Mss. Bamberg. SB Jur 4, fo. 21rb and Florence BML 392, fo. 11rb: "singula re; qui enim a fisco hereditatem emit, utili petitiione hereditatis tenetur. ut ff. de pet. her. Nec ulla § Item si quis [D. 5.3.13.9]. az." Others said that C. 7.37.2 prevailed. See Accursius, gloss s.v. *'Statim'* ad Inst.Just. II.66.14.

90 Cf. Accursius, gloss s.v. *'Consecuti sunt'* ad C. 7.37.2.

chaser is immediately safe from claims – apparently in contrast to acquirers from private persons who need to invoke usucapion or prescription.

The acquirer, De Révigny argued, is immediately safe from claims, because the prince is thought to own private property.[91] In his line of thought, a buyer is safe from claims, because he acquired ownership through transfer of possession by an owner – which the emperor is considered to be.[92] To solve the contradiction with D. 13.6.5.15 (*Duorum in solidum dominium esse non potest*) De Révigny applied this statement to private persons only.[93]

Having discussed whether everything in the world belongs to the prince, De Révigny turned to the question if the prince can transfer ownership of one of his subjects to another. Accursius had denied this,[94] but De Révigny argued, that the prince could do so as sovereign, irrespective of whether one attributes ownership of everything in the world to him.[95] Cinus da Pistoia, whose lectures on the Codex were published in 1314, agreed with De Révigny that the prince could expropriate the property of one of his subjects,[96] but denied that he owned everything in the world;[97] so did Albericus de Rosate,[98] and Bartolus

---

91 Cf. Jacques de Révigny, *Lectura super Codice* (Paris: Du Pre, 1519; repr. Bologna: Forni, 1967), fo. 345va: "Vnde illi qui exponunt, non intelligunt legem istam, quia hic loquitur de rebus priuatorum uenditis a fisco. Vnde exponitur: est hoc quod uenditio facta de re aliena procuratore fisci uel procuratore priuati patrimonii [caesaris] statim ualet. Et est emptor securus, nam omnia que sunt priuatorum principis esse intelliguntur".

92 In this respect, De Révigny differs from Accursius (gloss s.v. '*Exercere*' ad C. 7.37.2), who preferred the view of Irnerius that the acquirer of the fisc is a possessor against whom the owner's action for recovery is barred by privilege (C. 7.37.2).

93 Cf. Jacques de Révigny, *Lectura super const. Omnem* (as quoted by Cortese, *La norma giuridica*, II: 452): "Responde ad argumentum b[ulgari]: imperator est dominus, ut tu dicis, et subjectus est dominus; concedo quod duo erunt domini eiusdem rei in solidum, immo et tertius dominus. Vnde, cum dicitur plures non possunt esse domini eiusdem rei, uerum est plures priuati, sed imperator non ponitur in numerum".

94 See Accursius, gloss s.v. '*Quotiens*' ad C. 1.19.2 discussed in Ugo Nicolini, *La proprietà, il principe e l'espropriazone per publica utilità, Studi sulla dottrina giuridica intermedia* (Milan: Giuffrè, 1952), 127 ff.

95 Ibid., 453.

96 Cf. Cinus de Pistoia. *Lectura super Codice* (Frankfurt aM, 1578; repr. Turin: Bottega d'Erasmo 1969), fo. 36va nr 12 (super C. 1.19.2): "Ergo si mutari potest [ius gentium] in parte per principem, dici potest per illam quod licet imperator non possit totaliter facere ut omnes amittant dominium, potest saltem particulariter facere, ut unus amittat, et sic potest rescribere quod res tua sit mea".

97 Cf. Cinus, *Lectura super Codice,* fo. 445v no. 4 (super C. 7.37.3).

98 Cf. Albericus de Rosate, *Commentaria in Codice* (Venice, 1585–1586; repr. Bologna: Forni, 1979), vol. I, fo. 68vb – 69rb (super C. 1.19.2), no. 6–10.

de Saxoferrato.[99] Using the analogy with ownership of a flock he argued that the emperor could nevertheless be "the owner of the world" without owning everything in it. Hence, if someone else holds his territory, he may reclaim it, just like private persons their land.[100] In support he cited D. 6.1.1.3: "we own the flock, even if particular animals may not belong to us; for what is vindicated is the flock, not the individual beasts". Citing Bartolus, Paulus de Castro (c. 1360–1441) expressed the same view in his commentary on D. 30.48.pr.[101]

6 Ownership Liable to Reversal and Ownership *in spe*

As Odofredus reported, Johannes Bassianus and Azo already taught that the husband was the sole owner of the property that his wife had transferred to him as dowry. She was the owner *in spe*, knowing that upon dissolution of the marriage the ownership would return to her. As they had pointed out, it also implied that the husband cannot dispose of dotal property as his own, because he must return the property she transferred to him upon dissolution of the marriage.[102]

The Commentators used the notion of an ownership that is liable to reversal not only in the context of dotal property (C. 5.12.30) but also in other situations, for instance, in case an owner finds his captured slave is now serving

99 Cf. Bartolus de Saxoferrato, *Opera omnia* (Venice, 1526–1528), I: fo. 2va (ad const. Omnem) nr 3. Bartolus did not discuss this issue at C. 7.37.3.

100 Cf. Bartolus, *Opera omnia,* I: fo. 180va (ad D. 6.1.1.3) no. 2: "Pro hoc ego sum consuetus dicere in prima con(stitutione) huius libri, quod imperator sit dominus totius mundi. Et glosa dicit eum dominum quo ad protectionem, quia cum alii sint domini singulariter, plures non poterunt esse domini in solidum. Ego dico quod imperator est dominus totius mundi uere. Nec obstat quod alii sunt domini particulariter, quia mundus est uniuersitas quaedam. Vnde potest quis habere dictam universitatem, licet singulares non sint suae. Vnde si alius teneret mundum, ipse imperator posset uendicare". Bartolus said the same in his commentary to the const. *Ad reprimenda* of Henry VII. See Dante Fedele, *The medieval foundations of international law, Baldus de Ubaldis (1327–1400) Doctrine and Practice of the Ius Gentium* (Leyden: Brill, 2021), 46. On Bartolus' thesis, see Constantin Fasolt, *Limits of history* (Chicago–London: University of Chicago Press, 2004), 190–191; Pier Giuseppe Monateri, *Dominus Mundi: Political Sublime and the World Order* (Oxford: Hart, 2018), 44.

101 Cf. Paulus de Castro, *In secundam Infortiati partem commentarii* (Venice, 1550), fo. 26vb (ad D. 30.48.pr) no. 3. He comments on the gloss s.v. '*In factum*' ad D. 30.48pr which said that the heir owns the bequeathed thing because it is part of the inheritance: "inspecta universitate in qua continetur res legata, haec sicut cetere est heredis".

102 Cf. Odofredus, ad D. 13.6.5.15 (Rüfner, "The Roman Concept of Ownership," 132) and ad C. 5.12.30 (above, note 57).

someone else (D. 49.15.12.7). Bartolus' and Baldus interpretation of the texts that suggest double ownership thus provided leads for Socini's exceptions to the rule that ownership in entirety cannot be in two persons.

Both father and son seem to be owners of the same thing, when children under paternal control are said to be in some sense owners of the estate during his lifetime (D. 28.2.11). Bartolus affirmed that this is not proper ownership.[103] As Accursius had said, their *dominium* is more imaginary than real.[104] Baldus elaborated that they are in some sense owners, because by a fiction of law father and son are thought of as one person (C. 6.36.11).[105] During his father's lifetime the son has ownership *in spe*, after his father's demise *in re*. Baldus equated these with *dominium* in potency (*in potentia* or *habitu*) and in act (*actu*)[106] – a dichotomy the medieval jurists borrowed from Aristotelian philosophy.[107] Paulus de Castro argued that this ownership by fiction of law is not true ownership, because his father can disinherit him. During his lifetime the father is the true owner of his assets, the son only fictitious.[108]

Bartolus taught that the husband is sole owner of the property his wife has transferred to him as dowry[109], but Baldus used the difference between *dominium directum* and *dominium utile* to argue that both husband and wife can be owner in entirety of the dotal property, as C. 5.12.30 suggests. Of such property the husband has no free power of disposal, and the wife retains a relic of her dominative power[110] as *dominium utile*, which is subordinate to her husband's

103 Cf. Bartolus, *Opera*, III: fo. 110rb (ad D. 28.2.11) no. 4: "Oppone quod duo non possunt esse domini in solidum. l Si ut certo § Si duobus uehiculum supra commo. [D. 13.6.5.15]. Solutio. Dicitur filius dominus improprie uiuo patre, ut patet ex textu, qui dicit 'quoddammodo'".

104 Ibid. "Et hoc est quod dicit glosa quod hoc dominium filii consistit in nudo et puro intellectu, qua dicit magis est in imaginatione quadam quam in ueritate".

105 Baldus, *Super infortiato*, fo. 53vb (super D. 28.3.11) no. 3: "et hoc est artificio iuris, nam fingit in personis unitatem. C. de impu. et aliis subs. l. fi. [C. 6.26.11] et sic plures non censentur ut plures, sed ut unus".

106 Ibid. "quod primo erat in potentia et in spe, nunc est in actu et in re".

107 The English canonist Alanus, for instance, wrote about 1210 that the pope had the temporal sword *in habitu* (in his power without exercising it) and the emperor *in actu*. Cf. Walter Ullmann, *Medieval Papalism. The political theories of the medieval canonists* (New York: Routledge, 1941), 195.

108 Cf. Paulus de Castro, *In primam Infortiati partem commentarii* (Venice, 1550), fo. 62vb (ad D. 28.2.11) no. 1: "Et est sensus quod uterque est dominus, pater uere et filius ficte, non enim possunt esse duo domini eo(dem) respectu".

109 Cf. Bartolus, *Opera*, VII: fo. 181ra (ad C. 5.12.3) and 181vb (ad C. 5.12.30).

110 Cf. Baldus, *Lectura super Codice*, vol. III (Venice, 1471, no. fol.), *In Quartum et Quintum Codicis* (Lyon, 1552), fo. 169ra (ad C. 5.12.30) no. 4: "Tu dic quod aut consideramus dominium essentialiter et proprie, et tunc est penes maritum; aut consideramus uestigia

ownership like that of a long term lessee is subordinate to the *dominium* of the bare owner.[111]

When someone has built on his own land with another one's building material, the building is his, but the other is said to remain the owner of the building material (D. 41.1.7.10 and Inst.Just. II.1.29).[112] As long as the building exists, he has no action to recover possession of the material, but against a builder who knew to build with another's material, he can bring a *rei uindicatio* for as much as he values it.[113] The issue of double ownership arises when all the materials used to build the house were of one person, as the *casus* of the Guido de Cumis (ca 1210–1263)[114] to Inst.Just. II.1.29 suggests, saying: Who is the owner of the building, if Titius built on his own land with another's material, Titius or the owner of the building material? Answer that, though Titius acquires *dominium directum* of the building, the owner of the material retains *dominium utile* of it, while he has no action for recovery as long as it is connected to the building.[115]

et reliquiias dominii, et tale dominium est penes mulierem. Non enim transit dominium in uirum absolute, sed dotis causa, in qua dote uir imaginem mulieris representat arg. infra de praescr. xxx. ann. Cum notissimi § i. [C. 7.39.7.1]. Sed contra hoc immediate oppone: nam ex hoc sequitur quod duo sunt domini in solidum, quod esse non potest". See also Baldus, *In Quartum et Quintum Codicis* (Venice: Giunti, 1577), no fol. (ad C. 5.12.30): "Glosa quærit utrum uxor sit domina rei dotalis constante matrimonio. Et dic quod sic si sit dominium large sumptum. Sed si stricte, pro uero dominio, secus ut de rei uend. l. Dote ancillam [C. 3.32.9]. Non potest negari quin penes ea quædam reliquiæ dominii remaneant re et nomine; inde habet comoditate et alimenta ex re".

111 Ibid. "Breuiter ergo dico quod uir habet dotale dominium proprietatis, sed mulier cum eo concurrit cum utili. ut supra de rei uend. l. Doce [C. 3.32.9] et supra De his que in [C. 5.12.11]. Quod autem dictum est de concursum indiuisibilium apud plures insolidum non habet locum in proprietate uel dominio eiusdem consideratione et speciei. Sed sub diversa consideratione, puta sunt duo dominia, quorum unum est sub altero, ut emphyteutico sub proprio, bene possunt concurrent insolidum".

112 Bartolus, Baldus and Paulus did not discuss one of these texts in their works.

113 Cf. Accursius, gloss s.v. *'Sciens'* ad D. 6.1.23.7: "Quo casu non aget ut eximatur, sed ut pretium peteret iurando in litem, quia dolo desiit possidere. Infra de tigno iniunc. l.i. in fi. [D. 47.3.1.2] et de sol. Qui res in fine [D. 46.3.98.8] secundum Joan[nem]".

114 Cf. Robert Feenstra, "Les Casus Institutionum de Guido de Cumis," in *Fata Iuris Romana*, ed. Robert Feenstra (Leiden: Leiden University Press, 1974), 260–282, at 280.

115 The casus is included in 16th-century editions of the Corpus Iuris with the Gloss. The earliest Feenstra mentioned is Paris 1506. The Lyon 1604 edition (published online at https://amesfoundation.law.harvard.edu/digital/CJCiv) reads: "Domine, Tititus in solo suo aedicauit ex materia aliena, modo quaero quis sit dominus illius aedificii, utrum Titius qui aedificauit, an ille qui erat dominus materiae? Ad hoc repond[e] quod Titius aedificator dominus est aedicii [...] Et quamuis Titio directum dominium aedificii acquiratur, ille tamen qui dominus fuit materie, dominus eius non desinit esse, sed

If anyone ransoms a slave that was captured by the enemy, he is thenceforth the property of the ransomer, but, the price he paid being offered to him, the slave is thought to have returned to his master (D. 49.15.12.7). The next paragraph discusses, whether someone who unwittingly ransomed a captured slave, believing him to belong to the seller, can be regarded as having usucapted him if the former master offered him the purchase price after more than three years. I cannot be regarded to usucapt what is my own, but nothing is left for the slave's master, D. 49.15.12.8 rules, after the time has lapsed in which I would have acquired ownership through usucapion, had it not been a captured slave.[116] Accursius had deduced a statutory limitation of the right to repurchase the slave (*ius luendi*)[117] in analogy to usucapion, but Bartolus concluded that the ransomer is capable of usucapting the slave he owns, because a slave that he must return is not irrevocably his.[118] His line of thought implies there are two owners.

In case a testator bequeathed the same thing twice and made it clear that each legatee is to receive the thing in entirety, the legatee who first joins issue has the choice of the thing itself or its value (D. 30.33). According to the Gloss, before that moment neither of the legatees was an owner. Bartolus affirmed this, adding that the heir was still the owner. The legatee's future ownership depended on his choice.[119] Baldus argued differently. In his opinion, in this case, ownership in entirety can be in more people, because each legatee's ownership is liable to reversal (*commutabilis*), depending on the future choice of the legatee who first joins issue.[120]

---

utile dominium retinet, sed tamdui materia suo inuncta est aedificio, neque eam uindicare neque ad exhibendam de ea agere potest".

116 Cf. D. 49.15.12.8.

117 Cf. Accursius, gloss s.v. '*Ius*' ad D. 49.15.12.8: "Tertio nota quod prescribitur iuri luendi".

118 Cf. Bartolus, *Opera*, VI: fo. 245va (ad D. 49.15.12.7): "Valde notabilis paragraphus est. Nota duo: quod seruus est redimentis, item quod redimens usucapit. [...] Oppone [ad secundum] l. Sequitur § Lana supra de usuca. [D. 43.3.4.19]. Solue: vera ponit in tex. 'eodem modo' quia res mea irreuocabiliter non potest usucapi in contrario, secus si reuocabiliter ut hic. Hoc habuistis notata.in l Sequitur § Fructus supra de usuc. [D. 43.3. 4.4] & ibi dixi". See Bartolus, *Opera*, V: fo. 101v.

119 Cf. Bartolus, *Opera*, IV: fo. 12v (ad D. 30.33): "Dicendum est ergo quod dominium interim nullius est ex legatariis, nec in totum nec in partem, sed est heredis. Quod patet, quia potest transferre in alium, ut dixi. Praeterea consequitur per contestationem legatarius ius eligendi, ut hac lege. Sed in relicto alternatiuo, non habet quis dominium ante electionem. ut l. Apud Aufidium de op. lega. (D. 33.5.20)".

120 Cf. Baldus, *Super infortiato*, fo. 130va (ad D. 30.33) no. 6: "In ea glosa ['*Contestatus est*'] ibi 'Sed et dici potest pro parte cuique quaesitum, sed sub conditione insolidum': Non est proprie conditio, quia non suspendit natiuitatem obligationis uel dominii, nam si suspenderet interim non esset dominium quaesitum. Ego dico quod dominium est unicui-

7 Bartholomeo Socini's Exceptions to the *regula*

There are several texts in Justinian's Corpus iuris, which suggest that ownership in entirety can be in two persons. Socini used five of them as the basis for exceptions to the rule found in D. 13.6.5.15. Some as cases in which the rule does not apply, others as examples thereof.

The rule does not apply, Socini argued, when several people are jointly owners of a thing or right, but without designated shares; for example, of a perpetual lease of municipal land, which a father gave as dowry for his daughter under paternal control.[121] In support he cited C. 5.12.30 and D. 24.3.2.1. The first concerns a dowry given by the wife herself, the latter a dowry given by her father. It states that after dissolution of the marriage the action[122] for return of the dowry – that is to be restored in possession of the property or to receive its value – can only be brought jointly. It is not a case, he said, where each of them has a separate claim in entirety.

In fact, this is not a case, where each is owner in entirety. Father and daughter are thought of as one person.[123]

D. 28.2.11 provides a second exception to the rule, Socini wrote, because during his lifetime the *pater familias* is true owner of his assets, while by

que quaesitum insolidum, sed commutabiliter quia pendet ex futura electione. Et illud quod dicitur quod duo non possunt esse in solidum domini habet locum in dominio incommutabili, non [in] commutabili".

121 It is the first exception to the rule (published in the appendix). Socini cited C. 3.36.6, but this constitution does not concern dowries. It states, that the heirs' shares in debts due to the estate are designated by law.

122 The Paris 1510 edn. has "persona communis iure uectigali" which is changed into "actio communis iure uectigali" in editions after 1150. Cf. Lyon, 1564; Frankfurt, 1586; Cologne, 1592.

123 The notion of a joint ownership without designated shares can already be found in Baldus' commentary to D. 24.3.2.1. Baldus maintained that, upon dissolution of the marriage, the ownership returned to the father, although one could argue from their joint action and the fact that father and daughter were considered to be one person that the subsisting right of ownership was also joint. Cf. Baldus, *Lectura super infortiato* (Venice, 1481, no fol); *In primam et secundam infortiati partem commentaria* (Venice, 1577), fo. 5rb (ad D. 24.3.3) no. 3: "res autem seu rei dominium uidetur reuerti ad ipsum patrum. Si quis uellet tenere quod ipsi iure reuerteretur domnium ad patrem et filiam in solidum, posset hoc defendere exemplo actionis. Non obstat l.iii. § Ex contrario de acquir. poss. [D. 41.2.3.5] quia ibi loquitur in dominio non connexo, ubi dominium cuiuslibet per se discernitur. Hic in dominio connexo, in quo plura representantur ut una persona". Ibid. fo. 5va "Hoc etiam probo quia actio est communis, cum pro dote competat triplex actio personalis, hypothecaria et rei uendicatio, ut l. In rebus [C. 5.12.30]. Statim sequitur, si rei uendicatio competit cuilibet in solidum, ergo et dominium".

legal fiction his son under paternal control is an owner as well. The son has no power of administration, but the fiction has several consequences for him, for instance, that he will not be able to usucapt as heir something his father possesses in bad faith.

The rule does thirdly not apply, Socini argued, to owners in different respects. In illustration he cited D. 6.3.1 and one of the interpretations of C. 5.12.30. The Digest-fragment states that perpetual lessees cannot be removed as long as the rent-charge is paid. The Accursian Gloss gives the reading of C. 5.12.30, to which Socini referred: the wife is owner of the dowry in respect to its use and fruits.[124]

A fourth reason why the rule does not apply could be that one is owner *actu* the other owner *habitu*, as for instance a legatee, who has ownership in potency (*habitu*) of the legacy, which he seems to renounce when he claims its value. At Roman law a legatee can choose between the bequeathed thing and its value. By legal fiction he is thought to be its owner from the testator's death, therefore even before an external heir accepts the inheritance, but he may prefer to receive its value from the heir (C. 6.43.1). According to Socini, from the moment the external heir accepted the inheritance, there are two owners in entirety: the heir and the legatee.

The rule does not apply in D. 41.1.7.10, Socini argued, because two persons are the owners of the same thing, but not in the same way. The Digest fragment states that someone who builds on his own land with building material of someone else becomes the owner of the building, while the owner of the material remains the owner thereof. They are owners in different ways, Socini argued, because the owner of the land is the owner of the building *in concreto*, the owner of the material used to erect the building remains its owner without regard to its current form.

A sixth exception to the rule is based upon D. 49.15.12.7, from which Socini deduced that ownership can be in two persons, when one of them has an ownership that is liable to reversal (*commutabilis*). In support he cited D. 49.15.12.7, which states that the person who ransoms a captured slave becomes thenceforth his owner, but must restore the slave to his master when he offers him the purchase price. Apparently, to Socini there are two owners from the moment the ransomer bought the slave. The buyer's ownership being liable to reversal, both rights may concur.

His seventh exception Socini based upon the Accursian Gloss rather than Justinian's legislation. The rule does not apply, he argued, to the bare owner

---

124 Cf. Accursius, gloss s.v. '*Rei ueritas*' ad C. 5.12.30, above footnote 49.

and the usufructuary. Which specific gloss Socini had in mind, however, cannot be determined,[125] and it was not the dominant view that usufruct was comparable to the right of a long-term lessee, vasal, superficiary, or a person who held land of a church or monastery *in precario*.

8 Conclusion

Socini included a maxim in his collection of *regulae* which, as Thomas Rüfner wrote, "at the end of the period of the commentators had become almost meaningless".[126] In contrast to what Rüfner asserted, however, Justinian's *Corpus iuris* does not contain a clear rule, for too many texts contradicted the statement in D. 13.6.5.15. The early Glossators were able to harmonise these conflicting texts by distinguishing between natural-law and civil-law ownership, but their interpretation of the rule became obsolete. Socini did not even mention it as an exception to the rule. Whether the same is true for the new interpretation that emerged, is unclear. Perhaps Socini meant to distinguish between *dominium directum* and *utile* when he wrote that the rule does thirdly not apply to owners in different respects, as for instance the bare owner and the long-term lessee. If so, his third and seventh exceptions coincide.

A comparison with the discussion in the works of the medieval jurists shows that the number of exceptions varied, and early-modern writers might, therefore, recognise other exceptions than Socini. Antonio Perez (1583–1672), for instance, claimed that the rule does not apply to the artist and the owner of the panel.

Appendix

Bartolomeo Socini, Regulae cum suis fallentiis (*Pavia 1510; Paris 1514*), *regula 99*

Domini in solidum plures eiusdem rei uel iuris esse non possunt.

1. Si ut certo §. Duobus uehiculum ff. commo. [D. 13.6.5.15] et l.iii. §. Ex contrario ff. de acquir poss. [D. 41.2.3.5] cum simili.
   Primo fallit ratione sed non communionis denominatione partium, sicut in lege Ea que C. fam. ercisc. [C. 3.36.6], [1]ubi persona communis iure vectigalis que est in dote in solidum penes patrem et filiam connexa,

125 Socini refers to a gloss to the thirteenth *lex* of an unspecified title.

126 Rüfner, "The Roman Concept of Ownership," 142.

tantummodo plures in quo nec una persona representatur in solidum. Et hoc per legem[1] In rebus C. de iure dot. [C. 5.12.30] de qua in l.ii. §.i. et legem per totam ff. solut matr. [D. 24.3.2.1-2], quia communis est in d.l. In rebus [C. 5.12.30] arg. l. Precipimus in fin. C. de appel. [C. 7.62.32.5].

2. Fallit in l. In suis ff. de liber. et posthum [D. 28.2.11] quia pater dominus est uere, filius autem ficte et sine administratione uiuente patre, licet hoc in filio operetur plures effectus, inter quos est quod in filiis non datur titulus pro herede, l. Nihil <§> pro herede [C. 7.29.2] facit l.i. §. Si impuberi de collat. bon. [D. 37.6.1.21] et quod Dynus et Bartolus in l. fin. ff. de liber agnosc. [D. 25.3.9] et per doctores et Baldem In repetitio in d. l. In suis [D. 28.2.11].

3. Fallit quando diversis respectibus possunt; l.i. si ager vectigal. [D. 6.3.1.1] et in dicta lege In rebus [C. 5.12.30] secundum unum intellectum per litteram ibi cum eodem[2] res ab initio uxoris fuerit et naturaliter in eius permanserit dominio, quamuis per legum subtilitatem earum transitus in mariti patrimonium uideretur fieri"; et per hoc l. Quamuis ff. de iure dot. [D. 23.3.75] et l. Dote ancillam ff. de rei uend. [C. 3.32.9].

4. Fallit quia unus potest esse actu alter[3] habitu, ut in legatario, qui etiam adita hereditate est dominus habitu rei legate, et potest intentare rei uendicationem cui uidetur renunciare eligendo actionem personalem uel hypothecariam. l.i. C. commun. deleg. [C. 6.43.1] l. Cum filius §. Variis ff. de legat. ii. [D. 31.76.8].

5. Fallit in casu l. Adeo § Cum in suo ff. de acq. rerum domin. [D. 41.1.7.10], ubi duo sunt domini: [dominus] [4]soli, ut est dominus aedificii super quo aedificat(ur) et primus dominus elementorum remanet dominus ipsorum elementorum. Sed hoc contingit aliter et aliter, quia dominus soli est dominus in concreto saltem ipsius materiae, sed dominus simpliciter[4] non habitu respectu ad formam edificii sicut in simili in l. Eorum iuncta l. Labeo et l. Eum qui aedes ff. de usucap. [D. 41.3.30pr – 1? & 23].

6. Fallit quando unus potest esse dominus commutabiliter. l. In bello §. Si quis seruus ff. de capi. dim. [D. 49.15.12.7].

7. Fallit in l. xiii. ut ibi not. per glosam. ff. de usufructuario et proprietario, sicut in simili sunt dominus et emphyteuta uel feudatarius uel superficiarius (ue)l qui habet precariam et d. l. i. ff. si ager uectigal [D. 6.3.1.1] et l.i. de iure emphy. [C. 4.66.1] et in tit. ff. de superfic. [D. 43.18] et in tit. de feud. [X 3.20] et in tit. extra de precario [X 3.14].

8. Fallit quia legatarius et dominus rei legatae tenetur ficte a morte testatoris, sed heres uere tenetur ab aditione et in seruitutibus iuxta l. Prop-

ter cum sua materia ff de seruit. [D. 8.1.11?] et in l.ii. § Ex his et l. Stipulationes non diuiduntur ff. de uerbo. obligatio [D. 45.1.2.2 & 72].

1. ubi – per l. *om.* (Paris, 1514) 2. eadem] heredibus (Pavia, 1510) 3.actu alter] actualiter (Pavia, 1514) 4. soli – simpliciter] eiusdem; sed hoc contingit aliter et aliter, quia dominus soli est dominus totius aedificii in concreto, sed dominus materiae remanet simpliciter dominus ipsius. (Paris, 1514).

Bibliography

Manuscripts

Admont, Stiftsbibliothek 188 (Placentinus, *Summa Codicis*)
Admont, Stiftsbibliothek, 88 (Johannes Bassianus, *Lectura Institutionum*; *Dissensiones Dominorum*)
Bamberg, Staatsbibliothek, Jur. 21 (*Digestum Vetus* with Azo's Apparatus)
Bamberg, Staatsbibliothek, Jur. 4 (*Institutiones* with Azo's Apparatus)
Bamberg, Staatsbiblitohek, Jur. 12 (*Digestum Vetus* with 12th-century glosses)
Bamberg, Staatsbiblothek, Jur. 22 (*Digestum Vetus* with Azo's Apparatus)
Berlin, Staatsbibliothek, 408 (*Codex* with Hugolinus' Apparatus)
Brussels, Koninklijke Bibliotheek, 125 (*Codex* with Hugolinus' Apparatus)
Düsseldorf, Universitäts- und Landesbibliothek, 9A (Placentinus, *Summa Codicis*)
Florence, Biblioteca Medicea Laurenziana, 392 (*Institutiones* with Azo's Apparatus)
Grenoble, Bibliothèque municipale, 391.1 (Placentinus, *Summa Codicis*)
Leipzig, Universitätsbibliothek, 921 (Johannes Bassianus, *Lectura Institutionum*)
Leyden, Universiteiteitsbibliotheek, d'Ablaing 3 (Johannes Bassianus, *Lectura Institutionum*)
London, British Library, Ms. Royal 11 C. III (*Digestum Vetus* with Hugolinus' Apparatus)
Melk, Stiftsbibliothek, 73 (*Codex* with Azo's Apparatus)
Paris, Bibliothèque Nationale, lat. 4450 (*Digestum Vetus* with 12th-century glosses)
Paris, Bibliothèque Nationale, lat. 4461 (*Digestum Vetus* with Hugolinus' Apparatus)
Paris, Bibliothèque Nationale, lat. 4536 (*Codex* with Azo's Apparatus)
Seu d'Urgel, Biblioteca de la Cathedral, 2063 (*Digestum Vetus* with Hugolinus' Apparatus)
Stockholm, Konigliga Bibliotheket, 680 (*Digestum Vetus* with 12th-century glosses)
Vaticano, Biblioteca Apostolica Vaticana, Vat.lat. 11152 (*Codex* with Azo's Apparatus)
Vaticano, Bibliotheca Apostolica Vaticana, Ottobat. 1298 (*Dissensiones dominorum*)

Vienna, Österreichische Nationalbibiothek, 2157 (Pillius, *Libellus disputatorius*)
Vienna, Österreichische Nationalbibiothek, 2268 (*Codex* with Hugolinus' *Apparatus*)

Printed Sources

Accursius. *Glossa in Codicem*. Venice: Baptista de Tortis, 1488; reprint, Turin: Bottega d' Erasmo, 1968.

Accursius. *Glossa in Digestum Infortiatum*. Venice: Baptista de Tortis, 1488; reprint, Turin: Bottega d' Erasmo, 1968.

Accursius, Glossa in *Digestum Novum*. Venice: Baptista de Tortis, 1487; reprint, Turin: Bottega d' Erasmo, 1968.

Accursius. *Glossa in Digestum Vetus*. Venice: Baptista de Tortis, 1488; reprint Turin: Bottega d' Erasmo, 1969.

Albericus de Rosate. *Commentaria in Codice*. 2 vols. Venice: 1585–1586; reprint, Bologna: Forni, 1979.

Axiomata legum ex receptis iuris utriusque libris ordine alphabetico. Frankfurt, 1546; Lyon, 1547.

Azo. *Brocarda*. Naples, 1568; reprint, Turin: Ex Officina Erasmiana, 1967.

Azo. *Lectura super Codice*. Paris, 1577; reprint, Turin: Bottega d'Erasmo, 1966.

Baldus de Ubaldis. *In primam et secundam Infortiati partem commentaria*. Venice, 1577.

Baldus de Ubaldis. *In Quartum et Quintum Codicis Partem Commentaria*. Lyon, 1552; Venice, 1577.

Bartolomeo Socini. *Regulae cum suis ampliationibus et fallentiis*. Paris: 1514.

Bartolomeo Socini. *Regulae fere super toto corpore iuris cum omnibus fallentiis suis*. Paris: 1510.

Bartolus de Saxoferrato. *Opera omnia*. Venice: Torti, 1526 –1528.

Bilsten, Johannes. *Iustiniani Institutionum … axiomatis seu regulis … illustrati*. Hannover: Apud Guilielmum Antonium, 1596.

Brocardica iuris. Paris: Berthold, 1515; Paris: Guillard, 1541.

Brocartica iuris [Paris], 1495; Paris: Jehan Petit, 1505, Paris: 1508; Paris: 1511.

Cinus de Pistoia. *Lectura super Codice*. Frankfurt aM, 1578; reprint Turin: Bottega d'Erasmo, 1969.

Corpus iuris civilis (with the Gloss), edited by Dionysius Gothofredus. 6 vols. Lyon: 1604.

Corpus iuris civilis, edited by Paul Krüger and Theodor Mommsen. 3 vols. Berlin: Weidmann, 1900 – 1905.

Damasus. *Burchardica siue regulae canonicae*. Cologne: Birchmann, 1564.

Dissensiones dominorum, edited by Gustav Hänel. Leipzig: Hinrich, 1834; reprint, Aalen: Scientia, 1964.

Dumoulin, Charles. *Prima Pars Commentariorum in Consuetudines Parisiensis*. Paris: 1536.

Fina, Giovanno Donato. *Enchiridion conclusionum et regularum utriusque iuris*. Frankfurt: 1574.

Galvani, Marcaurelio, *Dissertationes variae de usufructu*. Geneve: 1626.

Huber, Ulric. *Praelectiones iuris civilis secundum Institutiones*. Franeker: Amama & Taedama, 1687.

Révigny, Jacques de. *Lectura super Codice*. Paris: Du Pre, 1519; repr. Bologna: Forni, 1967.

Libellus de preparatoriis litium, edited by Giovanni B. Palmieri (*Scripta Anecdota Glossatorum*, vol. 3). Bologna: In aedibus successori Monti, 1901.

Loci communes iuris civilis. Lyon: Gryhpius, 1545.

Mynsinger a Frundeck, Joachim. *Apotelesma. Hoc est corpus perfectum scholiorum …* Basel: apud Nicolaum Episcopum, 1563.

Odofredus. *Lectura super Codice*, vol. I. Lyon: Marchant, 1550, reprint, Bologna: Forni, 1968.

Odofredus. *Lectura super Digesto Novo*. Lyon: Marchant, 1550; reprint, Bologna: Forni, 1968.

Odofredus. *Lectura super Digesto Veteri*, vol. I. Lyon: Marchant, 1550; reprint, Bologna: Forni, 1967.

Paulus de Castro. *In secundam Infortiati partem commentaria*. Venice, 1550.

Paulus de Castro. *In secundam Digesti veteri partem commentaria*. Venice, 1575.

Perez, Antonio. *Institutiones … ex ipsis principiis regulisque iuris … explicate*. Amsterdam: 1654.

Placentinus. *Summa Codicis*. Edited by Nicolaus Rhodius. Mainz: Shoeffer, 1536; reprint, Turin: Bottega d'Erasmo, 1962.

Pothier, Robert. *Pandectae Justinianeae in novum ordinem digestae*, 3 vols. Paris: Saugrain, Desaint & C, 1748–1752.

Roffredus Beneventanus. *De libellis et ordine iudiciorum*. Avignon: 1500; reprint Turin, Bottega d'Erasmo, 1968.

Rogerius. *Summa codicis*, edited by Giovanni B. Palmieri (*Scripta Anecdota Glossatorum*, vol. 1). Bologna: In aedibus Societatis Azzoguidianae, 1913.

Rolando da Lucca, *Summa trium librorum (1195–1197)*, edited by Emanuele Conte and Sara Menzinger. Rome: Viella, 2012.

Sententiae sive loci communes utriusque iuris. Cologne: Baumius, 1585.

Wilhelmus de Cabriano. *Casus Codicis*, edited by Tammo Wallinga. Frankfurt a.M: Klostermann, 2005.

Literature

Ballentine, James A. *A Law Dictionary*. Indianapolis: The Bobbs-Merill Co., 1916.

Bellomo, Manlio. *Ricerche sui rapporti patrimoniali tra coniugi, Contributo alla storia delta famiglia medievale*. Milan: Giuffrè, 1961.

Coing, Helmut. "Zum Eigentumslehre des Bartolus." *Savigny Zeitschrift für Rechtsgeschichte, Romanistische Abteilung* 70 (1953), 348–371.

Conte, Emanuele. "Defensa. Resistance against unjust power in the medieval learned law (12th–13th centuries)." In *Revolten und politische Verbrechen zwischen dem 12. und 19. Jahrhundert: Rechtliche Reaktionen und juristisch-politische Diskurse*, edited by Angela de Benedictis and Karl Härter, 21–134. Frankfurt aM: Klostermann, 2013.

Cortese, Ennio. "Controversiae medievali sul dominium utile: Bartolo e il quidam doctor de Aurelianis." In *Amicitiae pignus: studi in ricordo de Adriano Cavanna*, edited by Antonio Padoa Schioppa e.a., vol. 1, 613–635. Milan: Giuffrè, 2003.

Cortese, Ennio. *La norma giuridica*. Milan: Giuffrè, 1964.

Endemann, Friedrich. *Lehrbuch des bürgerlichen Rechts*. Berlin: Heymans, 1905.

Fasolt, Constantin. *Limits of history*. Chicago–London: The University of Chicago Press, 2004.

Fedele, Dante. *The medieval foundations of international law, Baldus de Ubaldis (1327–1400) Doctrine and Practice of the Ius Gentium*. Leyden: Brill Nijhof, 2021.

Feenstra, Robert. "Der Eigentumsbegriff bei Hugo Grotius im Licht einiger mittelalterlicher und spätscholastiker Quellen." In *Festschrift für Franz Wieacker*, edited by Okko Behrends, Malte Diesselhorst, Hermann Lange e.a., 209–234. Göttingen: Vandenhoeck und Ruprecht, 1978.

Feenstra, Robert. "Dominium utile est chimaera; nouvelles réflexions suur le concept de propriété dans le droit savant." *Tijdschrift voor Rechtsgeschiedenis* 66 (1998): 381–397.

Feenstra, Robert. "Les Casus Institutionum de Guido de Cumis." In *Fata Iuris Romani*, edited by Robert Feenstra, 260–282. Leyden: Leidse Universitaire Pers, 1974.

Gruyaert, Dorothy. *De exclusiviteit van het eigendomsrecht* [Diss. Leuven]. Antwerpen: Interscientia, 2016.

Jouanneau, Auguste. *Recueil de maximes et citations latines à l'usage du monde judiciaire*. Paris: Administration et librarie des Annales de justices de paix, 1912.

Levy, Ernst. *West Roman vulgar law: the law of property*. Philadelphia: American Philosophical Society, 1951.

Liebs, Detlef. *Lateinische Rechtsregeln und Rechtssprichwörter*. Darmstadt: Wissenschaftliche Buchgesellschaft, 1982.

MacNair, Mike. "The Case of the Careless Purchaser, or Bonitary Ownership and Ownership." In *Principle and Pragmatism in Roman Law*, edited by Benjamin Spagnolo and Joe Sampson, 33–55. Oxford: Hart Publishing, 2020.

Madero, Marta. *Tabula Picta,* translated by Monique D. Inciarte and Roland D. Valayre. Philadelphia: University of Pennsylvania Press, 2009.

Maffei, Paola. *Tabula picta. Pittura e scrittura nel pensiero dei glossatori.* Milan: Giuffrè, 1988.

Masmejan, Lucien. *La Protection possessoire en droit romano-canonique médiéval: (XIIIe – XVe siècles).* Ph.D. Diss., University of Lausanne. Montpellier: Société d'Histoire du Droit et des Institutions des Anciens Pays de Droit Écrit, 1990.

Monateri, Pier Giuseppe. *Dominus Mundi: Political Sublime and the World Order.* Oxford: Hart Publishing, 2018.

Nicolini, Ugo. *La proprietà, il principe e l'espropriazone per publica utilità, Studi sulla dottrina giuridica intermedia.* Milan: Giuffrè, 1952.

Peloubet, Seymour S. *A collection of legal maxims in law and equity.* New York: George Diossy, 1880.

Pennington, Kenneth, *The Prince and the Law, 1200 – 1600, Sovereignty and Rights in the Western Legal Tradition.* Berkeley: University of California Press, 1993.

Pluss, Jacques A. "Baldus de Ubaldis of Perugia on dominium over dotal property." *Tijdschrift voor Rechtsgeschiedenis* 52 (1984): 399–411.

Reinach, Adolf B.P. "Die apriorischen Grundlagen des bürgerlichen Rechts." *Jahrbuch für Philosophie und phänomenologische Forschung* 1 (1913): 685–847.

Rüfner, Thomas. "The Roman Concept of Ownership and the Medieval Doctrine of dominium utile." In *The Creation of the Ius commune, From Casus to Regula,* edited by John W. Cairns and Paul J. du Plessis, 127–142. Edinburgh: Edinburgh University Press, 2010.

Silveira Marchi, Eduardo C. "La proprietà per piani nel diritto romano." *Index* 18 (1990): 265–274.

The Digest of Justinian, English language translation, edited by Alan Watson. 4 vols. Philadelphia: University of Pennsylvania Press, 1998.

Ullmann, Walter. *Medieval Papalism. The political theories of the medieval canonists.* New York: Routledge, 1941.

Waelkens, Laurent L.J.M. *Amne adverso, Roman legal heritage in European Legal Culture.* Leuven: Leuven University Press, 2015.

Zaera García, Ana, *La superficies en derecho romano.* Madrid: Dykinson, 2017.

Zwalve, Willem. "Text and Commentary: The Legal Middle Ages and the Roman Law Tradition, Justinian's Const. *Omnem* and its Medieval Commentators." In *Neo Latin Commentaries and the Management of Knowledge in the Late Middle Ages and the Early Modern Period (1400–1700),* edited by Karl Enenkel and Henk Nellen, 349 – 386. Leuven: Leuven University Press, 2013.

CHAPTER 8

Quod quis ex sua culpa damnum sentit, damnum sentire non videtur

Emanuel G.D. van Dongen

1 Introduction

In Italian law, the contribution of the negligent act of the injured party in extracontractual cases is known as *concorso di colpa del danneggiato*:[1] the contributory negligence of the injured party. In such a case, the principle is applied that the amount of compensation is reduced according to the seriousness of the fault of the injured party and the extent of the resulting consequences.[2] One of the *brocardi* mentioned on www.brocardi.it, linked to Article 1227 *Codice civile* (*concorso del fatto colposo del creditore*), is the following: *Quod quis ex sua culpa damnum sentit, damnum sentire non videtur*.[3]

Before this rule applies, however, it must be established that this is a case where the law provides that the damage must be compensated by someone else. If not, the general rule applies, namely that an owner has to bear the risk of accidental loss (casus) himself. An accident can be defined as an event for which a third party cannot be blamed. In that case, the injured party has to suffer the damage himself, e.g. in cases when someone brings damage on himself, the loss should lie where it falls (*casum sentit dominus*).[4]

The Latin words of the *brocardo* just mentioned are taken *verbatim* from D. 50.17.203, a Digest text from the title *De regulis iuris antiqui*, and it demonstrates the interest therein that still exists among lawyers today. This rule had no general scope in its classical origin; however, in the literature, it is often

1 See, e.g., the decision of Supreme Court of Cassation of Italy, Cass. 6 May 2016, n. 9241.

2 Art. 1227(1) Cc. See also, e.g., Franco Anelli and Carlo Granelli, eds., *Manuale di diritto privato* (Milan: Giuffrè, 2019), 919.

3 Editor's note: This *regula* is registered in the FWO.OPR.2020.005001 database under No. 975.

4 Cf. Corjo Jansen, "Accidental Harm under (Roman) Civil Law," in *The Challenge of Chance. A Multidisciplinary Approach from Science and the Humanities*, ed. Klaas Landsman & Ellen van Wolde (Springer, 2016), 233–234.

 | DOI:10.1163/9789004736092_010

connected to *lex Aquilia* texts and thus with extracontractual liability.[5] This contribution will focus on this *regula* and describe how its role and meaning developed and changed over time.

2 The Text of D. 50.17.203 in the Original Classical Roman Law Context

Before discussing the meaning of D. 50.17.203, it is important to realise that there is a question of the distribution of damages only if there is contributory negligence. This is a modern concept, a (modern) juridical qualification, and it is – as will be shown below – superfluous when discussing (classical) Roman law.[6] D. 50.17.203 derives from Pomponius' commentary on Quintus Mucius Scaevola, which contained a systematic treatise of the *ius civile*. Lenel, in his *Palingenesia*, placed this fragment in the commentary of Pomponius on Quintus Mucius under the title *De legatis*.[7] The wording of D. 50.17.203, as delivered to us, is: *Quod quis ex culpa sua damnum sentit, non intellegitur damnum sentire.*[8]

When Pomponius wrote the lines of D. 50.17.203, they probably formed an integral part of a larger text which is now lost. The text may have been shortened by the compilers of Justinian when they included it in the Digest.[9] One can assume that this fragment, like all the *regulae*, originally referred to a

5 I have elaborately discussed this development, i.e. the role of contributory negligence in extracontractual liability, in Emanuel G.D. van Dongen, *Contributory Negligence. A Historical and Comparative Study* (Leiden: Brill, 2014).

6 See also, Maria F. Cursi, "Il concorso della colpa del danneggiato nel risarcimento e la rilevanza penale dell'azione aquiliana," *Index: Quaderni camerti di studi romanistici* 47 (2019): 191.

7 Otto Lenel, *Palingenesia iuris civilis* (Leipzig: Ex Officina Bernardi Tauchnitz, 1889), II: col. 68, pal. no. 6.260.

8 In Van Dongen, *Contributory negligence*, 18, I translated this text in the following way: "Because the one, who suffers loss as a result of his own negligence (*culpa*), is not considered to suffer any loss". I also gave an alternative translation: "He who suffers a loss through his own negligence is not considered to have suffered a loss", which could be preferred, from a philological point of view. Differently, Rolf Knütel, "Neues zur 'contributory negligence'?," *Index: Quaderni camerti di studi romanistici* 44 (2016): 350, stated that *quod* should be understood as referring to *damnum*, or as a factual *quod* in the sense of 'with regard to' or 'if'.

9 According to Paul Jörs, *Römisches Recht: Geschichte und System des römischen Privatrechts* (Berlin: Springer, 1927), 119, this fragment is interpolated. See also Ernst Levy and Ernst Rabel, *Index interpolationum quae in Iustiniani Digestis inesse dicuntur* (Weimar: Hermann Böhlaus Nachfolger, 1935), III: col. 600. I have argued that "a part is missing before the word '*Quod*'"; see: Van Dongen, *Contributory negligence*, 22.

concrete case,[10] in this case one of legacy. This fragment comes from a larger text, part of a *responsum* to a concrete case, rather than being meant as a general (didactical) rule. Although some argue that the content can no longer be reconstructed,[11] I have attempted to reconstruct the factual case of D. 50.17.203 in the past.[12] In view of the original legal case in which Pomponius made his comment, one can assume that the text was an interpretation of a rule of the law of legacies, which contained the word "*damnum*". In the case to which Pomponius was replying, he obviously aimed to interpret this notion of *damnum* in a way which allowed him to solve the problem that arose in that particular case.[13] The question in the original case was whether the loss resulting from the damage to a (material) object could be explained as "*damnum*" in the legal sense. Considering the close connection in Roman times between rhetoric and law, and the acquaintance with rhetoric, it is also plausible that the jurist considered the case to be a problem of *definitio* (could the damage be considered as *damnum?*) and argued his case on the basis of a *locus a differentia*: a distinction between what was *damnum* and what was not *damnum* based on the fact that the loss was incurred because of one's own negligence.[14]

3 D. 50.17.203 in Justinianic Law

D. 50.17.203 therefore probably did not have anything to do with a situation of compensation of fault (*culpae compensatio*) – it refers to the *culpa* of the

---

10 Hermann Lange, *Schadensersatz und Privatstrafe in der mittelalterlichen Rechtstheorie* (Munster/Cologne: Böhlau-Verlag, 1955), 71.

11 Cursi, "Il concorso della colpa," 190.

12 Van Dongen, *Contributory negligence*, 21ff., 24ff., see also: Sara Galeotti, "Colpa della vittima e risarcibilità del danno ingiusto," *Quaderni Lupiensi* 8 (2018): 418, – although Knütel, "Neues zur 'contributory negligence'?," 350–351, did not find this to be plausible, he has not himself provided an alternative, which does not advance this matter any further.

13 In Van Dongen, *Contributory Negligence*, 21ff., I discussed reconstructions of the original classical context, those of Peter Aumann, "Das mitwirkende Verschulden in der neueren juristische Dogmengeschichte" (Ph.D. diss., Universität Hamburg, 1964), and Christian Wollschläger, "Das eigene Verschulden des Verletzten im römischen Recht," *Zeitschrift der Savigny-Stiftung für Rechtsgeschichte. Romanistische Abteilung* 93 (1976): 115–137, and made some suggestions myself.

14 Van Dongen, *Contributory negligence*, 24. On the *locus a differentia*, see Quintilianus, *Institutio Oratoria*, v.10.58–63. An alternative option would be to consider the second part of the text to be a fiction: if the damage suffered was the consequence of one's own negligence, the damage caused to the harmed person was presumed not to be *damnum*.

injured party, but not in relation to a possible liability of a wrongdoer.[15] The compilers extracted D. 50.17.203 from its original context in Pomponius' work and placed this fragment in the title *De diversis regulis iuris antiqui*, and it became a general rule (*regula*). The precise function of the last title of the Digest is, nevertheless, not clear today and was probably not clear to the compilers themselves, but they probably attributed a certain ornamental function to the title. According to Stein, it rounded off the Digest in a neat and conclusive manner.[16] Pugsley emphasises that the title is not *De regulis juris*, 'On legal rules', which sounds important, but *De diversis regulis juris antiqui*, 'On miscellaneous rules of ancient law', which certainly does not.[17] This title was not originally planned but was 'thought up' at the last moment when it became clear that D. 50.16 was not going to be long enough to reach the end of book 50 as required.[18]

Making it a general rule (*regula*) in Justinian's compilation, to be understood in the sense of Paul, D. 50.17.1, it was generally set up as an abstract principle, valid for both delictual and contractual remedies. A kind of principle might have existed according to which someone who suffered a disadvantage resulting from his "own fault", in a legal sense, was not considered to have suffered any damage for which compensation could be claimed. Because of his 'own fault' it would be unreasonable to punish a wrongdoer. In Justinian's time, all relevant texts on a topic were part of the same compilation. Therefore, *lex Aquilia* texts could possibly be explained in combination with D. 50.17.203.[19] However, one should beware that, unlike the binding force of a modern provision, the *regula* of Pomponius could not be attributed with too much binding force.[20] However this may be, the solution of D. 50.17.203

15 Cf. also Cursi, "Il concorso della colpa," 190–191.

16 Peter Stein, *Regulae Iuris. From juristic rules to legal maxims* (Edinburgh: Edinburgh University Press, 1966), 122–123.

17 See also: Stein, *Regulae Iuris*, 163–164, citing Cujas, who stressed that the rubric was called *de diversis regulis iuris antiqui* and not *de omnibus regulis iuris*.

18 David F. Pugsley, "On compiling Justinian's Digest(6): Twin texts and working methods," *Orbis Iuris Romani: Journal of Ancient Law Studies* 1997: 53. Although Stein, *Regulae Iuris*, 115, argued that 'as each sub-committee read through the works allotted to it for digesting, its members would have been instructed to look out for *regulae* suitable for insertion in the last title', Pugsley is of the opinion that this is very unlikely.

19 For example, D. 9.2.11pr., especially the final phrase (*se queri debere*) could be read and explained in conjunction with D. 50.17.203.

20 Knütel, "Neues zur 'contributory negligence'?," 355. On page 359 he even called it the '*Verabsolutierung*' of the rule of D. 50.17.203.

became an "all or nothing" rule which was rapidly adopted and provided a common foundation for jurists in Western Europe in the past.[21]

4 The *Regula* in Medieval Roman Scholarship

One of the important starting points to solve the problem of contributory negligence in the Civilian tradition[22] in medieval legal scholarship was the rule of D. 50.17.203. The contributory negligence of the injured party seems to have been regarded as reproachable misconduct that was sanctioned by a refusal to grant a claim for damages. Bulgarus (†1166), one of the Four Doctors, the leader of the "orthodox party",[23] systematically studied the title D. 50.17 in his *apparatus*,[24] serving as the basis of later glossatorial work on this title.[25] He attempted to interpret this rule by providing an example of a case in which it applied. This example, D. 17.2.52.18, was mentioned in most (later) glosses and commentaries on the *regula* as an example.

The text of D. 17.2.52.18 concerns a partner in all goods (*socius omnium bonorum*) against whom a judgment was rendered for having insulted someone (an *actio iniuriarum*). The question was whether the partner, after having paid the *poena*, could reclaim payment from the community. The answer provided by the text is that, if the partner had been unjustly condemned, he would be entitled to recourse. However, if the injury resulted from some illegal act that he had committed, he had to bear the entire loss.

Suppose now – as Bertrandus Metensis (Bertram, bishop of Metz (1180–1212)) did – that one of the partners stole an object (for example, a horse) and brought it into the community. Then, that partner was sued and had to

---

21 See also Dmitry Poldnikov, "Contributory Negligence: A Historical and comparative study," *Journal on European History of Law* 5, no. 2 (2014): 135.

22 Roman law was not received in English Common law to the degree that it was received on the continent. It nevertheless had some influence on the concepts, terminology, and principles of English common law. See, elaborately: Edward D. Re, "The Roman Contribution to the Common Law," *Fordham Law Review* 29, no. 3 (1961): 447ff. Some thoughts on the topic of contributory negligence have been taken from Roman law as well. See Francis Wharton, *A Treatise on the Law of Negligence* (Philadelphia: Kay and brother, 1874), 265, who even claimed that the principle of Pomponius in D. 50.17.203 – stating that he who suffers loss due to his own negligence is not considered to have suffered loss – was reaffirmed in Anglo-American jurisprudence.

23 Stein, *Regulae Iuris*, 132.

24 Bulgarus, *De diversis regulis iuris antiqui commentarius*, ed. Friedrich G.C. Beckhaus (Bonn: Henry u. Cohen, 1856; Frankfurt am Main: Minerva, 1967), 154, ad D. 50.17.203.

25 Stein, *Regulae Iuris*, 136.

return the object. Furthermore, he had to pay a fine. Could he claim this from his associate? According to Bulgarus, one has to make a distinction: did the other partner know about the *furtum* or not? If the associate was unaware of the theft, the partner could only claim the whole value of the stolen object, but not the *poena*. However, if the other partner was aware of the fact, he would also be liable to pay the penalty, as it is just that he who participated in the profit should also share in the loss.[26] The *regula* does not apply (i.e. an exception to the *regula* applies) when *culpa* can be attributed to someone else.[27] Johannes Bassianus (†1197), who took over the role of Bulgarus as the leader of the conservative part of the Glossators,[28] described the case in which someone tried to impute the risk of a *res* given in *depositum* or the loss suffered in a *societas* to somebody else's *culpa*. If it was not possible to impute the damage to someone else, or to *fatum* or *vis maior*, the general rule of the *regula* applied and the *damnum* was imputed to the injured party.[29]

In his Gloss, Accursius starts with the example of one of the partners in all goods who was sentenced by the judge due to a contract because he did not come to trial, but had he been present, he would have been absolved. The sentenced partner had no recourse against the community (with reference to D. 17.2.52.18 and D. 17.2.53). Another example of the application of the *regula* that Accursius (c. 1182–1263) gave in his Gloss is that of D. 9.2.31: a person crossed over a place where there was no road, neither public nor private; while crossing over, a branch of a tree fell on him, and in that case the *lex Aquilia* was not applicable. Under those circumstances, this act could be considered to be the person's own fault, and thus the victim would not be considered to have suffered any damage. Therefore, the *regula* applied to the claims based on the *lex Aquilia*, making the link with the law of delicts. Therefore, D. 50.17.203 applied to the claim of the one whose corporeal possessions were damaged (action based on the *lex Aquilia*) at the end of the Accursian gloss, and so directly concerned the question of extracontractual liability.[30] According to

---

26 Bulgarus, *De diversis regulis*, 154; also Bertrandus Metensis, *De regulis iuris*, ed. Severino Caprioli (Perugia: University, Faculty of Law, 1981), 211, ad D. 50.17.203.

27 This is also stated a.o. by Rainerius de Forlivio, *Lectura super Digesto novo* (Lyon, 1523; Bologna: Forni, 1968), fo. 153v.

28 Stein, *Regulae Iuris*, 137.

29 Johannes Bassianus, "*Apparatus ad titulum De diversis regulis iuris antiqui*," ed. Severino Caprioli, *Annali di storia del diritto: rassegna internazionale* VI (1963): 238, ad D. 50.17.203.

30 Accursian *Glossa Magna ad* D.50.17.203(-204), s.v. '*Quod quis*' (*Accursii Glossa in Digestum Novum* (Torino: ex officina Erasmiana, 1968), 305); Nils Jansen, "§ 254. Mitverantwortlichkeit des Geschädigten," in *Historisch-kritischer Kommentar zum BGB*, Bd. II/1, ed.

Accursius, the injured party's own negligence deprived him of the right to claim damages from someone else. Accursius read the *ratio* of the *regula* as applying to both the cases in which the negligence of the injured party was the only factor and the cases of the concurrence of faults, namely in which the negligence of the wrongdoer and the injured party were at stake.[31] That is not the case for the examples of the *regula* given by Odofredus in his *Lectura*: an instituted heir who refused an inheritance and subsequently was regarded as having suffered a loss due to his own negligence, and a creditor who concluded a *pactum de non petendo* with a debtor of his own free will.[32]

The later civilians ('Commentators' – but also canonists, see below) even extended the examples of the *regula* given in the Gloss. The first case is that of a procurator (agent) who was condemned because of his own fault and who paid the *poena*, as the fault had to be attributed to him and not to his principal. Also, in another case, if the payment by a procurator or manager of another's affairs was undue, the loss had to be imputed to him and not to the principal.[33] Jacobus Butrigarius (c. 1273–1348), a student of Bartolus, discussed the case of a party that, after having accepted arbitration, had to comply with the decision of the arbiter in the matter under dispute, regardless of whether this decision was just or unjust. Therefore, if the party suffered any damage, the blame was attributed to that party if he had agreed to arbitration.[34] Furthermore, when a person lost a trial, he had to pay the costs (of the lawsuit) to the victorious party, except for expenses incurred by that party due to his contumacy (*contumax*).[35] A final example is that of a surety who could not recover interest from the principal if it was paid due to the negligence (*culpa*) of the

Mathias Schmoeckel, Joachim Rückert and Reinhard Zimmermann (Tübingen: Mohr Siebeck, 2007), 664.

31 Accursian *Glossa Magna* s.v. '*Quod quis*' ad D. 50.17.203(-204).

32 C. 6.27.6 and D. 2.14.7.10; Odofredus, *Lectura super Digesto Novo* (Lyon: Pullon, 1552; Bologna: Forni, 1968), fo. 202rb.

33 D. 3.3.46.5 and D. 3.5.24; both mentioned by Dynus de Mugello, *Preclarus et insignis tractatus allegabilis et quotidianus de regulis iuris* (Pavia, 1518), fo. CXXIIIIv/CXXVr.

34 D. 4.8.27.2; see the commentary on this text by Jacobus Butrigarius, *Commentaria in primam et secundam veteris Digesti partem* (Rome, 1617), 307.

35 See also D. 48.19.5pr. – obviously a person who did not obey notices or the edicts of Governors. This case was already mentioned by Guillaume Durand (Guilelmus Durantis), Panormitanus (Nicolaus de Tudeschis) and, later, by one of the last Commentators Philipphus Decius. See Guilelmus Durantis, *Speculum iuris* (Torino: apud heredes Bevilaquae, 1578), II, *De expen. § Nunc de expensis*, uers. 'ceterum', fo. 228r; Nicolaus de Tudeschis, *Commentaria in quinque decretalium libros* (Venice: al segno della Fontana, 1571), II, fo. 254r ff, ad X 2.14.5; Philippus Decius, *In tit. ff. De regulis iuris* (Venice: Apud Cominum de Tridino Montisferrati, 1564), fo. 210v.

surety himself.[36] In all of these cases, the victim suffered damage because of his own negligence (*culpa*).

5 The *Regula* in Medieval Canon Law

Pope Bonifacius VIII[37] (c. 1235–1303) in his *Liber Sextus* (1298) followed his predecessor Pope Gregory IX (1170–1241) in including the title on *regulae*, but in contrast to Gregory's *Liber Extra*, where 11 were included, Bonifacius included 88 – a symbolic number.[38] The Roman *regula*, D. 50.17.203, found its counterpart in the compilation by Pope Boniface in VI. 5.12.86:[39]

> *Idem. Reg.* LXXXVI. *Damnum, quod quis sua culpa sentit, sibi debet, non aliis, imputare.*[40] The same [=Pope Bonifacius VIII]. Regula 86. One has to impute damage, which someone suffers due to one's own negligence, to himself, not to others.

This rule concerns the injured party's own negligence, not contributory negligence (i.e. when two parties have been negligent – the wrongdoer and the injured party). So, the canonists were not influenced by Accursius on this point that much. Several examples of this maxim are provided by canonists, which show that the *ratio* of this maxim was used in a wide range of cases.[41] The examples of the maxim of VI 5.12.86 are partly the same as those already mentioned by the medieval civilians in their comments on the *regula*; apart from those, the following examples can be cited: the case in which a person who lost his trial was not obliged to pay certain costs which took place after

---

36 Decius, *De regulis iuris*, fo. 211r.

37 See also Emanuel G.D. van Dongen, "The Defence of Contributory Negligence in (Medieval) Canon Law and in Conflict Resolution in Italy in the Early Modern Period," *Zeitschrift der Savigny-Stiftung für Rechtsgeschichte. Kanonistische Abteilung* 100 (2014): 599ff.

38 Stein, *Regulae Iuris*, 148–149, stating that the duplication of the figure 8 represented the Pope's double power (spiritual and temporal), while the number 8 also had symbolic references, e.g. being 2 to the power of 3, it could suggest the two natures of Christ together with the three persons of God.

39 Although the rule of VI 5.12.86, in fact, has its origin in D. 50.17.203, Dynus de Mugello referred to some other Digest texts as a general confirmation of this rule, namely, to D. 46.8.22.4, D. 14.3.7.2, and D. 10.2.44.5.

40 Emil A. Friedberg, ed., *Corpus Iuris Canonici*, II (Leipzig: Tauchnitz, 1881), col. 1122.

41 See, e.g., the commentaries of Johannes Monachus Picardus, Dynus de Mugello and Johannes Andreae in their commentaries on the text, as well as gloss s.v. '*Damnum*' in the *Glossa Ordinaria* on this text.

the *litis contestatio* to the victor, namely, those which the victor paid or had to pay due to his contumacy (*contumax*);[42] the bailiff (*fideiussor*) who paid undue interest (*usura*) and thus suffered damage because of his own negligence (*culpa*), and therefore he could not recover this interest from the debtor.[43] In another case, a cleric was suspected of having committed a very serious crime for which he was sentenced to life imprisonment. To evade this judgment and prison, he threw himself from his horse in front of his bishop and was thereby injured and subsequently died. His death had to be imputed to the cleric himself.[44] Another case concerned a cleric to whom the prospect of receiving a prebend was given. In that case, the cleric negligently did not claim the prebend when he could have done so, and, as a result of this, the prebend went to someone else. He had to blame himself for his own negligence in that he had not claimed the first vacant prebend.[45] The general principle in fact corresponds to the rule of personal responsibility: he who is at fault will impute the loss to himself.[46]

In the early modern times, a change occurred as to the use of the *regula*, namely by applying it to cases of mutual fault, i.e. when two parties were (to some degree) at fault. Another concept came into being, namely that of *culpa admixta* (literally 'mixed fault'), which originated in the contractual sphere. These words were used to give a legal qualification to the act of the injured party in the situations in which a harmful action by the wrongdoer is mixed with a fault on the part of the injured party.[47] It was then thereafter extended to the extracontractual sphere. A wrongdoer was not held liable when an injured party brought danger or risk on himself – in that case, the damage would also result from the contributory negligence of the injured party.[48] Interestingly, the Italian jurist Hyppolytus Bonacossa (1514–1591), who adopted the concept of *culpa admixta*, stressed the fact that no liability for

42 Durantis, *Speculum*, II, fo. 228r.

43 The question of whether the bail could get back from the debtor the interests, paid to the creditor, is extensively dealt with by Johannes Andreae, *In I-V decretalium libros Novella commentaria* (Venice, 1581; Torino: Bottega d'Erasmo, 1963), fo. 14r and v.

44 C.23 q.4 c.38.

45 VI 3.4.11. See Johannes Monachus Picardus, *Glossa aurea* (Paris: Petit, 1535; Aalen: Scientia Verlag, 1968), fo. 447r, ad VI 5.12.86. Finally, in the case of a purchaser of a piece of land who did not show up at the trial and lost the land due to eviction, this purchaser could then not bring an action against the vendor (C. 8.44.8); in the *Glossa Ordinaria*, Johannes Andreae even provided further examples of the rule of VI 5.12.86.

46 Victorius Bartocetti, *De regulis juris canonici* (Roma: Belardetti, 1955), 252.

47 Van Dongen, "The Defence of Contributory Negligence in (Medieval) Canon Law," 601–602.

48 Van Dongen, *Contributory Negligence*, 144–145.

any damage exists in the event of *culpa admixta* on the part of the injured party[49] – thenceforward, the concept of *culpa admixta* was cited in relation to D. 50.17.203 (or VI 5.12.86) and the idea of *culpae compensatio* – i.e. the idea, which originated in the Medieval period, that, if both parties were the cause of the damage, the negligence of both parties had to be compensated: negligence (*culpa*) of the wrongdoer was nullified by the negligence (*culpa*) of the injured party, and therefore also excluded liability – this was not the case if the wrongdoer acted with *dolus*[50] – until the 18th century. Legal sources show that with the application of the *regula* the jurists regarded it as a problem of mutual blame.[51] The same idea gave rise to the much-used concept of *culpa communis*.[52]

6 Humanistic Thoughts on the *Regula*

The (legal) humanists lectured on D. 50.17 (and D. 50.16), which they regarded as a sort of summary of legal thinking.[53] As to their comments, in their attempt to reconstruct the contextual origin of D. 50.17.203, some humanists used palingenesis to put the text back into its original context, i.e. the law of legacies.[54] The prevailing interpretation of the rule of D. 50.17.203 among the humanists was that if someone suffered damage due to his own negligence, no compensation for the damage could be claimed from the wrongdoer.[55] Nevertheless, a minority interpreted the *regula* differently: specifically, Petrus Faber (1540–1600), Johannes de Sande (1568–1638), and later Hugo Donellus (1527–1591). They argued that the person who gave the *causa* (or *occasio*) that produced

---

49 Ippolito Bonacossa, *Quaestiones criminales* (Venice: apud Zenarum, 1573), fo. 56r, *De damno dato*, uers. '*damnificans*'.

50 See Van Dongen, *Contributory Negligence*, 111ff.

51 Klaus Luig, "Überwiegendes Mitverschulden," *Ius Commune* 2 (1969): 200–201.

52 Luig, "Überwiegendes Mitverschulden," 201, with reference to Franciscus N. Cyriacus, *Controversiarum forensium* (Venice: apud Brogiollum, 1664), I: 576, Controv. 197, n. 21 ss.

53 Govaert C.J.J. Van den Bergh, *Geleerd recht. Een geschiedenis van de Europese rechtswetenschap in vogelvlucht*, 3rd ed. (Deventer: Kluwer, 1994), 53.

54 See Jacobus Raevardus, "*Ad titulum Pandectarum De diversis Regulis Iuris Antiqui commentarius,*" in *Opera Omnia* (Naples: ex officina Manfredii, 1779), I: 225, ad D. 50.17.203; Hugo Donellus, "*Commentarii,*" in *Opera omnia*, IV (Lucca: ex typis Riccomini, 1764), 784–786, ad D. 50.17.203; Van Dongen, *Contributory Negligence*, 197–198.

55 See, e.g., Everardus Bronchorst, *Commentarius in titulum Digestorum de [diversis] regulis iuris antiqui* (Antwerp: apud Verdussen, 1676), 355–357.

the damage through his own *culpa* (or *negligentia*) could not *partially* or totally claim compensation for the damage from someone else.[56]

According to Donellus, to the extent that the damage had resulted from the actions of the injured party, actions taken at the injured party's own risk – in such a case there could be no claim as the person was not considered to have suffered damage, like in the *regula*. Furthermore, from D. 50.17.155pr. and D. 50.17.173.2, in connection with D. 50.17.203 – not a self-evident connection, as the latter text was written by a different Roman jurist – the general rule could be established that in such a case any act had to be to the detriment of the actor himself, not to the other party.[57] Donellus mentioned two consequences of the *regula*. Firstly, the risk had to rest with the person by whose negligence the damage was caused, e.g. the purchaser for whom the vendor had made a *stipulatio duplae* as a guarantee against eviction. If the purchaser/promisee lost possession through his own fault, then he had no right to bring an action either under a stipulation for double selling prices or on the contract for purchase against the vendor (D. 21.2.29.1). Secondly, the person who suffered damage because of his own negligence could not claim anything from the other person of a community (*communio*): e.g. when one of the co-heirs makes a payment under an inheritable stipulation as a consequence of his own act, he cannot reclaim anything from his co-heir (D. 10.2.44.5). Donellus mentioned various examples of the application of the *regula*, among which is an example of the *lex Aquilia*. These examples show the application of the rule that when someone suffered damage because of his own negligence, and only this injured party suffered damage because of his own act, no liability could be imposed upon the wrongdoer, because the damage to the injured party was not considered to be claimable.[58]

Most examples from the *regula* provided by the humanists had already been mentioned by medieval scholars, but they extended the *ratio* of the rule to new cases. One interesting added example is that by the humanist Johannes Wissenbach (1607–1665): someone who lost ownership as a consequence of usucapion could not file a complaint, since the loss had to be imputed to this person's *negligentia* and careless inactivity of not having bet-

56 Petrus Faber, *Commentarius ad titulum de diversis Regulis Iuris antiqui* (Lyon: apud Fabrum, 1590), 424–428; Johan van den Sande, *De diversis regulis iuris antiqui commentarius* (Groningen: Lens, 1681), 201; Donellus, "*Commentarii,*" 784–786.

57 Donellus, "*Commentarii,*" loc. cit. See also Gregorius Majansius, *Ad triginta jurisconsultorum omnia fragmenta quae estant in juris civilis corpore commentarii* (Geneva: apud Fratres de Tournes, 1764), I: ad D. 50.17.203, no. I.

58 Donellus, "*Commentarii,*" loc. cit.; Van Dongen, *Contributory Negligence*, 200.

ter searched to find his thing for a certain period of time nor having tried to claim it back by vindication (D. 41.3.1).[59] Also cases of delictual liability based on the *lex Aquilia* were mentioned by the French lawyer Petrus Faber (Pierre du Faur; 1540–1600) as examples of non-liability based on the *regula*, amongst which is the famous case of the shopkeeper (D. 9.2.52.1).[60] Interesting is also the Dutch jurist Gerard Noodt (1647–1725) – belonging to the 'antiquarian' branch of the Dutch Elegant School[61] – in his interpretation of the latter text: the injury inflicted in self-defence would be forgiven by human nature, especially in this case, where the damage was due to the negligence of the injured party, who was therefore not considered to have suffered any claimable damage (cf. D. 50.17.203).[62]

7 The *Regula* of D. 50.17.203 in the Roman-Dutch, *usus modernus* and Natural Law

The foundation upon which the law of contributory negligence has been built in Roman-Dutch law is to be found in certain passages in the Digest, among which the most important is D. 50.17.203. Particular attention may be given to D. 9.2.28, which includes the general rule that an injured plaintiff is refused relief if it had been in his power to avoid the danger created by the defendant. The words '*culpa sua*' in the rule of D. 50.17.203 could be understood as applying to any carelessness in safeguarding a person's own life or property. That would be negligence in the sense of failing to look after a person's own interests.[63] The *regula* comes into effect in cases in Roman-Dutch law, in ship collisions, if both parties had acted negligently. Although one could argue that, in this case, both parties should pay for each other's damage, this solution was not found in collision cases. But one can find two different views in Roman-Dutch law. In one instance, the contributory negligence of the injured party was mentioned by the Supreme Court of Holland, Zeeland and West

59 Johannes J. Wissenbach, *In extremum pandectarum titulum De diversis regulis iuris antiqui exercitationes cathedrariae* (Franeker: Idzardus Alberti, 1656), 422, ad D. 50.17.203.

60 Faber, *Commentarius*, 426.

61 Jeroen M.J. Chorus, "History," in: *Introduction to Dutch Law*, 6th edn., ed. Larissa van den Herik, Ewoud Hondius, and Wim Voermans (Alphen aan den Rijn: Wolters Kluwer, 2022), 11.

62 Gerard Noodt, "*Ad legem Aquiliam liber singularis,*" in *Opera omnia* (Leiden: Apud Theodorum Haak, 1767), 143, c. XIX.

63 Aquarius, "Causation and Legal Responsibility," *The South African Law Journal* 58 (1941): 248.

Friesland (*Hoge Raad van Holland, Zeeland en West-Friesland*), and the Court of Holland (*Hof van Holland*), in a case recorded by Cornelis Neostadius. The case concerned a collision between two ships, as a result of which one of them sank. In this case, both parties blamed each other and the courts came to the conclusion that since the fault appeared to be equal on each side, the loss had to be borne equally (an approach based on maritime law).[64] However, the Dutch jurist Corneli(u)s van Bijnkershoek (1673–1743) argued that it would have been more correct to conclude that neither side could bring an action and that each ship had to bear its own damage. Whoever acted negligently could not bring an action.[65] The damage suffered by the plaintiff was due to his own negligence and he was therefore considered as not having suffered any damage (D. 50.17.203).[66] This approach, adopted by some legal scholars, was supported by two municipal laws of the cities of Rotterdam and Dordrecht.[67]

The *regula* was applied as a specific principle to concrete cases by the jurists of the *usus modernus*[68] as an argument to deny the right to claim damages in cases in which both the wrongdoer and the injured party had acted negligently, and so together caused the damage to the injured party. In order to provide a basis for the fact that contributory negligence leads to the annulment of the negligence of the wrongdoer, the jurists based themselves on the idea of *culpae compensatio* or the rule of D. 50.17.203.[69] If both the wrongdoer and the injured party had acted negligently, the *actio legis Aquiliae* was not applicable.[70] This 'all or nothing' approach, in which the degree of mutual participation or the more subtle differentiations within the concept of *culpa* were not taken into account, was at first mainly followed in practice and rep-

64 Cornelis Neostadius, *Utriusque Hollandiae Zelandiae Frisiaeque curiae decisiones* (The Hague: Apud Joannem & Danielem Steuckerios, 1667), 196–197, *decisio* no. 49.

65 See also Petrus J. Kotzé, "Die aanspreeklikheid van mededaders en afsonderlike daders" (Ph.D. diss., Leiden Universiteit, 1953), 68.

66 Cornelius van Bijnkershoek, *Quaestiones juris privati* (Leiden: Joannem van Kerckhem, 1744), 468, IV.22.

67 Van Dongen, *Contributory Negligence*, 253–254.

68 See, e.g., Johann Brunnemann, *Consilia sive responsa academica*, 2nd edn., ed. Samuel Stryk (Frankfurt an der Oder, 1704), 47, *cons.* II.143: "Sed damnum, quod quis sua culpa sentit, sibi non aliis debet imputare".

69 Van Dongen, *Contributory Negligence*, 259–260. See also Nils Jansen, "§ 254. Mitverantwortlichkeit," 664.

70 See already the German humanist Ulrich Zasius (1461–1535): Ulrich Zasius, *Opera omnia* (Frankfurt am Main: Feyerabend, 1590), I: 87, ad D. 9.2, no. 11.

resentatives of this line applied it until the second half of the 18th century.[71] This becomes clear from various 17th-century *consilia* from the Law Faculty of Tübingen,[72] but also in two decisions by the *Reichskammergericht*, applying the rule of D. 50.17.203.[73] Another example in which the rule of D. 50.17.203 was applied in the case of Aquilian liability was mentioned by the German jurist Wolfgang A. Lauterbach (1618–1678), according to whom (based on this text), ethically seen, nobody was considered to have suffered damage if that damage was caused by the negligence of the injured party – the wrongdoer was not considered to have committed a delict.[74] This was the first time the problem was really considered in terms of the concurrence of faults.[75]

As to the question whether the *regula* was directly applied under the *ancien regime*, it has been stated that this rule could not be considered a generally binding rule, although the scholars of the *ancient droit* no doubt knew of the rule.[76] Only concrete applications can be found, namely in the event of damage caused by an animal or in the event of the theft of objects from a traveller at an inn.[77] According to some natural law scholars, the problem of contributory negligence could be solved by simply denying the claim for damages if the injured party had acted with negligence, possibly with the application of the *regula* of D. 50.17.203. This view – which does not permit a partition of dam-

71 Van Dongen, *Contributory Negligence*, 261–262. See already Horst Kaufmann, *Rezeption und Usus Modernus der actio legis Aquiliae* (Cologne: Böhlau, 1958), 78.

72 See Van Dongen, *Contributory Negligence*, 262, esp. nt. 372.

73 Adrian Gilmann, *Decisionum sive rerum in camera imperiali iudicatarum libri duo* (Frankfurt: Wolfgang Richter, 1602–1603), I: 62 (dec. 65, no. 75); II: 407 (dec. 41, no. 50).

74 Wolfgang A. Lauterbach, *Collegium theoretico-practicum Pandectarum* (Tübingen: Cottae, 1784), IV: 566–567, ad D. 9.2 § 7.

75 Van Dongen, *Contributory Negligence*, 263. See also already Reinhard Zimmermann, "Usus modernus legis Aquiliae and Delictual Liability Today," *Stellenbosch Law Review* 1 (1990): 80; *id.*, *The Law of Obligations. Roman Foundations of the Civilian Tradition* (Oxford: Clarendon Press, 1996), 1030.

76 Marguerite Haller, *Essai sur l'influence du fait et de la faute de la victime sur son droit a réparation* (Paris: Barnéoud, 1926), 21; Volker Neumann-Schniedewind, "Mitverursachung. Mitverschulden. Haftungsausschluß und Schadensteilung im französischen außervertraglichen Schadensersatzrecht" (Ph.D. diss., Kiel Universität, 1969), 73f.; Van Dongen, *Contributory Negligence*, 315.

77 François Bourjon, *Le droit commun de la France et la Coutume de Paris* (Paris: Grangé, 1770), II: 499, livre VI, titre III, chap. III, sect. I, § V and § IX; Jean Domat, *Les loix civiles dans leur ordre naturel, le droit public, et legum delectus* (Paris: Durand, 1777), I: 208, Liv. II, Titre VIII, sect. 2 § 10. See also Léon Mazeaud et al., *Traité théorique et pratique de la responsabilité civile délictuelle et contractuelle*, 6th edn. (Paris: Montchrestien, 1970), II: 543; Thomas Hinrichs, *Die Berücksichtigung des Mitverschuldens bei der Haftung für Personenschäden im französischen und deutschen Recht* (Baden-Baden: Nomos, 1991), 55f.

age – can also be found among the early modern scholastics,[78] and also in the works of Domat and Pothier.[79] The renowned French jurist Jean Domat (1625–1696), in his *Les loix civiles*, wrote that if someone provoked or irritated a dog or another animal and caused it to bite, the provoker was to be held liable. If the provoker and the injured party were one and the same person, he only had himself to blame[80] (a reasoning which seems to be based on VI 5.12.86).[81] An affirmation of the use of the *regula* can be found in the applications given in the *Pandectae* of the French jurist Robert Pothier (1699–1772). The *regula* appears as rule no. 13, and within this rule Pothier arranged applications from the Digest, amongst which was the example of a partner (*socius*) who suffered damage due to his own negligence.[82]

8 The Revival of Roman Law in 19th-Century Germany and the Netherlands

According to the German pandectist theory, if the damage was caused by both the *culpa* of the wrongdoer and the *culpa* of the injured party, the *culpa* of the wrongdoer was cancelled out by the *culpa* of the injured party. The pandectist theory of compensation of fault rested in essence on D. 50.17.203, which was understood as a generally binding statutory norm (‘*als gesetzliche Norm verstandenen Satz*’).[83] This *regula* also dominated the practice in the areas of the *gemeine Recht* until the coming into effect of the *Bürgerliche Gesetzbuch*.[84] The pandectist theory contained the rule that, if the injured party could have avoided (or lessened) the damage by proper care,[85] he could not claim

78 See Luis de Molina, *De iustitia et iure* (Cologne: sumptibus Hermanni Mylii, 1614), tract. II, disp. 697, col. 1267–1269, nrs. 11, 12 and 14.

79 Van Dongen, *Contributory Negligence*, 286–287. This view could also have been held by Grotius, while it can also be argued that the relevant fragments in his work did not really concern the problem of contributory negligence (p. 287ff., 302).

80 Domat, *Les loix civiles*, I : 208, Liv. II. Titre VIII sect. 2 § 10.

81 In the same sense, Luig, “Überwiegendes Mitverschulden,” 217.

82 Robert J. Pothier, *Pandectae Justinianeae, in novum ordine Digestae* (Lyon: sumptibus Bernusset, 1782), 700. See Van Dongen, *Contributory Negligence*, 290–291.

83 Wollschläger, “Das eigene Verschulden des Verletzten im römischen Recht,” 118; Van Dongen, *Contributory Negligence*, 319–320.

84 Horst – Eberhard Henke, “Mitverursachung und Mitverschulden – Wer den Schaden herausfordert, muss den Schädiger schonen,” *Juristische Schulung* (1988): 757.

85 Friedrich Mommsen, *Zur Lehre von dem Interesse* (Braunschweig: Schwetz, 1855), 157; Bernhard Windscheid, *Lehrbuch des Pandektenrechts*, 9th edn., II, ed. Theodor Kipp (Frankfurt am Main: Literarische Anstalt Rütten & Loening, 1906), 64, § 258.

damages.[86] An exception was made by the Pandectists (as in the medieval and early modern period) in the event that the wrongdoer had acted *in dolo*.[87] In that event, the damage would be recovered in total.[88] On the other hand, some considered equity to be the correct basis for the theory of the denial of the claim by the injured party.[89] According to Victor von Leyden, from the nature of the subjective right it follows that everyone has to bear his own damage (*casum sentit dominus*), unless someone else was the cause of his damage – an exception based on equity. An exception to the latter rule based on equity is the re-entrance of the first rule – the damage was caused by the contributory negligence of the injured party (the rule of D. 50.17.203).[90] After the enactment of the natural law solution in the German provision of § 254 BGB, § 254 BGB also remained as a minimum to be regarded as an expression of the rule of D. 50.17.203.[91] Also, the case law of the *Reichsgericht* seems to have used § 254 BGB to limit the amount of damages without applying a distribution (of damage) in the form of quotas – with reference to D. 50.17.203.[92] The fact that in cases where the injured party had contributed to his own loss Dutch case law did not balance the causal contributions or the faults could be explained, according to the Dutch jurist Paul Scholten (1875–1946), by adhering strictly to the rule of D. 50.17.203.[93] In the Dutch case law, before 1916, a partition of damage in the event of the contributory negligence of the injured party was

86 See, e.g., Eduard Heilfron and Jacques Stern, *Römisches Recht* (*Rechtsgeschichte und System des Privatrechts*) *als Grundlage des heutigen Rechts*, 7th edn. (Mannhem/Berlin/Leipzig: J. Bensheimer, 1920), 245, and later Dirk Looschelders, *Die Mitverantwortlichkeit des Geschädigten im Privatrecht* (Tübingen: Mohre Siebeck, 1999), 21.

87 See, e.g., Carl C. Burckhardt, "Sinn und Umfang der Gleichstellung von dolus und lata culpa im Römisches Recht" (Ph.D. diss., Göttingen Univesität, 1885), 109; Oscar Priester, "Compensatio culpae" (inaug. diss., Würzburg Universität, 1896), 10f.; Norbert Labowsky, "Eigenes Verschulden bei Schadenersatz-Ansprüchen nach gemeinem Recht und Bürgerlichen Gesetzbuch" (Ph.D. diss., Friedrich-Alexander-Universität Erlangen, 1898), 37f.

88 Mommsen, *Zur Lehre von dem Interesse*, 157, 257ff.; Windscheid, *Lehrbuch des Pandektenrechts*, 64f, § 258.

89 Hans J. Wieling, *Interesse und Privatstrafe vom Mittelalter bis zum Bürgerlichen Gesetbuch* [Forschungen zur Neueren Privatrechtsgeschichte] (Cologne/Vienna: Böhlau, 1970), 226.

90 Victor von Leyden, *Die sogenannte Culpa-Compensation im Bürgerlichen Gesetbuch* (Berlin: Heymann, 1902), 24, 35f.; Van Dongen, *Contributory Negligence*, 320–321, nt. 104.

91 Thomas Honsell, *Die Quotenteilung im Schadenersatzrecht. Historische und dogmatische Grundlagen der Lehre vom Mitverschulden* (Ebelsbach am Main: Gremer, 1977), 88.

92 Honsell, *Die Quotenteilung im Schadenersatzrecht*, 91f.; Van Dongen, *Contributory Negligence*, 334.

93 Paul Scholten, "De 'schuld' in de leer der onrechtmatige daad," *Weekblad voor Privaatrecht, Notariaat en Registratie* (1915), no. 2350: 17ff.

only rarely applied. Usually, the claim for damages was denied, (implicitly) based on the rule of D. 50.17.203 or the doctrine of *culpae compensatio*.[94]

9 Conclusion

The *regula* of D. 50.17.203 probably had no general scope in its classical origin, but originated from a solution given by a jurist to a conflict that had arisen in the area of legacy law. Furthermore, D. 50.17.203 probably had nothing to do with a situation of *culpae compensatio* – it refers to the *culpa* of the injured party, but not in relation to the possible liability of a wrongdoer. The meaning and/or application changed, however, and was broadened over time, according to: i. the area of the law; ii. the situation of (mutual) blame.

In medieval *ius commune* various examples of the *regula* were mentioned, outside the law of legacies. Nevertheless, in medieval learned law D. 50.17.203 became one of the starting points to solve issues of contributory negligence. In medieval *ius commune* various examples were mentioned, but it was only Accursius who linked D. 50.17.203 with the law of delicts. Besides, he understood this rule to be *not only* about cases in which the negligence of the injured party was the only factor and in which the negligence of the wrongdoer was absent, but also where both demonstrated some degree of negligent behaviour.

The maxim was included, slightly differently, in the *Liber Sextus* – the examples of this maxim were provided by canonists and showed a wide range of cases where there was *only* negligence on the side of the injured party, but *not* contributory negligence – although Accursius opened the door to such an approach. The examples given by the humanists fitted the ones mentioned by medieval scholars, but also included *lex Aquilia* cases. Some humanists held the view that the text dealt with common participation in the total damage, i.e. in situations where both parties acted negligently.

In Roman-Dutch law, D. 50.17.203 became one of the important foundations of the theory on contributory negligence. In the early modern period, the harshness of this rule was mitigated by some scholars by requiring that when the fault of the wrongdoer and the injured party were unequal, the person whose negligence was considered to be more serious was held liable/

94 See Emanuel G.D. van Dongen, "Hollandsche IJzeren Spoorwegmaatschappij/Morré. Enige Rechtsvergelijkende en Rechtshistorische Beschouwingen over de Gevolgen van Eigen Schuld van de Gelaedeerde voor de Aansprakelijkheid voor Onrechtmatig Handelen," *Pro Memorie – Bijdragen tot de rechtsgeschiedenis der Nederlanden* 16, issue 1 (2014): 76–101.

responsible – Gerard Noodt formulated the idea of *maior culpa*, and thereafter also Johannes Voet accepted it.[95] Contributory negligence, when less serious in comparison to the fault of the wrongdoer, does not cancel out his claim. Others, however, still advocated the Roman law rule, meaning that any contributory negligence led to the denial of the claim. Jurists of the *usus modernus pandectarum* used D. 50.17.203, together with other tools, to solve concrete cases of contributory negligence, leading to the injured party's claim being denied. Natural law scholars used D. 50.17.203 in cases of contributory negligence leading to the denial of a claim, an approach which was also followed by Domat and Pothier. The Pandectists interpreted the maxim of D. 50.17.203 as a statutory norm; legal practice influenced by Pandectism did not change immediately by the enactment of § 254 of BGB. The *regula* was (explicitly or implicitly) used once again in the 19th- and 20th-century German and Dutch case law and doctrine.

Acknowledgements

This contribution is based on a presentation delivered at the *Regulae iuris and maxims of law in the legal historical perspective Workshop*, University of Ghent, 21 January 2022, where the author was working as a TPR Chair at that time. This contribution, to a large extent, is a reworked version of parts already published in Emanuel G.D. van Dongen, *Contributory Negligence. A Historical and Comparative Study* (Leiden: Brill, 2014).

Bibliography

Accursius, Franciscus. *Glossa in Digestum Novum*. Venice, 1487.

Andreae, Johannes (Giovanni d'Andrea). *In I–V decretalium libros Novella commentaria*. Venice, 1581. Reprint, Torino: Bottega d'Erasmo, 1963.

Anelli, Franco, and Carlo Granelli, eds. *Manuale di diritto privato*. Milan: Giuffrè, 2019.

Aquarius (ps). "Causation and Legal Responsibility." *The South African Law Journal* 58 (1941): 232–263.

Aumann, Peter. "Das mitwirkende Verschulden in der neueren juristische Dogmengeschichte." Ph.D. diss., Universität Hamburg, 1964.

Bartocetti, Victorius. *De regulis juris canonici*. Roma: Belardetti, 1955.

95 Van Dongen, *Contributory Negligence*, 217–220, 232–233, 240–241.

Bassianus, Johannes. "*Apparatus ad titulum De diversis regulis iuris antiqui.*" Edited by Severino Caprioli. *Annali di storia del diritto: rassegna internazionale* VI (1963): 131–248.

Bertrandus Metensis. *De regulis iuris*. Edited by Severino Caprioli. Perugia: University, Faculty of Law, 1981.

Bijnkershoek, Cornelius van. *Quaestiones juris privati*. Leiden: Joannem van Kerckhem, 1744.

Bonacossa, Ippolito. *Quaestiones criminales*. Venice: apud Zenarum, 1573.

Bourjon, François. *Le droit commun de la France et la Coutume de Paris*. Paris: Grangé, 1770.

Bronchorst, Everardus. *Commentarius in titulum Digestorum de [diversis] regulis iuris antiqui*. Antwerp: apud Verdussen, 1676.

Brunnemann, Johann. *Consilia sive responsa academica*. 2nd edn. Edited by Samuel Stryk. Frankfurt an der Oder, 1704.

Bulgarus, *De diversis regulis iuris antiqui commentarius*. Edited by Friedrich G.C. Beckhaus. Bonn: Henry u. Cohen, 1856. Reprint, Frankfurt am Main: Minerva, 1967.

Burckhardt, Carl C. "Sinn und Umfang der Gleichstellung von dolus und lata culpa im Römisches Recht." Ph.D. diss., Göttingen Univesität, 1885.

Chorus, Jeroen M.J. "History." In *Introduction to Dutch Law*. 6th edn. Edited by Larissa van den Herik, Ewoud Hondius, and Wim Voermans, 3–12. Alphen aan den Rijn: Wolters Kluwer, 2022.

Cursi, Maria F. "Il concorso della colpa del danneggiato nel risarcimento e la rilevanza penale dell'azione aquiliana." *Index: Quaderni camerti di studi romanistici* 47 (2019): 165–194.

Cyriacus, Franciscus N. *Controversiarum forensium*. 4 vols. Venice: apud Brogiollum, 1664.

Decius, Philippus. *In tit. ff. De regulis iuris*. Venice: Apud Cominum de Tridino Montisferrati, 1564.

Domat, Jean. *Les loix civiles dans leur ordre naturel, le droit public, et legum delectus*. 2 vols. Paris: Durand, 1777.

Donellus, Hugo. *Opera omnia*, IV. Lucca: ex typis Riccomini, 1764.

Dongen, Emanuel G.D. van. "Hollandsche IJzeren Spoorwegmaatschappij/Morré. Enige Rechtsvergelijkende en Rechtshistorische Beschouwingen over de Gevolgen van Eigen Schuld van de Gelaedeerde voor de Aansprakelijkheid voor Onrechtmatig Handelen." *Pro Memorie – Bijdragen tot de rechtsgeschiedenis der Nederlanden* 16, issue 1 (2014): 76–101.

Dongen, Emanuel G.D. van. "The Defence of Contributory Negligence in (Medieval) Canon Law and in Conflict Resolution in Italy in the Early Modern Period." *Zeits-*

chrift der Savigny-Stiftung für Rechtsgeschichte. Kanonistische Abteilung 100 (2014): 580–607.

Dongen, Emanuel G.D. van. *Contributory Negligence. A Historical and Comparative Study*. Leiden: Brill, 2014.

Durantis, Guilelmus (Guillaume Durand). *Speculum iuris*. 2 vols. Torino: apud heredes Bevilaquae, 1578.

Dynus de Mugello. *Preclarus et insignis tractatus allegabilis et quotidianus de regulis iuris*. Pavia, 1518.

Faber, Petrus. *Commentarius ad titulum de diversis Regulis Iuris antiqui*. Lyon: apud Fabrum, 1590.

Forlivio, Rainerius de. *Lectura super Digesto novo*. Lyon, 1523. Reprint, Bologna: Forni, 1968.

Friedberg, Emil A., ed. *Corpus Iuris Canonici*. 2 vols. Leipzig: Tauchnitz, 1879–81.

Galeotti, Sara. "Colpa della vittima e risarcibilità del danno ingiusto." *Quaderni Lupiensi* 8 (2018): 393–422.

Gilmann, Adrian. *Decisionum sive rerum in camera imperiali iudicatarum libri duo*. 2 vols. Frankfurt: Wolfgang Richter, 1602–03.

Haller, Marguerite. *Essai sur l'influence du fait et de la faute de la victime sur son droit a réparation*. Paris: Barnéoud, 1926.

Heilfron, Eduard, and Jacques Stern. *Römisches Recht (Rechtsgeschichte und System des Privatrechts) als Grundlage des heutigen Rechts*. 7th edn. Mannhem/Berlin/Leipzig: J. Bensheimer, 1920.

Henke, Horst-Eberhard. "Mitverursachung und Mitverschulden – Wer den Schaden herausfordert, muss den Schädiger schonen." *Juristische Schulung* (1988): 753–761.

Hinrichs, Thomas. *Die Berücksichtigung des Mitverschuldens bei der Haftung für Personenschäden im französischen und deutschen Recht*. Baden-Baden: Nomos, 1991.

Honsell, Thomas. *Die Quotenteilung im Schadenersatzrecht. Historische und dogmatische Grundlagen der Lehre vom Mitverschulden*. Ebelsbach am Main: Gremer, 1977.

Jacobus Butrigarius. *Commentaria in primam et secundam veteris Digesti partem*. Rome, 1617.

Jansen, Corjo. "Accidental Harm under (Roman) Civil Law." In *The Challenge of Chance. A Multidisciplinary Approach from Science and the Humanities*, edited by Klaas Landsman and Ellen van Wolde, 233–247. Springer, 2016.

Jansen, Nils. "§ 254. Mitverantwortlichkeit des Geschädigten." In *Historisch-kritischer Kommentar zum BGB*, Bd. II/1, edited by Mathias Schmoeckel, Joachim Rückert and Reinhard Zimmermann, 655–714. Tübingen: Mohr Siebeck, 2007.

Johannes Monachus Picardus. *Glossa aurea*. Paris: Petit, 1535. Reprint, Aalen: Scientia Verlag, 1968).

Jörs, Paul. *Römisches Recht: Geschichte und System des römischen Privatrechts*. Berlin: Springer, 1927.

Kaufmann, Horst. *Rezeption und Usus Modernus der actio legis Aquiliae*. Cologne: Böhlau, 1958.

Knütel, Rolf. "Neues zur 'contributory negligence'?" *Index: Quaderni camerti di studi romanistici* 44 (2016): 349–360.

Kotzé, Petrus J. "Die aanspreeklikheid van mededaders en afsonderlike daders." Ph.D. diss., Leiden Universiteit, 1953.

Labowsky, Norbert. "Eigenes Verschulden bei Schadenersatz-Ansprüchen nach gemeinem Recht und Bürgerlichen Gesetzbuch." Ph.D. diss., Friedrich-Alexander-Universität Erlangen, 1898.

Lange, Hermann. *Schadensersatz und Privatstrafe in der mittelalterlichen Rechtstheorie*. Munster/Cologne: Böhlau-Verlag, 1955.

Lauterbach, Wolfgang A. *Collegium theoretico-practicum Pandectarum*. 4 vols. Tübingen: Cottae, 1784.

Lenel, Otto. *Palingenesia iuris civilis*. 2 vols. Leipzig: Ex Officina Bernardi Tauchnitz, 1889.

Levy, Ernst, and Ernst Rabel. *Index interpolationum quae in Iustiniani Digestis inesse dicuntur*. 5 vols. Weimar: Hermann Böhlaus Nachfolger, 1929–35.

Leyden, Victor von. *Die sogenannte Culpa-Compensation im Bürgerlichen Gesetzbuch*. Berlin: Heymann, 1902.

Looschelders, Dirk. *Die Mitverantwortlichkeit des Geschädigten im Privatrecht*. Tübingen: Mohr Siebeck, 1999.

Luig, Klaus. "Überwiegendes Mitverschulden." *Ius Commune* 2 (1969): 187–238.

Majansius, Gregorius. *Ad triginta jurisconsultorum omnia fragmenta quae estant in juris civilis corpore commentarii*. 2 vols. Geneva: apud Fratres de Tournes, 1764.

Mazeaud, Léon, Henri Mazeaud, et al. *Traité théorique et pratique de la responsabilité civile délictuelle et contractuelle*. 6th edn. 3 vols. Paris: Montchrestien, 1965–83.

Molina, Luis de. *De iustitia et iure*. Cologne: sumptibus Hermanni Mylii, 1614.

Mommsen, Friedrich. *Zur Lehre von dem Interesse*. Braunschweig: Schwetz, 1855.

Neostadius, Cornelis. *Utriusque Hollandiae Zelandiae Frisiaeque curiae decisiones*. The Hague: Apud Joannem & Danielem Steuckerios, 1667.

Neumann-Schniedewind, Volker. "Mitverursachung. Mitverschulden. Haftungsausschluß und Schadensteilung im französischen außervertraglichen Schadensersatzrecht." Ph.D. diss., Kiel Universität, 1969.

Noodt, Gerard. *Opera omnia*. Leiden: Apud Theodorum Haak, 1767.

Odofredus. *Lectura super Digesto Novo*. Lyon: Pullon, 1552. Reprint, Bologna, Forni, 1968.

Poldnikov, Dmitry. "Contributory Negligence: A Historical and comparative study." *Journal on European History of Law* 5, no. 2 (2014): 134–135.

Pothier, Robert J. *Pandectae Justinianeae, in novum ordine Digestae*. Lyon: sumptibus Bernusset, 1782.

Priester, Oscar. *Compensatio culpae*. Inaug. diss., Würzburg Universität, 1896.

Pugsley, David F. "On compiling Justinian's Digest (6): Twin texts and working methods." *Orbis Iuris Romani: Journal of Ancient Law Studies* 3 (1997): 40–56.

Quintilianus, Marcus Fabius. *Institutio Oratoria*. Cambridge/Massachusetts: Harvard University Press, 2002–06.

Raevardus, Jacobus. *Opera Omnia*. 2 vols. Naples: ex officina Manfredii, 1779.

Re, Edward D. "The Roman Contribution to the Common Law." *Fordham Law Review* 29 (1961): 447–494.

Sande, Johan van den. *De diversis regulis iuris antiqui commentarius*. Groningen: Lens, 1681.

Scholten, Paul. "De 'schuld' in de leer der onrechtmatige daad." *Weekblad voor Privaatrecht, Notariaat en Registratie* (1915), no. 2350: 17–20.

Stein, Peter. *Regulae Iuris. From juristic rules to legal maxims*. Edinburgh: Edinburgh University Press, 1966.

Tudeschis, Nicolaus de (Nicoló Tedeschi, Abbas Panormitanus). *Commentaria in quinque decretalium libros*. 8 vols. Venice: al segno della Fontana, 1571.

Van den Bergh, Govaert C.J.J. *Geleerd recht. Een geschiedenis van de Europese rechtswetenschap in vogelvlucht*. 3rd ed. Deventer: Kluwer, 1994.

Wharton, Francis. *A Treatise on the Law of Negligence*. Philadelphia: Kay and brother, 1874.

Wieling, Hans J. *Interesse und Privatstrafe vom Mittelalter bis zum Bürgerlichen Gesetbuch* [Forschungen zur Neueren Privatrechtsgeschichte]. Cologne/Vienna: Böhlau, 1970.

Windscheid, Bernhard. *Lehrbuch des Pandektenrechts*. 9th edn. Vol. II. Edited by Theodor Kipp. Frankfurt am Main: Literarische Anstalt Rütten & Loening, 1906.

Wissenbach, Johannes J. *In extremum pandectarum titulum De diversis regulis iuris antiqui exercitationes cathedrariae*. Franeker: Idzardus Alberti, 1656.

Wollschläger, Christian. "Das eigene Verschulden des Verletzten im römischen Recht." *Zeitschrift der Savigny-Stiftung für Rechtsgeschichte. Romanistische Abteilung* 93 (1976): 115–137.

Zasius, Ulrich. *Opera omnia*. 6 vols. Frankfurt am Main: Feyerabend, 1590.

Zimmermann, Reinhard. "Usus modernus legis Aquiliae and Delictual Liability Today." *Stellenbosch Law Review* 1 (1990): 67–93.

Zimmermann, Reinhard. *The Law of Obligations. Roman Foundations of the Civilian Tradition*. Oxford: Clarendon Press, 1996.

Conclusion. *Regulae Iuris:* The Medieval Understanding

James Gordley

Ilya Kotlyar's able summary of the proceedings depicts a tension. On the one hand, as David De Concilio observed, the medieval jurists "tended to see the *regulae* as objective generalizations of the solutions to the groups of related legal cases: they revealed certain 'reasons of law' (*causae legis*) underlying the solutions".[1] David Deroussin described the dream of Cicero, "to reduce law to an art" based upon ultimate principles. Cicero envisioned "a complete art of the common law, magnificent and copious but neither inaccessible nor mysterious".[2] Deroussin observed that French writers of the ancient regime such as Jean Domat tried to realise this dream by using the "concept of *regulae iuris* to identify the general rules".[3] As the work of the other contributors shows, that was not how the medieval jurists used *regulae iuris*. The, Justinianic title *De diversis regulis* remained a heterogeneous collection of rules[4] (Paul Du Plessis); the Glossators who collected *regulae* and *brocarda* pursued no systematic purpose[5] (David De Concilio); exceptions to the rule and juristic "explaining away" of those exceptions could produce more legal content than the rule itself[6] (Harry Dondorp); the meaning of a rule might depend on the mental (conceptual) context in which the rule was read[7] (Emanuel van Dongen). Gero Dolezalek showed, in Kotlyar's words, how "the *regulae* started appearing in juristic Mss. very early; yet, later on, the interest to them was declining, and the old *regulae*, formulated by the early Glossators, were often erased, as, probably, not fitting the new conceptual legal contexts".[8]

What, then, did the medieval jurists think of *regulae iuris*? For centuries, the discussions of the jurists focused on the text of D. 50.1.17 (Paulus).

1 See the introduction to this volume.
2 M. Tullius Cicero, *De oratore,* XLII, trans. E. W. Sutton (Havard Univ. Press, Cambridge, Mass. 1958).
3 See David Deroussin's contribution to this volume.
4 See the introduction to this volume.
5 Ibid.
6 Ibid.
7 Ibid.
8 Ibid.

 | DOI:10.1163/9789004736092_011

> [T]he law is not taken from a rule, but a rule is made according to the law. Consequently, by a rule a brief description is given of things [*res* – facts or cases], and, as Sabinus said, a rule is a connection[9] of cases [*causae*] which loses it force when it becomes defective in any way.[10]

They often cited Pomponius who said, "[i]n law, every definition is dangerous. It is rarely indeed that one cannot be undermined".[11]

In these texts, a Roman jurist reflected the method actually employed by Roman jurists. That method was case-oriented.[12] I have described elsewhere, that the Romans refined general concepts, not by defining them, as a Greek philosopher might have done, but by giving particular examples of their scope.[13] To explain consent, they put cases of copper sold for gold or vinegar for wine.[14] To explain negligence, they put cases of tree branches cut over public streets,[15] muleteers losing control of their animals,[16] and fires that spread when stubble is burned on a windy day.[17] To explain when possession was transferred, they put cases of goods delivered to someone's door[18] and land viewed from a nearby tower.[19] They thought that one could tell what result was right in a particular case without first formulating a rule or definition.

In the classical period of Roman law, a jurist was a person considered to be competent to give an opinion on any legal question that was put before him. He rarely cited authority for his opinion, although he might, like Paul, refer to the opinion of another jurist such as Sabinus. Medieval jurists had a different

9 In the version of the Digest that he was using, the word was not connection – *coniectio* – but *coniunctio,* which suggests a closer union or joining. Bulgarus' opinion would actually have been more faithful to the text if his version had said *coniectio.* As Conte noted, *coniunctio* sits more easily with the view that one *causa* means one *ratio.* Emanuele Conte, "*Ordo Iudicii et Regula Iuris* Bartolus et les origines de la culture juridique (XIIe siècle)," in *Frontières de savoir en Italie à l'époque des premières universités* (*XIIIe – IVe siècles*), ed. Joël Chandelier and Robert Aurélien (Rome: École Française de Roma, 2015), 157–176 at 173.

10 D. 50.17.1.

11 D. 50.17.202 [vulg. 203].

12 Peter Stein, *Regulae Iuris From Juristic Rules to Legal Maxims* (Edinburgh: Edinburgh University Press, 1966), 102.

13 James Gordley, *The Jurists: A Critical History* (Oxford: Oxford University Press, 2013), 13.

14 D. 18.1.9.

15 Ibid.

16 D. 9.2.8.1.

17 D. 9.2.30.3.

18 D. 9.2.28.pr.; see D. 9.2.29.pr.

19 D. 9.2.28.pr.

conception of their task. It was to interpret the Roman texts. A jurist was an expert on these texts. Whenever possible, he supported his opinion by citing a text.

Consequently, it can be misleading to read the medieval jurists' comments on D. 50.17.1 as though they were discussing their own method. They were discussing a text written by a Roman jurist who was discussing the quite different method of Roman jurists. The medieval jurists were reflecting neither on the method of the Romans nor on their own. Their task, here as elsewhere, was to interpret a text. In interpreting this text, they considered what a rule is, how one arises, and how far it extends. As I have discussed elsewhere, they anticipated some of the perennial questions that jurists have asked about the formulation and application of rules. Yet their task was to pin down the exact meaning of each word in their text. That task occupied them for centuries. It was a mistake to think their conclusions about the meaning of this text describe their own method. Yet, if we examine the way they went about reaching these conclusions, we can see their own method at work.

Citing Pomponius, Bulgarus observed that "a rule loses its force when it fails in a particular case. Consequently, definitions in law are dangerous ...; there are few that cannot be undermined".[20] For example, there is a rule of what belongs to no one becomes the property of the first to take possession. For example, a fish belongs to the first person to catch it.[21] But suppose one takes possession of something that cannot be owned by any person, such as a river, a free man, or, in Roman law, a shrine.[22] He does not own it. So, with this rule, as with nearly every other, there are exceptions. If so, how can one trust a rule?

According to Bulgarus, the application of the rule on ownership by possession did not work in the case of the shrine because of a logical fallacy. He was familiar with Aristotle's works on logic. The fallacy, he said, is that of using the middle term of a syllogism in two different senses. The rule is that what belongs to no one belongs to the person who takes possession. A shrine belongs to no one. It would seem that a shrine must belong to whoever takes possession of it. But the term "belongs to no one" has two meanings. In the case of the fish, it refers to what belongs to no man. In the case of the shrine, it refers to what belongs not to man but to god.[23]

20 Bulgarus, *Bulgari ad digestorum titulum De diversis regulis iuris antiqui commentarius et Placentini ad eum additiones sive exceptiones*, ed. F.G.C. Beckhaus (Bonn: Henry u. Cohen, 1856), to D. 50.17.1.

21 Inst.Just. II.1.12.

22 Inst.Just. II.1.8; D. 1.8.6.3.

23 Bulgarus, *Ad digestorum titulum De diversis regulis*, to D. 50.17.65.

Those remarks suggest that rules can be trusted provided they are formulated precisely. But that suggestion conflicts with Bulgarus' idea of how rules are made. A rule or a definition is a collection of particular cases.

> [A] rule is like a collection of singulars forming a universal. For example, following nature, it is laid down that wild beasts which previously did not belong to anyone belong to the possessor, like birds and fish. And when this is first laid down as to singulars, afterward it is laid down in common, as a universal, that what belongs to no one goes to the possessor.[24]

Suppose that in the first case to arise, a person captured a wild bird. In the second, he caught a fish. In both cases, the appropriate result is that he owns it. We generalise: an object unowned by anyone belongs to the first to take possession of it. But in a third case, a person takes possession of a shrine. Our rule was made to apply to a bird and a fish. To say it applies to anything that no one else owns is to overgeneralise. Consequently, to apply the rule to a new case, we first must decide whether or not that case should fall within the rule. If so, following rules is not only dangerous. It seems to be futile. What would be the point of having rules?

An answer was given by Joannes Bassianus, Azo, and Accursius. To Bulgarus, the word *causa* meant a particular case. In contrast, they said that "one *causa* means one *ratio*" – that is, one reason or rationale. "[C]*ausa*, indeed, is said to be *ratio*". Azo said, in a passage that may have been written or inspired by his teacher Iohannes Bassianus:[25]

> [T]his is the force of rules: given one *causa*, to attribute to one, many other things in which the same equity is found: for example, first it was laid down for fish that they belong to the possessor because they belonged to no one; and indeed for this *ratio*, it was so also for lions and other wild animals, because they belonged to no one: wherefore it was well and generally received that what belongs to no one goes to the possessor. The origin or birth of rules thus proceeds from this general source, whose rivulets flow into the various habitations of the law which may be so expressed: where there the *ratio* is the same, the law is the

24 Ibid., to D. 50.17.1.

25 Stein, *Regulae iuris*, 140–41.

> same. And so the force of rules is not that they make the law: rather a rule is constituted by the law.[26]

According to this view, the cases of fish, lions and other wild animals were not simply collected in formulating a rule, the way one might throw various objects in a bag. The result in these cases had something in common: the same *ratio*.

Azo, perhaps following Bassianus, said that it is difficult for a jurist to frame a rule because of "the jurist's inability to discriminate among men [...] or the mutability of human affairs, the weakness of the human mind, or the variety of wrongs".[27] Consequently, the rules should be applied carefully but they should not be distrusted. Accursius concluded that although the rules do not make law "in the cases [in which they are] laid down", nevertheless, "in cases in which the equity is the same, and are not established in law, they do make law".[28] He said: "stand firmly by rules, as the Bolognese do by their Caroccio" – their war chariot – "lest others wrest it from their grasp".[29]

Having raised this profound and perennial question about the sources and values of rules, one might have expected the medieval jurists to have searched for answers. They did not. They had gone as far as the text would take them. They turned to other questions.

One such question had been raised by Bulgarus. How was it possible for a rule to be true if sometimes it did not apply? That seemed to be a logical contradiction. As we have seen, Bulgarus said the contradiction was only apparent because the middle term had two different senses. To say that a fish belongs to no one means that it belongs to no man. To say that a shrine belongs to no one means that it belongs not to man but to god.[30]

The trouble with that solution is that sometimes, the middle term might not have two different senses. Azo drew a distinction that later writers followed. Some terms, "universals", referred to every single thing denoted by the term, and, to so indicate, one could formulate a rule by using words such as "all", "none", or "always". Other terms are "indefinite" in the sense that they need not apply to every single thing that they denote.[31] Examples are "man"

26 Azo, *Summa Codicis* (Basel: per Joannem Hervagium, 1563), to D. 50.17 pr. no. 4.

27 Ibid. no. 6.

28 *Glossa ordinaria* to D. 50.17.1 s.v. '*Regula est*'.

29 Ibid. to D. 50.17.202 [vulg. 203] s.v. '*Omnis diffinitio*'.

30 Bulgarus, *Ad digetorum titulum De diversis regulis,* to D. 50.17.65.

31 Azo, "*Summa in rubrica Digestis Novi* ad D *de diversis regulis iuris,*" in Azo, *Summa Aurea* (Lyon: Petrus Fradin, 1558), f. 308r., nos. 1–2.

and "phoenix".[32] When one says "men are ..." one might mean "all men are ..." or one might not.

The question was how to tell whether an indefinite term in a rule should be applied as though it were universal. According to Azo, it should be when "a substantive term applies to many things such as man, phoenix" according to its natural signification.[33] Dynus pointed out that it need not be so. "[T]he word marble in a legacy only refers to the raw material and not the kinds of things made out of marble".[34] The same was true of the word "wool". "Therefore", he concluded, "it is false that indefinite terms are equivalent to universals". "When there is not the same *ratio* and *conditio* in all the particulars included in the universal term, indefinite terms are not equivalent to universal affirmative terms".[35] Later jurists agreed. According to Bartolus, when "there is no reason (*ratio*) why it should refer to more to one that to another, it refers to all".[36]

Another question was what the Roman text meant when it said that "the law (*ius*) is not taken from a rule". Accursius gave an explanation which was followed by later jurists. A rule makes law "in the cases in which the equity is the same and which are already a matter of law (*in iure positi*). It does not make law in cases that have already been resolved (*statutis*)": as the text says, the rule is taken from the law that is found in these cases. Moreover, "a rule does not make law when there are exceptions": the rule cannot apply to them since they are not decided in accordance with the rule.[37]

Dynus saw a problem. Some rules are new. They are not founded on the law (*ius*) that is already established. So, it would seem they make law. For example, "[t]he Catonian rule was newly made". So "it would seem that *ius* can be made *de novo*".[38] As Celsus said, "The Catonian Rule (*Catoniana regula*) is as follows: 'Any legacy which would have been invalid at the time of the making of the will is invalid whenever he dies'".[39] But to say that a rule can make law (*ius*) contradicts the text of D. 50.17.1. Dynus responded that the law (*ius*) "which is already determined" before a rule is made need not be the law (*ius*) from

32 Ibid. no. 3.

33 Ibid.

34 Dynus, *Tractatus super Regulis Juris cum accessionibus et correctionibus* (1515), ff. 7–8.

35 Ibid. f. 9.

36 Bartolus de Saxoferrato, *Commentaria in Digestum novum* (Venice: Giunti, 1602), to 50.17.1 no. 3.

37 *Glossa ordinaria* to D. 50.1.17 s.v. '*Regula*'.

38 Dynus, *Tractatus*, f. 10.

39 D. 34.7.1.

which the rule is taken". It may be "a law (*ius*) which comes from elsewhere, not from the law that is established".[40]

Iohannes Andreas (Giovanni d'Andrea) did not want to posit a law (*ius*) on which the *regula Catoniana* is based, which is not *ius* already established but *ius* which comes "from elsewhere". The rule of the *lex Catoniana* does not make law, he said, because the "rule is *per se* not a rule of law".[41] This solution seems circular. What is a rule *per se*? One that does not make law. Why is it that such a rule does not make law? Because otherwise it would contradict D. 50.1.17.

Bartolus claimed that the opinions of Dynus and Iohannes Andreas "both … can be saved". "I believe that Iohannes Andreas says the truth as to those rules which are dealt with here by this text notwithstanding the *regula Catoniania* because you ought to say that a rule of law (*regula iuris*) is a rule which is law (*regula quae est ius*)".[42] "A rule of law is a law which is a rule".[43] Some rules are law because they are founded on law previously established. The *regula Catoniana* is a rule which is law although not founded on law previously established. It is law but does not make it.[44]

Yet another question was whether a rule can be valid and still be subject to exceptions. Placentinus said that exceptions belong to a rule. Iohannes Bassianus said that they are departures from it.[45] Accursius said that it would seem from the text of D. 50.17.1 that a rule cannot have exceptions although there are cases to which the rule does not apply. The text said that "a rule … loses its force when it becomes defective in any way". "[I]t is objected," he observed, that in that event "no rule can be vitiated". He answered that since a rule extends only to cases in which the same equity is to be found as in the cases that were used to formulate the rule, a rule would fail only if it did not apply even in a case in which the same equity is found. If there is no such case, then, properly speaking, the rule has no exceptions.[46] The apparent exceptions are not within its purview.

If the exceptional cases are not within the purview of the rule then they are not truly exceptions to it. According to Dynus, Bassianus "is to be understood

40 Dynus, *Tractatus*, f. 11

41 Described by Bartolus, *Commentaria.*, to D. 50.17.1 no. 4.

42 Ibid. no. 4

43 Ibid.: "*regula iuris, id est, ius quod est regula*".

44 For more detail on the discussion between Dynus, Johannes d'Andrea and Bartolus on the issue of the relationship between law and *regulae*, see Ilya A. Kotlyar's contribution to this volume.

45 Dynus, *Tractatus*, f. 12.

46 *Glossa ordinaria* to D. 50.17.1, s.v. '*Regula est*'.

to be speaking of cases in which a rule does not apply because the same equity is not to be found". If these are not true exceptions, his opinion can be reconciled with that of Accursius: "It seems to me that both opinions contain truth".[47] "If the rule concerns 'man' an exception must be as to 'man' and must not concern an ass or a goat or some other species. Again, if the rule concerns real actions, it not does rightly follow that there is an exception in personal actions or the reverse". Again, the exceptional cases do not fall within the scope of the rule. "In this way it is plausible to understand Placentinus".[48]

The difficulty is that cases in which the same equity is not found may nevertheless fall within the wording of the rule. For example, the words of the rule "what belongs to no man belongs to a person who takes possession" extend to possession taken of a free man or a temple. Bartolus said: "I ask whether a rule has an exception ... and some say that yes and others no. You are to say, and this is true that as to the words ... and as to the disposition of law (*ius*) it is not".[49]

Outside the law schools, the works of Aristotle and Thomas Aquinas transformed the work of scholars. Inside the law schools, it did not, at least insofar as their explanation of *regulae iuris* is concerned. Thomas Aquinas explained that sometimes, because of the circumstances of a case, applying a general rule will lead to the wrong result. Following Aristotle, he said that, as a matter of *epikeia* or equity, the rule should not be followed.

> [S]ince human actions, with which laws are concerned, are composed of contingent singulars and are innumerable in their diversity, it was not possible to lay down rules of law that would apply to every single case. Legislators in framing laws attend to what commonly happens: although if the law be applied to certain cases it will frustrate the equality of justice and be injurious to the common good, which the law has in view. Thus the law requires deposits to be restored, because in the majority of cases this is just. Yet it happens sometimes to be injurious – for instance, if a madman were to put his sword in deposit, and demand its delivery while in a state of madness, or if a man were to seek the return of his deposit in order to fight against his country. In these and like cases it is bad to follow the law, and it is good to set aside the letter of the law and to follow the dictates of justice and the common good.

47 Dynus, *Tractatus,* f. 12.

48 Ibid., f. 13

49 Bartolus, *Commentaria,* to D. 50,17.1, no. 4.

> This is the object of 'epikeia' which we call equity. Therefore it is evident that 'epikeia' is a virtue.[50]

Bartolus was familiar with Aristotle and Aquinas. As I have described elsewhere, he sometimes read an Aristotelian meaning into the Roman texts.[51] Had he wished, he could have done so here. He could have explained that because words are general, there will be cases in which they lead to the wrong result and therefore should not be followed. A rule that whatever belongs to no man belongs to a person who takes possession of it should not be followed in the case of a free man or a temple. Yet when Bartolus discussed a possible objection to Dynus, even if he had the Aristotelian idea of *epikeia* in mind, he did not say so.

Aquinas had defined "law" (*lex*) as "a rule of reason laid down for the common good by those in authority and promulgated". Bartolus might have had this definition in mind when he began his own discussion by noting:

> The word rule is taken in two ways. In one way, a rule is what rules (*regit*) and gives order such as the rule of the Friars Minor and in things written that have rules which give order of writing, and in his way it is understood that every law (*lex*) that rules and gives an order of living. In the other way, a rule is as is said here (in D. 50.17.1).[52]

Perhaps he had in mind Aquinas' definition of law as a rule of reason when he spoke of a rule in the first sense. Aquinas was describing all the law that give order to the universe, nature and society: eternal law, natural law, positive law. Be that as it may, Bartolus introduced this idea of what a rule was only to distinguish it from a "rule" within the meaning of D. 50.1.17 and to exclude it from his discussion.

If we wish to better understand the method of the medieval jurists, we will be helped neither by examining their conclusions about the meaning of D. 50.17.1 nor by the influence of Aristotle and Aquinas. We will do better if we step back from their conclusions and examine the method by which they arrived at them.

The method is to reconcile conflicting texts. They would observe a possible conflict and then introduce a distinction to resolve it.

---

50 Thomas Aquinas, *Summa theologiae*, II-II Qu. 120, a. 1.

51 James Gordley, *The Philosophical Origins of Modern Contract Doctrine* (Oxford: Oxford University Press, 1991), 50–55 (*causa*), 59–60 (*error in substantia*).

52 Bartolus, *Commentaria*, to 50.17.1 nos. 1–2.

Can a rule be true if there are cases in which it does not apply? One might say, like Bulgarus, that one of the terms of the rule has two different senses, and that it applies invariably only when the term is used in its first sense. Or, like the later jurists, one can distinguish between terms that apply universally and those that do not. How can it be that a rule does not make law (*ius*)? The *regula Cantoniana* seems to do so. One can say that rule is "from elsewhere", or that it is a "rule *per se* and not a rule of law (*regula iuris*) or that it is a *regula iuris*, and since every such *regula* is *ius*, it is law but does not make it. Are the cases to which a rule does not apply truly exceptions? They need not be if we say that the rule extends only to the cases in which the equity is the same as in the ones used to formulate the rule. But since the rules may extend beyond these cases, we need another distinction between exceptions that concern the words and those that concern the result.

One can see the same pattern in the descriptions of other contributors to this volume of the treatment of particular *regulae iuris* by medieval jurists. Harry Dondorp discussed the rule *duorum in solidum dominium esse non potest*, "Ownership in entirety cannot be in two persons",[53] taken from Ulpian, D. 13.6.5.15. That rule seemed to fail in the case of land in a dowry. According to C. 5.12.30, ownership of that land naturally remains with the wife although according to Roman statute it belongs to her husband's estate. Henricus de Bayla, Martinus and Bulgarus drew a distinction. D. 13.65.15 refers to ownership by more than one person of the same land under the same law. In C. 5.12.30, the wife was the owner of the land under natural law, and the husband was the owner under civil law. Johannes Bassianus and Azo drew a different distinction. In C. 5.12.30, the husband and wife did not have the same interest in the land: he was the actual owner and she was the owner *in spe*.

One can see the same pattern in Piotr Alexandrowicz's account[54] of the Canon law rule *utilius scandalum nasci permittitur, quam veritas relinquatur*,[55] "It is better to permit the birth of scandal than to sacrifice the truth". But was that true of every truth? Laurentius Hispanus and Geoffrey of Trani distinguished three kinds of truth: the truth of good life (*veritas bonae vitae*), applicable to everyone, truth of justice (*veritas iustitiae*), applicable to the judge, and truth of discipline (*veritas disciplinae*), applicable to the prelate. The first could not be sacrificed to prevent scandal although the others might.

One can see the same pattern when the medieval jurists interpreted texts which did not purport to formulate a *regula iuris*. In discussing fraud (*dolus*),

53 See the contribution by Harry Dondorp to this volume.
54 See the contribution by Piotr Alexandrowicz to this volume.
55 X 5.41.3.

they distinguished between fraud in the *causa*, which led a person to contract, and incidental fraud, which affected the price at which he contracted. The seller of a horse commits causal fraud if he convinces the buyer that his own horse will soon die; he commits incidental fraud if he gets a better price by lying about the age of the horse. The jurists further distinguished between two types of incidental fraud: in one, *dolus ex proposito*, one party lied; in the other, he did not but the price was too low or too high. They are described in the 12th-century *Collectio Senensis*.[56]

> When fraud gives a contract of good faith its *causa*, the contract is invalid ipso iure, and no action arises on it. ... When the contract is affected by fraud that does not give the contract its *causa* but affects it in some other way, then the fraud is either committed intentionally (*ex proposito*) or it appears from the thing itself (*ex re ipsa*). If the fraud is Good intentionally, it is purged away by an action on the contract no matter how small the amount of money. [D. 4.3.9; D. 19.6.6; D. 19.1.13.4]. If the fraud appears from the thing itself, then one must distinguish as to whether the equity of the contract will tolerate it or not. If the equity of the contract will tolerate it there is no action, for by nature the parties are permitted to circumvent each other. If, however, the deception is such that the equity of the contract cannot tolerate it, as, for example, if one buys for more than twice the just price or sells for less than half the just price, what has been done unequally ought to be reformed. ... [C. 4.44.2; C. 4.44.8; D. 23.3.13 [3.12]; D. 38.5.1.12].

These distinctions are not to be found in the texts that are cited. One, however, seemed to explain why sometimes fraud invalided the transactions but at other times it gave rise to an action for damages. Another identified two situations in which a price might be unfairly high or low: the advantaged party had lied, or without telling a lie, he had charged too much or paid too little. In the latter case, one Roman text gave a remedy for land sold at less than half its

56 "*Collectio Senensis, Antiquissimorum glossatorum distinctiones,*" in *Scripta Anecdota Glossatorum*, vol. II, ed. G.B. Palmerio (Bologna: In aedibus Petri Virano, 1892), 152. The collection has been ascribed to Ugo de Porta Ravennate und Albericus de Porta Ravennate, see Aleksander M. Grebieniow, "Die *laesio enormis* und der *dolus re ipsa* heute: die Verschuldensfrage," *Tijdschrift voor Rechtsgeschiedenis* 85 (2017), 192, 206, n. 59; Christoph Becker, *Die Lehre von der laesio enormis in der Sicht der heutigen Wucherproblematik, Ausgewogenheit als Vertragsinhalt und § 138* (Köln: Carl Heymann, 1993), 59 n. 78.

just price, a remedy which the Glossators generalised so that it was available to buyers as well as sellers, in goods as well as land, and in leases as well as sales, provided the contract price deviated by the just price by more than half:[57] then, according to the *Collectio Senensis*, the equity of a contract cannot tolerate it.

For centuries thereafter, jurists discussed fraud by drawing the same distinctions. Neither they nor the author of the *Collectio* presented or organised their discussion as though their task was to formulate rules based on a similarity of *rationes* to be found in established law, although it might have been easy enough for them to do so had they wished. They drew a series of distinctions to explain the differences among Roman texts. Their task, as they understood it, was to resolve apparent conflicts among their texts.

The task was the same whether, as here, they were explaining texts that did not purport to contain *regulae iuris*, like those cited in the *Collectio Senensis*, or with texts that did, like those discussed by Dondorp and Alexandrowicz. The task was the same when they dealt with the text of D. 1.17.50, which described what a *regula iuris* is and how one is formulated. As the task was the same, so was their method. It was not the one sketched in D. 50.17.1. That text described how general rules might be formulated on the basis of existing law and applied to new cases in which the *ius* was the same. The medieval jurists did believe that rules should be formulated and applied in that way: the Roman text said so. But their method was one of reconciling contradictions by distinguishing texts, not of formulating rules and applying them to new cases.

This method may have had its roots in dialectics and rhetoric, as some of the contributors suggest. It was founded on a rule of logic: the law of non-contradiction. It may, as Ilya Kolyar suggests, have parallels in the method of structural linguistics.[58] The method, however, presupposed only the validity

57 The *Brachylogus*, written at the beginning of the 12th century, does not speak of land but of objects sold. *Brachylogus,* iii.xiii.8. The *Dissensiones dominorum* of the early-13th-century reports a dispute in which all participants take it for granted that the buyer has a remedy. The disputed question is whether, for him to have it, the sales price must be twice or one and one-half times the just price. The participants are said to be Placentinus, Albericus, who wrote in the 12th century, and Martinus, a student of Irnerius. (Hugolinus de Presbyteris, *Diversitates sive dissensiones dominorum*, ed. G Haenel (Leipzig: Hinrich, 1834), § 253) According to Accursius, it was agreed among the jurists that the remedy would be available generally in contracts *bonae fidei. Glossa ordinaria* to C. 4.44.2 s.v. '*Auctoritate iudicis.*

58 See Ilya Kotlyar's contribution to this volume.

of the law of non-contradiction and the authority of the Roman texts. If the texts were authoritative and seemed to contradict, the contradiction must be resolved. How else could it be resolved than by drawing distinctions?

Consequently, *regulae iuris* were not interesting to the medieval jurists for the same reasons that they interest modern scholars. As Adolfo Giuliani points out, "the huge wave of studies on maxims (*regulae*) produced during the 1950-60's ... sought an alternative normativity, distinct form legislative rules, and felt that a broader normativity extended beyond the state". "Maxims were rules not made but found, unsuitable for logical deduction ("*jus non ex regula sumatur*", D. 50.17.1) ... to be understood not *more geometrico* but through the rich dialectical methodology, dismissed by the rise of modern states".[59] These writers hoped to escape the difficulties of 19th-century positivism in which the only source of law was the lawmaker, and these rules had to be interpreted by logical deduction. But the medieval jurists were not troubled by the problems of the 19th-century positivism. Nor were they concerned with epistemological problems which, as Giuliani describes, have led more recent scholars to look to *regulae iuris* for insight into "the cognitive purposes of legal actors".[60]

They did raise a question which, as described elsewhere,[61] haunts modern discussions about rule scepticism: if a rule cannot be applied as written, if one has to ask what result is appropriate in a new case before one applies a rule, then what is the point of having rules at all? Bulgarus concluded that one could not trust rules. Accursius urged his contemporaries to stand by them. But the problem did not trouble them as it does modern jurists who see their task as the application of rules. The medieval jurists saw their task as the reconciliation of authorities. They raised the question of how far one could trust rules without resolving it and then turned elsewhere.

We began by noting the tension that Kotlyar observed within the contributors' accounts of *regulae iuris*. De Concilio observed that the medieval jurists "tended to see the *regulae* as objective generalizations of the solutions to the groups of related legal cases: they revealed certain 'reasons of law' (*causae legis*) underlying the solutions". Yet they never realised the dream of Cicero and some 17th-century French jurists described by Deroussin: reduce law to an art by examining its underlying principles. From what other contributors have

59 See Adolfo Giuliani's contribution to this volume.

60 Ibid.

61 James Gordley, "*Regulae Juris* and Legal Principles: Whence and Whither?'," *Tulane European & Civil Law Forum* 37 (2022), 201–207.

said of their work, it was a goal that the medieval jurists did not achieve and probably did not attempt. We can see why they did not. Their task, as they understood it, was not to formulate general rules, let alone assemble them into “a complete art ... magnificent and copious but neither inaccessible nor mysterious”. It was to reconcile their authoritative texts.

Index of *Regulae* (Maxims)

The number in the brackets refers to the number under which the relevant *regula* is registered in the database of the FWO.OPR.2020.005001 project.

Index of Matters

www.ingramcontent.com/pod-product-compliance
Lightning Source LLC
Chambersburg PA
CBHW051401240926
51852CB00002B/84
9789004736078